AF147418

Tradition Principally With Reference To Mythology And The Law Of Nations

By

Lord Arundell Of Wardour

Tradition Principally With Reference To Mythology And The Law Of Nations
by Lord Arundell Of Wardour

Copyright © 2023

All Rights reserved.

No part of this publication may be reproduced,
stored in a retrieval system, or transmitted in any
form or by any means, electronic, mechanical,
photocopying or Otherwise, without the written
permission of the publisher.
The author/editor asserts the moral right to
be identified as the author/editor of this work.

ISBN: 978-93-59950-40-2
Published by

DOUBLE 9 BOOKS

2/13-B, Ansari Road
Daryaganj, New Delhi – 110002
info@double9books.com
www.double9books.com
Tel. 011-40042856

This book is under public domain

ABOUT THE AUTHOR

Lord Arundell of Wardour, whose complete name changed into John Francis Arundell, become a British author and student recognized for his widespread contributions to the fields of mythology and global regulation all through the nineteenth century. His book, "Tradition, principally with Reference to Mythology and the Law of Nations," reflects his deep interest in those topics and showcases his widespread studies and insights. Arundell's paintings explores the concept of subculture, particularly as it pertains to mythology and the development of worldwide law. He delves into the ways wherein traditional testimonies, ideals, and customs have motivated and maintain to influence the prison structures and diplomatic relationships among nations. Arundell's book affords a comprehensive examination of the role of mythology and traditional narratives in shaping the principles and practices of global regulation. He argues that many criminal principles and global agreements have their roots in ancient myths and cultural traditions, dropping light on the interconnectedness of human records and the improvement of criminal norms. "Tradition, principally with Reference to Mythology and the Law of Nations" is a testomony to Lord Arundell of Wardour's scholarly acumen and interdisciplinary method.

CONTENTS

PREFACE

I shall have no hope of conveying to the reader, within the narrow limits of a preface, any fuller idea of the purport of this work than its title expresses; and as the chapters are necessarily interdependent, I can indicate no short-cut in the perusal by which this information can be obtained.

I venture to think that those who are interested in the special matters referred to will find something in these pages which may attract on account of its novelty—and some other things, new at least in their application—e.g. the comparison of Boulanger's theory with the narratives of Captain R. Burton and Catlin.

The frequent introduction and the length of the notes, must, I am aware, give to these pages a repellent aspect, but the necessity of bringing various points under comparison has compelled this arrangement; and I regret to say that the argument runs through the whole, and that almost as much matter requiring consideration will be found in the notes and appendices as in the text.

I trust that these imperfections may not be so great as to estrange the few, among whom only I can hope to find much sympathy, who wish to see the true foundations of peace and order re-established in the world, and who may therefore to some extent be indulgent towards efforts which have for their aim and motive the attempt to erect barriers which would render the recurrence of the evils which have lately deluged mankind difficult, if not impossible.

There are others whom the recent scenes of horror have inspired with a love of peace and order, or of whom it would be more true to say, that the horrors of the late war and revolution have deepened in them the sentiment of peace and order which they have always entertained, but who still do not desire these things on the conditions upon which alone they can be secured. From them I can only ask such passing examination as may be demanded for the conscientious rejection of the evidence I have collected, or for its adjustment with more accepted theories.

There will remain for me much ground in common with all who retain their faith in the inspiration of Holy Writ, and who wish to see its authority sustained against the aggressive infidelity of the day; and even among those who reject the authority of divine revelation, there may be still some who are wearied in the arid wastes, and who would gladly retrace their steps to the green pastures and the abundant streams. Among such I may perhaps expect to find friendly criticism.

At the same time, I do not disguise from myself that, in its present mood, the world is much more anxious to be cut adrift from tradition than to be held to its moorings; and that it will impatiently learn that fresh facts have to be considered before its emancipation can be declared, or before it can be let loose without the evident certainty of shipwreck. Although the exigencies of the argument have compelled research over a somewhat extended field of inquiry, the exploration has no pretensions to being exhaustive, but at most suggestive; not attempting to work the mine, or, except incidentally, to produce the ore, but only indicating the positions in which it is likely to be found.

In the main position of the mythological chapters, that the heroes of mythological legend embody the reminiscences of the characters and incidents of the biblical narrative, I do nothing more than carry on a tradition, as the reader will see in my references to Calmet, Bryant, Palmer, and others.[1] I should add, that I limit the full application of De Maistre's theory to the times preceding the coming of our Lord.

My attention was first drawn to the coincidences of mythology with scriptural history by the late Colonel G. Macdonell.[2] Colonel Macdonell's coincidences were founded upon a peculiar theory of his own, and must necessarily have been exclusively upon the lines of Hebrew derivation. There is nothing, however, in these pages drawn from that source. I may add, for the satisfaction of Colonel Macdonell's friends, that as Colonel Macdonell's MSS. exist, and are in the possession of Colonel I. J. Macdonell, I have (except at p. 243, when quoting from Boulanger,) expressly excluded the consideration of the influence of the Hebrew upon general tradition, which, however, will be necessary for the full discussion of the question.

Whatever, therefore, Colonel Macdonell may have written will remain over and above in illustration of the tradition. But whether on the lines of Hebrew or primeval tradition, these views will inevitably run counter to the mythological theories now in the ascendant. These views, indeed, have been so long relegated to darkness, and perhaps appropriately, on account of their opposition to the prevalent solar theories, "flouted like owls and bats" whenever they have ventured into the daylight, that it will be with something amounting to absolute astonishment that the learned will hear that there are people who still entertain them: "itaque ea nolui scribere, quæ nec indocti intelligere possent, nec docti legere curarent" (Cic. Acad. Quæs., 1. i. § 2).

I can sincerely say, however, that although my theories place me in a position of antagonism to modern science, yet that I have written in no spirit of hostility to science or the cause of science.

I have throughout excluded the geological argument, for the first and sufficient reason that I am not a geologist; and secondly, by the same right and title, that geologists, *e.g.* Sir C. Lyell, in his "Antiquity of Man," ignores the arguments and facts to which I have directed special attention.

Nevertheless, I find that competent witnesses have come to conclusions not materially different from those which have been arrived at, on the ground of history, within their own department of geology. I have more especially in my mind the following passage from a series of papers, "On Some Evidences of the Antiquity of Man," by the Rev. A. Weld, in the *Month* (1871), written with full knowledge and in a spirit of careful and fair appreciation of the evidence. He says:—

> "These evidences, such as they are, are fully treated in the work of Sir C. Lyell, entitled 'Antiquity of Man,' which exhausted the whole question as it stood, when the last edition was published in the year 1863. It is worthy of note that though the conclusion at which the geologist arrives is hesitating and suggestive, rather than decisive, and though nothing of importance, as far as we are aware, has been added to the geological aspect of the question since that time—except that the reality of the discovery of human remains has been verified, and many additional discoveries of a similar character have been made—*still the opinion, which was then new and startling, has gradually gained ground*, until we find writers assuming as a thing that needs no further proof, that the period of man's habitation on the earth is to be reckoned in tens of thousands of years."—*The Month* (May and June 1871).

Among various works, bearing on matters contained in these pages, which have come to hand during the course of publication, I may mention—

"The Mythology of the Aryan Nations," by the Rev. G. W. Cox, referred to in notes at pp. 158, 165, 396.

The third edition of Sir John Lubbock's "Pre-historic Times."

Mr E. B. Tylor's "Primitive Culture," referred to in notes at pp. 41, 136, 300.

Mr St George Mivart's "Genesis of Species."

Mr F. Seebohm on "International Reform."

Sir H. S. Maine's "Village Communities."

The Archbishop of Westminster's paper, read before the Royal Institution, "On the Dæmon of Socrates."

"Orsini's Life of the Blessed Virgin," translated by the Very Rev. Dr Husenbeth.

"Hints and Facts on the Origin of Man," by the Very Rev. Dr P. Melia, 1872, who says (p. 59), "Considering the great length of life of the first patriarchs, Moses must have had every information through non-interrupted tradition. If we reflect that Shem for many years saw Methuselah, a contemporary of Adam, and that Shem himself lived to the time of Abraham, ... that Abraham died after the birth of Jacob, and that Jacob saw many who were alive when Moses was born, we see that a few generations connect Moses not only with Noah, but also with Adam." I quote this passage as it is important to place in the foreground of this inquiry the unassailable truth that (apart from revelation) the historical account of the origin of the human race, to which all others converge, is consistent with itself, and bears intrinsic evidence of credibility.

An analogous argument with reference to Christian tradition was sketched in a lecture by Mr Edward Lucas, and published in 1862, "On the First Two Centuries of Christianity."

With reference to other parts of these pages, much supplemental matter will be found in—

"Historical Illustrations of the Old Testament," by the Rev. G. Rawlinson, M.A., Camden Prof., where, at pp. 19, 20, will be found direct testimony to what I had conjectured from indirect evidence at pp. 270, 271—viz., that the Polynesian islanders "have a clear and distinct tradition of a Deluge, from which one family only, *eight in number*, was saved in a canoe."

Also, but from a different point of view, in "Legends of Old Testament Characters," by Rev. S. Baring Gould, M.A.

The articles in the *Tablet* "On Arbitration instead of War," to which I have referred in chap. xiv. at p. 380, have recently been collected and reprinted by Lord Robert Montagu, M.P.

If I have exceeded in quotation, I must direct my readers, for the defence of this mode of composition, from the point of view of tradition, to a work which I trust some in this busy age still find leisure to read, Mr Kenelm Digby's "Mores Catholici," i. 40.

I must, moreover, add a passage from the general preface to the recent republication of Mr Disraeli's works, which I came upon too late to introduce into the body of this book, but which I feel sure the reader, even if he has met with it before, will not be reluctant to reperuse:—

"The sceptical effects of the discoveries of science, and the uneasy feeling that they cannot co-exist with our old religious convictions have their origin in the circumstance that the general body who have suddenly become conscious of these physical truths are not so well acquainted as is desirable with the past history of man. Astonished by their unprepared emergence from ignorance to a certain degree of information, their amazed intelligence takes refuge in the theory of what is conveniently called progress, and every step in scientific discovery seems further to remove them from the path of primæval inspiration. But there is no fallacy so flagrant as to suppose that the modern ages have the peculiar privilege of scientific discovery, or that they are distinguished as the epochs of the most illustrious inventions. On the contrary, scientific invention has always gone on simultaneously with the revelation of spiritual truths; and more, the greatest discoveries are not those of modern ages. No one for a moment can pretend that printing is so great a discovery as writing, or algebra as language. What are the most brilliant of our chemical discoveries compared with the invention of fire and the metals? It is a vulgar belief that our astronomical knowledge dates only from the recent century, when it was rescued from the monks who imprisoned Galileo; but Hipparchus, who lived before our Divine Master, and who, among other sublime achievements, discovered the precession of the equinoxes, ranks with the Newtons and the Keplers; and Copernicus, the modern father of our celestial science, avows himself, in his famous work, as only the champion of Pythagoras, whose system he enforces and illustrates. Even the most modish schemes of the day on the origin of things, which captivate as much by their novelty as their truth, may find their precursors in ancient sages; and after a careful analysis of the blended elements of imagination and induction which characterise the new theories, they will be found mainly to rest on the atom of Epicurus and the monad of Thales. Scientific, like spiritual truth, has ever from the beginning been descending from Heaven to man. He is a being who organically demands direct relations with his Creator, and he would not have been so organised if his requirements could not be satisfied. We may analyse the sun and penetrate the stars; but man is conscious that he is made in God's own image, and in his perplexity he will ever appeal to our Father which art in Heaven."

MEMOIR
OF
COLONEL GEORGE MACDONELL, C.B.

The following notice appeared in the *Times*, May 23, 1870—"In our obituary column of Saturday we announced the death of Colonel George Macdonell, C.B., at the advanced age of ninety. This officer, who was a cadet of the ancient and loyal Scottish house of Macdonell of Glengarry, was the son of an officer who served under the flag, and who, as we have been told, was on the staff, of Prince Charles Edward Stuart at the battle of Culloden, where he was severely wounded. His son, the Colonel now deceased, was born in 1779, or early in the following year; obtained his first commission in 1796, and was nominated a Companion of the Bath in 1817. He saw active service in the war in North America with the 79th Foot, and received the gold medal for the action at Châteaugay; and had he not accepted the retirement a few years since, he would have been, at his death, almost the senior officer in the army holding Her Majesty's commission. The late Colonel Macdonell, who adhered to the Roman Catholic religion professed by his ancestors, and for which they fought so gallantly under the Stuart banners, married, in 1820, the Hon. Laura Arundell, sister of the Lord Arundell of Wardour, but was left a widower in May 1854." His son, Colonel I. J. Macdonell, now commands the 71st Highlanders.

I take this opportunity of adding a few facts, not without interest, to the above brief summary of a not uneventful life, as they might otherwise pass unrecorded. In the sentiment of the Gaelic saying—"Curri mi clach er do cuirn" (Wilson, "Archæol. Scot.," p. 59)—"I will add a stone to your cairn."

Colonel Macdonell's father, as stated in the above account, was wounded at Culloden in the thigh, but was able to crawl on all-fours, after the battle, eighteen miles, to a barn belonging to a member of the Grant family. He there remained in concealment for six months, leaving nature to heal the wound; but the search in the neighbourhood in time becoming too hot, he had to decamp, and walked with a stick all the way to Newcastle, where he was not greatly re-assured by meeting a soldier who had just been drummed out of his regiment as a Catholic, with the word "Papist" placarded on his back. He, however, escaped all dangers, and reached Hull, and subsequently Versailles or St Germains, where he remained three years, or at least till the events following the Peace of Aix-la-Chapelle dispersed the Prince's adherents. He then returned to England under the Act of Indemnity, entered the royal army, and was present with General Wolfe at the taking of Quebec. If I remember rightly, he had the good fortune to take an aide-de-camp of Montcalm's prisoner, with important dispatches.

Colonel Macdonell's maternal uncle, Major Macdonald (Keppoch), was taken prisoner at the battle of Falkirk. He was said to have been the first man who drew blood in the war. By a curious revenue of fortune, he was carried back into the enemy's ranks by the horse of a trooper whom he had captured. He was executed at Carlisle, and the circumstances of his execution supplied Sir Walter Scott, I believe, with the incidents which he worked up into the narrative of MacIvor's execution in "Waverley." His sword is in the possession of Mr P. Howard of Corby Castle, near Carlisle.

Fortune, however, had in store another revenge; for the Duke of Cumberland being present, many years afterwards, at a ball at Bath, by a most unhappy selection indicated as the person with whom he wished to dance a beautiful girl who turned out to be no other than the daughter of Major Macdonald (afterwards married to Mr Chichester of Calverley) the circumstances of whose execution have just been referred to. She rose in deference to royalty, but replied, in a tone which utterly discomfited, and put his Royal Highness to flight—"No, I will never dance with the murderer of my father!"

With these antecedents, it is needless to add that Colonel G. Macdonell was a warm admirer of the Stuarts, and not unnaturally extended his sympathy and adhesion to the kindred cause of legitimacy in France; and the one event to which he always looked forward, and confidently predicted—the restoration of the monarchy in the person of Henri V.— is now, if not imminent, at least "the more probable of possible events." There was, however, a belief which somewhat conflicted in his mind with the above anticipation—namely, his unshaken conviction that the Dauphin did not die in the Temple. He was frequently at Holyrood when the palace was occupied by Charles X., and he accompanied the Duchess de Berri to the place of embarkation for her unfortunate expedition to France. Colonel Macdonell also acted as the medium of communication between the French Royalists and the English Government; and on one important occasion conveyed intelligence to Lord Bathurst or Lord Sidmouth respecting the movements of the secret societies in Spain in 1823 some hours before it reached them by the ordinary channel. Part of the communication was made on information supplied by the Abbé Barruel; and in reply, Lord Sidmouth said—"Well, I remember Edmund Burke telling me that he believed every word that Barruel had written, and I fully accept the authority."

Colonel Macdonell was under the impression that he was unwittingly and remotely the cause of the break up of the Ministry of "all the talents." As this is an obscure point in history, it may be worth while to give the following facts. The impression produced by Marengo and Austerlitz had led to the Army Reform Bill of 1806, in which the points discussed were almost identical with those which lately excited the public mind. The disasters which accompanied our descent on Egypt in 1807, and the consequent evacuation of Alexandria, created considerable discontent and re-opened the question, and as further reforms on minor points were contemplated, suggestions from officers in the army were invited.

Colonel Macdonell (then only lieutenant), wrote to Mr Windham, the Secretary at War, to point out that any broken attorney might create considerable embarrassment at any critical moment, seeing that, as the law then stood (an Act of George I. had extended the obligation of taking the sacrament to privates), any soldier could obtain, if not his own, his comrade's discharge by pointing him out as a Papist. The danger was recognised, and Mr Windham brought in a bill directed to meet the case, but its introduction revived the larger question of the repeal of the Tests' Acts and of the Catholic claims; and the discussion eventuated in Lord Howick's bill, which was met by the King's refusal, and the consequent resignation of the Ministry. This may explain the statement (mentioned in the obituary notice in the Times of the Marquis of Lansdowne), that he (Lord Lansdowne) could never understand how the Ministry came to be dissolved. "He had heard instances of men running their heads against a wall, but never of men building up a wall against which to run their heads."[3]

It has been mentioned that Colonel Macdonell entered the army when quite a boy; and there were few men, I fancy, living, when he died last year, who could boast, as he could, of having served in the Duke of York's campaign in the last century, but I am not able to state in what regiment. He was for some time previously in Lord Darlington's regiment of Fencibles. He was at one period in the 8th, and at another in the 50th regiment, in which latter, I think, he went out to the West Indies and Canada.

It was in Canada, however, that his principal services were rendered, which indeed were considerable, and have never been adequately acknowledged.

When the Americans invaded Canada upon the declaration of war in 1812, it is hardly necessary to remind the reader that almost all our available troops were engaged in the Peninsula, and that Canada was pretty well left to its own resources.

Under these circumstances it will be recognised as of some importance that Colonel Macdonell was able to raise a regiment among the Macdonells of his clan who had settled there. But the conditions made with him were not fulfilled, and the command of the regiment, almost immediately after it was raised, was transferred to the command of a Protestant and an Orangeman, which caused a mutiny which was with difficulty suppressed. Now, it must be borne in mind that the regiment was only raised through his personal influence with the clan, and through that of its pastor, Bishop Macdonell, and that the adhesion of the Catholic Macdonells went far to determine the attitude of the French Canadians also. There were not more than 1200 regular troops in Upper Canada during the war.[4]

Before referring to the actions in which Colonel Macdonell was engaged, I will add the following particulars as to the Highland settlement which Colonel Macdonell gave me. In 1798, the submission of the Highland chiefs to the House of Hanover having been of some standing, and their adhesion being, moreover, cemented in a common sentiment of abhorrence of the French Revolution, they were willingly induced to raise regiments among their clans. This was done by Glengarry, Macleod, and others. At the peace these regiments were disbanded, but finding that complications of various sorts had necessarily arisen during their absence respecting their lands and holdings at home, and, in point of fact, that they had no homes to return to, the greater part remained temporarily domiciled at Glasgow, the place of their disbandment. I infer that they remained under the charge and direction of Bishop Macdonell, who had accompanied them in their campaigns as chaplain, and was the first Catholic priest officially recognised in the capacity of regimental chaplain. At Glasgow (previously only served as a flying mission), he hired a storehouse, which he opened as a chapel, but stealthily only, as two of the congregation were always posted as a guard at the entrance on Sunday. He found only eighteen Catholics at Glasgow at that time, i.e., I suppose, previously to the disbandment of the Highlanders. Through Bishop Macdonell's influence with Lord Sidmouth— who, although a strong opponent of the Catholic claims, always acted in his relations with him, he said, in the most honourable and straightforward way—the emigration of the Highlanders to Canada was shortly afterwards arranged.

Colonel Macdonell was subsequently partially reinstated in his command of the Glengarry regiment. The important services rendered by Colonel Macdonell in Canada, to which I have alluded, were—1. The taking of Ogdensburg at a critical moment, on his own responsibility, and contrary to orders, which had the effect of diverting the American attack from Upper Canada at a moment when it was entirely undefended; and, 2. Bringing the regiment of French Canadian militia, then temporarily under his command, from Kingston, by a forced run down the rapids of the St Lawrence without pilots (passing the point where Lord Amherst lost eighty men), in time enough (he arrived the day before, unknown to the Americans) to support De Saluberry at the decisive action at Chateaugay. De Saluberry indeed had only 300 French Canadians under his command, which, with the 600 brought up by Colonel Macdonell, only made up a force of 900 (with about 100 Indians), with which to check General Hampton's advance with some 7000 (the Americans stated the force at 5520 infantry and 180 cavalry, James, i. 305) in his advance on Montreal. In point of fact, Colonel Macdonell must be considered, on any impartial review of the facts, to have won the day (*vide infra*), yet he was not even mentioned in Sir G. Prevost's dispatch.

Colonel Macdonell received the Companionship of the Bath for the taking of Ogdensburg, and the gold medal for his conduct in the action at Chateaugay.

I append the following accounts of the affairs at Ogdensburg and Chateaugay, adding a few particulars in correction and explanation— Alison, "History of Europe," xix. 121 (7th ed.), says—"Shortly after Colonel M'Donnell (Macdonell), with two companies of the Glengarry Fencibles, and two of the 8th, converted a *feigned* attack which he was ordered to make on Fort Ogdensburg into a real one. The assault was made under circumstances of the utmost difficulty; deep snow impeded the assailants at every step, and the American marksmen, from behind their defences, kept up a very heavy fire; but the gallantry of the British overcame every obstacle, and the fort was carried, with *eleven guns, all its stores,* and *two armed schooners* in the harbour." The difficulties, as I have understood from Colonel Macdonell, were not so much from the impediments of the snow, as from the dangerous state of the St Lawrence at the time, the ice literally waving under the tramp of his men as he passed them over (ten paces apart). The stroke of the axe, by which they judged, told it indeed to be only barely safe, and it had never been crossed by troops before at that point, as it was deemed insecure, being within three miles of the Gallops Rapids. (Among the guns were some taken from General Burgoyne.)

A fuller account of the taking of Ogdensburg may be read in Mr W. James' "Full and Correct Account of the Military Occurrences of the late War between Great Britain and the United States of America," vol. i. p. 135–141: London, 1818; he adds, "Previously to dismissing the affair at Ogdensburg it may be right to mention that Sir G. Prevost's secretary, or some person who had the transcribing of Major (Colonel) Macdonnell's (Macdonell's) official letter, must have inserted by mistake the words 'In consequence of the commands of his Excellency.' Of this there needs no stronger proof than that Major (Colonel) Macdonnell (Macdonell) while he was in the heat of the battle, received a private note from Sir G. dated from 'Flint's Inn at 9 o'clock,' repeating his orders not to make the attack; and even in the first private letter which Sir G. wrote to Major Macdonnell (Colonel Macdonell) after being informed of his success, he could not help qualifying his admiration of the exploit with a remark that the latter had *rather* exceeded his instructions—(*Note.*—Both of these letters the author has seen"), vol. i. 140. Colonel Macdonell's explanation to me of his taking this responsibility on himself was simply that he saw that the fate of the whole of Upper Canada depended upon it. Colonel Macdonell had received information that 5000 American troops were moving up in the direction of Ogdensburg, and they, in fact, came up a week after it was taken, under General Pike; but seeing the altered aspect of affairs, they moved off, and fell back upon Sackett's Harbour, anticipating a similar attack at that point.

Colonel Macdonell always spoke with much emotion of the gallant conduct of a Captain Jenkins, a young officer under his command, who, although he had both arms shattered by two successive shots, struggled on at the head of his men until he swooned. He survived some years, but died of the overcharge of blood to the head consequent on the loss of his limbs.

As Ogdensburg was a frontier town on the American side of the St Lawrence, Sir G. Prevost authorised payment for any plunder by the troops, but Colonel Macdonell received a certificate from the inhabitants that they had not lost a single shilling—which must be recorded to the credit of the Glengarry Highlanders under his command.

As I have already said, although Colonel Macdonell commanded the larger force, and by an independent command, at the action of Chateaugay, his name is not mentioned in Sir G. Prevost's dispatch, nor in Alison, who apparently follows the official account (xix. 131, 7th ed.) In Alison, De Saluberry is called, by a clerical error, De Salavary—such, after all, is fame! saith Hyperion. Although his troops, raw levies, broke, and Colonel De Saluberry was virtually a prisoner when Colonel Macdonell came up to the support, it was through no fault of his disposition of his men—(Colonel Macdonell always spoke of him as an excellent officer, who behaved on the occasion in the most noble and intrepid manner).

The American troops at Chateaugay are variously stated at 7000 to 5700 (Alison says, "4000 effective infantry and 2000 militia, and 10 guns," xix.

131). The British, 300 French Canadian militia, under De Saluberry; 600 under Colonel Macdonell, and some Indians, without artillery.

A full, but, Colonel Macdonell said, inaccurate account (from imperfect information) will be found in Mr W. James' "Military Occurrences," above referred to.

I extract the following passages, i. 307:— "The British advanced corps, stationed near the frontiers, was commanded by Lieutenant-Colonel De Saluberry of the Canadian Fencibles, and consisted of the two flank companies of that corps and four companies of voltigeurs, and six flank companies of embodied militia and Chateaugay chasseurs, placed under the immediate orders of Lieutenant-Colonel Macdonell, late of the Glengarrys, who so distinguished himself at Ogdensburg. The whole of this force did not exceed 800 rank and file. There were also at the post 172 Indians under Captain Lamotte." Colonel Macdonell's account differed substantially. It has been already mentioned that he had brought up his troops by a forced march the night before, and held them under a separate command. I conclude with the following passage as bearing out Colonel Macdonell's version:— "The Americans, although they did not occupy one foot of the 'abatis,' nor Lieutenant-Colonel De Saluberry retire one inch from the ground on which he had been standing, celebrated this partial retiring as a retreat.... By way of animating his little band when thus momentarily *pressed*" [Colonel Macdonell's version was, that although the troops were driven back, Colonel De Saluberry literally "refused to retire one inch himself," and virtually remained a prisoner until—] Colonel De Saluberry ordered the bugleman to sound "the advance. This was heard by Lieutenant-Colonel Macdonell, who thinking the Colonel was in want of support, caused his own bugles to answer, and immediately advanced with two ['six'] of his companies. He at the same time sent ten or twelve buglemen into the adjoining woods with orders to separate ['widely'], and blow with all their might. This little 'ruse de guerre' led the Americans to believe that they had more thousands than hundreds to contend with, and deterred them from even attempting to penetrate the 'abatis.'"

For the rest of the account I must refer my readers to Mr W. James' "History," as above; though, if a complete and accurate account of an engagement which probably saved British Canada were ever thought desirable, Colonel Macdonell's commentaries (MS.) on the above and the official accounts, would afford valuable supplementary information.[5]

CHAPTER I
THE LAW OF NATIONS

The increasing number of essays, pamphlets, works, and reviews of works on speculative subjects, with which the literature of England at present teems, compels the conclusion that the public mind has been greatly unsettled or strangely transformed since the days when John Bull was the plain matter-of-fact old gentleman that Washington Irving pleasantly described him.

Remembering the many sterling and noble qualities whimsically associated with this practical turn of mind, it will be felt by many to be a change for the worse. But if old English convictions, maxims, and ways of thought have lost their meaning; if in fine it is true that the mind of England has become unsettled, it says much for the practical good sense of Englishmen that they should have overcome their natural repugnances, and should so earnestly turn to the discussion of these questions, not indeed with the true zest for speculation, but in the practical conviction that it is in this arena that the battle of the Constitution must be fought.

There is, as it has been truly observed,[6] "an instinctive feeling that any speculation which affects this" (the speculation in question being the effect of the Darwinian theory on conscience), "must also affect, sooner or later, the practical principles and conduct of men in their daily lives. This naturally comes much closer to us than any question as to the comparative nearness of our kinship to the gorilla or the orang can be expected to do. *No great modification of opinion takes place with respect to the moral faculties, which does not ultimately and in some degree modify the ethical practice and political working of the society in which it comes to prevail.*"

There is perhaps no question which lies more at the root of political constitutions, and which must more directly determine the conduct of states in their relations to each other, than the question whether or not, or in what sense, there was such a thing as natural law, *i.e.* a law antecedent to the formation of individual political societies, and which is common to and binding on them all.

It may be worth while, therefore, to examine whether a stricter discrimination may not be made between things which are sometimes confounded, viz.:—The Law of Nations and International Law, natural law and the state of nature; and even if the attempt at discrimination should fail in exactitude, it may yet, by opening out fresh views, contribute light to minds of greater precision, who may thus be enabled to hit upon the exact truth.

This view was partially exposed in an article which was inserted in the Tablet, September 28, 1861,[7] entitled "International Law and the Law of Nations," and, all things considered, I do not think that I can better consult the interests of my readers, than by reproducing an extract from it here, as a convenient basis of operation from which to advance into a somewhat unexplored country:—

> "It has been the fashion since Bentham's[8] time, to substitute the phrase 'International Law' for the 'Law of Nations,' as if they were convertible terms. The substitution, however, covers a distinction sufficiently important.

> "The 'Law of Nations' is an obligation which binds the consciences of nations to respect the eternal principle of justice in their relations with each other. 'International law' is the system of rules, precedents, and maxims accumulated in recognition of the eternal law. But as men may build a theatre or a gambling-house upon the foundations constructed for a religious edifice, and upon a stone consecrated for an altar, so has it been possible for diplomacy to substitute a system of chicanery for the simple laws which were intended to facilitate the intercourse of nations, and with such effect as in a great number of cases to place international law in contradiction with the law of nations—as, for instance, when in a certain case the law of nations says that it is wrong to invade a neighbour's territory, international law is made to say that it is lawful to invade in such a case, because such-and-such monarchs in past history have done so.

> "Practically the effect of the substitution is, that the sentiment of justice disappears, that wars which formerly were called unjust, are now called inevitable, so that good men, disheartened at the conflicting evidence of precedents, yield their sense of right and wrong, and defer to the adjudication of diplomatists. This is particularly satisfactory to the modern spirit which will admit nothing to be law which is

superior to, and distinct from, that which the human intellect has determined to be law.

"But the sense of right and wrong in good men is that which gives its whole efficacy to the law of nations. There is nothing else in the last resort, to restrain the ambition and passion of princes, but the reprobation of mankind — nothing but the fear of invading that "moral territory"[9] which even bad men find it necessary to conquer, 'dans l'ame des peuples ses voisins.' On the other hand, the whole mass of precedents to which diplomatists appeal, which are rarely carefully collated with those which legists have accumulated and digested, is nothing but a veil which thinly covers the supremacy of might and the right of force.

"In fact, the conventional deference which is paid to them, is at best only the hypocritical homage which force is constrained to pay to justice before it strikes its blow.

"International law, therefore, as accumulated in the precedents of diplomatists, is a parasitical growth upon that tree which has its roots in the hearts of nations, and which may be compared to one of those old oaks under which kings used to sit and administer justice. It was a dream of Dodwell's that the 'law of nations was a divine revelation made to the family preserved in the ark.' In the grotesqueness and wildness of this theory we detect a true idea. The law of nations is an unwritten law, tradited in the memories of the people, or, so far as it is written, to be found in the works of writers on public law, like Grotius, whose authorities, as Sir J. Mackintosh remarks, are in great part, and very properly, made up of the sayings of the poets and orators of the world, 'for they address themselves to the general feelings and sympathies of mankind.' It is in this that the Scriptural saying about the people is so true — 'But they will maintain the state of the world.' And it is a just observation, that 'the people are often wrong in their opinions, but in their sentiments rarely.' You may produce state papers and manifestoes, written with all the dexterity of Talleyrand, and the lying tact of Fouché, but you will not convince the people. You have your opportunity. The Liberal press of Europe, at this moment, may be said to be in possession of the whole field of political literature; nevertheless, nothing will prevent its being recorded in history,[10] that Victor

Emmanuel in seizing upon the patrimony of St Peter was a robber, and his conquest an usurpation."

I have observed that International Law is the more appropriate term from Bentham's point of view, and as Bentham is the most redoubtable opponent of natural right and the law of nations, I will quote him at some length:—

"Another man says that there is an eternal and immutable rule of right, and that that rule of right dictates so-and-so. And then he begins giving you his sentiments upon anything that comes uppermost; and these sentiments (you are to take it for granted) are so many branches of the eternal rule of right.... A great multitude of people are continually talking of the law of nature; and they go on giving you their sentiments about what is right and what is wrong, and these sentiments, you are to understand, are so many chapters and sections of the law of nature. Instead of the phrase, law of nature, you have sometimes law of reason, right reason, natural justice, natural equity, good order. Any of them will do equally well. This latter is most used in politics. The three last are much more tolerable than the others, because they do not very explicitly claim to be anything more than phrases. They insist, but feebly, upon the being looked upon as so many positive standards of themselves, and seem content to be taken, upon occasion, for phrases expressive of the conformity of the thing in question to the proper standard, whatever that may be. On most occasions, however, it will be better to say utility—utility is clearer, as referring more especially to pain and pleasure."

In truth, although Mr Bentham indulges a pleasant ridicule, yet the ridicule and the thing ridiculed being eliminated, the fact that there is a belief in a law of nature remains untouched. It is probable, therefore, that appeals will be frequent to what is believed to be "the eternal and immutable rule of right," "to the law of nature," &c., *i.e.* each and every individual, all mankind distributively, so appeal, because there is a deep conviction among mankind, severally and collectively, that there is this eternal and immutable rule of right, blurred and obscured though it may be, or concealed behind a cloud of human passion and error: and most men, moreover, will have an instinct which will tell them when an individual is substituting his own ideas for the eternal and immutable law,—as, for instance, when at the conclusion of the sentence quoted, Mr Bentham seeks to substitute his own peculiar crochet, as embodied in the word "utility" (which may be used indifferently in the sense of the absolute or relative, the supernatural or the natural, the immediate or the remote utility), as synonymous with "natural justice," "natural equity," and "good order."

So, again, when Mr Bentham comes to the discussion of "International Law," after pointing out, very properly, that whereas internal laws have always a super-ordinate authority to enforce them, "that when nations fall into disputes there is no such super-ordinate impartial authority to bind them to conformity with any fixed rules," Mr Bentham goes on to say, "though there is no distinct official authority capable of enforcing right principles of international law, there is a power bearing with more or less influence on the conduct of all nations, as of all individuals, however transcendently potent they may be, this is the power of public opinion." Public opinion! not then of public opinion threatening coercion, for in that case we should have "a super-ordinate impartial authority binding to conformity with fixed rules," but public opinion as a moral expression. If, however, you take from it the expression of right and wrong, of natural justice, and of the eternal and immutable law; if its expression is not reprobation, and, so to speak, a fore-judgment of the retribution of the Most High, but only dissatisfaction or the mere pronouncement of the inutility of the action, whatever it may be, what even with Benthamites can be its efficacy and worth? The vanquished say to their conqueror, the multitudes to their oppressor, this oppression is not according to utility. Utility! he replies, useful to whom? To you! Fancy the look of Prince Bismarck as he would reply to such an address. What are men if you take away the notion of right and wrong but "the flies of a summer?" How different was the expression of Napoleon after his ill-usage of Pius VII., "J'ai frissonè les nations." Napoleon had a conscience,[11] and in his moments of calm reflection felt in its full force the reprobation of mankind.

When Bentham, still speaking of public opinion, adds:—

> "The power in question has, it is true, various degrees of influence. The strong are better able to put it at defiance than the weak. Countries which, being the most populous, are likely also to be the strongest, carry a certain support of public opinion with all their acts *whatever they may be.* But still it is the only power which can be moved to good purposes in this case; and, however high some may appear to be above it, there are in reality none who are not more or less subject to its influence."

Here Bentham is again in imagination gathering men together like the flies of a summer,—the force of their opinion depending on their numbers. But what, again, is the force of all this buzzing if it is the mere expression of "pleasure," or "pain," of satisfaction or dissatisfaction in the masses? Conquerors may not always be relentless, they may at times exhibit some sympathy with their fellow men; but as a rule they are so dominated by some one idea or passion, or at best are so absorbed in the interests of their own people, as to be deaf to such appeals. Prince Bismarck's sentiments towards France during the late war are pretty well known; but it is said that after the conflict was over, and when France was in the throes of its terrible internecine conflict, he was asked, "What is your Excellency's opinion of the present state of France?" he replied, "Das ist mit ganz wurst," which is equivalent to "I don't care two straws about it."[12] How are men of this stamp to be affected by any exclamations of pleasure or pain? If on the contrary it is the voice of reprobation which they hear, and if in their case the saying "vox populi vox Dei" is felt to have its full application, there is then a public opinion expressed which is calculated to strike the conscience and inspire terror, and that is quite another matter.

De Tocqueville, from his own point of view, puts the argument in favour of natural justice very forcibly, and in a certain construction would express the identical truth for which I contend.

> "I hold it to be an impious and an execrable maxim that, politically speaking, a people has a right to do whatever it pleases; and yet I have asserted that all authority originates in the will of the majority. Am I, then, in contradiction with myself? A general law which bears the name of Justice has been made and sanctioned, not only by a majority of this or that people, but by a majority of mankind. The rights of every people are consequently confined within the limits of what is just. A nation may be considered in the light of a jury which is empowered to represent society at large, and to apply the great general law of justice. Ought such a jury, which represents society, to have more power than the society in which the laws it applies originate." —M. de Tocqueville's "Democracy in America", ii. 151.

Although M. de Tocqueville's view does not go to the full length of the argument, still, regarded in this light, the voice of the majority of mankind, or of any large masses of mankind, has a very different significance from what it bears in the writings of Bentham.

Let us now consider the doctrines of Bentham in their more recent exposition.

The *Pall Mall Gazette*, Oct. 6, 1870, says:—

> "Laws have been described as definitions of pre-existing rights, relations between man and man, reflections of divine ordinances, anything but what they really are,—forms of organised constraint. It says little for the assumed clear-headedness of Englishmen, that they have very generally preferred the ornate jargon of Hooker, to the accurate and intelligible account of law and government which forms the basis of Bentham's juridical system."

It says much, however, for their strong political sense and sagacity. If this is the true and only description of law, it is tantamount to saying that law is force and force is law; in other words, that the commands of a legitimate government need not be regarded when it is weak, but that the enactments of power must always be obeyed, however it is acquired, and whether its decrees are in accordance with right or contrary to justice. It is a ready justification for tyranny, equally sanctioning the "lettres de cachet" of the ancient regime, and the proscriptions of the Convention, equally at hand for the National Assembly at Versailles, or for the Commune at Paris. But however much it may be disguised, it is the only alternative definition of law, when once you say that law is not of divine ordinance and tradition. If no regard is to be had to the definition of right, but the term law is to be applied to any adequate act of repression, there is in truth nothing but force. Yet why should force adequate to its purpose seek to cloak itself in the forms of law? I suppose the question must have been put and answered before; but the answer can only be because law is felt to import a totally different set of ideas from force.

It is necessary, more especially now that the utilitarian theory is dominant, to enter a protest according to the turn the argument may take, but in the end nothing more can be said than was said by Cicero in the century before our Lord:—

> "Est enim unum jus, quo devincta est hominum societas, et quod lex constituit una; quæ lex est recta ratio imperandi atque prohibendi: quam qui ignorat is est injustus, sive est illa scripta uspiam, sive nusquam. Quod si justitia est obtemperatio scriptis legibus institutisque populorum, et si, ut iidem dicunt utilitate omnia metienda sunt, negliget leges, easque perrumpit, si poterit, is, qui sibi eam rem fructuosam putabit fore. Ita fit, ut nulla sit omnino justitia; si neque naturâ est, eaque propter utilitatem constituitur, utilitate alia convellitur."—*De Legibus*, i. 15.

It is only upon this construction that the Law of Nations can be said to exist, as "there is no superordinate authority to enforce it." It is accordingly asserted that the law of nations is not really law. But is not this only when it is regarded from the point of view of "organised constraint?"[13] If it is regarded as a divine ordinance, or even as under the divine sanction, then it is law in a much higher degree than simple internal or municipal law, for it more immediately and directly depends upon this sanction; and hence nations may more confidently appeal to heaven for the redress of wrong here below than individuals—seeing that, as Bossuet somewhere says, God rewards and chastises nations in this world, since it is not according to His divine dispensation to reward them corporately in the next.

More recently, however, the extraordinary successes and subversions which we have witnessed during this last year, have brought the *Pall Mall Gazette* face to face with problems pressing for immediate and anxious settlement; and in a series of articles it has discussed the question of the law of nations with much depth and earnestness.

I there observe phrases which I can hardly distinguish from those I have just employed. Combating Mr Mill's view, the writer says:—

"Nobody knows better than he that International Law is not really law, and why it is not law; but he seems to have jumped to the conclusion that it is therefore the same thing as morality.... There cannot, in truth, be any closer analogy than that which we drew the other day between the law of nations and the law of honour, and between public war and private duelling." [This is upon an assumption that there is nothing "essentially immoral in the code of honour," as "to a great extent it coincided with morality."] "But it differed from simple morality in that its precepts were enforced, not by general disapprobation, but by a challenge to the offender by anybody who supposed himself to be aggrieved by the offence. The possible result always was, that the champion of the law might himself be shot, and this was the weakness of the system. But this is exactly the weakness of international law, and the *original idea* at the *basis* both of *public war* and of private duelling was precisely the same,— *that God Almighty somehow interposed* in favour of the combatant *who had the juster cause.* There is clear historical evidence that the feuds which became duels were supposed to be fought out under divine supervision, *just as battles* were believed to be decided by the God of battles."

I believe that if history could be re-written from this point of view that many startling revelations would be brought to light. It is with reluctance that I turn from the points upon which I approach to agreement with the writer, to those upon which we fundamentally differ.

And here I must remark, that "the accurate and intelligible account of law and government which forms the basis of Bentham's juridical system"[14] (supra, p. 9), is not distinguishable from, and in any case ultimately depends upon, his theory of utility as a foundation, or, as his later disciples say, a "standard" of morals. Such a standard is the negation of all morality; and if it ever came to stand alone every notion of morals would be obliterated, because, being open to every interpretation, and incapable of supplying any definite rule itself, it would abrogate every other, and under a plausible form abandon mankind to its lusts and passions.

In the *Pall Mall Gazette,* April 12, 1871, an article entitled "Mr Darwin on Conscience," discusses Benthamism with reference to Darwinism. There is a fitness in this which does not immediately appear.

The writer says:—

> "What is called the question of the moral sense is really two: how the moral faculty is acquired, and how it is regulated. Why do we obey conscience or feel pain in disobeying it? And why does conscience prescribe *one kind* of actions and condemn another kind? To put it more technically, there is the question of the subjective existence of conscience, and there is the question of its objective prescriptions."

I will avail myself of this distinction, and, setting aside the questions referring to the "subjective existence of conscience," I will ask attention only to "its objective prescriptions." Assuming, then, the operations of conscience in the individual man, there will necessarily also have been in the course of history some outward expression of this inward feeling in maxims, precepts, and laws, if not also reminiscences of primeval revelations and divine commands.

It will be true, therefore, to say, without touching the deeper question of the foundation of morals, that there has been a tradition of morals which cannot but have had its influence in all ages upon the "social feelings" in which, according to the Pall Mall Gazette, "it will always be necessary to lay the basis of conscience." Now is this tradition of morals identical with utilitarian precept? If the tradition of morals is identical with "the greatest happiness principle," then that principle was no discovery of Bentham's,[15] neither can Benthamism be regarded as "the new application of an old principle." Bentham in that case simply informed mankind that they had been talking prose all their lives without knowing it! Benthamism, however, in point of fact, is felt as a new principle precisely in so far as it discards the old morality. The question which I ask is, how does it account for these old notions of morality obtaining among mankind? How is it that mankind has so long and so persistently, both in their notion of what was good and their sense of what was evil, departed from the line of their true interests, as disclosed in the utilitarian philosophy? If the history of man is what the Scriptures tell us it was, the manner in which this has come about is sufficiently explained; and there is no mystery as to the notion of sin, the necessity of expiation, the restraints and limitations of natural desires, the excellence of contemplation, and the obligation of sacrifices and prayers. Now, if the history of mankind is not to be invoked in explanation, it is difficult to see how these notions should not conflict with any theory and plan of life based on a principle of utility.[16] It is not unnatural, therefore, that the utilitarians should turn to Darwinism and other such kindred systems for the solution of their difficulties.

The *Pall Mall Gazette*, April 12, 1871, says:—

"Between Mr Darwin and utilitarians, as utilitarians, there is no such quarrel as he would appear to suppose. The narrowest utilitarian could say little more than Mr Darwin says (ii. 393):—'As all men desire their own happiness, praise or blame is bestowed on actions and motives according as they tend to this end; and as happiness is an essential part of the general good, the greatest happiness principle indirectly serves as a nearly safe standard of right and wrong.'"

Now, there is nothing in this reiteration of Benthamism which has not been thrice refuted by Lord Macaulay in the Essays above referred to. I append an extract more exactly to the point.[17]

I refer to it because it will be interesting to see how the argument looks in its application to Darwinism.

It will be seen that if the conditions of unlimited enjoyment anywhere existed, Lord Macaulay's strictures would lose something of their force. If, indeed, there was superabundance and superfluity of everything for all in this life, then anything which conduces to the satisfaction of the individual would add to, or at least would not detract from, the sum of happiness of all mankind. But unless you can show this—if even the reverse of this is the truth—then "the greatest happiness" will be in proportion to the self-abnegation of those who possess more, or have the greatest faculties or facilities of producing more.

Now, if there is one view more prominent than another in Mr Darwin's work, it is embodied in the phrase to which he has given a new sense and significance, "the struggle for existence." In the midst of this struggle for existence, what is there in the greatest happiness principle to bind the individual to abnegation? Why should he postpone his certain and immediate gratification to the remote advantage of others, or of distant and contingent advantage to himself? If, on the other hand, he regards the transitoriness of the enjoyment, and balances it against the fixity and eternity of the consequences, the argument takes altogether different proportions, and the temptation to enjoyment is inversely to the intensity of the struggle for existence.

I will take another test of Benthamism by Darwinism, which will more exactly bring out the argument for which I contend. We have a traditional horror of infanticide which revolts all our best feelings and shocks our principles. But if Mr Darwin has demonstrated this struggle for existence existing from all time; if also we are disembarrassed from all advertence to another world; if, further, Mr Malthus, before Mr Darwin, has shown reason to believe that over-population is the cause of half the evils of this life, what is there in Benthamite principles which should prevent our sacrificing these unconscious innocents to the greatest happiness of the greatest number? Nothing, except the horror we should excite among mankind still imbued with the old superstitions! A person who did not hold to Mr Malthus' views might demur; but a Malthusian, who was also a disciple of Mr Bentham, could only hold back because his feelings were better than his principles. A disciple of Mr Darwin's would probably stand aloof, and would merely see in our notions an artificial interference with the working of his theory, preventing the struggle for existence going on according to natural laws. This seems to me to be almost said in the same article from the *Pall Mall Gazette*, from which I have quoted. Mr Darwin, in his "Origin of Species" (p. 249), has pointed out that "we ought to admire the savage instinct which leads the queen-bee to destroy her young daughters as soon as born, because this is for the good of the community." And in his new book he says, firmly and unmistakably (i. 73), that "if men were reared under precisely the same conditions as hive-bees, there can hardly be a doubt that our unmarried females would, like the worker-bees, think it a sacred duty to kill their brothers, and mothers would strive to kill their fertile daughters, and no one would think of interfering." The *Pall Mall* continues—

"If, from one point of view, this is apt to shock a *timorous* and *unreflecting* mind, by asserting that the most cherished of our affections might have been, under *certain* circumstances, a vicious piece of self-indulgence, and its place in the scale of morality taken by what is *now* the most atrocious kind of crime; nevertheless, from another point of view, such an assertion is as reassuring as the most absolute of moralists could desire, for it is tantamount to saying that the foundations of morality, the distinctions of right and wrong, are deeply laid in the very conditions of social existence; that there is, in the face of these conditions, a positive and definite difference between the moral and the immoral, the virtuous and the vicious, the right and the wrong, in the actions of individuals partaking of that social existence."

This is very well. It is so *now*, because of the traditional sentiments and principles which still retain their force—but how long will it continue?

I invite attention to the following passage from Mr Hepworth Dixon's "New America" (vol. i. p. 312, 6th edition), which I must say struck me very forcibly when I read it. He narrates a conversation which he had with Brigham Young on the subject of incest:—"Speaking for himself, not for the church, he (Brigham Young) said he saw *none at all* (*i.e.* no objection at all). He added, however, that he would not do it himself,—'my prejudices prevent me.'" Upon which Mr Hepworth Dixon observes—

"This *remnant* of an old feeling brought from the Gentile world, *and this alone*, would seem to prevent the saints (Mormons) from rushing into the higher forms of incest. How long will these Gentile sentiments remain in force? 'You will find here,' said elder Stenhouse to me, talking on another subject, 'polygamists of the third generation. When these boys and girls grow up and marry, you will have in these valleys the *true feeling* of patriarchal life. The *old world is about us yet*, and we are always thinking of what people may say in the Scottish hills and the Midland shires.'"

Here, and in the previous extract, we seem to catch glimpses of what the morality of the future is likely to be, at any rate in such matters as infanticide and incest, if old notions are to be discarded, and men are left, in each generation, to no higher rule than their own individual calculation as to pleasure and pain, or to the prevailing sense or determination of the community as to what the conditions of utility may permit.

The nineteenth century is now verging on its decline, and of it, too, may we say that it has been better than its principles. Yet, in spite of its philanthropy, and its aspirations for good, the destructive principles which it has nursed are rapidly gaining on its instincts: and if we may not truly at this moment paint its glories, as they have been depicted, I think by Alexandre Dumas, as "the livery of heroism, turned up with assassination and incest," is the time very remote when the description will apply?

CHAPTER II
THE LAW OF NATURE

But underlying the question of the law of nations, and determining it, is the question whether or not there is a law of nature—a rule of right and wrong, independent of, and anterior to, positive legislative or international enactment. To prevent misconception, however, as to the scope of the inquiry, it is as well that I should state that I am only regarding the law of nature as the law of conscience (by which the Gentiles "were a law unto themselves," Rom. ii. 14), in so far as it has manifested itself in laws and maxims; and the question I am here concerned with is, whether in any sense which history can take cognizance of, there was a rule of right and wrong previous to legislative enactment?

At the first glance, the question would seem sufficiently disposed of by saying that men never were in a state of nature; which is true in this sense, that mankind never formed a multitude of isolated individuals, or a promiscuous herd of men and women. A totally different solution supposes a state of nature; but which, whether it depicts it as a golden age or an age of barbarism, still contemplates mankind in this state as a mere congeries of individuals, without law, or else without the necessity of law—in either case an aggregate of isolated individuals, eventually to be brought into the state of civil society by a social compact.

Now my intention is not to combat this view—which at the present moment may be considered to be exploded—but to account for it.

I think that I shall do something towards clearing up this mystery by pointing out that this latter solution, although in great vogue with the publicists of the seventeenth and eighteenth centuries, is traced beyond them to the classical times, and was derived by them through the tradition of the Roman law from Paganism. A theory of the lawyers, and a theory of the philosophers, concreted with a true but distorted fact in tradition in order to produce this belief, viz., that society was founded by a contract among men who were originally equal.[18]

I shall in a subsequent chapter state to what extent I believe it to be true that society was founded upon a contract, and also the way in which this impression was confirmed, from the actual circumstances of the formation of the early communities of Greece and Italy; and I shall then examine the true tradition, such as I believe it to be, of a state of nature associated with the reminiscence of a golden age, as contrasted with the distinct yet parallel tradition of a state of nature identified with a state of barbarism (vide ch. vii. and ch. xiii.)

This latter tradition I believe to have been a recollection of that period of temporary privation after the Flood, when mankind clung to the caverns and the mountains (vide p. 137), until, incited by the example of Noah, they were brought into the plains, and instructed in the arts of husbandry by the patriarch; and the notion of the primitive equality[19] of condition I believe to have originated in the Bacchanalian traditions of the same patriarch.[20]

If we start with a belief in the primitive equality of conditions, the only way out of the mesh is apparently by a theory of a compact.

> "From the Roman law downwards," says Sir G. C. Lewis, "there has been a strong tendency among jurists to deduce recognised rights and obligations from a supposed, but non-existing contract. When an express contract exists, the legal rights and duties which it creates are in general distinct and well-defined. Hence, in cases where it is wished that similar legal consequences should be drawn, which come within the spirit of the rules applicable to a contract, though they do not themselves involve any contract, the lawyer cuts the knot by saying that a contract is presumed, that there is a contract by intendment of law, that there are certain rights and obligations "*quasi ex contractu.*" Thus the Roman law held that a guardian was bound to his ward by a *quasi* contract." — *Sir G. C. Lewis, "On the Methods of Observation, &c, in Politics,"* i. 423; *"On the Social Compact,"* pp. 424–431.

It is not difficult to see how such a fiction of the law would tend to give shape and system to the vague tradition as to the fact among the populace.

The way in which the philosopher came to his conclusion was somewhat more complex. It will have been seen that the notion of the state of nature and the social compact was, among the ancients, in the main, a figment of the imagination, and not a tradition. But there was also a tradition of a law of nature which did not at all correspond to a state of license, of equality, and of barbarism, such as the state of nature was conceived to be. It was, on the contrary, a law of decorum and restraint. What, then, the Roman probably meant by the law of nature was a reminiscence of a primitive revelation, or a tradition of the maxims of right and wrong by which men were guided in their relations to one another, when fresh from the hand of God—"a *diis recentes"* —when family life still subsisted, and before men had settled down into states and communities. It was not a law of nature as nature then was, but an aspiration after a lost rule of life, as after a higher standard, and an attempt to trace it back, through the corruption of mankind. Dim and uncertain as these notions were, they were not without their influence.

But their ideas as to the cosmogony were more shadowy still. When, then, in reasoning from a law of nature to a state of nature, mankind discovered that they knew or remembered nothing of their origin, or of the history of the human race, except indirectly through legendary lore, they then had recourse to the philosophers. These latter then did what philosophers incline to do in such cases of difficulty. They regarded the existing state of things, and finding it to be artificial, they, by a process of abstraction, resolved it into its elements, and, having thus reduced society into an assemblage of individuals, substituted their last analysis for the commencement of all things. In this analysis they found men, what historically and in fact they had never been, alike free, equal, and independent.

The theory of the social compact among men individually free and equal was in the main a fiction, started *à posteriori* to account for relations otherwise obscure, or, as Sir Henry Maine explains, to facilitate modifications which were felt to be desirable; and we cannot be astonished that Paganism should take this view, unless we are prepared to believe that the traditions truly embodying the history of the world were more direct, vivid, and potential than I suppose them to have been. It is at least remarkable, that in proportion as men lose their faith, they fall back, as if by some necessary law, upon some theory which directly or indirectly contemplates mankind as a collection of atoms; and if ever society should lose again the history of its origin, as would happen if ever infidelity were to gain complete ascendancy, it would return by the same processes to the same conclusion. But however sceptical individual minds may become, or however general may be the disposition to reject or ignore the scriptural narrative, the general framework of its statements is now too firmly embedded in the belief of mankind to be easily overthrown.

The notion of a social compact, in more recent times, obtained a certain credence[21] so long as the discussion was confined to Hobbes, Locke, and their disciples. And it must be borne in mind that this is a very taking theory, a ready and convenient starting point, and conformable to much that is true in history and politics. But it is long since exploded; and even the fervid advocacy of Rousseau, in an age peculiarly predisposed for its reception, could not secure for it even temporary recognition among mankind; and why? Because, whenever the discussion cools, men will inevitably ask each other the question, If such a compact took place, where shall we locate it consistently with the evidence recorded in Genesis? Remove the evidence in Genesis, and such a theory becomes at once a tenable and plausible conjecture.

As I shall have occasion, later on, to come into collision with Sir Henry Maine upon some points, I have the greater satisfaction here in invoking his testimony. This acute and learned writer ("Ancient Law," p. 90) regrets that the Voltairean prejudices of the last century prevented reference "to the only primitive records worth studying—the early history of the Jews[22].... One of the few characteristics which the school of Rousseau had in common with the school of Voltaire was an utter disdain of all religious antiquities, and more than all of those of the Hebrew race. It is well known that it was a point of honour with the reasoners of that day to assume, not merely that the institutions called after Moses were not divinely dictated, ... but that they and the entire Pentateuch were a gratuitous forgery executed after the return from the Captivity. Debarred, therefore, from one chief security against speculative delusion, the philosophers of France, in their eagerness to escape from what they deemed a superstition of the priests, flung themselves headlong into a superstition of the lawyers."

CHAPTER III
PRIMITIVE LIFE

The scriptural narrative seems to establish:—(1.) That human society did not commence with the fortuitous concurrence of individuals, but that, though originating with a single pair, for the purposes of practical inquiry it commences with a group of families—the family of Noah and his sons, together with their families, and whose dispersion in other families is subsequently recorded. (2.) That men were not primitively in a state of savagery, barbarism, and ignorance of civil life; but that, on the contrary, it is presumable that Noah and his family brought with them out of the ark the traditions and experiences of two thousand years, and, not to speak of special revelations, the arts of civil life and acquaintance with cities. (3.) That, although everything in the early state of mankind would have led to dispersion, and although there is mention of one great and complete dispersion, yet this dispersion of mankind was a dispersion of families and not of individuals.

In all our speculations, therefore, as to society and government, it is the family and not the individual whom we must regard as the elementary constituent.

Moreover, so long as family government sufficed, there was nothing but the family. The state would have existed only in germ (vide infra, p. 341), and would have remained thus inchoate even during that subsequent period when families were affiliated in tribal connection, though not yet coalesced into tribal union. It is my impression, that the period during which family government sufficed, continued much longer than is generally supposed; for, until the world became peopled and crowded, everything led to dispersion and the continuance of the pastoral state of life. From the necessities of pastoral life, mankind in early times could not have been gregarious—herds would have become intermixed, keep would have become short, the broad plains were spread out before them;[23] e.g. Gen. chap. xiii.—

"But Lot also, who was with Abraham, had flocks of sheep, and herds and tents. 6. Neither was the land able to bear them, that they might dwell together. 7. Whereupon there arose a strife between the herdsmen of

Abraham and Lot; and at that time the Canaanite and the Perizzite dwelt in that country. 8. Abraham therefore said, Let there be no quarrel. 9. Behold the whole land is before thee."[24]

It is scarcely to be believed, that in such a state of society there would have been feuds, in the sense of inherited or hereditary quarrels, but at most contentions for particular localities; in which case the weaker or the discomfited party would have pushed on to other ground. There was no long contest, because there was nothing worth contesting. It has been noticed that only the highly civilised man, and the savage who has tasted blood, love fighting for the mere sake and ardour of the conflict. The simple barbarian does not fight until he is attacked, neither do the wild animals of the desert; their ferocity is limited and regulated by the necessity and the provocation. It is the exception, rather than the rule, for animals to fight among themselves. It is not in the nature of man or beast to fight without a reason. Accordingly, there is no such fomenter of war as war. Carver notices that the wars carried on between the Indian nations are principally on motives of revenge, and, when not on motives of revenge, their reasons for going to war are "in general more rational and just than such as are fought by Europeans, &c"—Carver's "Travels in North America," pp. 351, 297.[25]

The same tendencies, under similar circumstances, where the tribes were not crowded or in fear of warlike neighbours, was noticed among the Red Indians some forty years ago. Now, I suppose, instances would be rare.

"When a nation of Indians becomes too numerous conveniently to procure subsistence from its own hunting-grounds, it is no uncommon occurrence for it to send out a colony, or, in other words, to separate into tribes.... The tribe so separated maintains all its relations independent of the parent nation, though the most friendly intercourse is commonly maintained, and they are almost uniformly allies. Separations sometimes take place from party dissensions, growing generally out of the jealousies of the principal chiefs, and, not unfrequently, out of petty quarrels. In such instances, in order to prevent the unnecessary and wanton effusion of blood, and consequent enfeebling of the nation, the weaker party moves off usually without the observance of much ceremony."[26]

Mr Grote in his "Plato"[27] says—

"There existed," even "in his (Plato's) time, a great variety of distinct communities—some in the simplest, most patriarchal, cyclopian condition, nothing more than families; some highly advanced in civilisation, with its accompanying good and evil, some in each intermediate stage between these two extremes. Each little family or sept exists at first separately, with a patriarch whom all implicitly obey, and peculiar customs of its own. Several of these septs gradually coalesce together into a community, choosing one or a few lawgivers to adjust and modify their respective customs into harmonious order."[28]

In the situations, however, where the more powerful families had seized the vantage-ground, or established themselves in the richest and most coveted valleys, the tendency to consolidation and permanent settlement would have more rapidly manifested itself. As the tendency to family dispersion became restrained, and its scope restricted, disputes as to *meum* and *tuum* would have become more frequent as between families, some more central authority than the family headship would have been demanded for the protection, discrimination, and regulation of property. *In these* instances the state may be said to have arisen out of the expansion of the family into the tribes—the families, probably, never having ceased to dwell together in semi-aggregation; and, when greater concentration was required, they simply had to fall back upon the patriarchal chieftain. We seem to see a tradition of this in the Anax Andron.

But equally as regards the rest there must inevitably have come a time when, as the world became crowded, the same necessity of defending their possessions, would have caused families, among whom there was no affinity of race, to coalesce, intermix, succumb, and form communities and states.

These two modes of settlement into communities and states were, however, essentially dissimilar, and the basis thus laid would have remained permanently different. The one was the basis of custom, the other of contract; the one the settlement of the East, the other of the West; and it will be seen, I think, that whilst the one was more favourable to the conservation of traditions of religion and history, the other would have better preserved the tradition of right. These are points to which I shall return in a subsequent chapter, when I shall avail myself of the investigations of Sir Henry Maine.

This simple outline, however, of human history, conformable, as I believe it to be, with the scriptural narrative, conflicts with at least three theories now much in vogue. The first, which is substantially that of Sir John Lubbock, Mr Mill,[29] and Mr B. Gould, is thus conveniently summarised by Mr Hepworth Dixon.[30]

> "Every one who has read the annals of our race—a page of nature with its counterfoil in the history of everything having life—is aware that, in our progress from the savage to the civilised state, man has had to pass through three grand stages, corresponding, as it were, to his childhood, to his youth, and to his manhood. In the first stage of his career he is a hunter, living mainly by the chase; in the second, he

is a herdsman; ... in the third stage, he is a husbandman....
Then these conditions of human life may be considered as
finding their purest types in such races as the Iroquois, the
Arabian, the Gothic, in their present stage; but each condition
is, in itself and for itself, *an affair of development and not of
race*. The Arab, who is now a shepherd, was once a hunter.
The Saxon, who is now a cultivator of the soil, was first a
hunter, then a herdsman, before he became a husbandman.
Man's progress from stage to stage is *continuous* in its
course, *obeying the laws of physical and moral change*. It is
slow, it is *uniform*, it is silent, it is unseen. In one word, it
is *growth*.... These three stages in our progress upward are
strongly marked; the interval dividing an Iroquois from an
Arab being as wide as that which separates an Arab from a
Saxon."

Now, in the first place, I must remark that the Iroquois and the Arab
have never progressed;[31] neither does the Arab at the present show any
signs of a transition to the third stage of necessary growth, nor does Mr
Hepworth Dixon, although he gives some sound practical advice as to the
best mode in which the red man is to be restrained, venture to suggest any
mode by which he is to be reclaimed from the first to the third stage, either
with or without a transition through the second stage of development. The
conclusion therefore, one would think, would be inevitable that it is an
affair of race and not of development. The Arab and the Iroquois, after the
lapse of so many centuries, are still found with the evidences of primitive
life strong upon them; and so, I imagine, we shall find it wherever we come
upon a pure race of homogeneous origin. On the contrary, we shall find that
mixed races, by the very law and reason of their admixture, have shown
the greatest adaptibility, and, whenever circumstances were favourable,
very rapid growth. Again, I very much question whether the three
stages, or rather three phases of life were ever, as a rule, progressive; and
whether, in the cases in which they might chance to have been successive,
anything occurred in the transition at all resembling an uniform law of
growth. It is very much more probable that the three were from the earliest
period contemporaneous[32]—"and Abel was a shepherd, and Cain an
husbandman" (Gen. iv.)—the determination of the sons to the avocations of
shepherd, husbandman, and hunter respectively (the latter most probably
being the last selected), being influenced by taste, character, and the division
of the inheritance, the authority of the father, the geographical conditions of
the route, and chance circumstances.

And this is the more confirmed when we consider that when once the hunter started on his career, he would have determined their avocation also for his posterity. At his death he would not have had herds of cattle to apportion to any one of his sons, and thus the taste for wild life, necessarily perpetuated, would be bred in the bone, as an indomitable characteristic of race, and the first hunter by choice would inevitably come to be the progenitor of generations of hunters by instinct and necessity.

The second theory depicts the opening scene of human existence as a state of conflict, which, it must be allowed, is perfectly consistent with the theory that it was one of savagery. The theory I am now combating was originally the theory of Hobbes; and I might have regarded it as now obsolete, were it not that it has cropped up quite recently in a most respectable quarter. Mr Hunter, in his charming work, "The Annals of Rural Bengal," has a passage which, as I think, has been taken for more than it intends, though not for more than it expresses. Mr Hunter says.

"The inquiry leads us back to that far-off time which we love to associate with patriarchal stillness. Yet the echoes of ancient life in India little resemble a Sicilian idyl or the strains of Pan's pipe, but strike the ear rather as the cries of oppressed and wandering nations, of people in constant motion and pain. Early Indian researches, however, while they make havoc of the pastoral landscapes of Genesis and Job, have a consolation peculiarly suited to this age. They plainly tell us, that as in Europe so in Asia, the primitive state of mankind was a state of unrest; and that civilisation, despite its exactions and nervous city life, is a state of repose."

It is plain that there is here question of restlessness rather than of violence; but grant that there was violence too, the account of Mr. Hunter when examined, so far from conflicting with, appears to me to fall exactly into, the lines I have indicated. Is not the scene, from before which Mr. Hunter lifts the curtain, the scene of that age following the dispersion (of which, there is such distinct tradition in his pages), which is traditionally known to us as the iron age? The error, then, of Mr. Hunter is to confound the patriarchal with the iron age. It need not therefore cause surprise that in early Indian history we should hear of conflict, for it is just at the period and under the circumstances when we should consider the collision probable.

Mr. Hunter, indeed, speaks of the aboriginal races as mysterious in their origin. But from the point of view of Genesis, there seems to be no greater mystery about them than about their conquerors the Aryans. One representative, at least, of the aboriginal race, the Santals, retain to this day the most vivid traditions of the Flood and the Dispersion[33]. Now, if there had existed any race anterior to the Santals, I think we should have heard of them. On this point we may consider Mr. Hunter's negative testimony as conclusive, both on account of his extensive knowledge of the subject, and his evident predisposition to have discovered a prior race, if it had existed; and there is nothing to show that the same line of argument would not have applied to it if its existence had been demonstrated. It must be mentioned that besides their tradition of the dispersion, the Santals retain dim recollections—borne out by comparative evidence—of having travelled to their present homes from the north-east, whereas the Aryans came unmistakeably from the north-west.

Here, then, just as might have been predicted à priori, these rival currents of the dispersion met from opposite points, and ran into a *cul de sac*, from which, as there was no egress, there necessarily ensued a struggle for mastery.

Let us now regard the two people more closely.

"Our earliest glimpses of the human family in India, disclose two tribes of widely different origin, struggling for the mastery. In the primitive time, which lies on the horizon even of inductive history, a tall, fair-complexioned race passed the Himalaya. They came of a conquering stock. They had known the safety and the plenty which can only be enjoyed in regular communities. [34] They brought with them a store of legends and devotional strains; and chief of all they were at the time of their migration southward through Bengal, if not at their first arrival in India, imbued with that high sense of nationality, which burns in the heart of a people who believe themselves the depository of a divine revelation. There is no record of the newcomers' first struggle for life with the people of the land."—Hunter's Annals, p. 90.

Here we see the more intellectual, the more spiritual, monotheistic Aryan race overpowering the black race which had earliest pre-occupied the ground, and which was already tainted with demon worship. This contrast invites further inquiry; but first let me clear up and direct the immediate drift of my argument.

If we estimate—taking the minimum or the maximum either according to the Hebrew or Septuagint version—the time it would have taken these populations, according to the slow progress of the dispersion, to have arrived at their destinations from the plain of Sennaar (Mesopotamia), the period may be equally conjectured to correspond with that which tradition marks as the commencement of the iron age, when the world was becoming overcrowded, and the increasing populations came into collision.

Neither is it a difficulty,[35] it rather appears to me in accordance with tradition, that if this surmise be correct, the earliest arrival in the

Indian Peninsula should have been of those who took the longest route. For it is natural to suppose that the proscribed and weakest races, e.g. the Canaanitish, would have been the first to depart, and to depart by the north-east and west, the more powerful families having passed down and closed the south-east exit by way of the lower valleys of the Euphrates. These latter would have spread themselves out in the direction of India leisurely and at a subsequent period.

Following these lines of migration, the Aryan at some period came upon the black Turanian race (vide infra, Chap. v.); and Mr Hunter (p. 110) records the embittered feelings with which the recollection of the strife remained in tradition. Why should this have been? It might suffice to say, in consistency with what has already been advanced, that this was their first encounter, the first check in their advance.

Another solution seems to me equally ready to hand, and to solve so much more. But first, how does Mr Hunter account for this bitter feeling? He suggests contempt for their "uncouth talk," "their gross habits of eating," -will not this explain something of their animosity?

I must here remark that although scientific inquiry takes designations of its own, in order the more conveniently to express its distinctions, yet whether we accept the ethnological or philological demarcations of mankind, it is curious how inevitably, as I think De Maistre remarked, we are led back to Shem, Ham, and Japhet. And this is as true now after a half century of scientific progress, as it was when De Maistre wrote. Without asserting that the divisions may ever be distinctly traced with the minuteness of Bochart in his "Geog. Sacra," I still say, that the broad lines of the traditional apportionment of the world, and the three-fold or four-fold division of the race indicated in Scripture, is seen behind the ultimate divisions into which science is brought to separate mankind, whether into Caucasian, Ethiopian, Mongol, with two intermediate varieties, as by Blumenbach; or into Australioid, Negroid, Mongoloid, and Xanthochroic, as by Huxley; or into Brace's division into Aryan, Semitic, Turanian, and Hamitic. Behind these various systems, as behind a grill, we seem to see the forms and faces of the progenitors of the human race discernible, but their existence not capable of contact and actual demonstration, because of the intercepting bars and lattice work.[36]

I have spoken above of a three-fold and four-fold division as equally indicated in Scripture, and I think, from non-observance of this, the close approximation of these systems to Genesis is not sufficiently recognised. I refer to the three progenital races, and the Canaanite marked off and distinguished from the rest by a curse. I shall enlarge upon this point in another chapter (Chap. v).

I will only observe now that I do not venture to say that the Canaanite is co-extensive with the Turanian, which is more a philological than an ethnological division of mankind, or that their characteristics in all respects correspond.[37] I limit my argument now to indicating the correspondence between the Canaanite and the aboriginal tribes in India.

This correspondence I find not only in the features already noted—their blackness and their intellectual inferiority—but in their enslavement to the superior races of mankind whenever they came into contact and collision with them. Is not this everywhere also the mark of the Turanian race? are not these conflicts in primitive life always with the Turanian race? and are they not in Asia, as in Africa, in a state of subjugation or dependence?

At any rate, this is the condition in which we find the Turanian in India, so fully expressed in their name of "Sudras."[38]

Against this literal fulfilment of Gen. ix. 25—"Cursed be Canaan, a servant of servants shall he be to his brethren"—as regards the Indian Sudra, the text in Gen. x. 19—"And the limits of Chanaan were from Sidon ... to Gaza ... even to Sesa"—may be objected. But I construe this text only to refer to Chanaan proper, and to be spoken rather with reference to the limits of the Promised Land and the Hebrews, than to the allocation of the tribes of Chanaan; for the text immediately preceding seems to me to have its significance—viz. Gen. x. 18,[39] where it is said in a marked manner, and of the descendants of Chanaan alone, "The families of the Canaanites were spread abroad." But if we are to suppose the whole descent of Chanaan to have been confined between the limits of Sidon and Sesa, it could hardly have been said to have had the diffusion of the other Hamitic races, and the families of the Chanaanites will not have been "spread abroad" in any noticeable or striking manner. It appears to me, also, that it may be proved in another way. St Paul, Acts xiii. 19, says that God destroyed seven nations in the land of Chanaan, whereas Gen. x. enumerates eleven.

Again, Kalisch ("Hist. and Crit. Com. on Old Testament," trans. 1858) makes it a difficulty against Gen. ix. that "Canaan *should* not only fall into the hands of Shem, *i.e.* the people of Israel, but also of *Japhet*" (i. 226).

A remote fulfilment of the prediction may be seen in the Median conquest of Phœnicia, and the Roman destruction of Carthage; but if I have truly indicated the order of events, it will be seen that it had already come about in the earliest times.

The text, indeed, of Gen. ix. 27 — "May God enlarge Japhet, and may he dwell in the tents of Shem, and Canaan be his servant" — is so clear as almost to require some such fulfilment.

But the fulfilment is seen, not only in the degradation of Chanaan, but in the prosperity of Japhet;[40] and this is so correlative, that I shall still be enforcing the argument whilst connecting a link which may appear to be wanting, viz. the identity of Japhet with the more favoured nations of the world. The identity of the Indo-Germanic races with the descendants of Japhet may almost be said to be a truth "qui saute aux yeux," but it may still be worth while to collect the links of tradition which establish it.

In truth, it appears to us a self-evident proposition, simply because tradition has familiarised us with the belief that Europe was peopled by the descendants of Japhet, and because philology has recently demonstrated the Indo-Germanic race to include this demarcation (together with Central and Western Asia); but I think that if we exclude the testimony of tradition, we should have difficulty in establishing the point either upon the text of Gen. x. 5, or from the evidence of philology.

That the race of Japhet spread themselves over the islands, and colonised the coasts of the Mediterranean, is the traditional interpretation of that text; and it receives confirmation, in the first place, in the tradition that "Japetus being the father of Prometheus, was regarded by the Greeks as the ancestor of the human race." —Smith's "Myth. Dict." We have, I think, become familiar with such transpositions as "Deucalion the son of Prometheus," and "Prometheus the son of Deucalion," &c. Certainly Prometheus (vide Appendix to Chap. viii. p. 180, and Chap. x. p. 232), supposing Prometheus to be Adam,[41] would naturally stand at the head of every genealogy; but Japetus, supposing him to be identified with Japhet as the particular founder of the race (after so distinct and definite a starting-point as the Deluge), would also, in his way, have claims to be placed at the head of their genealogy; and probably about the time that he began to be called "old Japetus," and to be typical of antiquity, his claims would have been regarded as paramount, and Prometheus would have been accordingly displaced in his favour. This is conjectural, but must be taken as one link.

Well, the (Indian) Aryans also, according to Mr Hunter ("Rural Bengal," 103), "held (Book of Manu and the Vishnu Purana) that the Greeks and Persians were sprung from errant Kshatryas, who had lost their caste" — i.e. from their own race. They are called in the same books Yavanas and Pahlavas. Now no one, I think, will call it a forced analogy to see in Yavana the name of Javan, the son of Japhet.[42] This I may call link the second.

But the Aryans, as we have seen, are one of the three or four primitive races to which both philology and ethnology lead us back. They are contrasted, on the one side, with the Semitic, and, on the other, with the Hamitic or Turanian race. We will assume, then, on the strength of the philological and scriptural lines being so nearly conterminous, that at least, looking from the point of view of Scripture, the Aryan may be identified with great probability as the Japhetic race. If, then, the Aryan is the Japhetic race in its elder branch—to which its later migration would seem to testify—we should exactly expect that it would designate a kindred but collateral race, not by the name of their common ancestor, but by the name of the progenitor from whom they were more immediately descended—not as from Japhet, but from Javan. Thus the links seem to join; and here I leave them, till there may chance to come some one who will gather up all the links in the chain of tradition, dislocated and dispersed by the catastrophes which have been consequent upon the derelictions of mankind.

The third view to which I wish to advert, is that put forward by Mr John F. M'Lennan in his "Primitive Marriage," 1865, which also revives the theory of a savage state, and moreover professes to discover primitive mankind living in a state of promiscuity, little, if at all, elevated above the brute, and this during the long period which was required to develop 1. the tribe; 2. the gens; 3. the family.

It will be difficult for any one, who comes fresh from the perusal of Genesis, to realise the possibility of such a view being held; but, in truth, there is no view too grotesque for men in whose survey mankind appear originally on the scene as a mass of units coming into the world, no one knows how, like locusts rising above the horizon, or covering the earth perhaps like toads after a shower!

Yet Mr M'Lennan's theory is virtually endorsed (*vide infra*) by Sir J. Lubbock, who refers to it (p. 60, note), as "Mr M'Lennan's masterly work." If, then, we must discuss the theory upon its merits, the objection which I should take, *in limine*, is that it is a partial generalisation from facts, irrespective of the historical evidence as a whole. There stands against it, of course, the direct evidence of the Bible, also there stands against it the researches of oriental archaeology, and, again, what Mr M'Lennan calls the "so-called revelation of philology," which shows that mankind, in the period previous to their dispersion, "had marriage laws regulating the rights and obligations of husbands and wives, of parents and children." This evidence he rejects because "the preface of general history *must be* compiled from the materials presented by barbarism" (p. 9), thus *assuming* barbarism to have been the primitive state.

Mr M'Lennan struggles vainly for universal facts on which to build, and seems to find one in what he has termed exogamy (*i.e.* marriage outside the tribe), combined with the capture of wives and the infanticide of female children within the tribe. Impossible! If this state of things had been *universal*, the human race would have exterminated itself long before "the historic period!" The theory necessarily supposes that some tribes were addicted to these practices, whilst others were not. Exogamy, therefore, is not a universal fact; but neither could endogamy have been, *for "the conversion of an endogamous tribe into an exogamous tribe is inconceivable,"* p. 146. But as Mr M'Lennan is as much constrained to choose between exogamy and endogamy as was Mons. Jourdain between poetry and prose, he apparently elects in favour of the universal primitive prevalence of exogamy, *i.e.* he supposes mankind to have commenced under conditions which would have ensured its proximate extinction.

Mr M'Lennan says, "the two types of organisation (viz. exogamy and endogamy) may be equally archaic;" but it is evident that he inclines to the opinion that exogamy is the more archaic; and his analysis at, commencing with "Exogamy Pure, No. 1, and continuing on to ... Endogamy Pure, No. 6," is "the analysis of a series of phenomena which appears to form a progression" (141).

Moreover, the difficulties which I have just urged will immediately recur if we allow "the two types to have been equally archaic."

The supposed exogamous tribes, according to the theory, enforcing the infanticide of female children, and not permitting marriage within the tribe, must have been wholly dependent upon the endogamous groups for their women. These latter groups must either have succumbed, and so have become speedily extinguished through the loss of their women (for they could not have acquired others who were not of their stock, without ceasing to be endogamous); or they must have resisted successfully, and even if the matter went no farther, the exogamous tribes must have died out or abandoned exogamy; or the endogamous tribes must have resisted and retaliated, in which case we should have this further complication that they themselves would have ceased to be endogamous, and without any reason or necessity for becoming exogamous; for with the seizure of the females of the exogamous tribes, or even, under the special circumstances, with the recovery of their own, the element of "heterogeneity" would have been introduced, and the system of endogamy would have been no longer true in theory, or possible in fact. All these results must have been immediately consequent upon the first collision, which from the very conditions of exogamy, must have occurred at the outset! Postulating exogamy, it must therefore rapidly have extirpated or absorbed every other system, and yet it could never have stood alone.

Mr M'Lennan himself allows that wherever "kinship through females, the most ancient system in which the idea of blood relationship was embodied" (148) was known, there would have been a tendency among the exogamous groups to become heterogeneous, and that thus "the system of capturing wives would have been superseded."[43] In other words, exogamy would have become extinct. But if "kinship through females" was not discovered by the first children of the first mothers, how was it subsequently discovered? We are given no clue except that "the order of nature is progressive!"

This compels the remark that if Mr M'Lennan fails to prove that exogamy was universal, as a stage of human progress, or, to use a phrase of his own, "on such a scale as to entitle it to rank among the normal phenomena of human development," there is nothing to exclude the likelihood of its being much more satisfactorily and directly traced as the result of degeneracy. Mr M'Lennan should clear his ground by demonstrating that the circumstances exclude the possibility of this conjecture.

On the contrary, and on his own showing, they would appear much more certainly to affirm it. Although exogamy is the earliest fact which he believes to be demonstrable by evidence, he assumes an initial promiscuity; and seems to see his way out of this initial promiscuity through the system of "rude polyandry" (when one woman was common to a determinate number of men unrelated) as distinguished from "regulated polyandry" (where one woman was common to several brothers). It must be noted that before these polyandrous families, if we may so call them, at first necessarily limited, could theoretically or in fact have become the tribal exogamous groups, many difficulties must be disposed of, and many stages traced, of which we are told nothing more than that we are "forced to regard all the exogamous races as having originally been polyandrous". That these families, if it is not an abuse of terms to call them so, could not have become tribal by grouping, Mr M'Lennan himself maintains.

The two systems which Mr M'Lennan distinguishes as "rude" and "regulated polyandry," are so essentially different that I fail to trace the possibility of progression from one to the other. "Rude polyandry" is barely distinguishable from promiscuity, and not at all if we regard it as only promiscuity, necessarily limited through infanticide, or other causes destroying the balance of the sexes. The latter has peculiar features—arising in some way out of, and fixed in the idea of the relationship of brothers—

an idea which it is just conceivable might arise directly out of a state of promiscuity—where theoretically the children might be supposed to be in contact with the mother only, but which the system of "rude polyandry," by introducing conflicting and complicated claims, would immediately tend to weaken and obliterate.

Let us see, then, if we can trace the custom better on the lines of degeneracy.

If we start with the belief in the existence of many primitive ceremonies and regulations we may then suppose that in the downward progression to promiscuity, the stages of the descent will be traceable in the corruptions of these customs. Such surmises at least are as good as the contrary surmises of Mr M'Lennan.

Now, we have already seen[44] that Mr M'Lennan alludes to the law of Deuteronomy, which imposed the obligation of the younger brother marrying the widow of the elder—and it will, moreover, be seen (Mr M'Lennan, p. 219) that this was also prescribed in the law of Menu.

Whatever may be the true solution of this coincidence the least likely account would seem to be that they had both, under different conditions (different at any rate from the point of divergence, be it exogamy or polyandry), advanced to it independently and by similar stages. Such fortuitous coincidences would imply not merely a succession of similar developments, but also a corresponding succession of accidental circumstances.

If, however, the custom of the younger brother marrying the widow of the elder was of primitive institution (compare Genesis xxxviii. and the Code of Menu), the corruption of this custom into polyandry, in circumstances which may at any time have disturbed the balance of the sexes in the overcrowded East, though it revolts will not absolutely astonish us; whereas the converse, i.e. restriction to successive appropriation contingent upon widowhood, from a state of virtual promiscuity, is so uphill a reform and so contrary to probability that it requires some internal evidence of the stages, and some warrant in modern observation to make it plausible. None are given. For the fact that we find both the "rude" and the "regulated" form existing side by side cuts both ways;[45] and the discovery of a form of capture—the Rakshasa, among the eight forms sanctioned by the code of Menu, enforces our argument—it would exactly correspond to the military exemption among the Jews (Mr M'Lennan, p. 82), supposing we were able to read Deuteronomy xx. 10–14 in the same sense as Mr M'Lennan. In that case, therefore, it would be a departure from or relaxation of a rule laid down—a view which is confirmed when we find that the authority quoted (Dr Muir, "Sanscrit Texts," the Ramayana) tells that "Ravana, the most terrible of all the Rakshasas, is stigmatised as a destroyer of religious duties, and ravisher of the wives of others" (Prim. Mar. p. 309), which testifies to degeneracy at some period; whereas if Mr M'Lennan's view is true, this hero must be relegated to a time when the conception of "religious duties," and even of other men's "wives" were unknown.

We have seen (supra, 46), that when mankind had got, we know not how, into tribal exogamous groups, "kinship through females would have a tendency," and a moment's consideration will show an immediate tendency, "to render the exogamous groups heterogeneous, and thus to supersede the system of capturing wives." We ask why did they capture wives? Mr M'Lennan implies that their ideas of incest forbade marriage within the tribe.[46] Apparently, then, the groups must have been exogamous[47] previously to the time when they had attained to the knowledge of "kinship through females," else "kinship through females" would from the first have operated to produce a state of things which would have rendered exogamy unnecessary and inexplicable. The corollary is curious; they must, therefore, have had the idea of incest before they had the idea of kinship through females!

That some tribes should have arrived at some such state through a perverted traditional notion of incest, would, on the other hand, perfectly fit into the theory of degeneracy.

I had intended to have pursued this subject, but the chapter has already run to too great length. As allusion however, has been made to Sir John Lubbock, I append an extract (see p. 47) from which it will be seen that his view, although equally remote from historical truth, has a greater à priori probability. Indeed, if we could only consent to start on the assumption of "an initial state of hetairism," nothing would be more complete than the following theory:—

"For reasons to be given shortly, I believe that communal marriage was gradually superseded by individual marriages founded on capture, and that this led firstly to exogamy, and then to female infanticide; thus reversing M'Lennan's order of sequence. Endogamy and regulated polyandry, though frequent, I regard as exceptional, and as not entering into the normal progress of development. Like M'Lennan and Bachojen, I believe that our present social relations have arisen from an initial stage of hetairism or communal marriage. It is obvious, however, that even under communal marriage, a warrior who had captured a beautiful girl in some marauding expedition, would claim a peculiar right to her, and, when possible, would set custom at defiance. We have already seen that there are other cases of the existence of marriage, under two forms, side by side in one country, and that there is, therefore, no real difficulty in assuming the co-existence of communal and individual marriage. It is true that, under a communal marriage system, no man could appropriate a girl entirely to himself, without infringing the rights of the whole tribe.... A war-captive, however, was in a peculiar position, the tribe had no right to her; her capturer might have killed her if he chose; ... he did as he liked, the tribe was no sufferer." — *Sir J. Lubbock's "Origin of Civilisation,"*.

I will only ask one question. At what period does Sir J. Lubbock suppose the custom of inheritance through females arose? This as nearly approaches a universal fact as any which Sir J. Lubbock adduces (vide p. 105, et seq.); and, on the point of its having been a prevalent custom, I can have no difficulty. Whenever through degeneracy man arrived at the state of promiscuity or communal marriages, such inheritance as there might be, in such a community, would only be claimed through females, as the paternity would always be uncertain (vide infra, p. 129). If, however, mankind commenced with communal marriages, inheritance and relationship through females would also have been from the commencement.

Let us now turn to Sir J. Lubbock's theory, as expressed in the extract above, in which he shows us how marriage by capture would quite naturally have arisen out of the state of communal marriage. But if natural, it would have been natural from the commencement, *quid vetat?* There must then have been a system also in operation from the commencement, the inevitable tendency of which, by making paternity distinct and recognisable, would have been to substitute inheritance through males; and this system, by introducing a more robust posterity, would rapidly have gained upon the other system. Male inheritance, it would then appear, commenced and established itself at the outset, and to the displacement of inheritance through females. How, then, do we find traces of the latter custom so prevalent? From this point of view the more instances Sir J. Lubbock accumulates, the more he will excite our incredulity and surprise.

This theory again, equally with Mr M'Lennan's, supposes mankind originally in a state of hetairism, in which case it is futile to talk of tribes and of marriage out of the tribe; for how did they emerge into this tribal separation out of the state of promiscuity? The difficulty gets more complicated since, *ex hypothesi*, after emerging from, they still remain within the tribal limits, in the state of hetairism. These preliminaries must be settled before the argument can be carried further.

The usual philosophic formula is, of course, at hand—these changes must have required an indefinite lapse of ages! Into this swamp we shall see one philosopher after another disappear, leaving a delusive light behind him! If we could only, Dante like, recall one of these philosophers to life, after he has passed into his state of Nirvana, we would ask, as in this instance, why, supposing the state of promiscuity, it would require an indefinite lapse of ages to pass from it, according to the conditions of Sir John Lubbock's argument (*i.e.* to the state of exogamy); considering that, *vide supra*, "it is obvious that, even under communal marriage, a warrior who had captured, &c, would claim a peculiar right to her, and, when possible, would set custom at defiance." Clearly, then, it only required the man and the opportunity.

APPENDIX TO CHAPTER III.

The view substantially coincides with the lines laid down by Blackstone (compare Plato; Grote's Plato, iii. 337), which are the subject of Bentham's attack, and to which the recent contributions of Sir Henry Maine to our knowledge in these matters would seem to run counter. Blackstone, "Comm." i. 47, said— "This notion, of an actually existing unconnected state of nature, is too wild to be seriously admitted: and, besides, it is plainly contradictory to the revealed accounts of the primitive origin of mankind and their preservation two thousand years afterwards, both which were effected by the means of single families. These formed the first society among themselves, which every day extended its limits; and when it grew too large to subsist with convenience in that pastoral state wherein the Patriarchs appear to have lived, it necessarily subdivided itself by various migrations into more. Afterwards, as agriculture increased, which employs and can maintain a much greater number of hands, migrations became less frequent, and various tribes, which had formerly separated, reunited again, sometimes by compulsion and conquest, sometimes by accident, and sometimes, perhaps, by compact.... And this is what we mean by the original contract of society, which, though perhaps in no instance it has ever been formally expressed at the first institution of a state, yet, in nature, reason must always be understood and implied in the very act of associating together.... When society is once formed, government results, of course, as necessary to preserve and to keep that society in order ... unless some superior were constituted ... they would still remain in a state of nature."

Bentham says of this passage from Blackstone, that "'*society,*' in one place, means the same thing as a '*state of nature*' does: in another place, it means the same as '*government.*' Here we are required to believe there *never was* such a state as a state of nature: then we are given to understand there *has been*. In like manner, with respect to an original contract, we are given to understand that such a thing never existed, that the notion of it is even ridiculous; at the same time, that there is no speaking nor stirring without supposing that there was one." — *Bentham's "Fragment on Government,"* p. 9 (London, 1823).

The previous and subsequent chapters (ii., xiii.), will be found to meet these strictures of Bentham, although not originally written with reference to them.

CHAPTER IV
CHRONOLOGY FROM THE POINT
OF VIEW OF TRADITION

To many it may seem a fundamental objection that my theory supposes a chronology altogether out of keeping with modern discovery; and I fancy there is a somewhat general impression that modern science has an historical basis, to which not even the Septuagint chronology can be made to conform.

This really is not the case; but assuming it to be true, I must still remark, that if facts of primeval tradition have been established, the long lapse of ages will only enhance our notions of the persistency of tradition; or if the lapse of ages is disproved, this conclusion will be in recognition of a truth to which tradition testifies.

I shall now proceed to establish that the strictly historical testimony, and the direct historical evidence, is strikingly concurrent in favour of the scriptural chronology, allowing the margin of difference between the Hebrew and LXX. versions.[48]

With this view I shall successively examine the chronology of the principal nations whose annals profess to go back to the commencement of things—the Aryan (including the Indian, the Persian, the Greek, and the Roman), the Babylonian, the Chinese, Phœnician, and Egyptian. *Indian Chronology.*—There was a time when the Indian (Aryan) chronology was believed to attain to the most remote antiquity of all, and this belief was sustained by the apparently irrefragable testimony of astronomical evidence. Who upholds this evidence now? On this head I must refer to Cardinal Wiseman's seventh lecture ("On Science and Revealed Religion"), where the reader will find a clear and careful *precis* of the discussion on the subject between Bailly and Delambre, the *Edinburgh Review* and Bentley, to which I am not aware that anything of consequence has to be added.

If, on the other hand, we turn to what I am exclusively directing my attention—the strict historical investigation—we find that the cautious inquiries of such men as Sir W. Jones and Heeren concur in placing the Aryan invasion at the antecedently very probable date, from the point of view of Scripture, of some 2000 years B.C.

At the present moment the discussion takes the form of philological inquiry, and into the antiquity (upon internal evidence) of the ancient Sanscrit literature. In so far, therefore, as it is philological, it belongs to the indirect argument, which I am now excluding. In so far as the Sanscrit literature is historical, I have discussed the testimony which it brings in the preceding chapter. Professor Rawlinson, however, in his recent "Manual of Ancient History," refuses to discuss the question, as he does not regard the Maha-Bharata and Ramayana as "trustworthy sources of history," and commences his Persian history with the accession of Cyrus, previously to which he does not consider the Aryan migration and settlement to have been completed. Apart, then, from the peculiar line of argument to which I shall presently refer, it would appear that the Indian chronology, as reconstructed from history and tradition, falls easily within the lines, not only of the LXX., but of the Hebrew version.

The Indians, it is true ("Hales' Chron.," i. 196), themselves say that their history goes back 432,000,000 years. Although Hales gives a solution which may be deemed satisfactory, I think that, if considered in connection with the Babylonian computation, it will be seen that, though inexact in their figure, they are accurate in their tradition. The primary figure in their (Indian) calculation—432,000—is arrived at through the extended multiplication of the Chaldean sossos, neros, and saros, or of their own traditional figures corresponding to them (vide infra). In the Chaldean system (vide Rawlinson, "Anc. Mon.," i.), 6 and 10 were employed as alternate multipliers. Thus a "soss" = 60 years (10 × 6), a "ner" = 600 (60 × 10), a "sar" = 3600 (600 × 6); and if the multiplication be continued, the next figure would be 36,000 (3600 × 10), next 216,000 (36,000 × 6). The Indian figure 432,000,[49] is made up of twice 216,000.

Professor Rawlinson ("Anc. Mon.," i. 192) gives in detail, and endorses a remarkable *eclaircissement* of M. Gutschmid on the mythical traditions of Assyrian chronology. *Babylonian Chronology.*—Rawlinson says—

"Assuming that the division between the earlier and later Assyrian dynasty synchronises with the celebrated era of Nabonassar (747 B.C.), which is probable, but not certain, and taking the year B.C. 538 as the admitted date of the conquest of the last Chaldæan king by Cyrus, he obtains for the seventh or second Assyrian dynasty 122 years (747 to 625). Assuming, next, that B.C. 2234, from which the Babylonians counted their stellar observations, must be a year of note in Chaldæan history, and finding that it cannot well represent the first year of the second or Median dynasty, since in that case eleven kings of the third dynasty would have reigned no more than thirty-four years, he concludes it must mark the expulsion of the Medes and accession of the third dynasty (which he regards as a native dynasty). From his previous calculations, it follows that the fourth dynasty began B.C. 1976; between which and B.C. 2234 are 258 years, a period which may be fairly assigned to eleven monarchs. This much is conjecture ... the proof now suddenly flashes on us. If the numbers are taken in the way assigned, and then added to the years of the first or purely mythical dynasty, we get 36,000, equal to the next term, to the sar (saros, vide supra), in the Babylonian system of cycles."

It will be more apparent in the following table from Rawlinson, i.e. —

		Years.	B.C.
Mythical	86 Chaldæans	34,800	
	8 Medes	224	2458
	11 [Chaldæans]	(258)	2234
	49 Chaldæans	458	1976
Historical	9 Arab	245	1518
	45 [Assyrian]	526	1273
	8 [Assyrian]	122	747
	6 Chaldæans	87	625
		36,000	

Chinese Chronology.—The Chinese, also—though, be it observed, the Chinese of modern date, according to Klaproth ("Mem. Relatifs. à l'Asie," i. 405; Klaproth places the commencement of the uncertain history of China 2637 B.C., the certain history 782 B.C.),[50] in the first year of our era, but more systematically in the ninth century—forged a mythological history, which carried the empire back 2,276,000 years (another calculation, 3,276,000). He adds, however, that the Chinese themselves do not consider the Wai-ki, the authority for these statements, to be historical.

Again, if we allow ourselves to be entangled in certain astronomical disputations, the question may become complicated and confused; but the astronomical discussion must depend, in the end, upon a point which history must determine—i.e. whether the astronomical knowledge and observations referred to had come down in primitive tradition, or had been imported at a later date. Although it need not exclude a belief in a tradition of primitive knowledge of astronomy, yet the doubt will ever cause a fatal uncertainty in any calculations, since, if the knowledge, or the knowledge of the particular observations and facts, had at any time been imported, they might have calculated back their eclipses, as has been proved to have been done in India.

Let us then, excluding the purely astronomical calculations, closely scrutinise the evidence which tradition affords; for if we can discover tradition of "appearances of rare occurrence, and which are difficult to calculate, such as many of the planetary conjunctions," they "must," as Baron Bunsen observes ("Egypt," iii. p. 389), "either be pure inventions, or contemporary notations of some extraordinary natural phenomena." Baron Bunsen proceeds to say:—"One instance that may be cited is the traditional observation of a conjunction of five planets (among which the sun and moon are mentioned), on the first day of Litshin, in the time of Tshuen-hiü, the *second successor of Hoang-ti.* Suppose this should have been the great conjunction of the three upper planets which recurs every 794 years and four months, and to which Kepler first turned his attention in reference to the year of the nativity of Christ. It took place in the following years.

The one which occurred in historical times was in November, seven years B.C.; consequently the conjunctions prior to it occurred in—

	Yrs.	Mos.	Dys.
	794	4	12
	77	10	12
	7786	6	0
	7794	4	12
	71580	10	12
And the conjunction in	794	4	12
The time of Tshuen-hiü in	2375	2	24

According to the official Chinese tables, as given by Ideler, he reigned from 2513 B.C. to 2436 B.C.; but the dates vary to the extent of more than 200 years, and the year 2375 comes within the limits of these deviations."

Baron Bunsen, we may then assume, has very skilfully brought back Chinese chronology to within *two generations of Hoang-ti (supra).* If we could further identify Hoang-ti with Noah, two patriarchal generations would bring us close to the date of the Deluge as fixed by the Septuagint, if we referred them, in the first instance, to the death of Noah.

Before proceeding to this identification, I must point to another chronological fact in Chinese tradition, which would give to this identification an antecedent probability. It was stated (Bunsen, "Egypt," iii. 383) that Hoang-ti established the *astronomical cycle of 60 years* in the *sixty-first year* of his *reign*.

Bunsen says: "The scientific problem thus offered for our solution is the following—It is admitted that the Chinese, from the earliest times, made use of a sexagesimal cycle for the division of the year = 6 × 60 days (360 days), and they marked the years by a cycle of 60 years, running concurrently with the cycle of days. This cycle, therefore, must have been originally instituted at a time when the first day of the daily cycle coincided with the first year of the annual cycle, i.e. when they commenced on the same day. Ideler thinks it impossible to ascertain this, owing to the irregularity of the old calendar." We may ask, then, what year that could be named would so exactly satisfy these conditions as the sixty-first year of the reign of Noah after the Deluge?[51] Let us, moreover, consider how traditional this cycle of sixty years has been,—"Scaliger made the remark that the twelve yearly zodiacal cycle, which is in use among the Tartars (Mongols, Mandshus, Igurians), the inhabitants of Thibet, the Japanese and Siamese dated from the earliest times. Among the Tartaric populations, however, this is a cycle of sixty years (12 × 5); of the Indians we have already spoken."

It will have already been seen that the cycle of sixty years entered into the Chaldean system—viz. cycle of 60 years = a sossos, 600 years = a saros, 3600 years = a neros.

> "Now when we find (Bunsen, p. 387) that six hundred years *gives an excess of exactly one lunar month, with far greater accuracy* than the Julian year, such a cycle must have been indispensable when that of sixty years was in use, and consequently must have been employed by the Chinese, or, at all events, have been known to those from whom they borrowed the latter. Josephus also calls six hundred years the great year, which may have been observed by the patriarch."

And in summing up the general chronological result, he says:—

> "*a.* ... The earliest Chinese chronology rests upon a conventional basis peculiar to itself, that of limiting the lunar year by a cycle of six hundred years, which is common to the whole of North Asia and the Chaldeans; and probably (as it is also met with in India) to the Bactrians also: this basis is *historical*." "*b*. The communication took place before the Chaldees invented the cycle of six hundred years."

From our point of view, believing that the Chaldees never invented the cycle but held to it traditionally, the above conclusion must be construed to mean that the "communication," or diffusion of the knowledge, must have taken place before the lapse of the first six hundred years after the Deluge, which will be further confirmed by conclusion *c*.

"*c*. The Chinese observation is based upon the Babylonian gnomon,"

which appears to me tantamount to the admission that it took place, in the plains of Mesopotamia, previous to the Dispersion.

In arriving, then, at the sixty-first year of the reign of Hoang-ti, we are led up to such close proximity to the epoch of the Deluge, that the presumption that Hoang-ti was Noah would be strong, even if no other evidence was at hand to corroborate it.

It is with this supplementary evidence that I now propose to deal.

Although the tradition of the Chinese is remarkably accurate, up to a certain point, yet in the period beyond that point, where the confusion is manifest, there is no reason why we should not expect to find the same reduplications and amalgamations of ante and post diluvian traditions, which we have already found in the history of other nations.

Without attempting to unravel all complications, let us turn again to Bunsen (iii. 382), and setting aside Pu-an-ku, the primeval man who came out of the mundane egg and lived eighteen thousand years, and who has resemblances with the Assyrian Ra and Ana, and the Egyptian Ra, the son of Ptha (to whom thirty thousand are allotted, vide infra, p. 97–100), and Sui-shin, "who discovered fire," and who is the counterpart of Prometheus (vide p. 180). Regarding Pu-an-ku, the cosmical, and Sui-shin, as the mythical tradition of Adam, we come to the historical tradition in the person of Fohi.

"I. Fohi the great, the brilliant (Tai-hao) cultivator of astronomy and religion, as well as writing. He reigned one hundred and ten years. Then came fifteen reigns. II. Shin-nong (divine husbandman); institution of agriculture; the knowledge of simples applied as the art of medicine." [Compare pp. 210–214, Saturn, Bacchus, Æsculapius.] "III. Hoang-ti (great ruler) came to the throne in consequence of an armed insurrection (new dynasty), and was obliged to put down a revolt. In his reign the magnetic needle was discovered; the smelting of copper for making weapons;[52] vases of high art, and money; improvement in the written character, said to be borrowed from the lines on the tortoise-shell. It consists of five hundred hieroglyphics, of which two hundred can still be pointed out. He established fixed habitations throughout his dominions, and the astronomical cycle of sixty years in the sixty-first year of his reign (vide supra, 61); musical instruments. It was in his time also that the fabulous bird Sin appeared. The empire was considerably extended to the southward." —Bunsen, 382.

If we take Fohi as Adam, the fifteen reigns which follow will bear analogy with "the fifteen generations of the Cynic cycle" (vide Palmer i. p. 8, 23–37; also vide infra), and will correspond to the thirteen generations, viz. the ten antediluvian, and the three survivors (excluding Noah) of the Deluge in the Egyptian chronology (vide infra). Shin-nong, "the divine husbandman," will be Noah, and Hoang-ti, Shem or Ham, or else the two will be reduplicate traditions of Noah. Compare the attributions of Hoang-ti with those of Hoa in the Assyrian tradition, Certain statements regarding him —e.g. that he suppressed an insurrection, accord more nearly with epithets applied to Nin, the fish-god, whom I have considered a duplicate of Hoa e.g. "the destroyer of enemies," — "the reducer of the disobedient," — "the exterminator of rebels." Compare with the Phœnician tradition, of Saturn causing the destruction of his son Sadid by the Deluge. The appearance of the fabulous bird Sin, seems a reminiscence of the birds sent out of the ark, which is so frequent in tradition. Compare the mystery bird (the dove) in the Mandan ceremonies, —the worship of the pigeon in Cashmere,[53] &c. Other coincidences might be pointed if space allowed.

But analogous to the double tradition of the Deluge in Assyria in the persons of Hoa and Nin; and, again, by a distinct channel of tradition in Xisuthrus (vide pp. 208, 209), as in China, there seems to have been a similar reduplication in China in their kings Hoang-ti and Yao or Yu.[54]

Now under this Yao or Yu, according to Chinese tradition (preserved, moreover, in the inscription of Yu), there happened the Deluge, or a Deluge. But as there is a confusion between Hoang-ti and Yao, so there is between Yao and Yu. Bunsen, however, admits these latter to be identical.

But although Bunsen asserts the authenticity of the inscription (as also does Klaproth), he utterly scouts the idea that it is a tradition of the Deluge, and maintains that it is itself evidence of a local inundation. Let us see.

"All the confusion or ignorance," says Bunsen (398), "of the missionaries [in this matter], arises from their believing that this event referred to the Flood of Noah, which never reached this country." And he says the inundation in the reign of Yao had just as much to do with Noah's flood as the dams he created, and the canals he dug, had to do with the ark. This is said with reference to the "short Chinese account of it published by Klaproth," viz.—

"In the sixty-first year of the reign of the Emperor Yao, serious mischief was caused by inundations. The emperor took counsel with the great men of the empire, who advised him to employ Kuen to drain off the water. Kuen was engaged upon it for nine years without success, and was condemned to be imprisoned for life. His son Yu was appointed in his stead. At the end of nineteen years he succeeded in stopping the inundation, and made a report to the emperor upon the subject."

Let us turn, however, from this later gloss to the inscription itself, translated by Bunsen—

"The Emperor said, 'Oh thou Governor of the four mountains of the Empire!

The swelling flood is producing mischief;

It spreads itself far and wide;

It surrounds the hills, it overflows the dams;

Rushing impetuously along it rises up to Heaven:

The common people complain and sigh.'"

—*Vide supra*, p. 396.

"The venerable Emperor exclaimed with a sigh, 'Ho assistant Counsellor! the islands great and small up to the *mountain's top*;

The door of *the birds* and of beasts, all is overflowed together—

Is swamped: be it thy care to open the way, to let off the water.'"

He then says:—

"My task is completed; my sacrifice I have offered in the second month, trouble is at an end, the dark destiny is changed; the streams of the south flow down to the sea; garments are prepared; food is provided; all the nations have rest; the people enjoy themselves with gambols and dancing."—(Compare Commemorative Festivals, infra, p. 249).

I should have thought that all these phrases pointed much more to a universal Deluge than to a local inundation. But Bunsen says (398)—

"The fact is fully proved both by the inscription and the work of Yu itself. The inscription was on the *top* of the mountain, Yu-lu-fun, in the district of Shen-shu-lu. Owing to its having become illegible in early times, it was removed to *the top* of an adjoining mountain." ... "The former *locality* tallies exactly with the very interesting description of the empire in the time of Yu, which we find at the opening of the second book of the Shuking." And Bunsen concludes, "It may be presumed after this verification, that in future nobody will seriously doubt the strictly epic description of the Shuking in the Canon of Yu," as above.

So far from being impressed by the discovery of the monument on the top of the local mountain, as evidence of the local deluge, I can see in it only a memorial of the universal Deluge localised; and I cannot help considering it in connection with the worship of the tops of mountains, of which we shall find traces elsewhere (p. 244–46). Surely Baron Bunsen proves too much, and describes to us a deluge which must have been on the scale of the universal Deluge for all countries below the level of the mountain Yu-lu-fun. But, let it be said, that this description, so accordant with the description of the flood, was merely Chinese exaggeration. I here wish to point out two curious coincidences. What if we shall find works similar of those to Yao or Yu, ascribed to the original founders in Egypt and Cashmere? As in the first instance, I shall have to quote from Baron Bunsen himself, I am surprised that the coincidence should have escaped his observation.

"This is the account given of Menes [the first king of Egypt] by Herodotus—Menes, the first king of Egypt, as the priests informed me, protected Memphis by a dam against the river which ran towards the sandy chain of the Libyan Mountains. About 100 stadia above Memphis, he made an embankment against the bend of the river, which is on the south side. The effect of this was to dry up its ancient bed, as well as to force the stream between the two chains of mountains. This bend of the Nile, which is confined within the embankment walls, was very carefully attended to by the Persians, and repaired every year. For, if the river were to burst through its banks and overflow at this point, all Memphis would be in danger of being swamped. Menes, *the oldest of their kings*, having thus drained the tract of land by means of the dyke, built upon it the city now called Memphis, which lies in the mountain valley of Egypt. To the west and north he dug a lake round it, which communicates with the river—on the east it is bounded by the Nile—and afterwards erected in it a temple to Vulcan, a splendid edifice, deserving of especial notice" (ii. 48).

Bunsen fully endorses this account—"Herodotus, therefore, has recorded the following fact, that before the time of Menes the Nile overflowed the tract of country which he fixed upon as the site of his new metropolis" (p. 49 and p. 51). "There is no foundation whatever for Andriossy's hypothesis that the story originated in the fact of the Nile having once run westward from the Pyramid mountains to Bahr Bela Ma (stream without water) and the Natron and Mareotic Lakes. Herodotus mentions an historical fact, and describes the work of an historical king. Andriossy's hypothesis, if well founded, would belong to geology." A sagacious and well-founded remark on the part of Baron Bunsen, but, as I submit, equally applicable to the work of Yao or Yu.

Merely noting that, if the above work was really carried out by Menes, and it would have been, from the point of view of Genesis, so carried out at a period contemporary with that of Yao or Yu—and, moreover, conceding to it in any case (I mean the work of Menes) a certain historical basis—let us dispassionately compare both with the passage from Klaproth, which I shall now extract. It is taken from the Sanscrit History of Cashmere.[55]

Klaproth says:—

> "The Hindoo history of Kashmir assures us that the beautiful valley which forms this kingdom was originally a vast lake, called Satisaras. This account is also agreeable to the local traditions of this country. It was Kasy'apa, a holy person who, according to the Hindoo historians, caused the waters which covered this valley to escape. He was the son of Marichi, the son of Brahma. The Mahometan writers call him Kachef or Kacheb, and many of them pretend that he was a god, or a genius, and servant of Soliman, under whose orders he effected the drying up of Kashmir. To execute this task he made, near Baramanleh, a passage across the mountains, through which the water passed.... The territory, recovered in this way by Kasy'apa, was also peopled by this holy man, with the assistance of the superior gods, whom he brought for this purpose from heaven, at the commencement of the seventh manwantara, or that in which we are now." Klaproth adds:—"We must therefore suppose that Kashmir has been subjected to the same periodical revolutions as the other parts of the world, if we would reconcile this date with the ordinary chronology."[56]

It must, I think, be conceded that we have now before us three very similar accounts of works undertaken with reference to the reclamation of inundated land. All are undertaken by the first founders of their respective kingdoms—kingdoms widely separated and inhabited by people of diverse race—and all, more or less, contemporaneously. The Egyptians and Kashmerian have points in common as to their mode of reclamation, whilst the Chinese and Kashmerian have still more in common with the narrative in Genesis.[57]

Four solutions occur to me as possible. Either they were obscure or perverted traditions of the Deluge, or their works were traditions of similar works effected by Noah after the Deluge; or these works were actually carried out upon the precedent and model of similar works effected by Noah; or they were fortuitous coincidences.

Upon either of the three former conclusions, it will be shown that traditions of the Deluge, direct or indirect, exist both in Egypt and China, where it has been so confidently asserted that no tradition is to be found; and in the latter case, what is more especially to my purpose, a tradition which brings Yao into relation with Noah and Hoang-ti.

In conclusion, I must remark that when it is urged that there is no tradition, or but slight tradition, of the flood in Egypt, we have a right to reply that there is no country where we should have so little reason to expect it. If there is any country where we should think it likely that the reminiscences of the Deluge would be effaced, it would be in a country periodically subject to inundations, where the people are annually made familiar with its incidents, and where its recurrence is not to them a cause of alarm, but a matter of expectation and joy.[58]

CHAPTER V
CHRONOLOGY FROM THE POINT
OF VIEW OF SCIENCE

Although the testimony of history is definite and decisive as to the chronology of the world, within the limits of a few hundred years, there is a general assumption, in all branches of scientific inquiry, that man must have existed many thousand years beyond the period thus assigned to him. Lyell speaks of "the vastness of time"[59] required for his development, and Bunsen, as we have seen, requires twenty thousand years, at least, between the Deluge and the nativity of our Lord: and wherefore this discrepancy? Because of a fundamental assumption—not merely hypothetical for the convenience of inquiry—but confident and absolute; an assumption which, so far as the argument is concerned, is the very matter in dispute—that man must have progressed and developed to the point at which we see him.

At the same time, the actual chronology cannot be altogether ignored, and some cognisance must be taken of the facts which history presents to us; and it is this unfortunate exigency, interrupting the placid course of development, which not unfrequently lands scientific inquirers of the first eminence in difficulties from which it will take an indefinite lapse of time to extricate them; *ex. gra.*, Bunsen, in his "Egypt," iii. 379, says—

> "It has been more than once remarked, in the course of this work, that the *connection between the Chinese and the Egyptians* belongs, in several of its phases, to the *general history* of the world. The Chinese language is the furthest point beyond that of the formation of the Egyptian language, which represents, as compared with it, the middle ages of mankind,—viz., the Turanian and Chamitic stages of development."

The conclusion of philology (*vide* also Brace's "Ethnology," p. 114) is, therefore, that the Turanian or Chamitic grew out of the more inorganic and elementary Chinese.

Now, let us compare Lyell's conclusions with Bunsen's. Lyell equally believes ("Principles of Geology," ii. 471) "that three or four thousand years is but a *minute fraction* of the time required to bring about such wide divergence from a common parent stock, 'as between' the Negroes and Greeks and Jews, Mongols and Hindoos, represented on the Egyptian monuments."

At the same time, he endorses Sir John Lubbock's view, and pronounces, upon what appears to me very light and insufficient grounds (ii. 479), that "the theory, therefore, that the savage races have been degraded from a previous state of civilisation may be rejected:" and by implication that the civilised races have progressed from the savage state may be affirmed.[60]

I have, then, only to assume one point that Sir C. Lyell will concede, the order of progress or development to have been from black to white, and that he will pay us the compliment of being the more favoured race.

But of all the races that are akin to the Mongol or Turanian, the Chinese are the whitest, and most nearly approach the European in colour.

How many years, then, may we suppose that it took the Chinese to progress from the black state of the Egyptian? as many, let us conjecture, as it took the Egyptian to progress linguistically from the state of the Chinese or Mongol!

This is one instance of the entanglement in which the theory of progress, pure and simple, from a parent stock will involve us. The obvious mode of escape would be to deny the unity of the human race, a conclusion which would at once land us in the darkness of a still lower abyss, and convert our processes from being scientific in form and hopeful of result, into empirical and aimless conjectures. For either the theory is started that the various races of mankind were created separately, in which case we fly into the face of the only account we have of creation, and also of the multiform testimonies which history and science bring to attest this truth, and we, moreover, debar ourselves from falling back upon any uniform theory applicable to the whole human race; or if, without advertence to creation, we suppose mankind to have been variously developed, here again we shall equally find ourselves cut off from the application of any uniform historical theory, equally unable to account for or to exclude the testimony of history, and in the end reduced to the evidences, whatever they may be worth, of certain real or fancied analogies.[61] At this point, the historical inquiry will be virtually abandoned, and the records of the past merged in the phenomena of life, will be considered only in the light of some pantheistic or materialistic theory, or, so far as it is distinguishable, of some theory of evolution.

I am no longer concerned with any of these theories the moment they discard the historical element; and I shall, accordingly, return to the theory of Sir John Lubbock, which is honestly based upon it.

When all is said, I cannot make out that Sir John adduces any argument in favour of the antiquity of the human race which does not resolve itself into the contrast between our civilisation and the degradation of savages; and that the time which must have elapsed to bring about this transformation is measured by the fact that the negro, of the "true Nigritian stamp," appears upon the Egyptian monuments, at least as far back as B.C. 2400. "Historians, philologists, and physiologists have alike admitted that the short period allowed in Archbishop Usher's chronology could hardly be reconciled with the history of some Eastern nations, and that it did not leave room for the development either of the different languages or of the numerous physical peculiarities by which various races of men are distinguished."[62] As no facts in the history of Eastern nations are adduced, I shall consider that this part of the argument has been sufficiently disposed of in the preceding chapters, and if they had been adduced, I venture to think that they would have been interpreted by the latter part of the sentence, and would have been incompatible with the chronology, only because they did not allow sufficient time "for the development," &c. Of this sort of fact, I admit, nothing stronger can be adduced than the case of the negro on the Egyptian monuments, only I wish to direct attention to the different aspect these facts will bear when the theory of progress is not assumed as an infallible proposition. Moreover, as Mr Poole, whom Sir J. Lubbock very candidly quotes, points out, in the interval between this and 2400 B.C. we do not find "the least change in the negro or the Arab; and even the type which seems to be intermediate between them, is virtually as unaltered. Those who consider that length of time can change a type of man, will do well to consider the fact that three thousand years give no ratio on which a calculation could be founded." So that if Arch. Usher had expanded his chronology so as to take in the twenty thousand years Bunsen requires, it really would not appreciably have affected the argument. Sir J. Lubbock, indeed, says I am, however, not aware that it is supposed by any school of ethnologists that 'time' alone, without a change of external conditions, will produce an alteration of type." "Let us," he continues, "turn now to the instances relied on by Mr Crawford. The millions, he says, of African negroes that have, during three centuries, been transported to the New World and its islands, are the same in colour as the present inhabitants of the parent country of their forefathers. The Creole Spaniards ... are as fair as the people of Arragon and Andalusia. The pure Dutch Creole colonists of the Cape of Good Hope, after dwelling two centuries among black Caffres and yellow Hottentots, do not differ in colour from the people of Holland." [The strongest case is, perhaps, that of the American Indians, who do not vary from a uniform copper colour in north or south—in Canada or on the line.][63] In these instances, Sir J. Lubbock says:—"We have great change of circumstances, but a very insufficient lapse of time, and, in fact, there is no well authenticated case [he does not, however, advert to the case of the Indians, which seems to satisfy both conditions] in which these two requisites are united," ... and adds, "there is already a marked difference between the English of Europe and the English of America;" but is full allowance made here for admixture of race? and, also, is his instance to the point? Is not the difficulty rather that, whereas climate, food, change of circumstances have (for, I think, the balance of the argument is on that side), in many ways, modified other races (though whether to the extent of destroying the characteristic type, may be open to question), the negro has resisted these influences, and has remained the same negro that we find him 2400 B.C.? Consider that it is only a question of degree, and that it is merely true that the negro has resisted these influences more persistently than other races. [64] Still the contrast is not the less startling when we find the negro in the same relative position, and with the same stamp of inferiority, that we find indelibly impressed upon him four thousand years ago? It is a case which neither the theory of progress, nor the theory of degeneracy, seems to touch.

But it is a case which De Maistre's view exactly solves. Now, however much we may rebel against De Maistre's theory, that the early races of mankind were endowed with higher and more intuitive moral faculties than ours, and, whether or not, we accept his *dictum* that great punishments presuppose great knowledge, and reversely, that higher knowledge implies the liability to great punishments, I do not see how we can refuse to consider the matter, so far as to see whether the view solves all the difficulties of the question. It is not the first time that the blackness of the African race has been connected in theory with a curse; but De Maistre's theory throws a new light on the malediction—whether it be the curse of Cham or of Chanaan, or whether both were smitten, according to different degrees of culpability: and I maintain, further, that it is adequate to the explanation of the phenomena, that it does not clash with history, and that it is sustained by tradition.

Nevertheless, I apprehend that this view will be as much combated from the point of view of scriptural exegesis, as of scientific speculation.

Yet the curse of Cham, or of Chanaan, affecting all their posterity, ought not in reason to be more revolting even to those who have never realised what sin is, than the narrative of the fall of Adam and Eve with its direful consequences. The theory seems perfectly conformable to Scripture, and to what we know of the secrets of the Divine judgments. The picture of Cham, or Chanaan, stricken with blackness, does not present a more sudden or more terrible retribution to the mind than the Fall of the Angels. How many thousand years did it take to transform Lucifer into Satan? or the primitive

Adam into the Adam feeling shame, and conscious of decay, want, and the doom of death?

On the other hand, blackness, from the commencement, has been associated with evil. To this it may be replied that this is the sentiment merely of the white races—a natural prejudice of colour, an ex parte deduction; and to this argument, if such is the view really taken by the black races, and if no consciousness can be detected of their degradation amongst themselves, I see no other reply than this, That since, ex hypothesi, they are black because they are cursed, the tradition of this curse would be more naturally preserved by the white races than by the black. But is there no consciousness of this inferiority in the true negro? Without looking at the matter from the same point of view, I may appeal to Captain Burton's statements on this point as to a fully competent, if not the highest, authority that can be quoted on points of African travel. In the first place, he notices "the confusion of the mixed and the mulatto with the full-blooded negro. By the latter word I understand the various tribes of intertropical Africa, unmixed with European or Asiatic blood" ("Dahome," ii. 187); and p. 193, "I have elsewhere given reasons for suspecting, in the great Kafir family, a considerable mixture of Arab, Persian, and other Asiatic blood:" and as to the particular point in question, he says "The negro will obey a white man more readily than a mulatto, and a mulatto rather than one of his own colour. He never thinks of claiming equality with the Aryan race except when taught. At Whydat, the French missionaries remark that their scholars always translate 'white and black by master and slave.'" P. 189, "One of Mr Prichard's few good generalisations is, that as a rule the darker and dingier the African tribe, the more degraded is its organisation."[65] I find a very similar testimony in Crawford's "Hist. of the Indian Archipelago," i. 18. He says, "The brown and negro races of the Archipelago may be considered to present, in their physical and moral characters, a complete parallel with the white and negro races in the western world. The first has always displayed as great a relative superiority over the second, as the race of white men have done over the negroes of the west." Yet at p. 20 he says, "The Javanese, who live most comfortably, are among the darkest people in the Archipelago, the wretched Dyaks, or cannibals of Borneo, among the fairest." It must be noted, however, that the Javanese have also preserved something of primitive tradition—e.g. their marriage ceremony. And, moreover, it is not at all essential to the argument to prove that the negroes are the most degraded race. Let it be said that they have had their curse, and that the sign of the curse is in their blackness—this is merely equivalent to saying that they are cursed pro tanto; but it by no means follows that other races have not fallen to lower depths, and incurred a deeper reprobation.[66]

Among the Sioux Indians, and in the isle of Tonga (Oceanica), I find trace of the tradition of blackness as a curse, and I should think it likely that other instances might be discovered. The former (the Sioux), in their reminiscences of the Deluge, relate, "The water remained on the earth only two days (for the two months during which the Scripture says it was at its height), at the expiration of which the Master of Life, seeing that they had need of fire, sent it them by a white crow, which, stopping to devour carrion, allowed the fire to be extinguished. He returned to heaven to seek it. The Great Spirit drove it away, and punished it by *striking it black.*" — *"Annales de la Prop. de la Foi,"* l. iv. 537; Gainet, i. 211.

In Tonga, the tradition is connected with this history of Cain: —

> "The god Tangaloa,[67] who first inhabited this earth, is this Adam. He had two sons, who went to live at Boloton.... The younger was very clever. Tonbo (the eldest) was very different; he did nothing but walk about, sleep, and covet the works of his brother. One day he met his brother out walking, and knocked him down. Then their father arrived at Boloton, and in great anger said, 'Why has thou killed thy brother. Fly, wretched man; fly. Your race shall be black, and your soul depraved; you shall labour without success. Begone; you shall not go to the land of your brother, but your brother shall come sometimes to trade with you.' And he said to the family of the victim, 'Go towards the great land; your skin shall be white; you shall excel in all good things.'" —Gainet, i. 93.[68]

Cardinal Wiseman (in his "Science and Revealed Religion," lect. iii.), says, with reference to Aristotle's distribution of mankind into races by colour: —

> "There is a passage in Julius Firmicus, overlooked by the commentators of Aristotle, which gives us the same ternary division, with the colours of each race. 'In the first place,' he writes, 'speaking of the characters and colours of men, they agree in saying, — if by the mixed influence of the stars, the characters and complexions of men are distributed; and if the course of the heavenly bodies, by a certain kind of artful painting, form the lineaments of mortal bodies; that is, if the moon makes men white, Mars red, *and Saturn black,* how comes it that in Ethiopia all are born black, in Germany white, and in Thrace red?'" —*Astronomicon,* lib. i., c. i., ed. Basil. 1551, p. 3.

Now this passage seems to me to have a still further significance in the words I have italicised, with reference to the argument I have in hand. It transpires, therefore, that the ancients had the notion that Saturn made men black, which provoked the natural query, why then are only the Ethiopians black? That it should ever have been supposed that the distant Saturn, astronomically regarded, should have had such an influence is preposterous, but if the mythological personage, Saturn, ch. x., has been sufficiently identified with Noah, and the deification of the hero in the planet (comp. pp. 159, 161) probable, the notion that *he made men black,* must be the tradition of the event we are considering.

I have elsewhere traced the fulfilment of the text which says that Canaan shall be the "servant of servants to his brethren;" but as the following extract from Klaproth, in evidence of the same, has also its significance with reference to the point I am now considering—viz. the curse of blackness—I prefer to give it a place here:—"Sakhalian oudehounga est expliqué en Chinois par 'Khian chéon,' et par 'li chu,' ce qui signifie les *'têtes noires'* et le *'peuple noir,'* expression par laquelle on designe la 'bas peuple' ou les 'paysans.' Cette une expression *usitée dans plusieures pays Asiatiques ainsi qu'en Russie."—Klaproth, "Mem. Relatif a l'Asie;" vide strictures on Pere Amyot's "Mandchou Dict."*

In the oldest books of the Zendavasta, virtue and vice are personified as white and black. "The contrast between good and evil is strongly and sharply marked in the Gâthâs.... They go a step further and personify the two parties to the struggle. One is a 'white,' or holy spirit (*spentô mainyus*), and the other, a 'dark' spirit (*angrô mainyus*). But this personification is merely poetical or metaphysical, not real."—*Rawlinson's "Ancient Monarchies,"* iii. p. 106. The contrast, however, between good and evil, as white and black was the genuine expression of their idea or tradition. (Hung. ap. Bunsen, iii. p. 476, admits, at least in one instance in the Gâthâs, "an angra ('black') is put in opposition to the white, or more holy spirit.")

Mr Hunter ("Rural Bengal," p. 114) says of the primitive Aryans in India—"The ancient singer praises the *god* who 'destroyed the Dasyans and protected the *Aryan colour"* (Rig. Veda., iii. pp. 34–39), and "the thunderer, who bestowed on his white friends the fields," &c. Whatever obscurity may attach to the latter passage, there can be no doubt of the abhorrence with which the singers speak, *again* and *again,* of *"the black skin,"* ... *e.g.* "the sacrificer poured out thanks to his god for 'scattering the *slave* bands of black descent.'"

Although I believe the idea was traditional and had reference to the curse, I will concede that it might have arisen primarily in the contrast of night and day, light and darkness. But does this settle the question? On the contrary, fortified with this explanation, I return to my argument with those, who say that blackness is a mere prejudice of race, and that it is not demonstrable that it is the sign of a curse, or the mark of inferiority. Does not Nature herself proclaim it, in her contrast of light and darkness? Day and night, I imagine, would be recognised as apt symbols of error and evil as opposed to truth and goodness, even among the black races, irrespective of any consciousness or reminiscence of their degradation. Accordingly, the deeds of evil in Scripture are spoken of as the "works of darkness." It may be, therefore, that the idea of blackness as a curse is derived primitively from its association with the darkness of night; but the fact remains that blackness is connected in our minds with a curse,[69] and there is the further fact that a black race exists, and has existed during four thousand years, with this mark of inferiority upon it (compare sup. ch. iii. ix.) But a point of some difficulty remains to be determined—viz. what precisely was the race which came under this ban. Was it the whole descent of Ham, or only the posterity of Chanaan ?

Hales, in his learned work on chronology (i. p. 344), discusses this question. He says that, whereas—

"Even the most learned expositors (Bochart and Mede) have implicitly adopted the appropriation of the curse of servitude to Ham and his posterity." Yet "the integrity of the received text of prophecy, limiting the curse to 'Canaan' singly, is fully supported by the concurrence of the Massorite and Samaritan Hebrew texts, with all the other ancient versions except the Arabian; and is acknowledged, we see, by Josephus and Abulfaragi (sup.), who evidently confine the curse to Canaan—though they inconsistently consider Ham as the offender, and are not a little embarrassed to exempt him and the rest of his children[70] from the operation of the curse—an exemption, indeed, attested by sacred and profane history; for Ham himself had his full share of earthly blessings, his son Misr colonised Egypt, thence styled the land of Ham (Ps. cv. 23), which soon became one of the earliest, most civilised, and flourishing kingdoms of antiquity, and was established before Abraham's days (Gen. xii. 14-20), and in the glorious reign of Sesostris ... while Ham's posterity, in the line of Cush, not only founded the first Assyrian empire, under Nimrod, but also the Persian (?), the Grecian (?), and the Roman (?) empires, in direct contradiction to the unguarded assertion of Mede [that 'there hath never yet been a son of Ham that hath shaken a sceptre over the head of Japheth.'] How, then, is the propriety of the curse exclusively to Canaan to be vindicated?—evidently by considering him as the only guilty person ... upon the very ingenious conjecture of Faber, that the 'youngest son' who offended was not Ham, but Canaan—not the son, but the grandson of Noah. For the original, 'his little son,' according to the latitude of the Hebrew idiom, may denote a grandson, by the same analogy that Nimrod.... this (the former) interpretation is supported by ancient Jewish tradition, 'Boresith Rabba,' sec. 37, recorded also by Theodoret ... the tradition, indeed, also adds that Ham joined in the mockery, but for this addition there seems no sufficient grounds."

There is, however, the tradition, and, moreover, a distinct tradition that Ham was black. Sir J. Gardner Wilkinson, in his "Manners and Customs of the Ancient Egyptians," i., says—

"The Hebrew word Ham is identical with the Egyptian Khem, being properly written Khm, Kham, or Khem, and is the same which the Egyptians themselves gave to their country in the sculptures of the earliest and latest periods" (261). Egypt was denominated Chemi (Khemi), or the land of Ham, "as we find in the hieroglyphic legends; and the city of Khem, or Panopolis, was called in Egyptian Chemmo, of which evident traces are preserved in that of the modern town E'Khmim" (260). "Besides the hieroglyphic group, composed of the two above alluded to (260), indicating Egypt, was one consisting of *an eye*, and the sign land, *which bore the same* signification; and since *the pupil*, or *black* of the eye, was called *Chemi*, we may conclude this to be a phonetic mode of writing the name of Egypt, which Plutarch pretends was called Chemmia, from the *blackness* of its soil" (263). "*Chame* is *black* in *Coptic*, Egypt is *Chemi*, and it is remarkable that *khom* or *chom* is used in Hebrew for black or brown, as in Gen. xxx. 32–40." —Id.

Here then, at any rate, the name of Ham or Cham is curiously associated with blackness, and must have been so associated from the commencement of Egyptian history. I leave it to the Egyptologist to decide whether the presumption is stronger that the name of Egypt, identical with that of Ham, was originally derived from the blackness of its soil, or from the blackness of him whose name was identical with it ("the land of Ham" being both the scriptural and Egyptian appellation), more especially when "the eye" (apparently a personal or historical, not certainly a geographical allusion) was used as an equivalent hieroglyphic symbol for land.[71]

Here, as in other instances, if we follow the strict lines of tradition, it seems to me that we shall escape all the difficulties which are usually alleged against it. It will result then that, although according to the text of Scripture, the curse of servitude was limited to the posterity of Chanaan; yet, seeing that the criminality was common to Ham and Chanaan, according to the tradition referred to, and as is, moreover, implied in the marked manner in which Scripture (Gen. xviii. 22) indicates Cham as "the father of Chanaan," it is presumable that, if blackness was the concomitant of the curse, it extended to both Ham and Chanaan, and, by implication, to their posterity, but then *after the curse*. As Chanaan, according to the tradition, was then a boy, all his children would have been affected by the curse; but does it follow that all Ham's descent was involved in the malediction? This would be to suppose a retrospective curse, for which the only analogy would be the hypothesis that if Adam had sinned after the birth of Cain and Abel, they and their posterity would also have incurred the guilt of original sin. Now the sons of Ham were (Gen. x. 6) "Chus and Mesram and Phuth and Chanaan," *i.e.*, Chus and Mesram and Phuth were the elder brothers of Chanaan, and therefore not the children of Ham after the pronouncement of the curse. If, then, we find the children of Mesram dark, but without the negro features or the blackness of Canaan; if "Sesostris, his descendant, was a great conqueror;" if Nimrod, the son of Chus, was a powerful chieftain, and the founder of the Assyrian empire; if nothing is known of the posterity of Phuth beyond the conjecture that they were the Lybians—in a word, if the descent from these three sons does not bear out the evidence of the curse, can it be said to militate at all against the hypothesis of the curse of Ham as well as of Canaan?

Moreover, if there are differences among the black races which may present difficulties, would not the knowledge that there may have been a posterity of Ham, born after the curse,[72] go far to remove them? Hales, indeed, assumes that "Ham himself had his full share of earthly blessings; his son Misr colonised Egypt," &c. (as sup.); but this prosperity, as he indicates it, is only seen in the prosperity of his three sons, whom I assume to have been exempt from the curse. It must be remembered, however, that the occult science of the Cainites was said to have been preserved by the family of Ham, and, as we have seen, the taint was in the race.[73]

I am very far from claiming for these theories any special ecclesiastical countenance and authority. I have already intimated my opinion that, on the whole, they would be as much opposed from the point of view of scriptural exegesis as from that of unbelief. It will be said, for instance, that there is evidence in Scripture of the curse of Canaan, but no proof that blackness was the concomitant effect of the curse; and certainly it is not Scripture which affirms this, but only tradition.

To those who admit the curse, but deny the consequences which tradition attributes to it, I would oppose an almost identical argument with that which accounts for all differences in the human race by geographical location. I do not know where this argument is more forcibly put than in Latham's "Ethnology." There it is seemingly demonstrated that certain conditions, not merely of colour, but moral and intellectual, are the inseparable accompaniments of geographical location. Grant it, *pro argumento*, but I am arguing now upon the scriptural evidence, and with one with whom I assume I have a common belief in its inspiration.

It is true, then, that the curse of blackness is not recorded, but the distribution of the races is at least implied: Deut. xxxii. 8, "When the Most High divided the nations, when He separated the sons of Adam, he appointed the bounds of people according to the number of the children of Israel;" and Acts xvii. 26, "And hath made of one all mankind, to dwell upon the whole face of the earth, determining appointed times, and the limits of their habitation." (The Prot. version translates, "Having appointed the predetermined seasons and boundaries of their dwellings." Vide Hales's Chron., i. 351, who adds that this was conformable to their own allegory "that Chronos, the god of time, or Saturn, divided the universe among his three sons.")[74]

If, then, the different races of mankind, according to their merits or demerits, were apportioned to, or miraculously directed or impelled to, respective portions of the earth, which necessarily superinduced certain effects, is not the curse as apparent in its indirect operation as it would have been in its suddenness and directness?

This consideration must, I think, bring those who raise scriptural difficulties against the theory to the admission that blackness was a sign of inferiority, and that certain races were either smitten with, or were predestined to, in consequence of culpability, this degradation.

This, I admit, is no reply to those who argue from the evidence of the Egyptian monuments. But the evidence from the monuments, so far from embarrassing my conclusion, seems absolutely to enforce it. If, indeed, the evidence from the monuments did not stare one in the face, we might fall back upon the line of argument which I have just indicated, and whilst recognising in their blackness the operation of a curse, trace it in the lapse of centuries and the influences of the torrid zone. But they are recorded as being black on the earliest monuments known to us, and within a few centuries of the Deluge. The conclusion, therefore, seems inevitable, that they were so from the commencement, which exactly hits in with the tradition of the curse of Canaan.

Such, from his own point of view, is the conclusion of Sir J. Lubbock ("Prehistoric Times," p. 478)—

> "If there is any truth in this view of the subject (p. 478), it will necessarily follow that the principal varieties of man are of great antiquity, and, in fact, go back almost to the very origin of the human race. We may then cease to wonder that the earliest paintings on Egyptian tombs represent so accurately several various varieties still existing in those regions, and that the Engis skull, probably the most ancient yet found in Europe, so closely resembles many that may be seen even at the present day."

The following conclusion of Mr Wallace also exactly coincides with De Maistre's view.

Lyell, in his "Principles of Geology" (ii. 471) says—

> "Wallace suggests that at some former period man's corporeal frame must have been *more pliant and variable* than *it is now*; for, according to the observed rate of fluctuation in modern times, scarcely any conceivable lapse of ages would suffice to give rise to such an amount of differentiation. He therefore concludes, that when first the *mental* and *moral* qualities of man acquired predominance, his bodily frame *ceased to vary*."

But, although science in its own way may arrive at approximations to the truth, yet, if the traditional solution be true, assuredly it is not a solution which will be reached by any merely scientific process; and therefore, if it should be the truth, the ethnological difficulty will remain an enigma and embarrassment to the learned in all time to come.

CHAPTER VI
PALMER ON EGYPTIAN CHRONOLOGY

Having probed the chronologies of India, Babylonia, Phœnicia,[75] China, &c, and having found that one and all, when touched with the talisman of history, shrink within the limits of the Septuagint, and even of the Hebrew text, we come, perforce, to the conclusion, that there is one nation, and one only, which presents a primâ facie antiquity irreconcileable with Holy Writ—viz. Egypt.

This impression is sustained by the knowledge, somewhat indefinite and in something disturbed, that the Egyptian tradition had always attributed a fabulous antiquity to the dynasties of its kings, and that these dynasties have been marvellously resuscitated through the discovery which has enabled us to decipher the inscriptions on their tombs and monuments.

My reader need not fear, however, lest I should plunge him into the chaos of hieroglyphics; not, indeed, that much has not been rescued from the abyss, and that there is not good expectation of more to come, but when once it is established, as we may now consider to be the case, that many of these dynasties were cotemporaneous, and not successive, an uncertainty is introduced which again reduces the chronology to primitive chaos, although floating objects in it, the *débris* of tombs and dynasties, remain clearly distinguishable, and, in point of fact, have been perfectly identified. If we had no other evidence, I should feel irresistibly drawn to the dictum of M. Mariette (ap. Mgr. Meignan, "L'Homme Primitif," p. 391), "Le plus grand de tous les obstacles à l'établissement d'une chronologie égyptienne regulière, c'est que les Egyptiens eux-mêmes n'ont jamais eu de chronologie."

I shall, on the contrary, from another point of view, attempt to show, not only that they had a chronology, but that this chronology has actually been re-discovered and re-constituted.

In the conviction that this is the case, and that it is not sufficiently known that it is so, I shall devote some space to an abstract of Mr William Palmer's "Egyptian Chronicles" (1861), in which it appears to me that this exposition and solution is to be found.

Mr Palmer at least has brought the Egyptian chronology (upon the system of the Old Chronicle) to so close a reconciliation with Scripture (upon the basis of a collation of the Septuagint and Josephus), that we have a right to compare any Egyptologist making an attempt to advance into the interior to the monuments, whilst disregarding it, to a commander leaving an important fortress in his rear.[76] As Mr Palmer takes his stand upon the Old Chronicle, and as the Old Chronicle has been in considerable disrepute with Egyptologists (Bunsen, i. 216), I do not see that I can adopt a better plan of bringing the whole subject before the reader, than by confronting Mr W. Palmer's discovery and exposition with Baron Bunsen's strictures on the Old Chronicle.

Bunsen (i. 214–217) says (the italics are mine)—

"'The Egyptians,' says Syncellus, 'boast of a certain Old Chronicle, by which also, in my opinion, Manetho (the impostor) was led astray.' ... The origin of this fiction is obvious. Its object, as well as that of the pseudo-Manetho, is to represent the great year of the world of 36,525 years, or twenty-five Sothic cycles. The timeless space of the book of Sothis becomes the rule of Vulcan.... The number fixed for the other gods, 3984, is quite original; perhaps it may not be mere accident that it agrees with the computation of some chronographers for the period from the Creation to B.C. The dynasty of the demigods reflects the same judicious moderation as in the scheme of the pseudo-Manetho (214½). Then comes a series of corruptions of the genuine Manetho, i.e., of the Manetho of the thirty historical Egyptian dynasties. He is, however, confounded with the Manetho of the Dog-star, and hence it is that the fifteen dynasties of Manetho are called the fifteen dynasties of the Sothiac cycle. But how is the number 443 to be explained? Is this entry to be understood in the same sense as the similar one in Clemens, namely, that the first fifteen dynasties comprehended the 443 years prior to the beginning of the last cycle, consequently prior to 1322? or is it simply taken, with a slight alteration by Eusebius, to the fourteenth and fifteenth dynasties (435)? The following dates for the length of reigns are in the gross evidently borrowed from Eusebius.... In the sequel, there is no more reckoning by dynasties, but seventy-five generations are numbered, in order to make up the 113 of Manetho. So palpable is that,.... Lastly, the dates and numbers ... are brought into shape by various arbitrary expedients; but

Eusebius on all occasions appears as the authority.... As the dates of the individual dynasties now run, 184 years are wanting to make up the promised 36,525 years. It is scarcely worth while to inquire where the mistake lies." He finally pronounces the Old Chronicle to be the compilation of a Jewish or Christian impostor of the third century, or later.

As Mr Palmer has not directly adverted to this passage from Bunsen in his "Egyptian Chronicles," I will give an extract from a letter which I have received from Mr Palmer on the subject, which will clear off some of the tissues of confusion into which the strictures of Baron Bunsen have got entangled.

"I assert, in the first instance (there being nothing whatever to the contrary), that we have the Old Chronicle in a perfectly genuine form, i.e. in the text of Syncellus and Africanus, but by no means in Bunsen; and further, that it really is, and they from whom we have it tell us it was, the oldest Greco-Egyptian writing of the kind current in the time of Africanus.... Bunsen pronounces the Old Chronicle to be the compilation of a Jewish or Christian impostor of the third century ('Eusebius appearing on all occasions as the authority,' &c) In the Old Chronicle, as given by Syncellus and Africanus, there is nothing whatever borrowed from Eusebius; but Eusebius has borrowed from and altered the Old Chronicle, so as to suit his own sacred chronology. The 'Book of Sothis,' too, has worked up and altered the Old Chronicle, with which it is by no means to be identified.... But I deal with three so-called Manethos—viz. (1.) the original Manetho of Josephus and Eratosthenes, who had only twenty-three historical dynasties of his total of thirty dynasties (the Old Chronicle, from which he took the number of thirty, having twenty-nine historical and one [that of the sun god] unhistorical); (2.) the Manetho of Ptolemy of Mendes, which is the Manetho of Africanus, who has thirty-one dynasties, all pretending to be historical; and, lastly, the Manetho of the 'Book of Sothis,' used by Anianus and Panadorus (to which last alone Bunsen's ... mention of 'fifteen dynasties of the Dog-star' refers).... If any figures in the Manetho of the 'Book of Sothis' of the fifth century A.D., are borrowed from Eusebius, there is nothing in this, Eusebius himself having used and altered the Old Chronicle before, just as the author of the Book of Sothis or Anianus may have used Eusebius and the old chronicle. But I am not now dealing with the question of fact, whether Eusebius' figures were so followed or not.... When Bunsen says, 'Perhaps it may not be mere accident that the figures 3984 agrees,' &c; he should have said rather that some 'chronographers' 'agree' 'with it,' and perhaps so agree not by accident. I do not remember whether any one, or who in particular, of modern chronographers agree with it; but certainly if any do, it is quite by accident. The number 3984, as given by the Old Chronicle to Chronos and the other twelve gods, has no relation whatever to any reckoning of the year of the world to Christ; and a chronologer might as well adapt his sum of years from the Creation to Christ, or to any other fanciful number, as to this. The truth is, that with the shorter numbers of the Vulgate, many chronologers have made out sums of about four thousand years, some rather more, some less."

In the somewhat lengthened extract which I have made (sup. p. 94) from Bunsen, four figures (3984, 217, 443, and 184) will have struck the eye, which baffle even Bunsen's penetration, and only make twice confounded what was confused before. But what if these four figures should all be accounted for? and, when accounted for, fitted into the chronology so as to be in keeping, not only with the other figures of the Chronicle, but also with the systems of Manetho and Eratosthenes, as exactly as "the key fits the wards of the lock?" (vide infra, p. 332), will not the matter begin to wear a different aspect? When the figures are shown to be imbedded in all the different systems which have been transmitted to us, will it then be said that the figures "are evidently borrowed from Eusebius?" But, in fact, it is also demonstrated by internal evidence that the Chronicle, as we have it, must be referred to the date 305 B.C.

This, then, is how the argument stands; but it is a matter of some difficulty to compass Mr Palmer's elaborate argument, and I cannot attempt to do more than to indicate its most salient points.

Premising that the Sothic cycle (a period of 1461 vague, or 1460 fixed sidereal years) was connected by the Egyptians with their recurring periods of transformation and renovation ("common to the mythologies of Egypt and India"), and also that two such periods (1461 × 2) = 2922 corresponded with the antediluvian period, or rather with the sum of the lives or reigns of the antediluvian patriarchs, inclusive of survivors of the Deluge, with something added in order to throw the whole into cyclical form, all which is shown in detail in "Egyptian Chronicles," i. 23–37, I may now proceed to Mr Palmer's analysis of the scheme of the Old Chronicle, which is thus given by Syncellus, "probably from the Manetho of Africanus" (Palmer's "Egypt. Chron.," i. 7):—

"There is extant among the Egyptians a certain Old Chronicle, the source, I suppose, which led Manetho astray, exhibiting xxx dynasties and again cxiii generations, with an infinite space of time (not the same either as that of Manetho), viz. three myriads, six thousand five hundred and twenty-five years—1st, Of the Aeritæ; 2dly, Of the Mestræans; and, 3dly, Of the Egyptians,—being word for word as follows:—

[Dynasty I. to XV. inclusive of the chronicle of the gods]:—

Time of Phtha there is none, as he shines equally by night and by day [but all generations being from him]

[First dynasty] Ἥλιος [i.e. Ra, the sun-god], son of Phtha, reigned three myriads of years,	30,000
Then [Dynasty II. to XIV. inclusive, and generations II. to XIV. inclusive] Κρονος [or Χρονος], i.e. Seb], and all the other xii gods [who are the Aeritæ perhaps of Eusebius and Africanus], reigned years	3984
Then [Dynasty XV.] viii demigod kings [the Mestræans of Eusebius and Africanus] reigned [as viii generations but one dynasty], years	217
And after them xv generations of the Cynic cycle were registered in years	443
Then Dynasty XVI. of Tanites, generations viii, years	190
Then Dynasty XVII. of Memphites, generations iv, years of the same generations	103

After whom there followed—

Dynasty XVIII. of Memphites, generations xiv, years of the same generations	348
Then Dynasty XIX. of Diospolites, generations v, years	194
Then Dynasty XX. of Diospolites, generations viii, years of the same generations	228
Then Dynasty XXI. of Tanites, generations vi, years	121

Then Dynasty XXII. of Tanites, generations iii, years	48
Then Dynasty XXIII. of Diospolites, generations ii, years of the same generations	19
Then Dynasty XXIV. of Saites, generations iii, years	44

Besides whom is to be reckoned—

Dynasty XXV. of Ethiopians, generations iii, years of the same generations	44

After whom again there followed—

Dynasty XXVI. of Memphites, generations vii, years of the same generations	177

And then after—

Dynasty XXVII. [Here the designation, generations, and years are purposely omitted; but the years are implied by the sum total, which follows below, to be certainly	184]
Dynasty XXVIII. of Persians, generations v, years of the same generations	124
Then Dynasty XXIX. of Tanites, generations , years	39

And, lastly, after all the above—

Dynasty XXX. of one Tanite king, years

Generations cxiii, years	36,525

Sum of all the years of the XXX. Dynasties, three myriads, six thousand five hundred and twenty-five (Kings 1881 years)."

These 36,525 years, when divided by 1461, the Sothic cycle (as noted by Syncellus), give the quotient xxv. We need not digress into the conjectural reasons why twenty-five such periods were taken, rather than any other number. We will be content at starting to see in its relation to the cycle evidence of the purely fictitious character of its myriads of years, and a clue to the significance of the indication, "after them xv generations of the Cynic cycle," &c.

Mr Palmer (i. xxiii.) says, that the question which first suggested itself to him was—

"To what Sothic cycle are these 443 years or xv generations said to belong?" [for there was the doubt whether there was any real Sothic cycle at all.] "For a Sothic cycle is not merely a space of 1461 Egyptian years, but it is that particular space of 1461 such years, and that only, which begins from the conjunction of the movable new year or Thoth, with the heliacal rising of Sirius, fixed to 20th July of our Gregorian calendar for that part of Egypt which is just above Memphis.... For the author of a chronicle ending with Nectanebo, or at any date between the Sothic epochs, 20th July B.C. 1322 (the known commencement of a cycle), and 20th July A.D. 139, 'the Sothic cycle,' could only mean the cycle actually current" [i.e. B.C. 1322 to A.D. 139 = 1461]....

"After this discovery, if the perception of a truism can be called a discovery, it followed naturally to observe further that in constructing a fanciful scheme ... ending at any other date than a true cyclical epoch, the first operation ... must be to cut off all those years of the true current cycle which were yet to run out, below the date fixed upon, and to throw them back so that they might be reckoned as past instead of being looked forward to as future. This, then, was what the author of the Old Chronicle had done; and, with an ironical humour common among the Egyptians, he had told his readers to their faces the nature of his trick, ticketing and labelling the key to it (the 443 years) and tying it in the lock, or rather leaving it in the lock itself." Counting, then, back 139 years of the 443 "from the 20th July A.D. 139 to 20th July B.C. 1, and 304 more from 20th July B.C. 1, we come to 20th July in 305 B.C. (if the years be fixed, sidereal, or solar years), or to 8th November 305, if they be (as they really are) vague Egyptian years" (305 B.C. being the year in which Ptolemy Lagi assumed the crown).

[For the discrepancy between this date and the conquest of Ochus, "at which the series of the Chronicle ostensibly ends," vide_"Egypt. Chron.," p. xxiv.]

Let the reader now return to the scheme of the chronicle (sup. p. 97). The analysis of the whole sum, 36,525 years, gives 30,000 years (to the sun), + 3984 (to xiii gods), + 217 (to viii demigods), + 443 (to the Sothic cycle), + 1881 to kings from Menes to Nectanebo (the last native sovereign).

So far we have only 1881 years, corresponding to an historical period, + 443 of the cycle thrown up. It has been previously noted, however, that 2922 (two Sothic cycles) correspond to the antediluvian and patriarchal period (i. 37). The intricate part of the scrutiny will be found in the discrimination of the 2922 years (which, with 217 + 1881, make up the sequence of human time, A.M., to Nectanebo) from the figures 3984 years in the analysis above.

For the full and scientific discrimination, I must refer the reader to "Egyptian Chronicles," i. 17; but for a simple demonstration, we may take the historical figures as above—viz. 2922 + 217 + 1881, added to the figures thrown in to complete the cycle (*vide infra*), viz. 341 + 483, all which figures = 5844, and deduct them from the whole cyclical number thus—

$$36,525$$
$$\underline{5,844}$$
$$30,681$$

Now, reverting to the scheme of the Chronicle, we shall see the round number 30,000 years (being as it were an Egyptian month, in thousands of years instead of days) apportioned off to the sun-god. To obtain this round number, the fractional number 681 would have to be detached, and there being at hand the cyclical number 2922 years (two perfect Sothic cycles), any number in reason of fractional remainders might be added to it, since with the symmetrical nucleus, the agglomeration would always be recognisable by the initiated, *i.e.* by the priests. The 681 years were therefore added to 2922, and also the 341 fictitious years ("to make time from the beginning to run in the form of Sothic cycles") were added, because *there* they would cause no confusion; "whereas if they had been added to the 217 years of the demigods, no one could any longer have distinguished the original fraction."

We thus collect, therefore, those various figures into the sum which was the figure of difficulty—viz. 3984 (681 + 2922 + 341 + 40), the forty years included having merely reference to the point at which the current Sothic cycle was thrown up—being the years intervening between the flight of Nectanebo in B.C. 345, and the coronation of Ptolemy Lagi in B.C. 305.

Upon his own method, based upon Josephus, who follows in the main the Septuagint ("on a principle of compromise such as all readers, whatever may be their system, may agree in accepting provisionally, and as an approximation"), Mr Palmer (i. 22–29) brings the Scripture A.M. to B.C. 1, to a synchronism of "five years four months" and some days, with the Egyptian computation.

But the same key is made to unlock all the systems of Egyptian chronology, and in the course of his two volumes of close and learned investigation, Mr Palmer demonstrates that "Manetho, Eratosthenes, Ptolemy of Mendes, Diodorus, Josephus, Africanus, Eusebius, Anianus, Panodorus, and Syncellus, have, either of themselves or by following others, transferred dynasties, generations, and years of the gods and demigods of the Chronicle, and even fifteen generations of Ptolemies and Cæsars, as yet unborn at the date of the Chronicle, to kings after Menes."

Let the above scheme of the Chronicle be compared, for instance, with the scheme of Diogenes Laertius (which Mr Palmer conjectures, upon intrinsic evidence, to have been transmitted through Aristotle).

Diogenes Laertius' whole figure is 48,863 years, which contains for its fictitious part *thirty* times 1461 = 43,830, which, being deducted from

$$48,863,$$
$$\underline{43,830}$$
$$5,033$$

leaves 5033 for "true human time." Now 5033 years are equal to those 2922 years + 217 years + 1881 years, which alone in the Chronicle belong properly and originally to the xiii gods and viii demigods and the last xv dynasties of the kings from Menes to Nectanebo, with only thirteen surplus years, i.e. from the conquest of Darius Ochus to Alexander; "seemingly to the autumn of B.C. 332, when he first entered Egypt."

Here I might conclude my outline of Mr Palmer's scheme, so far as is necessary to the vindication of the Chronicle as against Bunsen, were it not for the remaining figure (all the others, if the reader will refer back, have been accounted for)—viz. 184, to which Bunsen refers.

This figure is shown to correspond with the 184 years of the Hyksos or Shepherds (i. 134, 135, *et seq.*, 155, 285, 299). Dynasty XXVII., to which the 184 years in the Chronicle are attributed, has been displaced from between Dynasties XVII. and XVIII. of the Chronicle, and its 184 years are "restored to their true place and to the Shepherds by Manetho," and are given "by the Theban priests, *i.e.* by Eratosthenes, suppressing the Shepherds, to the kings of Upper Egypt."

As regards Manetho (i. 284) "having, besides the 1881 years of the Chronicle, 1674 additional years of kings, of which (22 + 217 =) 239 only are in themselves, though not in their attributions, chronological, and having given of these 1491 (which are thrice 477 and 60 over) to his six early dynasties of *Lower* Egypt (and sixteen inconvenient years he isolated between his Dynasties XIV. and XV., so as to include them in his Book i.), he gave to the three early dynasties of *Upper* Egypt *no other unchronological years* than two complementary sums, the one of 43 (to the first), and the other, of 124 years, to the second of the three dynasties, that these same sums might both coalesce with the remainder of sixty years belonging to the sum of the six dynasties of Lower Egypt, so as to make with it, or rather to indicate, the one of them the sum of 103, the other the sum of 184."

Vide table, p. 285.... Sum of six dynasties of Lower Egypt, 1491. But this sum 1491 is equivalent to

$$190 + 103 + 184 \ = 477$$
$$190 + 103 + 184 \ = 477$$
$$190 + 103 + 184 \ \underline{= 477}$$

But 60

$$(1431 + 60) \ = 1491$$

43

$$(1431 + 60) \ + \ 43 =$$

103

(43 of Dyn. XIV. of Upper Egypt.)

$$(1431 + 60)$$

$$\underline{124}$$

184

(124 of Dyn. XV. of Upper Egypt in Book ii.)

The place of the 184 years of the Shepherd Dynasty will be seen as clearly in the analysis of Eratosthenes' scheme F. in "Egyptian Chronicles" (i. 299), and if I had space I should like to give it in extenso, because it is upon his 1076 from Menes to XVIII. Dynasty, that Bunsen mainly relies for his fundamental theory (Bunsen's "Egypt," ii. xvi.) As the confutation of Bunsen does not enter into Mr Palmer's plan, I think it worth while to add, that these 1076 years are thus made up 477, the true historical length of the epoch (from Menes to XVIII. Dynasty), as we know from the chronicle (vide Palmer's supra), hence the significance of this figure in table above, + 443 of the cycle added, + 156 of Dyn. XVIII. encroached upon[77] for the symmetrical purpose displayed in scheme F, in which scheme it will be seen that the 184 years of the Shepherds again enter as a constituent part.

But as I am merely indicating the scheme, and not elaborating the argument, I must here part company with Mr Palmer. If, however, any one wishes to examine the question more in detail, and seeks to know in what manner the years in the above scheme are apportioned among the different generations and dynasties, he must take up with Mr Palmer at i. p. 300. My purpose is sufficiently answered by establishing that a scheme exists, if not irrefutable, at least up to this unconfuted, which perfectly harmonises the scriptural with the Egyptian chronology.

CHAPTER VII
THE TRADITION OF THE HUMAN RACE

"Tradition reveals the past to us, and consequently it reveals to us also the future. It is the tie which binds the past, the present, and the future together, and is the science of them all. If we possessed the memory of mankind, as we do that of our personal existence, we should know all. But if we have not the memory of mankind, does not mankind possess it? Is mankind without memory, without tradition?... There is no nation which does not exist through tradition, not only historical traditions relative to its earthly existence, but through religious traditions relative to its eternal destiny. To despise this treasure, what is it but to despise life, and that which constitutes its connection, its unity, its light, as we have just seen?... When God spoke to men His Word passed into time ... Happily tradition seized upon it as soon as it left the threshold of eternity; and tradition is neither an ear, nor a mouth, nor an isolated memory, but the ear, the mouth, and the memory of generations united together by tradition itself, and imparting to it an existence superior to the caprices and weakness of individuals. Nevertheless, God would not trust to oral tradition alone ... Symbolical tradition was to add itself to oral tradition by sustaining and confirming it ... The five terms constituting the mystery of good and evil: the existence of God, the creation of the world and of man by God, the fall of man, his restoration by a great act of divine mercy, and, lastly, the final judgment of mankind ... and that which oral tradition declared, symbolical tradition should repeat at all times and in all places, in order that the obscured or deceived memory of man might be brought back again to truth by an external, a public, an universal, all-powerful spectacle. [Lacordaire is speaking principally with reference to sacrifice and the sacrifice of Mount Calvary.] ... Each time that oral tradition underwent a movement of renovation by the breath of God, symbolical tradition felt the effects of it.

The sacrifice of Abel marks the era of patriarchal tradition; the sacrifice of Abraham marks the era of Hebrew tradition; the sacrifice of Jesus Christ, the final and consummating sacrifice, marks the era of Christian tradition.... Such is the nature of tradition, and such its history. Tradition is the connection of the present with the past, of the past with the future; it is the principle of identity and continuity which forms persons, families, nations, and mankind. It flows in the human race by three great streams which are clearly perceptible—the Christian, the Hebrew, and the patriarchal or primitive; in all these three it is oral and symbolical, and whether as oral or symbolical it speaks of God, the creation, the fall, reparation and judgment.... Without occupying ourselves with the question as to whether Scripture was a gift from above or an invention of men, we see that there exists two kinds of it—human and sacred scripture. I understand by human scripture, that which is considered by men as the expression of the ideas of a man; I understand by sacred scripture that which is venerated by nations as containing something more than the ideas of a man.... There are in the world an innumerable quantity of books, nevertheless there are but six of them which have been venerated by nations as sacred. These are the 'Kings' of China, the Vedas of India, the Zend-Avesta of the Persians, the Koran of the Arabs, the Law of the Jews, and the Gospel. And at first sight I am struck with this rarity of sacred writings. So many legislators have founded cities, so many men of genius have governed the human understanding, and yet all these legislators, all these men of genius, have not been able to cause the existence of more than six sacred books upon earth!... Every sacred book is a traditional book, it was venerated before it existed, it existed before it appeared. The Koran, which is the last of the sacred writings in the order of time, offers to us a proof of this worthy of our thoughtful attention. Without doubt, Mahommed relied upon pretended revelations; however, it is clear to all those who read the Koran, that the Abrahamic tradition was the true source of its power.... The same traditional character shines upon each page of the Christian and Hebrew books; we find it also in the Zend-Avesta, the Vedas, and the Kings of the Chinese. Tradition is everywhere the mother of religion; it precedes and engenders sacred books, as language precedes and engenders scripture; its existence is rendered immovable in the sacred books ... a sacred book is a religious tradition which has had strength enough to sign its name.... The sacred writings are, then, traditional; it is their first character. I add that they are constituent, that is to say, they possess a marvellous power for giving vitality and duration to empires. Strange to say, the most magnificent books of philosophers have not been able to found, I do not say a people, but a small philosophical society; and the sacred writings, without exception, have founded very great and lasting nations. Thus the Kings founded China, the Vedas India, &c... Look at Plato ... how is it that Plato has not been able to constitute, I do not say a nation, but simply a permanent school? How is it that communities totter when thinkers meddle with them, and that the *precise moment of their fall* is that when men announce to them that mind is emancipated, that the old forms which bound together human activity are broken, that the altar is undermined and reason is all-powerful? Philosophers! if you speak the truth, how is it that the moment when all the elements of society become more refined and develop themselves, *is the moment of its dissolution?" —From Père Lacordaire's "Conferences." Conf. 9 and 10.* (Tran. H. Langdon; Richardson, 1852.)

I should also wish M. Auguste Nicolas' "Etudes Philosophiques sur le Christianisme"—particularly lib. I. chap. v., "Necessite d'une revelation Primitive;" and lib. II. chap. iv., "Traditions universelles" —to be read in connection with the following chapter. I did not become acquainted with M. Nicolas until after the chapter was concluded. I have, however, fulfilled my obligations in the above extract from L'Abbe Lacordaire, which lies more *au fond* of my view than the chapters referred to in M. Nicolas. I also wish to direct attention to a remarkable article in the *Home and Foreign Review*, Jan. 1864, entitled "Classical Myths in relation to the Antiquity of Man," signed F. A. P.

Tradition, in the sense in which we have just seen it used by Lacordaire, in what we may call its widest signification, is not limited to oral tradition, but may be termed the connection of evidence which establishes the unity of the human race; and, with this evidence, establishes the identity and continuity of its belief, laws, institutions, customs, and manners (Manners, *vide* Goguet's "Origin of Laws," i. 327–329). The more closely the tradition is investigated, the more thoroughly will it be found to attest a common origin, and the more fully will its conformity with the scriptural narrative be made apparent.

Now, although in all ages there have been men of great intellect who have held to tradition, it may be stated as one of those truths, *qui saute aux yeux*, and which will not be gainsaid, that the human intellect has been throughout opposed to tradition, has been its most constant adversary, equally when it was the tradition of a corrupt polytheism, as when it was the tradition of uncontested truth; and so active has been this antagonism, that the marvel is that anything of primitive tradition should have remained.

Hence arose the divergence between religion and philosophy—a divergence which, as it seems to me, is inexplicable from the point of view of those who believe that, in the centuries which preceded the coming of our Lord,[78] religion simply was not, had ceased to be; unless we suppose that a tradition of the antagonism had survived, which would still partially disclose how it came about that when religion had ceased to be (pro argumento), or had become corrupt, philosophy, which then (ex hypothesi) alone soared above the intellect of the crowd, did not, and could not become a religion to them, infra, pp. 142, 145, 146.

And the history of this antagonism seems to be, that the human intellect has ever had, and now more confidently than ever, the aim and ambition to substitute something better than the revelation of primitive tradition, and the experiences of the human race.

It is quite conceivable that human life and human institutions might have been arranged upon some scheme different from that of the divine appointment; and although we may believe that any such scheme would result in ultimate confusion and the final extinction of the human race, it is still theoretically possible that the experiment might have been made.[79]

Here comes in, with its full significance, the great saying of Lacordaire's— "Order I compare to a pyramid reaching from heaven to earth. Men cannot overthrow its base, because the finger of God rests upon its apex."

If the finger of God did not so rest, there is no assignable reason why this pyramid—this incubus, as some would call it—which goes back, stone upon stone, to the primitive ages, should not have been overturned, and some system purely atheistical, purely material, purely communistic, substituted for it. But I believe that no democratic organisation, however extended among the masses, will overthrow the established order of things, so long as the possessors of property, the upper classes, are true to the objects for which property was instituted.

Considering how much man has effected in the material order, and considering also the varied intellectual faculties with which he is endowed, it strikes one as strange, as something which has to be accounted for, that he has been able to effect so little in the moral order. It is the same whether we regard the action of the intellect upon the individual man, or upon society. And from this latter point of view it is so true, that it is more than doubtful whether those epochs in which man has attained the highest point of intellectual and material civilisation, are not those also in which he has reached the lowest depths of immorality;[80] and in which—having touched the lowest point of corruption—the human intellect is unable to devise any better plan for the government of mankind, than the repression of despotism.[81]

But if the human intellect cannot prevent or control corruption, cannot it disenchant vice of its evil, and so counteract its effects? Is there no new conception of virtue with which to allure mankind? No second decalogue which will attract by its novelty, or convince by logical cogency and force? The Comtists, I believe, have a scheme for setting all these things right. But what portion of mankind do they influence? They are at present formidable only as may be the cloud on the horizon, nor have they found sympathy even where they might have had some expectation of finding it. If there was any separate section of mankind which might have given them countenance, it would, one would think, be the rationalist section, whose principles would disincline them to regard old modes of thought with undue partiality. It is from this quarter, if I mistake not, that the unkindest cut has come, and that it has been said that "the latter half of Comte's career and writings is the despair and bewilderment of those who admire the preceding half;" yet in this latter half he only aimed at converting rationalism from a negative to a positive system. But, allowing that a system of some sort might thus be constructed, can positivism be defined as more than the system of those who are positive by mutual consent and agreement without faith or certainty, and who are the more positive in proportion as they recede from Catholic truth and tradition. We, however, who believe in the identity of Catholicism and Christianity, may still appreciate Professor Huxley's definition of positivism, viz.—"Catholicism minus Christianity."[82]

Can any one adduce a more typical representative of the clear, powerful, penetrating intellect of man than Voltaire! Voltaire, moreover, had the aim and ambition ("ecraser l'infame") to obliterate the tradition of the past; yet can there be a better example of the impotence of the intellect in the moral order? Does it not seem startling that, when the human intellect, as in the case of Voltaire, should be able to detect with so much acumen, so much wit, what is wrong, that it should be wholly struck with sterility when it attempts to tell us what is right, to reveal to man any truth in the moral order not traditionally known to them. And if the disciples of Voltaire have occasionally, in spasmodic efforts, attempted this, it has not been in the manner of Voltaire; it has been in the spirit of eclecticism, of reconstruction out of the elements of the past—that is to say (with pardon, if the phrase has been used before), an attempt to create, out of the elements he would have spurned, edifices which he would have derided.

Now, the pretension of the human intellect is quite contrary to this experience. It claims to have progressively elevated mankind out of a state of primitive barbarism, to have indoctrinated them with the ideas of morality which they possess, to have humanised them, and thus affirms the converse of the theory of tradition which it pursues with much unreasoning and implacable animosity.

The Saturday Review (July 24, 1869), in reviewing Mr Gladstone's "Juventus Mundi," says—"Mr Gladstone is doubtless well aware that there was no portion of his Homeric studies which was received with more surprise, or with more unfavourable comment, than his speculations on what he described as the traditive and the inventive elements in the Homeric mythology."[83] In consequence, Mr Gladstone says he has endeavoured to avoid in his more recent work "a certain crudity of expression." The Saturday Review, however, says—"That 'the crudity of expression' here referred to seems to have been corrected and modified to some extent by disguising the process of argument by which it was sustained, and by the adoption of a lighter touch and slighter treatment of the subject than in the former book. But the theory itself, we believe, remains the same."

I may assume, then, that the passage which I have elsewhere quoted from Mr Gladstone, and laid as the basis of my argument, still has his countenance and support, in spite of the manifest antagonism it has provoked. And this passage, I venture to think, acquires fresh light and an accession of force when placed in juxtaposition with the parallel passages from De Maistre and Dr Newman. These passages will present no difficulties to the believer in the Bible. How far the view is sustainable, with reference to the more recent conclusions in chronology, I shall consider in another chapter; but, assuming that it is not chronologically disproved, there is no intrinsic impossibility which will debar belief.

The general probability of tradition being thus avouched,[84] I proceed to examine certain statements that have been made as to its necessary variability, and as to the uncertainty and indefiniteness of its utterances.

In the first place, as to its variability, it is true that tested by the experience which we possess of the persistency and exactness of family and local traditions, tradition in the broader sense which I have indicated may appear to be of little value. I have elsewhere attended a closer argument on this point in reply to Sir John Lubbock (ch. xii.), but I may also make what appears to me, as regards this matter, a sufficiently important distinction.

Family tradition is so confused, because at each remove in each generation, it is necessarily crossed through marriage with the traditions of another family. These may be either rival or irreconcileable. But this remark will apply with much less force, it will only secondarily and accidentally apply at all to the common traditions, the inheritance of all families starting from a common origin. If these traditions acquired some dross through the intermarriage of families, they will, on the other hand, through the very action of intermarriages, have been more frequently compared, more vividly, therefore, kept in remembrance, and more recognisable in their distortion, because the distortion is more likely to have been in the way of super-addition of what was thought congruous and supplemental. And this seems to me to meet Mr Max Müller's objection in the *Contemporary Review* for April 1870. "Comparative philology," he says, "has taught again and again, that when we find *exactly* the same name in Greek and Sanscrit, we may be certain that it cannot be the same word;" for we here see reason why and how these traditions have been specially protected against the natural action and law which it is the peculiar province of philology to trace.

I say this more especially with reference to the etymology in Bryant's and other kindred works, which it is now the fashion to set aside with much hauteur; and I assert it without impugning in any way the results of modern philological inquiry, extending, of course, over a much wider field than the writers of the last century could embrace. But I do contend, that when the discussion has reference to the common progenitors of the human race, or the incidents of primitive life—for instance, the names of the ark, and what I may call its accessories, the dove and the rainbow[85]—a certain probability of identity may be presumed in such sort that it may chance that the probabilities of tradition must be held to override the conjectures, and in some cases even the conclusions of philology.[86]

I incline, moreover, to the belief that the fidelity and persistency of local tradition is greater than is generally supposed. Sir H. Maine[87] says—"The truth is, that the stable part of our mental, moral, and physical constitution is the largest part of it, and the resistance it opposes to change is such that, though the variations of human society in a portion of the world are plain enough, they are neither so rapid nor so extensive that their amount of character and general direction cannot be ascertained." This establishes a presumption, at any rate, in favour of tradition, although I admit that the quotation from Sir H. Maine does not go further than point to a tradition of usages; but I contend that a tradition of usage would enable us, after the manner of Boulanger,[88] to disclose "L'antiquite devoilée par ses usages," and to establish the main points and basis of the history of the human race, e.g. the Fall, the Deluge, the Dispersion, the early knowledge and civilisation of mankind, the primitive monotheism, the confusion of tongues, the family system, marriages, the institution of property, the tradition of a common morality,[89] and of the law of nations.

This inquiry might no doubt form a department either of scriptural exegesis, universal history, or of ethnological research; but, in point of fact, its scope is too large practically to fall within such limits; whereas, if it were recognised as a separate branch of study, it would, I venture to think, in the progress of its investigation, bring all these different branches of inquiry into harmony and completeness. And I further contend, that the conclusions thus attained are as well-deserving of consideration as the conclusions of science from the implements of the drift, or as the evidence of "some bones, from the pliocene beds of St Prest, which appear to show the marks of knives;"[90] which are adduced in evidence of a Palæolithic age. So that, when on one side it is said that science (meaning the science of geology or philology, &c) has proved this or that fact apparently contrary to the scriptural narrative, it can, on the other hand, be asserted that the facts, or the inferences from them, are incompatible with the testimony of the science of tradition. The defenders of Scripture will thus secure foothold on the ground of science, which, when properly entrenched, will stand good against the most formidable recognizances or assaults of the enemy.

I cannot help thinking that some such thought lurks in the following passage of Cardinal Wiseman's Second Lecture on "Science and Revealed Religion" (5th Edition, p. 73)—

> "Here again I cannot but regret our inability to comprehend in one glance the bearings and connections of different sciences; for, *if* it appears that ages must have been required to bring languages to the state wherein we first find them, other researches would show us that these ages never existed; and we should thus be driven to discover some shaping power, some ever-ruling influence, which could do at once what nature would take centuries to effect; and the Book of Genesis hath alone solved this problem."

No doubt a greater general acquaintance and power to grasp—or better still, an intuitive glance—with which to comprehend "the bearings and connections of different sciences," would tend to circumscribe the aberrations of any particular science; but the special intervention which appears to me destined to bring the various sciences into harmony, will be the elevation of the particular department of history or archæology which has to do with the traditions of the human race as to its origin into a separate and recognised branch of inquiry; and I am satisfied that if any portion of that intellect, which is cunning in the reconstruction of the mastodon from its vertebral bone, had been directed to the great lines of human tradition, that enough of the "reliquiæ" and vestiges of the past remain to establish their conformity with that "which alone has solved this problem—the Book of Genesis;" and which, apart from the consideration of its inspiration, will ever remain the most venerable and best attested of human records.[91]

It is much too readily assumed that traditions must be worthless where no records are kept. Gibbon,[92] I think, was the first who took this position. To this I reply, that although records are valuable for the attestation, they are not guarantees for the fidelity of tradition.[93] I do not assert that the tradition is more trustworthy than the record; but that, when mankind trust mainly to tradition, the faculties by which it is sustained will be more strongly developed, and the adaptation of society for its transmission more exactly conformed. In other words, tradition in ancient times seemed to flow as from a fountain-head, and the world was everywhere grooved for its reception. We may take in evidence the strange resemblances in mythological tradition in various parts of the world on the one hand, and on the other the oral tradition of the Homeric verses; the frequent concourse of citizens, and at recurring festivals of the surrounding populations, to listen to their recital. And not only was there oral tradition in verse, but all public events were recorded in the attestations of the market-place. When a treaty was ratified it was commonly before some temple, or in some place of public resort, and its terms were committed to memory by some hundred witnesses; and in like manner was the recollection of other public events and memorable facts preserved.[94] (Vide Pastoret's "Hist. de la Législation," i. 71; also, account of "Annales Maximi" in Dyer's "Rome," xvii.)

Yet, although during long periods oral transmission was for mankind the main channel of tradition, it must not necessarily be concluded that writing was unknown, and was not employed for monumental and other purposes. What strikes one most forcibly in contemplating these ages, is the contrast between their intellectual knowledge and their mechanical and material contrivances for its application. During these centuries in which the 30,000 hexameters of the "Iliad" and "Odyssey" were transmitted in memory, by repetition, at public festivals, oral tradition was doubtless employed, because during this period "paper, parchment, or even the smoothed hides, as adapted for the purposes of writing, were unknown."[95] This, whilst it certainly is in evidence of the paucity of their available resources, at the same time establishes the retentive strength of their memory,[96] and their intellectual familiarity with great truths.

And this seems to me the sufficient reply to Sir Charles Lyell's somewhat captious objection, that if the intellectual knowledge of the primitive age was so great, we ought now to be digging up steam engines instead of flint implements.

Every age has its own peculiar superiority, as hath each individual mind—non omnia possumus omnes—and it is as reasonable to object to an age of philosophic thought, or of intuitive perception, that it was not rich in the wealth of material civilisation, as it would be to object to Plato or Shakspeare, that they did not acquire dominion over mankind; or to Alexander, that he did not excel Aristotle; or to Sir C. Lyell, supposing geology to be certain, that he did not anticipate Darwin, supposing Darwinism to be true. And if it should be more precisely objected that, if in those ages there was the knowledge of writing for monumental purposes, we ought at least to find monuments,[97] I say that the onus probandi lies with the objector to prove the invention or introduction of writing in the interval between the age of Homer and the age of Pericles, as against us who believe in its primeval transmission; or to show that its introduction was more probable at this latter period than at the former.[98]

Schlegel says[99]—

> "I have laid it down as an invariable maxim to follow historical tradition, and to hold fast by that clue, even when many things in the testimony and declarations of tradition appear strange and almost inexplicable; or, at least, enigmatical; for so soon as, in the investigations of ancient history, we let slip that thread of Ariadne, we can find no outlet from the labyrinth of fanciful theories and the chaos of clashing opinion."

I propose to give a few instances of tradition, casually selected, which appear to me to be in illustration of this dictum of Schlegel's.

Take, in illustration, the question whether mankind commenced with the state of monogamy. Not that there is any obscurity on this point in the Book of Genesis. It is indeed sometimes loosely said that we find instances of polygamy in patriarchal times; but, as our Lord said, it was not so in the beginning; and the Book of Genesis exhibits mankind as commencing with a single pair, and subsequently as re-propagated through a group of families, all represented to us at their commencement as monogamous. But if this highest testimony is discarded, and men gravely discuss whether or not they commenced with a state of promiscuity, the argument from tradition will go for as much as the argument from the analogy of circumstances and conditions as inferred from the existing state of savages, since this state, from our point of view, must have been the result of degeneracy.[100]

I must, moreover, contend that the practice of monogamy, in any one case, must weigh for very much more than the practice of polygamy in ten parallel instances; because the natural degeneracy and proclivity of man in his fallen state is in this direction.

And also, polygamy is much more naturally regarded as the departure from monogamy, than the latter as the restraint of, or advance out of, a state of promiscuity.

It may further, I think, be maintained that monogamy—in the way of separation with a single woman by reason of strong love or preference— would be the more probable escape from the state of promiscuity than through the intermediary and progressive stage of polygamy.[101]

Now, I need scarcely say, that the opponents of monogamy can show no instance of an advance out of the state of promiscuity either to monogamy or polygamy. But they can point to certain communities in ancient and modern times in a state of polygamy.

Either, then, they must have degenerated into this state from the primitive monogamous family system, or they must have arrived at the stage in growth and progress out of a state of promiscuity.

Does tradition give any clue out of this labyrinth? To simplify the question, I will consent to appeal to the identical tradition to which the advocates of an original promiscuity direct our attention.

Mr J. F. M'Lennan, who, in his "Primitive Marriage," 1865 (*vide supra*), apparently describes mankind as originally in a state of promiscuity, subsequently limited by customs of tribal exogamy and endogamy, in a recent article in the *Fortnightly Review* (Oct. 1869), "Totems and Totemism," sees further evidence of his theory in the following traditions from Sanchoniathon:—

> "Few traditions respecting the primitive condition of mankind are more remarkable, and perhaps none are more ancient, than those that have been preserved by Sanchoniatho; or rather, we should say, that are to be found in the fragments ascribed to that writer by Eusebius. They present us with an outline of the earlier stages of human progress in religious speculation, which is shown by the results of modern inquiry to be wonderfully correct. They tell us for instance that 'the first men consecrated the plants

shooting out of the earth, and judged them gods, and worshipped them upon whom they themselves lived, and all their posterity, and all before them, and to these they made their meat and drink offerings.'[102] They further tell us that the first men believed the heavenly bodies to be animals, only differently shaped and circumstanced from any on the earth. 'There were certain animals which had no sense, out of which were begotten intelligent animals ... and they were formed alike in the shape of an egg. Thus shone out Môt [the luminous vault of heaven?], the sun and the moon, and the less and the greater stars.' Next they relate, in an account of the successive generations of men, that in the first generation the way was found out of taking food from trees; that, in the second, men, having suffered from droughts, began to worship the sun—the Lord of heaven; that in the third, Light, Fire, and Flame [conceived as persons], were begotten; that in the fourth giants appeared; while in the fifth, 'men were named from their mothers' because of the uncertainty of male parentage, this generation being distinguished also by the introduction of 'pillar' worship. It was not till the twelfth generation that the gods appeared that figure most in the old mythologies, such as Kronos, Dagon, Zeus, Belus, Apollo, and Typhon; and then the queen of them all was the Bull-headed Astarte. The sum of the statements is, that men first worshipped plants; next the heavenly bodies, supposed to be animals; then 'pillars;' ... and, last of all, the anthropomorphic gods. Not the least remarkable statement is, that in primitive times there was kinship through mothers only, owing to the uncertainty of fatherhood."[103]

The fragments of Sanchoniathon here referred to are found at earlier date than Eusebius, having been copiously extracted by Philo (*vide* Bunsen's "Egypt").

Sanchoniathon was to Phœnicia what Berosus was to Assyria; that is to say, the earliest post-diluvian compilers of history when tradition was becoming obscure. Let us scrutinise his testimony. We are here told "that the first men *consecrated the plants* shooting out of the earth, and *judged them gods*."... "Next they relate, in an account of the successive generations of men, that in the first generation *the way was found out of taking food from trees.*" Here, I submit, that we have plainly and unmistakably a tradition of that first commencement of evil, the first man and woman plucking the apple from the tree, thinking they would become as gods (Gen. iii. 4, 5), ... "and the serpent said ... for God doth know that in what day soever you shall eat thereof ... and you shall be as gods, knowing good and evil."

Then follows the succession of ages (vide infra, ch. xiii.), of which there is a curious parallel tradition in Hesiod and Apollodorus, and partial correspondences in the traditions of India, China, and Mexico (infra, ch. xiii.).[104]

It will be noted, however, that whilst running into the tradition of Hesiod on the one side (in Hesiod and in the Chinese tradition there is trace of a double tradition, ante and post-diluvian), Sanchoniathon still more closely runs in with the narrative of Genesis on the other, thus connecting the links of the chain of tradition.[105]

In the succession of ages we have in outline the history of mankind in the ante-diluvian period—the Fall, supra—followed in the succeeding age by a great drought—[compare this tradition with the following passage in Fran. Lenormant's "Histoire Ancienne," i. p. 5, 2d ed., Paris 1868—"and when geology shows us the first ante-diluvian men who came into our part of the world, living in the midst of ice, under conditions of climate analogous to those under which the Esquimaux live at the present day ... one is naturally brought to the recollection of that ancient tradition of the Persians, fully conformable to the information which the Bible supplies on the subject of the fall of man, ... which ranks among the first of the chastisements which followed the fall, along with death and other calamities, the advent of an intense and permanent cold which man could scarcely endure, and which rendered the earth almost uninhabitable."[106] It is to this period, and the short period immediately following the Deluge (vide ch. ii. p. 21, and infra, pp. 136, 137), that I am inclined to trace the notions of a primitive barbarism—compare, for instance, the facts which Goguet, in his "Origin of Laws," i. p. 72, adduces in proof of his progress from barbarism, with the above tradition of the Persians recorded by Lenormant.

Goguet says—"The Egyptians, Persians, Phœnicians, Greeks, and several other nations (vide his references, p. 72), acknowledged that their ancestors were once without the use of fire. The Chinese confess the same of their progenitors.... Pomponius, Mela, Pliny, Plutarch, and other ancient authors speak of nations, who, at the time they wrote, knew not the use of fire, or had only just learned it. Facts of the same kind are attested by several modern relations." Let this latter statement be compared with infra, pp. 136, 137.

In the third age we are told—"Light, Fire, and Flame (conceived as persons) were begotten," which looks like a tradition of Vulcan, Tubalcain,

&c. (vide ch. xii. infra); and "in the fourth, giants appeared;" while in the fifth, the corruption of mankind is indicated, as is declared in Genesis vi. 4: "Now giants were upon the earth in those days. For after the sons of God went in to the daughters of men and brought forth children," &c, ver. 12, "and when God had seen that the earth was corrupted (for all flesh had corrupted its way upon the earth), ver. 13, He said to Noe," &c. "It was not till the twelfth generation that the gods appeared that figured most in the old mythologies," says Mr M'Lennan, quoting Sanchoniathon, or what is believed to be his testimony. I trust that this fragment of tradition may be remembered in connection with what I have written in chapters viii., ix., x [107]

"The sum of the statements" then, so regarded, is to confirm the tradition of the human race as recorded in Genesis, that they sprang from three brothers and their three wives, forming three monogamous pairs who accompanied their father Noah into the ark, with his wife; and who again were more remotely descended from a single pair.

If, then, in the two most ancient traditions of which we have any record, we find concordance on some points and divergence on others, the circumstance of identity at all is so much more startling than the occurrence of discrepancy, that it will fairly be taken to warrant the presumption of a common origin; and this conformity will also be naturally claimed in support of our narrative as against the other on the points of disagreement, which will then be set down to the corruption of that which is deemed the most ancient and authentic. For those, therefore, who believe the Bible to be the revealed Word of God, and even for those who regard it as the most ancient record, the coincidences with Sanchoniathon will afford a striking testimony; whereas the coincidence of the fifth age of Sanchoniathon with Genesis (chap. vi. 1, 2, 4) and the tradition of Hesiod, must be an embarrassment to those who seek in this tradition evidence that what was characteristic of the fifth age, was true of the preceding and pristine ages.

To take a second instance, more exactly in illustration of the quotation from F. Schlegel, supra, p. 124, there is no such barrier to tradition (regarded retrospectively) as the notion, if we accept it, which crept over many nations, that they were "autochthones." Like the sand-drifts known to geologists as dunes, such notions, if they had been received absolutely, would have involved all tradition in a general extinction. But as the dunes, when minutely measured and submitted to calculation, have afforded the best evidence in favour of what may be called the diluvian chronology, so will this notion that men sprang out of the soil in which they dwelt, when analysed, contribute fresh evidence to the truth and persistence of tradition. But first of all, will any one start with the theory—that any nation that had this notion about itself—the Greeks, for instance, were really autochthones? There is, then, simply a confusion of ideas, a difficulty which has to be unravelled; but seeing that the Greeks notoriously believed themselves to be autochthones, it becomes an obstruction in the main channel of tradition, and it is especially incumbent upon us to consider the facts.

In the "Supplicants" of Æschylus—and I am not aware that the notion crops up at earlier date—Pelasgus is introduced as saying—

"Pelasgus bids you, sovereign of the land,

My sire, Palæcthon, of *high ancestry*,

Original with this *earth*; from me, their king,

The people take their name, and boast themselves

Pelasgians."

—v. 275.

Here the high descent, and the origin from the soil, the ancestry referred to in the same breath with the allusion to his sire, "original with this earth," strikes one as incongruous. And the incongruity appears still greater when we recollect that Pelasgus is the person whom all historical evidence proves to have been the first settler in the country; it being also borne in mind that the term "autochthones," whether in a primary or a secondary sense, is always applied to the supposed aboriginals of the country, and therefore excludes the hypothesis of any more primitive colonisation.[108]

But if we regard it as a corruption of the tradition that man was created out of the earth ("for dust thou art, and unto dust thou shalt return," Genesis iii. 19), does not this solve all difficulties? The extension of the knowledge that they were created out of the earth, to the notion that they were created out of this or that particular clay, is not violent. Is it not this same Æschylus[109] who has the allusion "to the earth drinking the blood of the two rival brothers, the one slain by the other." It will be seen at p. 175, that the Mexicans believed that the first race of men were created "out of the earth," and "the third out of a tree," a reminiscence of the creation, and of the fall, the intermediate event being probably the creation of Eve. In like manner, the Red Indians have a tradition that they were created out of the red clay by the Great Spirit; and to go to another part of the world, the supposed aboriginal tribes of China were called Miautze, or "soil children."[110]

This testimony must be connected with the phrase so startling in the seventh ode of the fourth book of Horace, "pulvis et umbra sumus," and with the text in Genesis iii. 19, "for dust thou art."[111] It may possibly be said that this is merely matter of every day's experience. But it is precisely at this point that we must ask those who dispute tradition to discard tradition. Do bodies—so far as the exterior senses tell us—return to dust, or to other forms of life? If it is true that we return to dust—Scripture apart—it is tradition and not experience which attests it, and yet so common is the belief, that it might readily pass as the result of common observation.

So general a tradition that man was created, and created out of the ground,[112] is so completely in accordance with the text of Genesis, that one can hardly see what more can be demanded; yet Catlin says[113]—"Though there is not a tribe in America but what has some theory of man's creation, there is not one amongst them all that bears the slightest resemblance to the Mosaic account." Catlin instances the traditions of the Mandans, Choctaws, and the Sioux—1st, The Mandans (who have the ceremony commemorative of the Deluge referred to, ch. xi.), believe that they were created "under the ground." 2d, The Choctaws assert that they "were created crawfish, living alternately under the ground and above it as they chose; and, creeping out at their little holes in the earth to get the warmth of the sun one sunny day, a portion of the tribe was driven away and could not return; they built the Choctaw village, and the remainder of the tribe are still living under the ground." The Iroquois, however, believe that they "came out of the ground," which is identical with the Greek notion of their being "autochthones" (vide Colden, ii. 103), where one of their chiefs speaks thus—"For we must tell you that long before one hundred years our ancestors came out of this very ground.... You came out of the ground in a country that lies beyond the seas." Now, even if we consent to detach the Iroquois tradition, there is still in both the Mandan and Choctaw tradition, a common idea of their having come from "under the ground," which seems to me the tradition that they were created out of the ground at one remove. To this it would seem the Choctaws have super-added their recollection of some incident of their tribe, possibly that they were an offshoot of the Esquimaux, or were at one period in their latitude and lived their life, which would be in accordance with the theory of their migrations from Asia by Behring's Straits. 3d, About the Sioux, the third instance of contrariety adduced by Catlin, it seems to me that there is no room for argument, the Sioux having the tradition referred to above, that the Great Spirit told them that "The red stone was their flesh." To these three instances Mr Catlin adds—"Other tribes were created under the water, and at least one half of the tribes in America represent that man was created under the ground or in the rocky caverns of the mountains. Why this diversity of theories of the Creation if these people brought their traditions of the Deluge from the land of inspiration?"[114]

Now, just as the tribes who said they were created "under the ground" implied the same tradition as those who said they were created *out of* the ground, so, too, the tribes who said they were created "under the water" probably held the tradition that the creation of the race preceded the Deluge.

The tradition which connects the creation with "the rocky caverns of the mountains" is more recondite—may it possibly be a recollection of the commencement of civil life after the Deluge, when Noah led them, according to tradition, from the mountains to the plains?

M. L'Abbé Gainet says (i. 176)—"The Lord repeated four times the promise that He would not send another deluge.... The children of Noah were long scared by the recollection of the dreadful calamity.... It is probable that they did not decide upon leaving the 'plateaux' of the mountains till quite late. Moreover, caverns have been found in the mountains of the Himalaya, and in many other elevated regions of Asia, which they suppose to have been formed by the first generations of man after the Deluge. The works of the learned M. de Paravey make frequent mention of them." This tradition is supported by the lines of Virgil referring to Saturn (vide infra, p. 210).

"Is genus indocile, ac dispersum *montibus altis*

Composuit; legesque dedit."—*Æn*. viii. 315.

I give these suggestions for what they may be worth.[115] Truly, where some see nothing but harmony, others see nothing but diversity. Only to put it to a fair test, I should like to see Mr Catlin or some one else group these various traditions round any one tradition which they believe to be at variance with the revelation of Genesis, and which, at the same time, they happen to consider to be the true one. It must be conceded that in one way the facts accord with Mr Catlin's theory—contradicted, however, by other evidence (infra, ch. xi.)—that the Indians were created on the American continent. But upon any theory that they were not created at all, but existed always in pantheistic transformation, or had progressed from the monkey, or had been developed in evolution from some protoplasm, is not the tradition incongruous and inexplicable?

To take another instance. The Hindoos had a fanciful notion that the world was supported by an elephant, and the elephant by a tortoise. Nothing can be imagined more incongruous and grotesque. Yet Dr Falconer has recently discovered, in his explorations in India, a fossil tortoise adequate to the support of an elephant. The incongruity then of the tradition disappears; its grotesqueness remains. I cannot help thinking, however, that it may have been the embodiment in symbol, or else the systematisation of the confused medley of their tradition of the order, i.e. of the sequence of days of the creation (vide Appendix to this chapter).[116]

I have alluded, p. 199, to the tradition preserved by Berosus, that Oannes, whom I identify with Noah, left writings upon the origin of the world, in which he says, "that there was a time when all was darkness and water, and that this darkness and water contained monstrous animals." Here, perhaps, two distinct traditions are confused; but is not the tradition of animals so much out of the ordinary nature of things as to be called monstrous sufficiently marked to make us ask if the discovery of the skeleton of the "megatherium" ought to have come upon the scientific world as a surprise? Might they not have anticipated the discovery if they had duly trusted tradition?

Other instances might doubtless be adduced. My present object is merely to suggest that there may be truths in tradition not dreamt of by modern philosophy. If the human intellect were as capacious as it is acute, we might then listen with greater submission to its strictures upon tradition; because then we might at least believe that its vision extended to all the facts. But in truth, no intellect, however encyclopædic, can grasp them all. Indeed, knowledge in many departments is becoming more and more the tradition of experts, and must be taken by the outside world on faith. How many facts, again, once in tradition, but at some period put on record, lie as deeply shrouded in the dust of libraries as they had previously lain hidden in the depths of ages? Who will say what facts are traditional in different localities? Barely do we move from place to place without eliciting some information strange and new. Who again will say what ideas are traditional in different minds? Barely is there a discussion which provokes traditional lore or traditional sentiment which does not bring to light some such thought or experience, re-appearing, like the lines in family feature, after the lapse of several generations.

Whenever, then, mankind is called upon to discard its traditions at the voice of any intellect, however powerful, is it unreasonable to demand that some cognizance should be taken of these facts.[117]

Let us now, returning to the tradition we have more especially in view, ask this further question,—What could the human intellect have done towards the regeneration of the race if there had been no revelation and no tradition?

It is not often that unbelief is constructive and supplies us with the necessary data with which to furnish the answer. But recently a work which is said to embody considerable learning has appeared, entitled, "The Origin and Development of Religious Belief," which is written "from a philosophic and not from a religious point of view;" in which "the existence of a God is not assumed, the truth of revelation is not assumed," and "the Bible is quoted

not as an authoritative, but as an historical record open to criticism." —Mr
Baring Gould, "Origin and Development of Religious Belief," preface, 1869.

Here then, if anywhere, we are likely to get the solution from the point
of view of unbelief.

At p. 119, Mr B. Gould thus summarises his views:—

"Religion, as has been already shown, is the synthesis
of thought and sentiment. It is the representation of a
philosophic idea. It always reposes on some hypothesis. At
first it is full of vigour, constantly on the alert to win converts.
Then the hypothesis is acquiesced in, it is received as final,
its significance evaporates. The priests of ancient times were
also philosophers, but not being able always to preserve
their intellectual superiority, their doctrines became void of
meaning, hieroglyphs of which they had lost the key; and
then speculation ate its way out of religion, and left it an
empty shell of ritual observance, void of vital principle.
Philosophy alone is not religion, nor is sentiment alone
religion; but religion is that which, based on an intelligent
principle, teaches that principle as dogma, exhibits it in
worship, and applies it in discipline. Dogma worship and
discipline are the constituents, so to speak, the mind spirit,
and body of religion." —"*Origin and Development of
Religious Belief.*" By S. Baring Gould, M.A. Rivingtons, 1869.
Part i., p. 119.

Here it is said that "religion is the representative of a philosophic idea.
It always reposes on some hypothesis." This philosophic idea may be that
there must necessarily be a Creator. But also it may not be, for "the existence
of God is not assumed" (vide preface). If it is not, then, according to this
definition, religion may be the representative of any philosophic idea (i.e.
any idea of any philosopher), even that which may be diametrically opposed
to the existence and goodness of God.[118] But if, on the other hand, the
existence of God is this primary philosophic idea, then all other philosophic
ideas must succumb to it. It is a point which you must settle at starting in
your definition of religion.

What follows seems to assume that some individual, or some set of
individuals, at a period more or less remote, evolved the idea of God and
religion out of their own consciousness; but that, as the descendants of these
individuals had not the same intellectual vigour, the conception lapsed,—
"their doctrines became hieroglyphs of which they had lost the key."
Nothing can be more conformable to the theory of tradition;[119] but from

the point of view of Mr Baring Gould, what was to forbid other individuals broaching fresh conceptions? Is there, however, any instance known to us? Is there any instance of a religion not eclectic or pantheistic (the one being the mere revivalism or reconstruction of the elements of former beliefs, and the other their absorption), any religion "based on an intelligible principle," heretofore unknown to mankind, rising up and obtaining even a temporary ascendancy among mankind? No; mankind, even in the darkness of Paganism, persistently distinguished between religion and philosophy, priests and sophists—though intellectually so much alike—and this I consider to be a master-key to the history of the past (ante, p. 109).

There is a further point which Mr Baring Gould must settle. Religion may be theoretically regarded as an affair of growth, progressive, or as an affair of revelation, or something so nearly counterfeiting revelation as to arise spontaneously; but it cannot well be both. Now, in the pages of Mr Baring Gould it appears at one time "springing into life", and, as in the passage above, analogously to a conception in the mind:—"At first it is full of vigour, constantly on the alert to win converts;" at another, "as a conception slowly evolved;" then all at once "a living belief, vividly luminous". Again, "Religion does not reach perfection of development at a bound; generations pass away, before," &c; and we find that in all primitive religions the idea of God is the idea of a devil, or (id.) "that the first stage in the conception of a devil is the attribution of evil to God," which is different, inasmuch as it supposes man to start with the knowledge of God, and is, moreover, inconsistent with what is said at page 113:—"The shapeless religion of a primitive people gradually assumes a definite form. It is that of nature worship. It progresses through polytheism and idolatry, and emerges into monotheism or pantheism." Of course this is said upon the assumption that the primitive man was barbarous. But however remote from the fact, it is theoretically as conceivable that man should worship nature as an ideal of beauty and power, as that he should regard it from the first as an apparition of terror; or, in other words, that taking nature-worship for granted, Mr Max Müller's view of it, viz.:—"He begins to lift up his eyes, he stares at the tent of heaven, and asks who supports it? He opens his eyes to the winds, and asks them whence and whither? He is awakened from darkness and slumber by the light of the sun, and Him whom his eyes cannot behold, and who seems to grant him the daily pittance of his existence, he calls 'his life, his breath, his brilliant Lord and Protector'" (Chips, i. 69, apud B. G., 139),—is as likely to be the true one as Mr Baring Gould's,[120] viz.:—"At first man is ... antitheist; but presently he feels resistances.... The convulsions of nature, the storm, the thunder, the exploding volcano, the raging seas, fill him with a sense of there being a power superior to his own, before which he must bow. His religious thought, vague and undetermined, is roused by the opposition of nature to his will" (p. 137).

Mr Baring Gould postulates, I am aware, the lapse of several generations for the evolution of these ideas. But there is nothing in Mr Baring Gould's statement of the progression or development of the conception of the Deity among mankind which might not pass in rapid sequence through the mind of the primitive man, — call him "Areios," if you shrink from close contact with history, and refuse to call him Adam. Why then the indefinite lapse of time? why the progressive advance of the idea through successive generations of mankind? Why, except that the primitive barbarism *must* be assumed; and because (p. 239), "in the examination of the springs of religious thought, we have to return again and again to the wild bog of savageism in which they bubble up." But if the savagery was so great, the perplexity how man ever came to make the first step in the induction is much greater than that, having made it, he should proceed on to make the last.

It is certain that reason can prove the existence of God and His goodness, and this knowledge evokes the instincts of love and worship. It is true also that man has a conscience of right and wrong, and that among its dictates is a sense of the obligation of love and worship. Still this will not account for the existence of religion in the world. Much less will Mr Baring Gould's theory of an induction by mankind collectively, spread over several centuries, account either for the notion or for the institution.

Neither, apart from direct or indirect revelation, would it prove more than that man was religious, though without religion; capable of arriving at the knowledge of God's existence, but without any knowledge how to propitiate him; seeking God, but not able to find Him.

Therefore, Mr Baring Gould truly says — "Philosophy alone is not religion." Philosophy, as we have seen, may prove the existence of God. But religion, from the commencement of the world, has conveyed the idea that there is a particular mode in which God must be worshipped. Here philosophy is entirely at fault. Mr Baring Gould again truly says that "dogma, worship, and discipline are the constituents, so to speak, the mind, spirit, and body of religion" (p. 119). But he goes no further, and does not explain how it came about that mankind in all ages have adhered with singular pertinacity to the notion that religion could teach that on which philosophy must perforce be silent. Has not the greater intellect ever been on the side of philosophy? Nay,[121] in the epochs in which intellectual superiority was undeniably on the side of philosophy, did the populace go to the academy or to the oracles? If the human intellect had originally framed the ritualistic observances, which bore so strange a resemblance in different parts of the world; if human sagacity had originated the idea of sacrifice (and wherefore sacrifice from the point of view of human sagacity?); if philosophy had revealed to them the religious conceptions which they retained, and had been able to define the relation of man to the Divinity—would not mankind, in all ages, have had recourse to its greatest intellects for the solution of its doubts, rather than to the guardians of an obscure and corrupt tradition? The question no doubt is complicated with the evidence as to demonolatry; but the extent to which this prevailed only enforces the argument against Mr Baring Gould, to whom, apparently, the demon is not a real existence, but only the embodiment of a phase of thought, and must seriously embarrass those who attribute the regeneration of man from savagery to intellectual growth and natural progress.

But demonology apart, what would have countervailed against the superiority of reason and the intellectual prestige of the world except a belief in a tradition of primitive revelation? What else will account for the different recognitions of philosophy and religion—priests and sophists? What else would have prevented mankind from resorting in their difficulties to where the greatest intellect was found?

this truth seems to gain partial recognition in the pages of Mr Baring Gould:—

> "In conclusion, it seems certain that for man's spiritual well-being, these forces ('the tendency to crystallise, and the tendency to dissolve') need co-ordination. Under an infallible guide, regulating every moral and theological item of his spiritual being, his mental faculties are given him that they may be atrophied, like the eyes of the oyster, which, being useless in the sludge of its bed, are re-absorbed. Under a perpetual modification of religious belief, his convictions become weak and watery, without force, and destitute of purpose. In the barren wilderness of Sinai there are here and there green and pleasant oases. How come they there? By basaltic dykes arresting the rapid drainage which leaves the major part of that land bald and waste. So in the region of religion, *revelations and theocratic systems have been the dykes saving it* from barrenness, and encouraging mental and sentimental fertility".

It is impossible that we should quarrel with this illustration, it is so exactly to our point. Is it not another way of affirming the position which I maintain against Sir John Lubbock? (ch. xii.) May not we, too, take our stand upon these "oases" of tradition, which "revelations" and "theocratic systems" have formed, and ask what the human intellect has been able to achieve for the spiritual cravings of man in the waste around?

Mr Baring Gould, indeed, says

"A power of free volition within or outside all matter in motion was a rational solution to the problems of effects of which man could not account himself the cause. Such is the origin of the idea of God—of God *whether many*, inhabiting each brook and plant, and breeze and planet, *or as* being a world-soul, *or as* a supreme cause, the Creator and sustainer of the universe. The common consent of mankind has been adduced as a proof of a tradition of a revelation in past times; but the fact that most races of men believe in one or more deities proves nothing more than that all men have drawn the same inference from the same premises. It is idle to speak of a 'Sensus Numinis' as existing as a primary conviction in man, when the conception may be reduced to more rudimentary ideas. The revelation is in man's being, in his conviction of the truth of the principle of causation, and thus it is a revelation made to every rational being."

Grant that it is so, there is nothing here which militates against our position, which is this,—not certainly that there is not a revelation of God in man's being, made to every rational creature, but that there has been an express revelation superadded to it; and that it is not true that "the common consent of mankind to the existence of God has been adduced as a proof of a tradition of a revelation in past times," but that the mode and manner of the consent attests the fact of tradition and the fact of revelation. But what have we just heard? That there is a revelation of God's existence in man's nature, *i.e.* in *each* man's nature—"it is a revelation made to every man's nature." Then the indefinite lapse of time demanded for the evolution of the ideas, which we have just been combating, is not after all necessary. "*Habemus reum confitentum.*"

But inasmuch as the consent of mankind is only "to one or more deities," it is only so far a testimony to the existence of God as it is shown that polytheism arose out of the corruption of this belief; and, moreover, by no means proves "that all men have drawn the same inference from the same premises," even if it were possible to reconcile this statement with what is said The shapeless religion of a primitive people gradually assumes a definite form. It is that of nature-worship. *It progresses through* polytheism and idolatry, *and emerges into* monotheism or pantheism" (*vide infra*).

At this point I should wish to put in the accumulation of evidence which L'Abbe Gainet has collected to prove that monotheism was the primitive belief.[122] When this evidence is dispersed, it will be time enough to return to the subject.

In any case, we may fall back upon the following testimony in Mr Baring Gould:—

"It is the glory of the Semitic race to have given to the world, in a compact and luminous form, that monotheism which the philosophers of Greece and Rome only vaguely apprehended, and which has become the heritage of the Christian and Mohammedan alike. Of the Semitic race, however, one small branch, Jewdom, preserved and communicated the idea. Every other branch of that race sank into polytheism (vide supra).... It is at first sight inexplicable that Jewish monotheism, which was in time to exercise such a prodigious influence over men's minds, should have so long remained the peculiar property of an insignificant people. But every religious idea has its season, and the thoughts of men have their avatars.... It was apparently necessary that mankind should be given full scope for unfettered development, that they should feel in all directions after God, if haply they might find Him, in order that the foundations of inductive philosophy might be laid, that the religious idea might run itself out through polytheistic channels for the development of art. Certainly Jewish monotheism remained in a state of congelation till the religious thought of antiquity had exhausted its own vitality, and had worked out every other problem of theodicy; then suddenly thawing, it poured over the world its fertilising streams" [123]

From all this it results that, so far as the testimony of the Semitic race is concerned (which, by the by, a concurrence of tradition points to as the oldest), the human race did not "emerge into monotheism," but "sank into polytheism;" that monotheism was their belief from "their earliest days," and their language bearing testimony to the same, shows also that it was primitively so. It moreover results, that although mankind may have been allowed to sink into polytheism, as a warning or a chastisement, it certainly could not have been "in order that the foundations of inductive philosophy might be laid;" for it is quite apparent from this extract that the induction was *never made* that man did *not* "emerge into monotheism;" but that having "*exhausted its vitality,*" and "worked out every problem of theodicy" in the way of corruption, it *received* monotheism back again from the only people who had preserved it intact.

At any rate, monotheism came to it *ab extra*, and before polytheism had attained the "full scope of that development" which was necessary for the perfection of art!

But Mr Baring Gould having a perception that this admission (although he has not apparently seen its full significance) is fatal to his theory, hastens to unsay it "Whence did the Jews derive their monotheism? Monotheism is *not* a feature of any primitive religion; but that which is a feature of secondary religions is the appropriation to a tribe of a particular god, which that tribe exalts above all other gods." In support of this view, Mr Baring Gould quotes certain texts of Scripture—Isa. xxxvi. 19, 20 (*i.e.* words spoken by Rabsaces the Assyrian), and Jos. xxiv. 15, "But if it seem evil to you to serve *the Lord*, you have your choice: choose this day that which pleaseth you, whom you would rather serve, whether the gods which your fathers served in Mesopotamia [query, an allusion to the idolatry in the patriarchal households? Gen. xxxv. 2, "the gods" being of the same kind with "the gods of the Amorites"], or the gods of the Amorites, in whose land you dwell; but as for me and my house, we will serve *the Lord*." One would have thought this text too plain to be cavilled at. Is not *the Lord* whom Josue invokes *the same Lord* who (Gen. i. 1) "in the beginning created heaven and earth," and who said to Noah (Gen. vi. 7), "I will destroy *man whom I have created*, from the face of the earth;" and who (Exod. iii. 2) appeared to Moses in a flame of fire in the bush which was not consumed; and to whom Moses said, "Lo, I shall go to the children of Israel, and say to them, *The God of your fathers* hath sent me to you; if they should say to me, What is His name? what shall I say to them? (ver. 14), God said to Moses, *I am who am*: He said thus shalt thou say to the children of Israel, *He who is* hath sent me to you." When or where has monotheism been more explicitly declared? Is there any phrase which the human mind could invent in which it could be more adequately defined? And when God speaks as "the God of Abraham, of Isaac, and of Jacob," is it not as if He would say, I am not only the God who speaks to the individual heart, but who is *also traditionally* known to you all collectively through my manifestations and revelations to your forefathers? Compare Matt. xxii. 32. *Inter alia*, Mr B. Gould also instances such unmistakable orientalisms as "'Among the gods there is none like unto Thee, O Lord,' says David, and he exalts Jehovah above the others as a 'King above all gods.'" Where, then, may we ask, is the monotheism, "the glory of the Semitic race," to be found, if not in the time of David?

The proof which follows is more clinching still—

> "Jacob seems to have made a sort of bargain with Jehovah that he would serve Him instead of other gods, on condition that He took care of him during his exile from home. The *next* stage in popular Jewish theology was a denial of the power of the Gentile gods, and the treatment of them as idols. Tradition and history point to Abraham as the first on whom the idea of the impotence of the deities of his father's house first broke. He is said to have smashed the images in Nahor's oratory, and to have put a hammer into the hands of one idol which he left standing, as a sign to Nahor that that one had destroyed all the rest."

Unfortunately for this view—according to the only authentic narrative we have of the facts, Gen. xii.—Abraham must have preceded Jacob by at least two generations!

I think that, after this, we may fairly ask Mr Baring Gould, who is learned in medieval myths, to trace for us more distinctly the notion of the chronicler who had a theory that Henry II. lived before Henry I.

With this passage I shall conclude this chapter, merely observing, that if any department of study existed which had for its special object the investigation of tradition,[124] it is simply impossible that a work (clever in many respects) such as that of Mr Baring Gould should ever have been written.

APPENDIX TO CHAPTER VII.

Cardinal Wiseman ("Lectures on Science and Religion," ii. 228–232), in speaking of what was characteristic of most Oriental religions—a belief "in the existence of emanated influences intermediate between the divine and earthly natures," is led on to give an account of the curious Gnostic sect, the Nazarians—"The first of these errors was common, perhaps, to other Gnostic sects; but in the Codex Nasaræus we have the two especially distinguished as different beings—light and life. In it the first emanation from God is the king of light; the second, fire; the third, water; the fourth, life." I wish to note that, whether or not their notions as to emanations originally meant more than the act of creation, a tradition as to the successive order of the creation seems clearly embodied in the text. God created first of all light; then the sun (the firmament) is fire (the distinct creation of the light and the sun in Genesis is so marked as to create a special difficulty in the cosmogony); then water; then life, in beasts, birds, reptiles, &c; lastly, man. Comp. with supra, p. 138, and with the above legend of Michabo.

"A Slavonian account of Creation.—The current issue of the Literary Society of Prague includes a volume of popular tales collected in all the Slavonian countries, and translated by M. Erben into Czech. We extract the shortest—'In the beginning there was only God, and He lay asleep and dreamed. At last it was time for Him to wake and look at the world. Wherever He looked through the sky, a star came out. He wondered what it was, and got up and began to walk. At last He came to our earth; He was very tired; the sweat ran down His forehead, and a drop fell on the ground. We are all made of this drop, and that is why we are the sons of God. Man was not made for pleasure; he was born of the sweat of God's face, and now he must live by the sweat of his own: that is why men have no rest.'" — *The Academy*, Feb. 12, 1870.

I wish also to examine, in greater detail than I should have had space for in a note, how far the case of the Samoyeds bears out Mr Baring Gould's theory of the development of idolatry from its grosser to its more refined manifestations, or of the progress of the human race from barbarism to the light of religion and of civilisation.

Mr Baring Gould says, p. 136—

"'When a Schaman is aware that I have no household god,' said a Samoyed to M. Castren, the linguist, 'he comes to me, and I give him a squirrel, or an ermine skin.' This skin he brings back moulded 'into a human shape.' ... 'This Los is a fetish; it is not altogether an idol; it is a spirit entangled in a material object. What that object is matters little; a stump of a tree, a stone, a rag, or an animal, serves the purpose of condensing the impalpable deity into a tangible reality.' Through this coarse superstition glimmers an intelligent conception. It is that of an all-pervading Deity, who is focussed, so to speak, in the fetish. This deity is called Num. 'I have heard some Samoyeds declare that the earth, the sea—all nature, in short—are Num.' 'Where is Num? asked Castren of a Samoyed, and the man pointed to the blue sea: but an old woman told him that the sun was Num. The Siethas, worshipped by the Lapps, had no certain figure or shape formed by nature or art; they were either trees or rough stones, much worn by water. Tomæus says they were often mere tree stumps with the roots upwards."[125]

It is curious to contrast this recent account of the Samoides with an account, apparently well informed and discriminating, in 1762. Pinkerton, i. 522—"The religion of the Samoides is very simple.... They *admit the existence of a Supreme Being*, Creator of all things, eminently good and beneficent; a quality which, according to their mode of thinking, dispenses them from any adoration of Him, or addressing their prayers to Him, because they suppose this Being takes no interest in mundane affairs; and consequently, does not exact nor need the worship of man. They join to this idea that of a being eternal and invisible, very powerful, though subordinate to the first, and disposed to evil. It is to this being that they ascribe all the misfortunes which befall them in this life. Nevertheless, they do not worship, although much in fear of him. If they place any reliance in the counsels of Koedesnicks or Tadebes (the 'Schamans' referred to above), it is only on account of the connection which they esteem these people to have with this evil being; otherwise they submit themselves with perfect apathy to all the misfortunes which can befall them." "The sun and moon, as well, hold the place of subaltern deities. It is by their intervention, they imagine, that the Supreme Being dispenses His favours; but they worship them as little as the idols or fitches (fetishes) which they carry about them according to the recommendation of their Koedesnicks." gives a similar account of the Lepchas), have lapsed, apparently through sun-worship, to a state of Pantheism, if not Fetishism.

Of the Tongusy, a people who, if not kin to the Samoides, have an analogous worship—("They are altogether unacquainted with any kind of literature, and worship the sun and moon. They have many Shamans among them, who differ little from those I formerly described."—Bell's "Travels in Asia, Siberia")—Bell, travelling in Siberia, 1720, says—"Although I have observed that the Tongusy in general worship the sun and moon, there *are many exceptions* to this observation. I have found intelligent people among them who believed there was a Being superior to both sun and moon, and who *created them and all the world.*" If, then, we may connect the Tongusy with the Samoides, it would appear that whereas Mr Baring Gould (*i.e.,* Castren) finds the latter sunk in Fetishism, they were, the one in 1762, the other in 1720, the worshippers of the sun and moon, joined with the knowledge and tradition of the true God still subsisting amongst them.

F. Schlegel ("Phil. of History," p. 138) says—"The Greeks, who described India in the time of Alexander the Great, divided the Indian religious sects into Brachmans and Samaneans.... But by the Greek denomination of Samaneans we must certainly understand the Buddhists, as among the rude nations of Central Asia, as in other countries, the priests of the religion of Fo bear at this day the name of Schamans." Compare Professor Rawlinson, "Ancient Monarchies," i. 139, 172. (Vide infra, p. 163, 164, 205.)

CHAPTER VIII
MYTHOLOGY

Since all antediluvian traditions meet in Noah, and are transmitted through him, there is an *à priori* probability that we shall find all the antediluvian traditions confused in Noah. I shall discuss this further when I come to regard him under the aspect of Saturn.

As a consequence, we must not expect to find (the process of corruption having commenced in the race of Ham, almost contemporaneously with Noah) a pure and unadulterated tradition anywhere; and I allege more specifically, that whenever we find a tradition of Noah and the Deluge, we shall find it complicated and confused with previous communications with the Almighty, and also with traditions of Adam and Paradise.

But inasmuch as the tradition is necessarily through Noah, and in any case applies to him at one remove, it does not greatly affect the argument I have in hand. There is a further probability which confronts us on the outset, that in every tradition, with the lapse of time, though the events themselves are likely to be substantially transmitted, they may become transposed in their order of succession. We shall see this in the case of Noah and his posterity. The principal cause being, that the immediate founder of the race is, as a rule, among all the nations of antiquity, deified and placed at the head of every genealogy and history. "Joves omnes reges vocârunt antiqui." Thus Belus, whom modern discovery seems certainly to have identified with Nimrod, in the Chaldean mythology appears as Jupiter, and even as the creator separating light from darkness (Rawlinson, "Ancient Monarchies," i. 181; Gainet, "Hist. de l'Anc. et Nouv. Test.," i. 120). But Nimrod is also mixed up with Jupiter in the god Bel-Merodach. In more natural connection Nimrod—("who may have been worshipped in different parts of Chaldea under different titles," Rawlinson, i. 172)—Nimrod appears as the father of Hurki the moon-god, whose worship he probably introduced; and, what is much more to the point, he appears as the father of Nin (whom I shall presently identify with Noah); whilst in one instance, at least, the genealogy is inverted, and he appears as the son of Nin. Thus, too, Hercules and Saturn are confounded, just as we find Adam and Noah confounded ("many classical traditions, we must remember, identified Hercules with

Saturn," vide Rawlinson, i. 166). Also in Grecian mythology Prometheus (Adam) figures as the son of Deucalion (Noah), and also of Japetus (Japhet); and so, too, Adam and Noah, in the Mahabharata, are equally in tradition in the person of Manou (vide Gainet, i. 199), and in Mexico in the person of the god Quetzalcoatl (vide infra, p. 326).

Before, however, pursuing the special subject of this inquiry further, it appears to me impossible to avoid an argument on a subject long debated, temporarily abandoned through the exhaustion of the combatants, and now again recently brought into prominence through the writings of Mr Gladstone, Dr Dollinger, Mr Max Müller, and others—the source and origin of mythology.[126]

Now, here, I am quite ready to adopt, in the first place, the opinion of L'Abbé Gainet, that every exclusive system must come to naught, "que toutes les tentatives qu'on ai faites pour expliquer le polythéisme par un système exclusif tombent à faux et n'expliquent rien."

Yet, whilst fully admitting an early and perhaps concurrent admixture of Sabaism,[127] I consider that the facts and evidence contained in the pages of Rawlinson will enable us to arrive at the history of idolatry by a mode much more direct than conjecture. The pages of Rawlinson prove the identity of Nimrod and Belus, and his worship in the earliest times. On the other hand, there has been a pretty constant tradition[128] that Nimrod first raised the standard of revolt against the Lord; and the erection of the tower of Babel seems to show a state of things ripe for idolatry. Here recent discovery and ancient tradition concur in establishing hero-worship as among the earliest forms of idolatry. But further, the Arab tradition of Nimrod's apotheosis, analogous to the mysterious and miraculous disappearance of Enoch (vide infra, p. 192), suggests how hero-worship might become almost identical with the worship of spirits, which L'Abbé Gainet inclines to think the first and most natural mode. If there was a tradition among them that one of their ancestors was raised up to heaven,[129] why may they not have argued, when their minds had become thoroughly corrupted, that their immediate ancestor, the mighty Nimrod, had been so raised? and when one ancestor was deified the rest would have been deified in sequence, or according to their relationship to him. What, again, more likely than that, when through the corruptions of mankind the communications of the Most High ceased, they should turn to those to whom the communications had been made, at first perhaps innocently in intercession, and, as corruption deepened, in worship?[130]

L'Abbé Gainet, in another part of his work, draws attention to the worship of ancestors in China, and asks whether the idols of Laban had reference to more than some such secondary objects?

It will be recollected that it was precisely the extent to which this veneration was to be considered culpable which was the subject-matter of the unfortunate disputes between certain religious orders in the seventeenth and eighteenth centuries (vide Huc's "Chinese Empire," and Cretineau Joly's "Hist. de la Com. de Jesus," vol. iii. chap. iii., and vol. v. chap. i.) Indeed, among the Semitic races it may never have degenerated into idolatry. Still it appears to me that weight should be attached to this tendency, more especially in primitive times, when the recollection of ancestors who had been driven out of Paradise, to whom direct revelations had been made, and who were naturally reputed to have been "nearer to the gods" (Plato, Cicero[131]), would have been all in all to their descendants. Then, again, as we have just seen, there was the tradition among them of one man who had been carried up into heaven, and accordingly, when hero-worship culminated in the deification of man, we are not surprised to find it taking the form of this apotheosis as in the identification of Nimrod and Enoch.

This tendency to idolatry through hero-worship seems to me so natural and direct, that I think, apart from the facts à priori, I should have been led to the conclusion that it was the actual manner in which it was brought about.[132] It is not denied, on the other hand, that there always has been a tendency to nature-worship also; and, indeed, there is probably a stage during which every mythology will be found to have come under its influence. But the inclination at the present moment is unmistakably to an exclusive astral or solar system. The point of interest which excites me to this inquiry is simply to determine the value of the historical traditions which may lie embedded in these systems; and I shall be content to find them, whether or not they form the primary nucleus, or whether only subsequently imported into, and blended with, solar mythology. It is easy to conceive how a mythology embodying historical traditions could pass into an astral system. In this case incongruity would not startle; but it is difficult to imagine a pure astral system which would not be too harmonious and symmetrical to admit of the grossness, inconsistency, and incongruity to which the process of adaptation would inevitably give rise, and to which hero-worship is inherently prone. As Mr Gladstone says (Homer, ii. 12):—

> "There is much in the theo-mythology of Homer which, if it had been a system founded on fable, could not have appeared there. It stands before us like one of our old churches, having different parts of its fabric in the different styles of architecture, each of which speaks for itself, and which we know to belong to the several epochs in the history of the art when their characteristic combinations were respectively in vogue."

Mr Gladstone (*passim*) victoriously combats the theory of nature-worship as applied to Grecian mythology; but it appears to me that his argument and mode of reasoning would apply with tenfold effect to the Chaldean mythology, where there is a likelihood at least that we shall view idolatry in its early commencements. I consider that this view is borne out by the following passage from Professor Rawlinson's "Ancient Monarchies," i. 139:—

"In the first place, it must be noticed that the religion was to a certain extent *astral*. The heaven itself, the sun, the moon, and the five planets, have each their representative in the Chaldean Pantheon among the chief objects of worship. At the same time it is to be observed, that the astral element is not universal, but partial; and that even where it has place, it is but one aspect of the mythology, not by any means its full and complete exposition. The Chaldean religion even here is far from being mere Sabeanism—the simple worship of the 'host of heaven.' The ether, the sun, the moon, and still more the five planetary gods, are something above and beyond those parts of nature. Like the classical Apollo and Diana, Mars and Venus, they are real persons, with a life and a history, a power and an influence, which no ingenuity can translate into a metaphorical representation of phenomena attaching to the air and to the heavenly bodies. It is doubtful, indeed, whether this class of gods are really of astronomical origin, and not rather primitive deities, whose characters and attributes were, to a great extent, fixed and settled before the notion arose of connecting them with certain parts of nature. Occasionally they seem to represent heroes rather than celestial bodies; and they have all attributes quite distinct from their physical and astronomical character.

"Secondly, the striking resemblance of the Chaldean system to that of the classical mythology, seems worthy of particular attention. This resemblance is too general and too close in some respects to allow of the supposition that mere accident has produced the coincidence."

The evidence in the "Ancient Monarchies;" seems to me to decide the point, not only for perhaps the earliest mythology with which we are acquainted, but also for the Grecian mythology, which has generally been the ground of dispute. It is curiously in illustration, however, of the common origin of mythology, that the mythology of Greece should be equally well traced to Assyria and Egypt. As evidence of the theory according to the Assyrian origin, let us turn, for instance, to Professor Rawlinson's identification of Nergal with Mars. It is true he appears as the planet Mars under the form of "Nerig," and he also figures as the storm-ruler; but can anything well be more human than the rest of his titles?

"His name is evidently compounded of the two Hamitic roots 'nir' = a man, and 'gula' = great; so that he is 'the great man' or 'the great hero.' His titles are 'the king of battle,' 'the champion of the gods,' 'the strong begetter,' 'the tutelar god of Babylonia,' and 'the god of the chase.'... We have no evidence that Nergal was worshipped in the primitive times. He is just mentioned by some of the early Assyrian kings, who regard him as their ancestor.... It is conjectured that, like Bil-Nipru, he represents the deified hero Nimrod, who may have been worshipped in different parts of Chaldea under different titles.... It is probable that Nergal's symbol was the man-lion. Nir is sometimes used in the inscriptions in the meaning of lion, and the Semitic name for the god himself is 'aria,' the ordinary term for the king of beasts both in Hebrew and Syriac. Perhaps we have here the true derivation of the Greek name for the god of war 'Ares' (Αρης), which has long puzzled classical scholars. The lion would symbolise both the hunting and the fighting propensities of the god, for he not only engages in combats, but often chases his prey and runs it down like a hunter. Again, if Nergal is the man-lion, his association in the buildings with the man-bull would be exactly parallel with the conjunction which we so constantly find between him and Nin in the inscriptions"[133]— Rawlinson, i. 172–174.

I must draw attention also to the remarkable absence here of all the monotheistic epithets we shall find attached to Ana, Enu, and Hoa.[134]

Let us now turn to the theory which is most in the ascendant, and which professes to see in the old mythological legends only the thoughts and metaphors of a mythic period.

This theory, which was Mr Max Müller's in the first instance, being not only exclusively drawn from the conclusions of philology, but also exclusive in itself, cannot be anywhere stronger than its weakest point.

If it is shown in the instance of one primary myth, that it was the embodiment of an historical legend, or theological belief, the whole ideal structure of a mythic period must collapse; for the rejection of eclecticism in any form, which would embrace a Biblical or euhemeristic interpretation of the myths, is at the foundation of Mr Max Müller's idea, and, indeed, would be incompatible with the theory of a mythic period such as he conceives it.

The connection of Nimrod with Nergal in the Assyrian mythology, of Nergal with their planet Nerig, and of the Semitic name of the god "Aria;" with the Greek Ἄρης and the Latin Mars, must, I think, form a chain of evidence destined to embarass Mr Max Müller and Mr Cox: for, apart from the numerous points of contact of the Assyrian and Egyptian with the Greek mythologies, it can hardly be contended that there was a mythic period for the Aryan which was not common to the whole human race.

It would be natural to suppose, that a mythology which was generated in a mythic period—which was the invention of mankind in a peculiar state of the imagination—would have been developed in its fulness and completeness, like Minerva starting from the brain of Jupiter, and would have borne the evidence of its origin in the symmetry of its form. Mr Max Müller, on the contrary, seems to yield the whole position, in what, from his point of view, looks like an inadvertent phrase, that "there were myths before there was a mythology" It is not that the view is not true, or that it is inconsistent with his analysis of the myths, but that it is so perfectly consistent with ours! Incongruity, such as would come from the confusion of separate myths, would be no difficulty for us; but it is hard to understand how mere fragmentary legends—sometimes attractive, but more frequently repulsive and revolting, having no hold on what is nearest the heart of a people, the traditions of its past—should have been so tenaciously preserved for so long a time under such different conditions in various countries.

Solar legends, spun out of confused metaphors, seem an inadequate explanation, unless we also suppose idolatry of the sun. In that case, the mythology, in so far as it was solar, would precede the myths; in other words, the myths would be radiations from a central idea. That in the day when mankind prevaricated after this fashion, and committed the act of idolatry in their hearts, everything, from the phenomena of nature to the remote events of their history, would come under the influence of a new set of ideas may be easily conceived.

At such a period—and the commencement of these things at least was not impossible in the days when, in the spirit of mistrust or defiance, men drew together to build the city and tower in the plain of Sennaar (Shinar)—much of what Mr Cox supposes to have been the common parlance of mankind becomes natural, and a mythic period within these limits conceivable.

But such a theory would not necessarily be exclusive of other forms of idolatry—as, for instance, the worship of ancestors—whilst it might clear up obscure points in the evidence which tends to establish the latter.

The theory, however, must embrace many shades and gradations— from the Hamitic extreme to the protomyths, which in time obscured the monotheism of the Aryan of ancient Greece, and of the Peruvian Incas. (p. 304.)

This would seem, unless they ignore all difficulties, a better standpoint for those who think, through the application of the solar legends, "to unlock almost all the secrets of mythologies;;" and any theory connected with the sun and sun-worship has this advantage, that it can be extended to everything under the sun!

It is sufficiently obvious that no system can be held to have settled these questions, which, if there were myths before there was a mythology, does not appropriate these antecedent myths, or exclude counter explanations; and it is equally clear that there can have been no mythology of which the solar legends were the offspring, if the legends embody thoughts which transcend the mythology; and no mythic period if they testify to facts and ideas incompatible with its existence.

Allowing for a certain confusion arising out of "polyonomy," this sort of confusion, if there were nothing else, ought not to baffle the ingenuity of experts like Mr Max Müller and Mr Cox. Such complications should be as easily disentangled as the superadded figures in Egyptian chronology (vide chapter vi.) when the key has been found.

But does Mr Max Müller profess to have brought the various legends into harmony? On the contrary (ii. 142), he frankly admits—"Much, no doubt, remains to be done, and *even* with the assistance of the Veda, the whole of Greek mythology will never be deciphered and translated."

I have no wish to push an admission unfairly, but this appears to me fatal as regards the argument with which I am dealing.[135] If there are myths which never will be deciphered, this must be because they have had some non-astral or non-solar origin, which I consider to be almost equivalent to saying that they must have had some pre-astral origin. What that precise origin was I think I have been able sufficiently to indicate in italicising the subjoined sentences from Mr Max Müller. If these enigmas can be shown to be strictly local and Grecian, cadit quæstio; but if they are common to other mythologies, and these the oldest, I must say they have the look of antecedent existence. At any rate, like those inconvenient boulders in the sand and gravel strata, they require the intervention of some glacial period to account for them.[136]

I have already hinted that a further consideration appears to me to incapacitate the theory of nature-worship, in any of its disguises, from being taken as the exclusive, or even the primitive form of idolatry, or of perverted tradition; and it is this,—that all the explanations, even the most ingenious, even those which would be accounted "primitive and organic," have their counter explanations, traceable in the corruptions of truth and the perversions of hero-worship. Take, for instance, the name Zeus, which is in evidence of the primitive monotheism, and which stood in Greece, as Il or Ra in Assyria, for the true Lord and God, and which has its equivalents in Dyaus ("from the Sanscrit word which means 'to shine';"); Dyaus-pater (Zeus-pater), Jupiter; Tiu (Anglo-Saxon, whence Tuesday); and Zia (High German)—*vide* Cox's "Mythology."

What more natural than to associate the Almighty with the heaven where He dwelt? Mr Max Müller ("Comparative Myth.," "Chips," ii. 72) says—"Thus Ζευς, being originally a name of the sky, like the Sanscrit Dyaus, became gradually a proper name, which betrayed its appellative meaning only in a few proverbial expressions, such as Ζευς ὕει, or sub Jove frigido." Taking this passage in connection with what is said (p. 148, of Welcker)—"When we ascend with him to the most distant heights of Greek history, the idea of God as the Supreme Being stands before us as a simple fact. Next to the adoration of one God, the Father of heaven, the Father of men, we find in Greece a worship of nature." I conclude that Mr Max Müller means, as Mr Cox means, that the names, Zeus or Dyaus, was applied to the one true God, whose existence was otherwise and previously known to them.[137] At starting, therefore, we find that the language borrowed from nature was only called in to give a colouring and expression to a previously known and familiar truth; and here, too, we also see the commencement of incongruity. The simple idea of the heavens might have been harmoniously extended by the imagination; but, complicated with the idea of personality, it gave birth to the awkward and incongruous expression, "Ζεύς ὕει, or sub Jove frigido," a phrase which never could have been originated by the Grecian mind, unless the personality of Jove had been the idea most prominently before the mind. But if the knowledge of the Deity, or even the conception of the personality of Zeus was operative in the mythic period, it must have been operative to the extent of embodying what was known or recollected of his dealings in love and anger with mankind, in the legends which they wove, and also of blending them with the confusions which "polyonomy;" occasioned. The introduction of this element would seriously embarass Mr Cox, and would give to Mr Gladstone's explanation an "à priori;" probability.

Take, again, the following passage from Mr Max Müller (p. 107)—"The idea of a young hero, whether he is called *Baldr*, or Sigurd, or Sigrit, or Achilles, or Meleager, or Kephalos, dying in the fulness of youth—a story so frequently told, localised, and individualised—was first suggested by the sun dying in all his youthful vigour, either at the end of a day, conquered by the powers of darkness, or at the end of the sunny season, stung by the thorn of winter."

Here is a myth evidently very widely diffused. Let it be interpreted by what is told us at p. 108—

> "*Baldr*, in the Scandinavian Edda, the divine prototype of Sigurd and Sigrit, is beloved by the whole world. Gods and men, the whole of nature, all that grows and lives, had sworn to his mother not to hurt the bright hero. The mistletoe alone, that does not grow on the earth, but on trees, had been forgotten, and with it Baldr was killed at the winter solstice....
>
> Baldr, whom no weapon pierced or clove,
>
> But in his breast stood fix'd the fatal bough
>
> Of mistletoe, which Lok, *the accuser, gave*
>
> *To Hoder,* and the unwitting Hoder threw;
>
> 'Gainst that alone had Baldr's life no charm."

"Thus Infendiyar, in the Persian epic, cannot be wounded by any weapon.... *All these are fragments of solar myths.*" One hardly likes to disturb such illusions. Solar myths! well, allow me at least to repeat the history which seems to me so very like this myth. Many centuries ago, in a beautiful garden which a concurrence of tradition places somewhere in Central Asia, a man, the first man of our race, framed according to the "divine prototype,;" dwelt beloved by the whole world. God and the angels, and the whole of nature—all that grows and lives, were agreed that nothing should do him harm. One fruit or growth alone—the mistletoe it may have been—something that does not grow on the earth, but on trees, was excepted; and it was told to this man, whose name was—but we will not anticipate—that on the day on which he touched this fruit he should die the death. It so came about that the accuser, whom some call the serpent, had previously handed it to his companion, and his unwitting companion gave it to him. He took it, and he died. Against that fatal bough his life had no charm. No weapon pierced or clove him; for Baldr—I should say Adam—was invulnerable, as was Achilles and Meleager, except in one single respect.

I believe that instances might be indefinitely multiplied. I shall content myself, however, with the following, which I think will be generally considered among the happiest illustrations of nature worship.[138]

"And as it is with this sad and beautiful tale of Orpheus and Euridike (Euridice). [The story of Euridice was this—'Euridice was bitten by a serpent, she dies, and descends into the lower regions. Orpheus follows her, and obtains from the gods that his wife should follow him if he promised not to look back, &c' It reads to me like a sad reminiscence of Adam and Eve.] Mr Max Müller proceeds—'so it is with all those which may seem to you coarse, or dull, or ugly. They are so only because the real meaning of the names has been half-forgotten or wholly lost. Œdipus and Perseus (vide Appendix), we are told, killed their parents, but it was only because the sun was said to kill the darkness from which it seemed to spring.'"[139]

But why is darkness called the parent of the sun, and not rather light the parent of darkness? and why not a contrary legend founded on this surmise? Is it merely accidental that the metaphor is not reversed?

Compare the above speculation of Mr Max Müller's with the following passage from Gainet, "Hist. de l'Ancien. Nouv. Test.," i.; "Les Souvenirs du genre Humain," p. 79:—

> "Chaos was placed at the commencement of all things in the Phœnician cosmogony (Euseb. Præp. Evan. l. i.), as in that of Hesiod (Theog., p. 5). The latter calls upon the Muses to tell him what were the beings that appeared first in existence, and he replies—'At the commencement of all things was Chaos, and from Chaos was born Erebus and dark night.'
>
> "Thus, in the order of existence, as in the order of time, there is a concurrence of profane tradition to place night before day. This is the reason why the Scandinavians, the Gauls, the Germans, the Kalmucks, the Numidians, the Egyptians, and Athenians, according to Varro and Macrobius, count their days, commencing with sunset and not with sunrise."

Curiously enough, in another chapter on a different subject, Mr Max Müller enables me to clinch this argument against himself. In an article on the "Norsemen in Iceland," he says—in proof of the genuineness of the Edda—"There are passages in the Edda which sound like verses from the Veda." But what are these verses from the ends of the earth which are identical? Let us listen—

> "'Twas the *morning* of *time*
> When yet *naught was*,
> Nor sand nor sea were there,
> Nor cooling streams;

Earth was not formed,

Nor *Heaven* above;

A yawning gap there was,

And grass nowhere."[140]

Under these conditions, I think it will be conceded that there was also darkness—and therefore, that the tradition of the precedence of chaos and darkness is confirmed.

"A hymn," continues Mr Max Müller, "of the Veda begins in a very similar way—

"Nor aught, nor naught existed; yon *bright sky*

Was not, nor Heaven's broad roof outstretch'd above,

What cover'd all? what shelter'd? what conceal'd?

Was it the waters' fathomless abyss?;" &c

Mr Max Müller adds, "There are several mythological expressions common to *the Edda* and *Homer*. In the Edda, man is said to have been created out of an *ash tree*. In Hesiod, Zeus created the third race of men out of *ash* trees, and that this tradition was not unknown to Homer we learn from Penelope's address to Ulysses—"Tell me thy family from whence thou art: for thou art not sprung from the olden trees, or from the rocks;" (Max Müller, ii. 195).

The tradition about the ash tree in Hesiod, Homer, and the Edda,[141] is curious but inexplicable: the general drift of the tradition may be determined by the recollection of two facts—that man was created, and that a tree was inseparably connected with his history from its earliest commencement. But I have quoted the passage more especially with reference to its confirmation of the extract from Gainet, which attests the wide-spread tradition—so exactly in accordance with the cosmogony of Scripture—that Chaos was at the commencement of all things, and that darkness existed before light.[142] I conclude by asking why this should be? When we are in the midst of solar and astral systems and legends, it seems natural that a theory of cosmogony should commence with light rather than darkness—at least, as well that it should commence with light as with darkness. But no, the universal tradition seems against it. Much more strange is this if we connect the solar and astral legends with any system of Sabaism. These considerations make it plain to me that the solar and astral legends embodied anterior traditions.

I think Mr Max Müller will at least recognise them as spots on the disk of his solar theory, and which must ever remain obscure to those who refuse the light of Scripture and tradition.

APPENDIX TO CHAPTER VIII.

"ŒDIPUS, PERSEUS."

Here again, the explanation of Mr Max Müller, "si non vrai est vraisemblable," and yet I cannot help seeing that the legends of Perseus and Œdipus may just as well be supposed to embody primitive tradition. Let us read the histories of Œdipus and Perseus in the light of the tradition concerning Lamech (Gen. iv. 23, 24). "And Lamech said to his wives, Adah and Zillah ... I have slain a man to the wounding of myself, and a stripling to my own bruising. Sevenfold vengeance shall be taken for Cain, but for Lamech seventy times sevenfold." The note to the Douay edition says—"It is the tradition of the Hebrews that Lamech, in hunting, slew Cain, mistaking him for a wild beast, and that having discovered what he had done, he beat so unmercifully the youth by whom he was led into that mistake that he died of the blows." Œdipus was the son of Laius, who had supplanted his brother. Œdipus was exposed to destruction as soon as born, because his father had been warned that he must perish by the hand of his son,—but was rescued and brought up by shepherds. Hearing from the oracle of Delphi (the tradition is of course localised), that if he returned home he must necessarily be the murderer of his father, he avoided the house of Polybus, the only home he knew of, and travelled towards Phocis (from west to east by the by). (Comp. with infra, p. 194.) He met Laius, his father, in a narrow road. Laius haughtily ordered Œdipus to make way for him, which provoked an encounter, in which Laius and his armour-bearer were slain. Other circumstances, either separate traditions of the same event, or distinct legends, are no doubt mixed up in the narration, but still four facts remain as a residuum available for the comparison.

Œdipus was the son, as Lamech was the grandson, of one who supplanted his brother, both kill their respective progenitors, and in the *casual* encounter in which in both instances the tragedy occurred, *two* persons were slain. In this there is a fair outline of resemblance.

In the legend of Perseus, certainly the legend is more indistinct, et, in one point, that he inadvertently killed his *grandfather*, the coincidence is perfect. And it must be borne in mind that it is not a question of absolute but of comparative resemblance—in fact, a choice between a mythical or an historical, an astral or a scriptural solution, and when you come to degrees of relationship, the astral or solar explanation becomes more attenuated at each remove,—"the father of the sun;" may be metaphorically intelligible, but the grandfather of the sun!

I see further trace of the tradition of Lamech in the Phrygian legend of Adrastus, somewhat confused in the tradition of Cain, and in some points reversed. Adrastus, the son of the Phrygian king, had *inadvertently killed* his brother, and was in consequence expelled by his father and deprived of everything. Whilst an exile at the court of Crœsus, he was sent out with Prince Atys as guardian to deliver the country from a wild boar. Adrastus had the misfortune to kill Prince Atys while aiming at the wild beast. Crœsus pardoned the unfortunate man, as he saw in this accident the will of the gods, and *the fulfilment of a prophecy*, but Adrastus killed himself on the tomb of Atys (Herod. i. 35; Smith, "Myth. Dict.")

Now let us take up the proof at another point. Will any one refuse to see in the following tale from the "Gesta Romanorum,"[143] at least a mediæval corruption of the legend of Œdipus:—"A certain soldier, called Julian, unwittingly killed his parents. For being of noble blood, and addicted as a youth frequently is to the sports of the field, a stag which he hotly pursued suddenly turned round and addressed him—'Thou who pursuest me thus fiercely shall be the destruction of thy parents.' These words greatly alarmed Julian.... Leaving, therefore, his amusement, he went privately into a distant country ... where he marries. It chances that his parents come into that country, and in his absence were received kindly by his wife, who, 'in consideration of the love she bore her husband, put them into her own bed, and commanded another to be prepared elsewhere for herself.' In the meantime, Julian returning abruptly home and discovering strangers in his bed, in a fit of passion slays them. When he discovers the parricidal crime he exclaims—'This accursed hand has murdered my parents and fulfilled the horrible prediction which I have struggled to avoid.'" Now, I submit that this is not a greater distortion of the classical stories of Œdipus, Adrastus, &c, than are the classical legends of the biblical traditions of Cain and Lamech.

For further trace read Bunsen, iv. 235, also, 253, 254. Mr Cox ("Mythology of Aryan Nations;") says:—"The names Theseus, Perseus, Oidipous, had all been mere epithets of one and the same being; but when they ceased to be mere appellatives, these creations of mythical speech were regarded not only as different persons, but as beings in no way connected with each other.... Nay, the legends inter-change the method by which the parents seek the death of their children; for there were tales which narrated that Oidipous was shut up in an ark which was washed ashore at Sikyon," p. 80. Sicyon was the oldest Greek city. Compare p. 157 of this ch., and ch. on Deluge. This was merely the traditional record that the tradition was preserved in the Ark, and subsequently emanated from Sicyon.

II. PROMETHEUS AND HERCULES OR HERAKLES.

I have elsewhere alluded to the confusion of Prometheus, as the creator of man, with Prometheus, the first man created. But the most curious instance of reduplication is the further confusion of what I may call the human Prometheus, with his deliverer Hercules,—Hercules and Prometheus both in different ways embodying traditions of Adam! Prometheus is the Adam[144] of Paradise and the Fall, Hercules is Adam the outcast from Paradise, with his skin and club sent forth on his long labours and marches through the world. But how can Hercules, who frees Prometheus from the rock, be the same as Prometheus who is bound to the rock? If, however, we are entitled to hope that Adam in the labour of his long exile worked off the sentence and expiated the guilt on account of which Adam, the culprit, was sentenced, may we not accept this as an adequate explanation? Is it a forced figure that he should be said to unbind him from the rock, to drive off the vulture which preys upon him, and thus finally liberate him?

This disjunction of Adam and separate personification in the two periods of his life, *before* and *after* the Fall, will accord well enough with the addition in some legends of a brother Epimetheus, and I submit that this explanation is as good as that (*vide* Smith's "Myth. Dict.") which regards the legend as purely allegorical, and *Pro*metheus and *Epi*metheus as signifying "forethought;" and "afterthought."

The travels of Hercules, it must be confessed, as traditionally recorded, are somewhat eccentric. But are they explicable on any solar theory? He begins by travelling from *west* to east; he then proceeds *south*, and although he traverses Africa westward, he diverges abruptly to the *north*, from which he proceeds south, and ends as he began by travelling from *west* to east. All this, however, is perfectly explicable if we are prepared to admit Bryant's ("Mythology," ii. 70) historical surmises, and to go along with him so far as to believe that the tradition was mainly preserved through Cuthite or *Chus*ite channels. We can, then, see a probability in the conjecture that the descendants of Chus, in preserving the tradition of the travels of Hercules (Herakles), superadded or substituted the scenes and incidents of their own wanderings, after they had settled down in the place of their final location.

CHAPTER IX
ASSYRIAN MYTHOLOGY

"But surely there is nothing improbable in the supposition, that in the poems of Homer such vestiges may be found. Every recorded form of society bears some traces of those by which it has been preceded, and in that highly primitive form, which Homer has been the instrument of embalming for all posterity, the law of general reason obliges us to search for elements and vestiges more primitive still.... The general proposition that we may expect to find the relics of scriptural traditions in the heroic age of Greece, though it leads, if proved, to important practical results, is independent even of a belief in those traditions, as they stand in the scheme of revealed truth. They must be admitted to have been facts on earth, even by those who would deny them to have been facts of heavenly origin, in the shape in which Christendom receives them; and the question immediately before us is one of pure historical probability. The descent of mankind from a single pair, the lapse of that pair from original righteousness, are apart from and ulterior to it. We have traced the Greek nation to a source, and along a path of migration which must in all likelihood have placed its ancestry, at some point or points, in close local relations with the scenes of the earliest Mosaic records: the retentiveness of that people equalled its receptiveness, and its close and fond association with the past, made it prone indeed to incorporate novel matter into its religion, but prone also to keep it there after its incorporation.

"If such traditions existed, and if the laws which guide historical inquiry require or lead us to suppose that the forefathers of the Greeks must have lived within their circle, then the burden of proof must lie not so properly with those who assert that the traces of them are to be found in the earliest, that is, the Homeric form of the Greek mythology, as with those who deny it. What became of those old traditions? They must have decayed and disappeared, not by a sudden process, but by a gradual accumulation of the corrupt accretions, in which at length they were so completely interred as to be invisible and inaccessible. Some period, therefore, there must have been at which they would remain clearly perceptible, though in conjunction with much corrupt matter. Such a period might be made the subject of record, and if such there were, we might naturally expect to find it in the oldest known work of the ancient literature.

"If the poems of Homer do, however, contain a picture, even though a defaced picture, of the primeval religious traditions, it is obvious that they afford a most valuable collateral support to the credit of the Holy Scripture, considered as a document of history. Still we must not allow the desire of gaining this advantage to bias the mind in an inquiry, which can only be of value if it is conducted according to the strictest rules of rational criticism." — *Gladstone on Tradition in "Homer and the Homeric Age,"* vol. ii. sect. i.

Having laid, as I think, in what has been premised in the last chapter, grounds for a presumption that primitive traditions may be shrouded in the ancient mythology, I proceed to seek traditions of the patriarch Noah among the inscriptions and monuments of the Chaldæans; for then we shall find ourselves in a period when the results of modern archæological science are in contact with the events and incidents of primitive patriarchal life recorded in Scripture; and, in seeking them where we shall best find them, in the able and discriminating pages of Rawlinson, we shall at least feel that we are treading on safe and solid ground.

The deities in the Chaldæan Pantheon are thus enumerated by Professor Rawlinson —

"The grouping of the principal Chaldæan deities is as follows: — At the head of the Pantheon stands a god Il or Ra, of whom little is known. Next to him is a triad, Ana, Bil or Belus, and Hea or Hoa, who correspond closely to the classical Pluto, Jupiter, and Neptune. Each of these is accompanied by a female principle or wife.... Then follows a further triad, consisting of Sin or Hurki the moon-god, San or Sanci the sun, and Vul (or Yem, or Ao, or In, or Ina, according to various readings of the hieroglyphics) the god of the atmosphere (again accompanied by female powers or wives).... Next in order to them we find a group of five minor deities, the representatives of the five planets, Nin or Ninip (Saturn), Merodach (Jupiter), Nergal (Mars), Ishtar (Venus), and Nebo (Mercury). [The bracket indications are Rawlinson's.]... These principal deities do not appear to have been connected like the Egyptian and classical divinities into a single genealogical scheme" (i. 141).

In a note at p. 142 it is said, "These schemes themselves were probably not genealogical at first ... but after a while given to separate and independent deities, recognised in different places by distinct communities, or even by distinct races;" (*vide* Bunsen's "Egypt," iv. 66; English Tran.)

Now to this opinion I venture unreservedly to adhere, and I connect it with the statement (id. i. 72), that "Chaldæa in the earliest times to which we can go back, seems to have been inhabited by four principal tribes. The early kings are continually represented in the monuments as sovereigns over the Kiprat-arbat, or 'Four Races' (vide supra, p. 30). These 'Four Races' are sometimes called the Arba Lisun or 'Four Tongues,' whence we may conclude that they were distinguished from one another, among other differences, by a variety in their forms of speech ... an examination of the written remains has furnished reasons for believing that the differences were great and marked; the languages, in fact, belonging to the four great varieties of human speech, the Hamitic, Semitic, Aryan, and Turanian." Compare.

If it is allowed that there may have been mythological systems corresponding to these divers nationalities, we may fairly conclude that the deities above enumerated may not necessarily have been different deities, but the same deities viewed in different lights, or included in duplicate in the way of incorporation, or in recognition of subordinate nationalities. If, therefore, I find the representation of Noah in any one of these deities, is there not a *prima facie* probability that I shall find the reduplication of him in others? I consider, at least, that I shall have warrant for thus collecting the scattered traditions concerning the patriarch who stands at the head of the second propagation of our race.

But first as to the god Il or Ra—

IL OR RA.

The form *Ra* represents, probably, the native Chaldæan name of this deity, while *Il* is the Semitic equivalent. *Il*, of course, is but a variant of *El*, the root of the well-known biblical *Elohim*, as well as of the Arabic Allah. It is this name which Diodorus represents under the form of *Elus*, and

Sanchoniathon, or rather Philo Biblius, under that of Elus, or *Ilus*. The meaning of the word is simply "God," or perhaps "The God;" emphatically. *Ra*, the Cushite equivalent, must be considered to have had the same force originally, though in Egypt it received a special application to the sun, and became the proper name of that particular deity. The word is lost in the modern Ethiopic. It formed an element in the native name of Babylon, which was *Ka-ra*, the Cushite equivalent of the Semitic *Bab-il*, an expression signifying "the gate of God."

Ra is a god with few peculiar attributes. He is a sort of fount and origin of deity, too remote from man to be much worshipped, or to excite any warm interest. There is no evidence of his having had any temple in Chaldæa during the early times. A belief in his existence is implied rather than expressed in inscriptions of the primitive kings, where the Moon-god is said to be "brother's son of Ana, and eldest son of Bil or Belus." We gather from this, that Bel and Ana were considered to have a common father, and later documents sufficiently indicate that that common father was Il or Ra." — *Rawlinson*, i. p. 143.

If in the Il or Ra of the Chaldæans the primitive monotheism is not revealed, I do not see how it can be discerned in the Zeus of the Greeks. We have the same god in the same relation in the Scandinavian, or at any rate in the Lapland mythology. Leems ("Account of Danish Lapland," Pinkerton, i. 458) says—"Of the Gods inhabiting the starry mansions the greatest is Radien, yet it is uncertain whether he is over every part of the sidereal sky, or whether he governs only some part of it. Be this as it may, I shall be bold to affirm that the Laplanders never comprehended, under the name of this false god, the true God; which is obvious from this, that some have not scrupled to put the image or likeness of the true God by the side of their Radien, on Runic boxes."[145] If, however, of their gods "the greatest was Radien," they would not have placed the true God by his side until they had become acquainted with the true God, or until they had come to commingle Christianity and Paganism; but then would they not have placed "Ra;" by the side of the true God as His counterpart? I am assuming that "Radien;" means simply the god Ra, as I suppose Mr Max Müller would recognise "dien;" as cognate to "Dyaus" ... "Dieu."

Yet it has been opposed, *in limine*, to M. L'Abbe Gainet's valuable chapter on the "Monotheisme des Peuples primitifs," "that he does not meet the specific assertions of historians such as Rawlinson, who finds idolatry prevalent among the Chaldæans on their first appearance on the stage of history."

I must submit, however, that although the discovery of idolatry at this early period may appear to disturb the particular theory, yet on closer examination it will be found to sustain L'Abbe Gainet's argument, on the whole, by sustaining the truth of tradition upon which his main argument reposes; for the idolatry which we find is intimately bound up with the worship of Belus, identified with Nimrod, whose rebellion against the Lord has always been in tradition, and is according to the more accepted interpretation of the sacred text. The discovery of idolatry, therefore, under the particular circumstances, is exactly what we should expect, and affords a remarkable confirmation of the fidelity of tradition.

Moreover, there are Chaldæans and Chaldæans, as we have just seen in Rawlinson (sup. p. 184), and as will be made more evident in the following passage from Gainet's "Monotheisme," &c.

> "It is sufficiently agreed, says Lebatteux (Mem. Acad. t. xxvii. p. 172), that the Babylonians recognised a supreme being, the Father and Lord of all (Diod. Sic. l. ii.) St Justin Cohortat. ad gent. Eusebi. Prep. Evan., l. iii. Porphyry (Life of Pythagoras) cites an oracle of Zoroaster, in which the Chaldæans are coupled in encomium with the Hebrews for the sanctity of the worship which they paid to the Eternal King. These are the words of the oracles—The Chaldeans alone with the Hebrews have wisdom for their share, rendering a pure worship to God, who is the Eternal King." —*Gainet*, iii. 408.

The pure monotheism here alluded to may have been preserved in Chaldæan families of Semitic origin, but the extract I have just given from Rawlinson seems to prove that the knowledge was preserved also, dimly and obscurely, among the predominant Chaldæans of Hamitic descent. This will be more apparent from the monotheistic epithets attached to the three next deities.

ANA.

"Ana is the head of the first triad which follows immediately after the obscure god Ra." "Ana, like Il and Ra, is thought to have been a word originally signifying God in the highest sense." "He corresponds in many respects to the classical Hades, who, like him, heads[146] the triad to which he belongs." In so far he is undistinguishable from Il or Ra, and may only transmit the monotheistic tradition through a different channel. But Ana has human epithets applied to him very suggestive of hero-worship. "His epithets are chiefly such as mark priority and antiquity." "He is the Old

Ana," "the original chief," "the father of the gods" [inter alia, of Bil Nipru, i.e. Nimrod]. He is also called—which imports another association of ideas—"the lord of spirits and demons," "the king of the lower world,"[147] "the lord of darkness or death," "the ruler of the far-off city."

Setting aside such titles as belong exclusively to the Deity, but assuming hero-worship—supposing man deified—who more appropriately placed in these primitive times at the head of the list, than their original progenitor Adam.[148] To whom would these titles, "the old Ana,"[149] "the original chief," "the lord of darkness and death," he who introduced death into the world, more exactly apply? Rawlinson also says—"His position is well marked by Damascius, who gives the three gods Anus, Illinus, and Aüs, as next in succession to the primeval pair, Assorus and Missara," i. 145. Now, it will not be contested, I think, that Assorus is the same as Alorus, the first of the ten antediluvian (deluge of Xisuthrus) Assyrian kings enumerated by Berosus, and which correspond to the ten antediluvian patriarchs. Consequently Assorus = Alorus = Adam.[150]

Here, then, we have a reduplication, or else what I have above referred to, the tendency to place the head of the dynasty at the top of the list superior to gods and men. In any case, granting this juxtaposition, would there not have been the proximate risk and probability of the two running into one another and becoming confounded, on the supposition that Ana and Alorus were not originally identical?

This will become more evident when we have considered the next in the triad—

BIL OR ENU.

But the evidence, though it will more clearly establish the fact of hero-worship, will perhaps raise a doubt whether we have rightly regarded Adam as the object of hero-worship in Ana, a point which we will then consider.

Rawlinson says of this god—"He is the Illinus (Il-Enu) of Damascius." "His name, which seems to mean merely lord" (again the primitive monotheistic appellation) "is usually followed by a qualificative adjunct possessing great interest. It is proposed to read this term as Nipru, or in the feminine Niprut, a word which cannot fail to recall the scriptural Nimrod, who is in the Septuagint Nebroth. The term *nipru* seems to be formed from the root *napar*, which is the Syriac "to pursue," to "make to flee," and which has in Assyrian nearly the same meaning. Thus Bil Nipru would be aptly translated as "the hunter lord" or the "god presiding over the chase," while at the same time it might combine the meaning of the "conquering lord" or "the great conqueror."

Here, at any rate, it must be admitted that "we have, in this instance, an admixture of hero-worship in the Chaldæan religion" (Rawlinson, i. 148). But if in one instance what à priori reason is there that it should not be so in others? Let us, then, examine further. The name of this deity, as Bel Nipru or Nimrod, has, I consider, been completely traced in the pages of Rawlinson (to which I must refer my readers). But what are we to say about the alternative name of Enu? And why, although no great stress can be laid upon the location of a deity in a genealogy or a system, yet why is Nimrod thus placed intermediate between Adam and the third of the triad Hoa, whom, on grounds quite irrespective of the similarity of name, I identify with Noah?[151]

If Ana is Adam, and Hoa Noah, why should not Enu, in another point of view, be Enoch? There is, I admit, an absence of direct evidence, but I think I discover a link of connection in a note in Rawlinson (i. p. 196). "Arab writers record a number of remarkable traditions, in which he (Nimrod) plays a conspicuous part." "Yacut declares that Nimrod attempted to mount to heaven on the wings of an eagle, and makes Niffers (Calneh) the scene of this occurrence (Lex. Geograph. in voc. Niffer). It is supposed that we have here an allusion to the building of the Tower of Babel." But I cannot help regarding it as much more certainly like an allusion to Enoch's disappearance from the earth. At p. 187, Prof. Rawlinson notices the confusion of Xisuthrus with Enoch, which proves that the tradition of Enoch was amongst them, and would have been common also to the Hamitic Arabs.[152]

I will now return to my doubt as to Ana. For although I feel tolerably certain that Ana in his human attributes represents one or other of the antediluvian patriarchs, it may well be that he is only a reduplication of Enu = Enoch. If we are to seek iñ the translation of Enoch the clue to the origin of the deification of man, and its commencement in the person of Nimrod (vide supra, p. 160), it is likely, in the legend of the apotheosis of Nimrod, that all the analogies should have been sought for in the striking historical event which was in tradition. There is, moreover, the analogy of name with Annacus, Hannachus = Enoch.[153] If he is Enoch, he naturally also falls into his place as second to Assorus.

I retain, however, my original opinion, that Ana is Adam (though possibly with some confusion with Enoch), in addition to the arguments already urged, upon the following grounds:— Rawlinson mentions (i. 147) "Telane," or the "*Mound* of Ana," distinct from Kalneh or "Kalana." We know that there has been a constant tradition that the bones of Adam were preserved in the ark, and this name of the "Mound of Ana" may be connected with it. If so, it will also account for Ana (Dis = Orcus) being the patron deity of Erech, "the great city of the dead, the necropolis of Lower Babylonia" (Rawlinson i. 146).

The son of Ana is Vul. If Vul could be identified with Vulcan, and Vulcan with Tubalcain, it would go far to decide the point that Ana was Adam.

But in the matter of etymology, I do not know that we can advance beyond the quaint phrase of old Sir Walter Raleigh in his "History of the World," that "there is a certain likelihood of name between Tubalcain and Vulcan." I rely more upon the wide-spread tradition of Tubalcain in the legends of Dædalus, Vulcan, Weland, Galant, Wielant, Wayland Smith, which approaches very nearly an identification. *Vide* Wilson's "Archæologia of Scotland," p. 210. Compare the Phœnician tradition, Bunsen's "Egypt," iv. 217, 219.

It is to be noted, however, that although Ana (*vide* Rawlinson) "like Adam had several sons, he had only two of any celebrity" (we can suppose that Abel had died out of the Cainite tradition), "Vul and another whose name represents 'darkness' or '*the west*,'" which might well be the view of Seth from a Cainite point of view (and it is traditional that the Cainite lore was preserved by Cham in the ark). Now it is remarkable that the Scripture (Gen. iv.) expressly says that Cain dwelt on the *east* side of Eden.

I now come to

HEA OR HOA.

"The third god of the first triad was Hea or Hoa, the Ana of Damascius. This appellation is perhaps best rendered into Greek by the Ωη of Helladius, the name given to the mystic animal, half man half fish, which came up from the Persian Gulf to teach astronomy and letters to the first settlers on the Euphrates and Tigris. It is perhaps contained in the word by which Berosus designates this same creature— Oannes (Ωάννης), which may be explained as Hoa-ana, or the god Hoa. There are no means of strictly determining the precise meaning of the word in Babylonian, but it is perhaps allowable to connect it provisionally with the Arabic Hiya, which is at once life and 'a serpent,' since, according to the best authority, 'there are very strong grounds for connecting Hea or Hoa with the serpent of Scripture, and the paradisaical traditions of the tree of knowledge and the tree of life.'

"Hoa occupies in the first triad the position which in the classical mythology is filled by Poseidon or Neptune, and in some respects he corresponds to him. He is 'the lord of the earth,' just as Neptune is γαιήοχος; he is the 'king of rivers,' and he comes from the sea to teach the Babylonians, but he is never called the 'lord of the sea.' That title belongs to Nin or Ninip. Hoa is the lord of the abyss or of 'the great deep,' which does not seem to be the sea, but something distinct from it. His most important titles are those which invest him with the character so prominently brought out in Oë and Oannes, of the god of science and knowledge. He is 'the intelligent guide,' or, according to another interpretation, 'the intelligent fish,' 'the teacher of mankind,' 'the lord of understanding.' One of his emblems is the 'wedge' or 'arrow-head,' the essential element of cuneiform writing, which seems to be assigned to him as the inventor, or at least the patron, of the Chaldæan alphabet. Another is the serpent, which occupies so conspicuous a place among the symbols of the gods on the black stones recording benefactions, and which sometimes appears upon the cylinders. This symbol here, as elsewhere, is emblematic of superhuman knowledge—a record of the primeval belief that 'the serpent was more subtle than any beast of the field.' The stellar name of Hoa was Kimmut.... The monuments do not contain much evidence of the early worship of Hoa. His name appears on a very ancient stone tablet brought from Mugheir (Ur), but otherwise his claim to be accounted one of the primeval gods must rest on the testimony of Berosus and Helladius, who represent him as known to the first settlers.... As Kimmut, Hoa was also the father of Nebo, whose functions bear a general resemblance to his own."—Rawlinson's Ancient Monarchies, i. 152.[154]

I have said that I shall not rely too much on the resemblance of name, Hoa; but I must draw attention to the curious resemblance which lurks in the name "Aüs" to the words upon which the Vicomte D'Anselme has founded an argument in the appended note.[155]

In the above extract from Rawlinson, although Hoa is said not to be "the true fish-god," yet he is called "the intelligent fish," and is associated with that mystic animal, half man half fish, which came up from the Persian Gulf to teach astronomy and letters to the first settlers on Euphrates and Tigris.

Let us compare this information with the following "History of the Fish," which the Abbé Gainet, i. 199, has translated from the Mahâbhârata.

The same history has been translated from the Bhagavad Pourana by Sir W. Jones ("Asiatic Researches"). Indeed, as the Abbé Gainet argues, as this same history is found in all the religious poems of India, there is a certain security that it would not have been taken from the Hebrews.

I shall merely attempt to give the drift of the legend from the Abbé Gainet's original translation of that portion of the Matysia Pourana which has reference to Noah:—

"The son of Vaivaswata (the sun) was a king, and a great sage, a prince of men, resembling Pradjapati in eclat. In his strength, splendour, prosperity, and above all, his penitence, Manou surpassed his father and his grandfather.[156]... One day a small fish approached him, and begged him to remove him from the water where he was, 'because the great fish always eat the little fish—it is our eternal condition.' Manou complies, and the fish promises eternal gratitude. After several such migrations, through the intervention of Manou, the fish at each removal increasing in bulk, he is at length launched in the ocean. The fish then holds this discourse with Manou:—'Soon, oh blessed Manou, everything that is by nature fixed and stationary in the terrestrial world, will undergo a general immersion and a complete dissolution. This temporary immersion of the world is near at hand, and therefore it is that I announce to you to-day what you ought to do for your safety.' He instructs him to build a strong and solid ship, and to enter it with the seven richis or sages.[157] He instructs him also to take with him all sorts of seeds, according to certain Brahminical indications. 'And when you are in the vessel you will perceive me coming towards you, oh well-beloved of the saints, I will approach you with a horn on my head, by which you will recognise me.' Manou did all that was prescribed to him by the fish, and the earth was submerged accordingly, as he had predicted. 'Neither the earth, nor the sky, nor the intermediate space, was visible; all was water.' 'In the middle of the world thus submerged, O Prince of Bharatidians, were seen the seven richis or sages, Manou, and the fish. Thus, O King, did this fish cause the vessel to sail' (with a rope tied to its horn), 'for many years, without wearying, in this immensity of water.' At length the ship was dragged by the fish on to the highest point of the Himalaya. 'That is why the highest summit of the Himaran (Himalaya) was called Nanbundhanam, or the place to which

the ship was attached, a name which it bears to this day—
Sache cela, O Prince des Bharatidians.' Then le gracieux,
with placid gaze, thus addressed the richis—'I am Brahma,
the ancestor (l'ancestre) of all creatures. No one is greater
than I. Under the form of a fish I came to save you from the
terrors of death. From Manou, now, shall all creatures, with
the gods, the demons (au souras), and mankind, be born....
This is the ancient and celebrated history which bears the
name of the 'History of the Fish.'"[158]

Here we seem to see what looks like the commencement of the
legendary origin of the fish symbol; and here also we see it unmistakeably
in connection with Noah. We have, moreover, seen the connection of Hoa
with the fish.[159]

Let us now turn to his reduplication, as I conceive, in Nin, or Ninip,
who is said to be "the true fish god."

"His names, Bar and Nin, are respectively a Semitic and a Hamitic
term, signifying 'Lord,' or 'Master,'" (p. 166). Astronomically Nin "should
be Saturn." However, a set of epithets which seem to point to his stellar
character are very difficult to reconcile with the notion that, as a celestial
luminary, he was (the dark and distant) Saturn. We find him called, "the
light of heaven and earth," "he who, like the sun, the light of the gods,
irradiates the nations." All this is very difficult to reconcile with legends
arising out of the simple worship of a celestial luminary, but perfectly
consistent with the supposition of the patriarch Noah, after deification,
being located in the planetary system. The phrase, "he who, like the sun, the
light of the gods, irradiates the nations," is perfectly applicable to him who,
as Oannes, we have ever regarded as "the god of science and of knowledge"
and who "taught astronomy and letters to the first settlers on the Euphrates
and Tigris." Let us glance at the other epithets applied to Nin in the
inscriptions. He is the "lord of the brave," "the champion," "the warrior
who subdues foes," "he who strengthens the hearts of his followers." [The
Scripture mentions the repeated assurances of the Almighty to Noah, that
there should not be another Deluge; and the above is in keeping with the
tradition that the early inhabitants long hesitated to quit the mountains for
the plains, and only did so incited by the example of the patriarch.] "The
destroyer of enemies," "the reducer of the disobedient," "the exterminator
of rebels," "he whose sword is good." Like Nergal, or Mars, he is a god
of battle and the chase. (I shall refer later on to these warlike epithets as
applied to Noah.) At the same time he has qualities which seem wholly
unconnected with any that have been hitherto mentioned. He is the true
"fish-god" of Berosus, and is figured as such in the Scriptures. (I hope I may

persuade some reader, who may be interested in this inquiry, to compare the figure of Nin, in Rawlinson, i. 167, with figure 23, Dupaix's "New Spain" in Lord Kingsborough's "Mexico," representing an emblematic figure with fish[160] (as in the representation of Nin) over a human head, which also has inverted tusks. Compare also with representations of Neph, associated with snake and ram's head, and also with "History of the Fish," supra, p. 197.) To continue—in this point of view he (Nin) is called the "god of the sea," "he who dwells in the deep" and again, somewhat curiously, "the opener of the aqueducts." Now, as applied to Noah, this is not at all strange, and corresponds to the Scriptural phrase, "He opened the fountains of the deeps." Subsequently to deification we cannot be surprised to find all that was done by the Almighty attributed to the individual to whom it was done; as in Prometheus we have a double legend of the Creator, who created man with the vital spark, and of Prometheus, the man who was so created. "Besides these epithets he has many of a more general character, as 'the powerful chief,' 'the supreme,' 'the favourite of the gods,' 'the chief of the spirits,' and the like."

I must, moreover, request attention to the following from Rawlinson, i. 168,—"Nin's emblem in Assyria is the man-bull, the impersonation of strength and power. He guards the palaces of the Assyrian kings, who reckon him their tutelary god, and gives his name to their capital city. We may conjecture that in Babylonia his emblem was the sacred fish, which is often seen in different forms upon the cylinders."[161]

I turn to Gainet, i. 198, and I find this legend concerning the man-bull from Bertrand's "Dict. des Religions," 38, i. ii.[162]

"D'après les livres Parsis, le souverain Créateur sut que le mauvais génie se disposait à tenter l'homme. Il ne jugea pas à propos de l'empêcher par lui-même; il se contenta d'envoyer des anges pour veiller sur l'homme. Cependant le mal augmenta; l'homme se perdit; Dieu envoya un Deluge, qui dura dix jours et dix nuits et détruisit le genre humain. L'apparition de Kaioumons (l'homme-taureau), le premier homme, y est aussi précédée de la creation d'une grande eau." Here, in a confused tradition, with Adam—just as Nin is confused with Hercules and Saturn—the man-bull is apparently associated with a great flood.

In the curious Etruscan monument commemorative of the Deluge—discovered in 1696—and to which Cardinal Wiseman draws attention in his "Conferences" (vide Gainet, i. 190), being a vase supposed to represent the ark, and containing figures of twenty couples of (12) animals, (6) birds, (2) serpents, &c., and several human figures represented in the act of escaping from an inundation, there were also discovered certain signets and amulets.

These consisted of hands joined, *heads* of *oxen*, and olives. Now the olive in connection with the Deluge will speak for itself,—the hands joined are the symbol of Janus (*vide* next chapter), and heads of oxen—here unmistakably connected with the Deluge—may also be conjectured to have allusion to the man-bull above referred to.

Thus Nin, through both his emblems (bull and fish), is brought into contact with the Noachic tradition.[163] It is also said (Rawlinson, i. 174) of Nergal, vide supra, who is clearly identified with Nimrod,—"Again, if Nergal is the man-lion, his association in the buildings with the man-bull would be exactly parallel with the conjunction which we so constantly find between him and Nin in the inscriptions."

It is true that the majority of the inscriptions, p. 169, assert that Nin was the son of Bel-Nimrod. This may be referred to that tendency, previously noted in ancient nations, to place the ancestor with whom they were themselves identified at the head of every genealogy. One inscription, however, "makes Bel-Nimrod the son of Nin instead of his father." Nin, in any case, is unquestionably brought into close historical relationship with Bel-Nimrod, an historical character, and we must, in fine, choose whether we shall admit him to be Noah—to whom all the epithets would apply— or whether, upon the more literal construction of the inscriptions, we shall believe him to be some nameless son or successor of Nimrod.

There is one god more in whom I fancy I see a counterpart of Noah, or at least a counterpart of Hoa and Nin—viz.

NEBO.

I base my conclusion upon the epithets applied to him in common with Hoa and Nin, and inconsistently applied if, according to the evidence, p. 177, "mythologically he was a deity of no very great eminence," but in no way conflicting with the supposition that he represented the tradition of Noah, the counterpart to the tradition of Hoa and Nin, among some subordinate nationality, and such appears to be the fact. "When Nebo first appears in Assyria, it is as a foreign god, whose worship is brought thither from Babylonia,".

Of Nebo it is said, "his name is the same or nearly so, both in Babylonian and Assyrian, and we may perhaps assign it a *Semitic* derivation, from the root '*nibbah*,' *to prophesy*. It is his special function to preside over *knowledge* and *learning*. He is called 'the god who possesses intelligence'—'he who hears from afar'—'he who *teaches*,' or 'he who teaches and instructs.' In this point of view he of course approximates to Hoa, *whose son* he is called in some inscriptions, and to whom he bears a general resemblance. Like

Hoa, he is symbolised by the simple wedge or arrow-head, the primary and essential element of cuneiform writing, to mark his *joint* presidency with that god over writing and literature. At the same time Nebo has, like so many of the Chaldæan gods, a number of general titles, implying divine powers, which, if they had belonged to him only, would have seemed to prove him the supreme deity. He is 'the lord of lords, who has no equal in power,' *'the supreme chief,' 'the sustainer,'* 'the supporter,' the 'ever ready,' 'the guardian over the heavens and the earth,' 'the lord of the constellations,' 'the holder of the sceptre of power,' 'he who grants to kings the sceptre of royalty for the *governance* of their people'" (Rawlinson, i. 177).

There is just a possibility, however, that Nebo may be Sem or Shem. He would be the son of Hoa as Nebo was stated to be.

I think, moreover, a striking resemblance will be seen between the above epithets and the traditions concerning *Shem,* collected by Calmet (Dict. "Sem.")

> "The Jews attribute to Sem the theological tradition of the things which Noah taught to the first men.... They say that he is the same as Melchisedek.... In fine, the Hebrews believe that he taught men the law of justice, the manner of counting the months and years, and the intercalations of the months. They pretend that God gave him the spirit of prophecy one hundred years after the Deluge, and that he continued to prophesy during four hundred years, with little fruit among mankind, who had become very corrupt. Methodius says that he remained in the isle of the sun, that he invented astronomy, and that he was the first king who ruled over the earth."[164]

The difficulty, however, is in understanding how the worship of Shem came to Assyria *from* Babylonia. I can only reconcile it upon a theory that *all* idolatry came from Babylonia, *i.e.* from the Hamitic race.

There remains a difficulty which will doubtless occur to every one who has read the chapter in Rawlinson to which I must acknowledge myself so much indebted, and it is a difficulty which I ought, perhaps, to have dealt with before; and that is, that there is in the pages of Rawlinson (I. vii. 184) the most distinct identification of Noah with Xisuthrus. Of this there can be no doubt, from his direct connection with the Deluge, the circumstances of which are perfectly recorded in the Babylonian tradition.[165] This establishes the fact that the tradition of Noah and the Deluge was still among them when Berosus wrote. But if Xisuthrus is Noah, then it may be said Hoa, Oannes, and Nin cannot be Noah. It is a non sequitur, but will still, I fear, be very influential with many. It is difficult to understand the tendency to reduplication, and still more difficult to realise how a tradition so clear and decided could be contemporaneous with other identical traditions so entangled and confused. I believe this explanation to be that the account of Xisuthrus was part of the esoteric tradition to which Rawlinson refers, and which was also the tradition of their learned men—"Vixere fortes ante Agamemnon";—and we cannot suppose that Berosus (of whom we should have known nothing if his works had not been preserved to us at third or fourth hand) was the first chronicler of his nation.[166]

I shall pursue this inquiry into the classical mythology in the next chapter, and then recapitulate the results as regards this inquiry.

CHAPTER X
THE TRADITION OF NOAH AND THE DELUGE

I now come to a different set of illustrations still more germane to my subject.

Calmet says:—"Plusieurs scavans out remarqué que les pagans ont confondu Saturne, Deucalion, Ogyges, le Dieu Cœlus ou Ouranus, Janus, Prothée, Prométhée, Virtumnus, Bacchus, Osiris, Vadimon, Nisuthrus avec Noë."

I must add that this enumeration by no means exhausts the list. It is not my purpose, however, to pursue the subject in all its ramifications. I shall limit myself to the examination of one or two of these counterparts of Noah.

I. And in the first place, "Him of mazy counsel, Saturn," the expression of Hesiod (τ' Ιαπετον τε ιδε Κρονον ἀγκυλομήτην), Hesiod. Theog. v. 19, which so well befits the intermediary between God and the survivors of the Deluge. "Under Saturn," as Plutarch tells us, "was the golden age." Calmet says (Dict. "Saturne"), "Quant aux traits de ressemblance qui se trouvent entre Noë et Saturne, ils ne peuvent être plus sensibles.[167] Il (Saturne) est représenté avec une faulx comme inventeur de l'agriculture[168]: Noë est nommé 'vir agricola' (Gen. ix. 20) et il est dit qu'il commença à cultiver la terre. Les Saturnales, qu'on célébrait dans le vin et dans la licence et où les serviteurs s'égaloient à leurs maitres—marquent l'ivresse de Noë et sa malédiction qui assujettit Chanaan à ses frères tout égal qu'il leur étoit par sa naissance." [I have little doubt that this Bacchanalian recollection originated the tradition of the equality of conditions in the golden age, contrary to the facts of Scripture and history.] "On disoit que Noë avait dévoré tous ses enfans à l'exception de Jupiter, de Neptune, et de Pluton. Noë vit périr dans les eaux du déluge tous les hommes de son temps dont plusieurs étoient ses parents et plus jeunes que lui. Dans la stile de l'écriture on dit souvent que l'on fait ce qu'on n'empêche pas, ou même ce que l'on prédit." Further resemblances are traced in Calmet.

Now, I find in Sanchoniathon,[169] i.e. in the most ancient Phœnician historian, a tradition running exactly parallel with this Greek tradition as interpreted by Calmet:—"Ces genies, ces sages, ces dieux, nous expliquent les autres dieux qui, d'après Berose, forment l'homme du sang de Bélus, et tous les dieux que Sanchoniaton nous représente saisis d'épouvante à la vue de Saturne, faisant périr par le déluge son fils Sadid." —(Le Peuple Primitif; Rougemont, i. 303, quoted by Gainet, iii. 561, with reference to the worship of spirits.) I adduce it in evidence of the connection in tradition between Saturn and the Deluge, and in corroboration of Calmet's interpretation, which clears the Greek myth of what is grotesque and repulsive in it.

If I have sufficiently identified Saturn with Noah and the period of the Deluge, the lines of Virgil (Æneid, 8th Book, 315), besides bearing testimony in the same direction, appear to me to acquire a new meaning and significance:—

"Primus ab ætherio venit *Saturnus* Olympo,

Arma Jovis fugiens, *et regnis exul ademptis,*

Is genus indocile, ac dispersum montibus altis

Composuit; *legesque dedit*; Latiumque vocari

Maluit."...

"*Aurea,* quæ perhibent, *illo sub rege* fuerunt

Sæcula; sed placidâ populos in pace regebat,

Deterior donec paulatim ac discolor ætas

Et belli rabies et amor successit habendi."[170]

Allowing for the confusion incidental to the deification of Noah in the person of Saturn, which necessitates his descent from heaven, the rest of the verses seem merely to describe what is recorded in tradition, if not implied in the scriptural narrative, that Noah, a voyager and exile, his possessions having been lost in the Flood, flying the wrath—not indeed as directed against himself, but the consequences of the wrath of the Almighty[171]— persuaded the survivors of the Flood to abandon the mountains, to which they clung in fear of a second Deluge, and brought them into the plains, incited and encouraged by his example,—he who, if he be the same (vide supra, 208, 209) with Nin and Nebo, we have seen called "the sustainer," "the supporter," "he who strengthens the hearts of his followers," who taught them the cultivation of the soil, and of whom it is now said more distinctly than we have seen it heretofore stated, legesque dedit.[172]

There is no doubt much that is monstrous and grotesque in the classical conception of Saturn, but I must again suggest that as all traditions met in Noah, and were tradited through him, we must not be surprised to find all antediluvian traditions confused in Noah. Thus even the tradition of Lamech, which we have seen (vide supra, 178) variously distorted in the legends of Perseus and Œdipus, are again repeated in the legends of Saturn.

There are, no doubt, also divers astral complications arising out of Saturn's place in the planetary system. When, however, we are told that Saturn was son of Cœlus and Tellus or Cœlus and Vesta,[173] the same as Terra (Montfauçon), it seems to occur to us, as a thing "qui saute aux yeux," that this was only a mode of expressing a truth, applicable to all men in general, and Saturn as a primal progenitor in particular, and having reference to the composite nature of man; in other words, that this was simply the tradition which Noah would have handed down that he was created,[174] as were all other men, out of the earth, yet with something ethereal in his composition which came direct from the Deity. What the astral explanation may be I am at a loss to imagine. It cannot by any possibility be supposed to have reference to their relative positions in the heavens.

I shall return to Saturn, under the representation of Oceanus, when I come to speak of Janus.

II. *Bacchus.*—The *Saturnalia* may be taken as the connecting link between *Saturn* and *Bacchus*, and I think that it is sufficiently remarkable that there should be this link of connection.

But as the legends of Saturn are not all derived from Noah, so neither do all the traditions concerning Bacchus appertain to Saturn. I shall simply separate and note such as appear to me to be in common, e.g. "that Bacchus found out the making of wine, the art of planting trees, and many things else commodious for mankind." ["And Noah, a husbandman, began to till the ground, and planted a vineyard, and drinking the wine was made drunk," Gen. ix. 20.][175] It is said there were several Bacchuses. This may be only a reduplication, such as we have seen in the case of Oannes, Nin, and Nebo, or as in the multiplications of Jupiter. "Joves omnes reges vocarunt antiqui."[176]

On this subject Montfauçon says (i. 155)[177] apropos of a point to which I shall again refer, viz. that Bacchus was Tauricornis.

> "Diodorus Siculus says that the horns are only ascribed to the second Bacchus, the son of Jupiter and Proserpine; but these distinctions of various Bacchus were minded only in the more ancient times, hardly known in their worship.... This will also hold good of most of the other gods who were multiplied in the same manner."

Vicomte d'Anselme (Gainet, i. 224), asks with reference to his Greek name of Dionysius, "Pourquoi les Grecs donnaient-ils le nom de Dionysos ou de divin Noush (dios nous ou Noë) à l'inventeur du vin?" —Vide supra, ch. ix.; vide also Gainet, i. 225.

Bacchus is by some called "Tauricornis" (compare supra, p. 203, Nin) "or Bucornis, and moreover he is frequently so represented," (i.e. not only with the horn in hand, a "bull's horn," as he is sometimes, which might be a drinking horn or cornucopia, in its way emblematical of the vir agricola"), "but also with horns on the head. Horace calls him "Bicorniger," Orpheus, Βουκερως; Nicander, Ταυροκερως."—Montfauçon, i. 147, 155; comp. p. 204, note to "Nin."

One Bacchus, Cicero tells us, "was King of Asia and author of the Laws called Subazian."—Montfauçon, i. 144. It is, moreover, said that Bacchus travelled through all nations as far as India,[178] doing good in all places, and teaching many things profitable to the life of man. His conquests are said to have been easy and without bloodshed. But it is also noted that amidst his benevolence to mankind, he was relentless in punishing all want of respect for his divinity, and indeed the conduct and punishment of Chanaan may be said to be narrated in the history of Pentheus.—Vide Montf. i. 161.[179]

III. *Janus.*—Janus represented the most ancient tradition of Noah in Italy; subsequent migrations brought in the legend of Saturn, and thus we find them variously confounded—Saturn sometimes figuring as his guest, sometimes as his son, sometimes as his colleague on the throne. Like Saturn he appears as double-headed or bifrons, he is said to have introduced civilisation among the wild tribes of Italy, and under him, as under Saturn, there appears to have been a golden age.

I have made reference to *Saturn* as Oceanus (*vide Montfauçon,* i. 5), and as Oceanus his representations are very remarkable. In one he appears as an old man sitting on the waves of the sea, with a *sea monster* on one side of him, and his spear or rod in his hand. In another as sitting on the waves of the sea with ships about him; he is "holding an urn and pours out water, the symbol of *the sea, and also of rivers and fountains.*"

But *Janus is also* represented in his medals "with a prow of a ship on the reverse," and he is said to have first invented crowns, *ships,* and *boats,* and to have coined the first money.

"According to the accounts of mythologists," says Macrobius, "*all families in the time of Janus* were full of religion and *holiness.*" "Xenon says he was the first that built temples and instituted sacred rites," and was therefore always mentioned at the beginning of sacrifices.

With reference to his description as "bifrons," Macrobius says (some say) he was so called "because he knew the past and future things.... Some pretend to prove that Janus is the Sun, and that he is represented with two faces, because he is master of the two doors[180] of heaven, and opens the day at his rising and shuts it at his setting."

A good secondary explanation is,[181] that "as Janus always began the year" (whence January) "the two heads do look on and import the old and new year" but then occurs the question—and this is why I submit that it is only a secondary explanation—how came Janus to commence the year?

In the nomenclature of the calendar connected with any system of hero worship, worship of ancestors, or even spirit worship, who more fitly chosen to commence the year than Janus, supposing him to be Noah?

There are, however, two what we may call primary explanations, and we must take our choice. The epithet is either applied to him, as exactly according with the reminiscence of Noah, who was pre-eminently acquainted with the past and the future; or we can take the astral explanation that Janus was called Bifrons,[182] because he opened the sun at his rising and shut it at his setting. As a symbol of Noah this double head appears to me very simple and natural, Noah forming the connecting link between the antediluvian and modern worlds; but as applied to the Sun or to Janus as in relation to the Sun, even allowing for personification, this twofold head of man strikes me as incongruous in the extreme. Besides, if it be allowed that it might apply to Saturn and Janus through the connecting idea of Chronos, how does it apply to Bacchus? Let us press this argument further. Here is a symbol common to Bacchus, Saturn, and Janus, and combining harmoniously in each instance with the representation of Noah. Can this symbol, common to these three, combine even congruously with any solar or astral legend? I have somewhere seen it noted as suspicious and as tending to confirm the solar theory that these mythological personages all "journey from east to west, and meet their fate in the evening." But is this so? Have we not just seen that Bacchus, according to mythology, travelled from the west into India?

But not only were Saturn, Janus, and Bacchus represented as "bifrons," but so also was Cecrops. Cecrops will present a difficulty the more in the way of any solar theory; but Cecrops,[183] like all founders or supposed founders of states, has something in common with Noah. Like Saturn and Janus in Italy, Cecrops was said to have brought the population of Attica into cities, to have given them laws, taught them the worship of the idols, planted the olive, and finally, was represented as half man, half serpent. [184]

To return to Janus. Before concluding I must note that Janus is called Eanus by Cicero, which may perhaps have analogy with "Hea and Hoa" (ch. ix., and with Eannes and "Oannes," although Cicero derives it from "eundo."

Janus was also called "consivius a conserendo," because he presided over generation, a title singularly appropriate to Noah as the second founder of the race, and through whom the injunction was given "to increase and multiply."[185] He is moreover called "Quirinus or Martialis," "because he presided over war," which is precisely the aspect under which it is the original and main purpose of this dissertation to consider Noah; and here I think I am entitled to urge, that if I have succeeded on other grounds in showing that Nin, Hoa, Janus, &c., represented Noah, then that these epithets, "Quirinus," "Martialis," "King of Battle," &c., can only be applied to him whose conquests were bloodless in the sense of controlling and regulating war.[186] In connection with this title of "Martialis," as applied to Janus—and, by the by, all the traditions concerning him are altogether peaceful and bloodless—it will be remembered that his temple was open in war and shut in peace, and closed for the third and last time at the moment of the birth of our Lord.

His name was also invoked first in religious ceremonies, "because, as presiding over armies," &c., through him only could prayers reach the immortal gods. Is not this a reminiscence of the communications of the Almighty to man through Noah?

IV. *Ogyges and Deucalion.*—I might pass over these traditions of Noah, since, having reference only to the fact of the Deluge and the personality of Noah, they will not furnish matter for the special purpose of this inquiry; but on these grounds the investigation may be justified, and moreover seems necessary, for the completion of this chapter, and to indicate the independent source and derivation of the classical tradition.

It appears to me manifest that the deluges of Ogyges and Deucalion were neither locally historical nor partial deluges, but merely the reminiscences of the universal Deluge. Of the universal Deluge, whether we call it the Mosaic Deluge or not, there is evidence and tradition in all parts of the world; though in every instance it is localised in its details and its history of the survivors.[187]

Since, however, there is nothing to be said against the possibility of subsequent partial inundations, there will, I suppose, always be found persons ready to maintain that the deluges of Ogyges and Deucalion were partial and historical; although I submit that the arguments which were formerly used to prove the priority of Ogyges to Deucalion, and the posteriority of both to the general Deluge, turned upon points of chronology which will hardly be sustained at the present day.

If, however, I can succeed in showing that the deluge of Deucalion is identical with the deluge of Noah, I shall consider that I shall have also proved the point for the deluge of Ogyges, which all agree to have been much older!

The following is Mr Grote's narrative collating the different traditions respecting the deluge of Deucalion:—

"Deukalion is important in Grecian mythical narration under two points of view. First, he is the person specially saved at the time of the general deluge; next, he is the father of Hellên, the great eponym of the Hellenic race; at least that was the more current story, though there were other statements which made Hellên the son of Zeus." [This was merely the incipient process of the apotheosis of their more immediate founder.] "The enormous iniquity with which the earth was contaminated, as Apollodorus says, by the then existing brazen race, or, as others say, by the fifty monstrous sons of Sykorôn, provoked Zeus to send a general deluge." "The latter account is given by Dionys. Halic. i. 17; the former seems to have been given by Hellenikus, who affirmed that the ark after the Deluge stopped upon Mount Othrys, and not upon Mount Parnassus (Schol. Pind. ut supra), the former being suitable for a settlement in Thessaly." [I have already pointed out how the general tradition is everywhere localised.] "An unremitting and terrible rain laid the whole of Greece under water except the highest mountain-tops, where a few stragglers found refuge. Deukalion was saved in a chest or ark, which he had been forewarned by his father Prometheus to construct. After he had floated for nine days on the water, he at length landed on the summit of Mount Parnassus. Zeus hearing, sent Hermes to him, promising to grant whatever he asked. He prayed that men and companions might be sent him in his solitude: accordingly Zeus directed both him and Pyrrha to cast stones over their heads, those cast by Pyrrha became women, those by Deukalion men. And thus the 'stony race of men' (if we may be allowed to translate an etymology which the Greek language presents exactly, and which has not been disdained by Hesiod, by Pindar, by Epicharmes, and by Virgil), came to tenant the soil of Greece. Deukalion on landing from the ark sacrificed a grateful offering to Zeus Phyxios, or the God of Escape; he also erected altars in Thessaly to the twelve great gods of Olympus. The reality of this deluge was firmly believed throughout the historical ages of Greece (localising it, however, and post-dating it to 1528 B.C.) Statements founded upon this event were in circulation throughout Greece even to a very late date. The Magarians ... and in the magnificent temple of the Olympian Zeus at Athens, a cavity in the earth was shown, through which it was affirmed that the water of the Deluge had retired. Even in the time of Pausanias the priests poured into this cavity holy offerings of meal and honey. In this, as in other parts of Greece, *the idea of the Deukalionian deluge was blended with the religious impressions of the people, and commemorated by their most sacred ceremonies."* —Grote's *"History of Greece," vol. i. ch. v. 132, 133, "The Deluge."* [188]

Mr Max Müller (comp. "Myth.," "Chips.," ii. 12), incidentally speaking of the legend of Deucalion, treats it with great contempt. "What is more ridiculous," he says, "than the mythological account of the creation of the human race by Deucalion and Pyrrha throwing stones behind them (a myth which owes its origin to a mere pun on λαός and λᾶας)." And ridiculous it certainly is from any point of view from which Mr Max Müller could regard it, i.e. either as the invention of a mythic period, or as a fugitive allegory arising out of some astral or solar legend: per contra, I shall submit that there is nothing forced in supposing that this legend arose out of some one of the processes of corruption to which all tradition is prone, of the known fact that the human race was re-propagated by Deucalion or Noah.[189] If I am asked to explain how it came about that there should have been this identity between the word for a "man" and a "stone," I must simply confess my ignorance. Perhaps if Mr Max Müller could be brought to look at things more from the point of view of biblical traditions, he might be enabled to see it. All that I can suggest is, that perhaps it may have a common origin with that Homeric expression quoted by Mr Max Müller at p. 175 (vide supra), "Thou art not sprung from the olden tree or from the rock." I consider that I shall definitely establish, however, that it originates in a tradition and not "a mere pun," and at any rate that it is not local, it is not Greek. It is no doubt singular that the word for man, λαός, populus, should so closely resemble the word for a stone, λᾶας; but not only is this coincidence found in the Greek, but we shall see that it is widely spread in all parts of the world. In proof, I adduce the following extract from Dr Hooker's inaugural lecture at Norwich in 1868, (since the publication of Mr Max Müller's work):—

"It is a curious fact that the Khasian word for a stone, 'man,' as commonly occurs in the names of their villages and places as that of man, maen, and men does in those of Brittany, Wales, Cornwall, &c.; thus Mansmai signifies in Khasia the Stone of Oath; Manloo, the Stone of Salt; Manflong, the Grassy Stone; and just as in Wales Pen mæn maur signifies the Hill of the Big Stone; and in Britanny a Menhir is a standing stone, and a Dolmen a table stone," &c.[190]

Here it is seen that the word for stone in these respective places is the same with our word "man" it is not specifically said that the word would carry this sense also in the places indicated, but I infer it from the analogy which runs through homo, homme, and by a connection of ideas through the Greek ὠμός to the Sanscrit—thus "âma-ad" (ὠμος-εδω]), are names applied "in the Sanscrit" to "barbarians" who are cannibals. (Max Müller, ii. p. 44.) And I am not sure that Mr Max Müller does not say so directly, in reference to the word "Brahman," for although the word originally is said to mean power (i. 363), yet "another word with the accent on the last syllable, is Brahmán, the man who prays."—Max Müller, i. 72.[191]

Also Kenrick ("Essay on Primæval History," p. 59), "Thus the Hindus attribute the origin of their institutions and race to Manu, whose name is equivalent to *man*. The Germans made Tuisto (Teutsch) and his son Mannus to be the origin and founder of their nation." Also Sir W. Jones' "Asiat. Res." i. 230; Rawlinson's "Bamp. Lect." lect. ii. 67:—"From *Manu* the earth was re-peopled, and from him *man*kind received their name *Manudsha*."

Gainet (i. 170) says:—"The stones changed then into men by Deucalion and Pyrrha, are they not their children according to nature? In Syriac the word 'Eben' signifies equally a child and a stone. In spite of these confusions their accounts of the Deluge are striking as well on account of their resemblance, as on account of their universality, as the reader will soon be able to convince himself."—Vide Gainet, i. 167.[192]

But if the whole human race were re-propagated by Deucalion and Pyrrha, how are we to locate the *anterior* legend of Ogyges, occurring among the same people? It is barely possible that the memory of a long antecedent and partial deluge may have remained in the memories of the survivors of the subsequent and universal calamity, but the much more reasonable conjecture seems to be that it was by a different channel the reminiscence of the same event. It must be remembered that it was the Ogygian deluge which was said to have been partial and to have inundated Attica. The deluge of Deucalion by all accounts, except by Pindar, was considered to have been universal, and corresponds in its details with Mosaic accounts, *e.g.* it was universal, covering the tops of the highest mountains; it was caused by the depravity of mankind; the single pair who were saved, were saved in a ship or an ark, and floated many days on the waters. In the end, they settled on the top of a mountain, went to consult the oracle (as Noah is said to have sacrificed and to have had communications with God), and re-peopled the earth. The version of Lucian gives particulars which brings the tradition to almost exact correspondence. Deucalion and his wife were saved (on account of their rectitude and piety) together with his sons and their wives. He was accompanied into the ark by the pigs, horses, lions, and serpents, who came to him in pairs. If the account of Lucian is somewhat recent, on the other hand it is the account of a professed scoffer, and moreover, shows what I do not remember to have seen noted from this point of view that the tradition was common to Syria as well as Greece.

This brings us to the contrary, but, as it appears to me, much less formidable objection—bearing in mind that the tradition of the Deluge is common to Mexico, India, China, the islands of the Pacific, &c. &c.—viz. that the tradition came to Greece from Asia.

This is Mr Kenrick's objection[193] (vide Preface to Grote's "History of Greece," 2d ed.) The most direct, and, as it appears to me, sufficient answer, seems to be that it was necessarily so; since, ex hypothesi, the population itself came to Greece from Asia. Mr Kenrick says, "It is doubtful whether the tradition of Deucalion's flood is older than the time when the intercourse with Greece began to be frequent," i.e. about the fifth century B.C. (p. 31.) But as the Septuagint, according to Mr Kenrick himself, could not have influenced Greece till the third century, this tradition can only have been the primeval tradition. Mr Kenrick is a fair opponent, and I must do him the justice to add that he repudiates the Voltairean suggestion that this tradition originated in a Hebrew invention. If then the inhabitants of Greece, who came originally from Asia, had not the tradition, or had it imperfectly, when they arrived, it can only have been because they had lost it; but as admittedly they recovered it at a later period, the presumption, even on this showing, is, at least for those who can realise how difficult it would be to make a pure fiction, as distinguished from a corrupt tradition, run current, more especially among different nationalities and during a lengthened period,— that when circumstances brought them again into contact with Asia, they added fresh incidents, only because they found the tradition fresher there than among themselves. Voila tout! for Mr Kenrick's whole argument depends entirely upon this—that "as we reach the time when the Greeks enjoyed more extensive and leisurely communication with Asia, through the conquests of Alexander ... we find new circumstances introduced into the story which assimilates it more closely to the Asiatic tradition."

It has been allowed (vide supra) that the tradition of Deucalion is as old as the fifth century B.C., and, not to speak of the deluge of Ogyges, connected with what was earliest in Grecian history, the following passage from Kenrick seems to me in evidence of long antecedent traditions among the Greeks themselves, which they must have brought with them originally from Asia.[194]

Mr Kenrick says (p. 31):—

"The account of Deucalion, given by Apollodorus (i. 7, 2), bears evident marks of being compounded of two fables originally distinct, in one of which, and probably the older, the descent of the Hellenes was traced through Deucalion to Prometheus and Pandora, without mention of a deluge. In the other, the destruction of the brazen race by a flood, the re-peopling the earth by the casting of stones, is related in the common way. That these two narratives cannot originally have belonged to the same myths is evident from their incongruity; for as mankind were created by Prometheus, the father of Deucalion, there was no time for them to have passed through those stages of degeneracy by which they reached the depravity of the brazen age."

Here are evidently two early traditions, ostensibly Greek, distinct, it is true, yet perfectly compatible. The one the tradition of Grecian descent through Noah to Adam and Eve, the other the tradition of the Deluge. But after what we have already seen (vide supra, pp. 157, 158) of reduplications and inversions, can a serious argument be based upon the expression that Deucalion (Noah) was the son of Prometheus (Adam)?[195] Is it not a most natural and inevitable façon-de-parler to connect the descendant directly and immediately with his remote ancestor, e.g. "Fils de St Louis—fils de Louis Capet—montez au ciel!"

I do not of course attempt, within this narrow compass, to grasp Mr Kenrick's entire view. I am merely dealing with the special argument; but it is curious to note how the line of reasoning adopted by Mr Kenrick, whilst it sustains the Greek traditions, as traditions (though not Greek), unconsciously neutralises the arguments which would dispose of the testimonies derived from them, by saying that they were not traditions of a general, but of a local and a partial deluge.

These latter arguments appear to have had weight with one against whom I hardly venture to run counter, Frederick Schlegel ("Phil. of Hist." p. 79)—"The irruption of the Black Sea into the Thracian Bosphorus is regarded by very competent judges in such matters as an event perfectly historical, or at least, from its proximity to the historical times, as not comparatively of so primitive a date." Compare with passage from Mr Kenrick.[196] Schlegel adds: — "All these great physical changes are not necessarily and exclusively to be ascribed to the last general Deluge. The presumed irruption of the Mediterranean into the ocean, as well as many other mere partial revolutions in the earth and sea, may have occurred much later, and quite apart from this great event". But it may also have occurred much earlier, as is clear from the following passage from Schlegel, to which I wish to direct the attention of geologists, and in which Schlegel speaks according to the original insight of his own mind, and not in deference to the opinions of others: —

> "These words ('the earth was without form and void, and darkness was upon the face of the deep; but the Spirit of God moved upon the face of the waters,' Gen. x.), which announce the presage of a new morn of Creation, not only represent a darker and wilder state of the globe, but very clearly show the element of water to be still in predominant force. Even the division of the elements, of the waters above the firmament, and of the waters below it, on the second day of creation, the permanent limitation of the sea for the formation and visible appearance of the dry land, necessarily imply a mighty revolution in the earth, and afford additional proof that the Mosaic history speaks not only of one but of many catastrophes of nature, *a circumstance that has not been near enough attended to in the geological interpretation and illustration of the Bible.*" —*Schlegel*, p. 82.

The point that is material to this discussion is to decide whether or not those disruptions in Thrace are historical and subsequent to the Deluge. Now, here Mr Kenrick's main theory, that "speculation is the source of tradition," comes in with fatal effect to dispose of the arguments I am combating, and yet in no way at this point militates against the view I am urging, that these supposed inundations were localisations of the tradition of the general Deluge which the Pelasgi brought with them from Asia.

Mr Kenrick says (p. 36): —

> "It was a λογος, a popular legend, among the Greeks, that Thessaly had once been a lake, and that Neptune had opened a passage for the waters through the vale of Tempe (Herod. 7, 129). The occupation of the banks of the rivers of this district by the Pelasgi tribes, which must have been *subsequent* to the opening of the gorge, is the *earliest* fact in Greek history, and the 'logos' itself no doubt originated

in a very simple speculation. The sight of a narrow gorge, the sole outlet of the waters of a whole district, naturally suggests the idea of its having once been closed, and, as the necessary consequence, the inundation of the whole region which it now serves to drain."

Now, if this reasoning is just, it seems to establish two things pretty conclusively: First, That the current legend among the Greeks was *not* the tradition of a local deluge; but, if not a reminiscence, was at any rate the observation of the evidences of a deluge previous to their arrival. Moreover, the deluge of their tradition exceeding the actual facts is in evidence of their recollection of an event adequate to such effects. Second, That the tradition, if it arose out of a speculation, must have arisen out of a speculation made in the earliest commencement of Greek history.

It is difficult to reconcile the latter conclusion with Mr Kenrick's view that the tradition was imported from Asia in the fifth century B.C.

It is impossible to reconcile the former with the acceptation of a local and historical inundation in the time of the Ogyges and Deucalion of popular history.

This digression on the legend of Deucalion has led me away from what is properly the subject-matter of this inquiry; and I therefore propose now to summarise the results of the last two chapters. To pursue the tradition of Noah in all its ramifications would extend the inquiry beyond the scope which is necessary for the purposes of my argument. It will have been seen, I think, that my object has not been merely antiquarian research. I have sought to bring into prominence the reminiscences of Noah, which recall him at any rate as the depository of the traditions, if not the expositor of the science of mankind, as the channel, if not the fountain-head, of law, which thus became the law of nations—as the intermediary through whom the communications of the Most High passed to mankind, and under whose authority mankind held together during some three hundred years.[197]

Let me collect more directly and more fully the epithets in this sense which are dispersed in the above traditions.

We have seen that Calmet properly identifies Saturn with Noah; that according to Virgil and Plutarch "under Saturn was the golden age" Saturn of whom Hesiod says:—"Him of mazy counsel, Saturn" that in the tradition, as we see it in Virgil, he is described as bringing his scattered people into social life, and the noticeable phrase is used legesque dedit;[198] that in Bacchus, directly connected with Saturn through the Saturnalia, we also see much in his characteristics in common with Saturn, all which equally identifies him with Noah; and Bacchus, as we are told by Cicero, was the author of the "laws called Subazian."[199] In Janus, too, we find great resemblances to Saturn, and in the very respects which would identify him with Noah. Under Janus as under Saturn was the golden age, and it is added that in the time of Janus, "all families were full of religion and holiness," and although his rule is described as singularly peaceful, he is called Quirinus and Martialis, as presiding over war. The closing and opening of his temple, too, had a conspicuous and direct connection with peace and war.

If we turn back to the mythological prototypes in Assyria we find him as Hoa in connection with "the mystic animal, half-man half-fish, which came up from the Persian Gulf to teach astronomy and letters to the first settlers on the Euphrates and Tigris," himself "known to the first settlers" he is called "the intelligent guide, or, according to another interpretation, the intelligent fish," "the teacher of mankind," "the lord of understanding" "one of his emblems is the wedge or arrow-head, the essential emblem of cuneiform writing, which seems to be assigned to him as the inventor, or at least the patron of the Chaldæan alphabet." In the Vedic tradition as Satiavrata (vide Rawlinson's "Bampton Lect.," lect. ii. 67), having been saved "from the destroying waves" in "a large vessel" sent from heaven for his use—which he entered accompanied "by pairs of all brute animals"—he is thus addressed, "Then shalt thou know my true greatness, rightly named the Supreme Godhead; by my favour all thy questions shall be answered and thy mind abundantly instructed" and it is added that "after the deluge had abated," Satiavrata was "instructed in all human and divine knowledge." In fine, if we recognise him as Hoa, we shall find his benefactions to mankind thus summed up in Berosus. (Vide the original in Rawlinson's "Ancient Monarchies," i. 154.)[200]

> "He is said to have transmitted to mankind the knowledge of grammar and mathematics, and of all the arts, of the polity of cities, the construction and dedication of temples, *the introduction of laws* (καί νομων εἰσηγήσεις); to have taught them geometry, and to have shown them *by example* the modes of *sowing the seed* and gathering the *fruits of the earth*," [the "vir agricola" of Genesis], and along with them to have tradited all the secrets which tend to humanise life. And no one else at that time was found more super-eminent than he."—*Vide* Rawlinson, i. 155.

We have seen that he was known to "the first settlers on the Euphrates and Tigris." The Abbé de Tressan says, Berosus begins his history with these words:—"*In the first year* appeared this extraordinary man" (Oannes). Now, with "the early settlers" on the Euphrates and Tigris the commencement of all things would have been naturally dated from the Deluge.

It appears to me worth while, in conclusion, to place more succinctly before the reader the *identical* terms in which the ancients (various authors) spoke of the first founders of states or their earliest progenitor—compelling the conclusion that allusion was made to one and the same individual and epoch.

Bryant ("Myth." ii. 253) says that Noah was represented as Thoth, Hermes, Menes, Osiris, Zeuth, Atlas, Phoroneus, and Prometheus, &c. &c. "There are none wherein his history is delineated more plainly, than in those of Saturn and Janus." These I will now omit, as we have just seen them to be identical—and so too Bacchus, who equally with them plants the vine, teaches them to sow, and gives them laws.

> *Phoroneus,* "an ancient poet quoted by Clemens Alex. (i. 380) calls him the first of mortals, φυρονευς πατηρ θνητων ανθρωπων." The first deluge took place under Phoroneus: "He was also the first who *built* an altar. He first collected men together and formed them into petty communities."—Pausanias, lib. 2, 145. He first gave laws and distributed justice.—Syncellus, 67, 125. They ascribed to him the distribution of mankind, "idem nationes distribuit" (Hyginus' Fab. 143), "which is a circumstance very remarkable."
>
> Poseidon's epithets connected with the ark are very striking (Bryant, ii. 269, Deucalion, vide ante, p. 232); but he is also said (Apollon. Rhod. lib. 3, v. 1085) to have been "the first man through whom religious rites were renewed, cities built, and civil polity established in the world."
>
> Cecrops (vide ante, p. 220), the identical terms are used.
>
> *Myrmidon,* "a person of great justice." "He is said to have collected people together, humanised mankind, enacted laws, and first established civil polity."—Scholia in Pindar, Ode 3, v. 21.
>
> Cadmus, vide ante, p. 221.
>
> *Pelasgus* also is described as equally a benefactor to mankind, and instructed them in many arts.—Pausanias, 8, 599. He is said to have built the first temple to the deity "ædem Jovi Olympis primum fecit Pelasgus."—Hyginus' Fab. 225, 346. Bryant says, "I have taken notice that as Noah was said

to have been ἄνθρωπος γης," a man of the earth—this characteristic is observable in every history of the primitive persons; and they are represented as 'νομιοι,' 'αγριοι', and 'γηγενεις.' Pelasgus accordingly had this title (Æschy. "Supplicants," v. 250), and it is particularly mentioned of him that he *was the first* husbandman. Pelasgus first found out all that is necessary for the cultivation of the ground."— Schol. in Eurip. "Orestes," v. 930.

Osiris.—The account of Osiris in Diodorus Siculus is exactly similar. He travels into all countries like Bacchus. He builds cities; and although represented as at the head of an army, is described with the muses and sciences in his retinue. In every region he instructed the people in planting, sowing, and other useful acts.—Tibullus, i. E. 8, v. 29. He particularly introduced the vine, and when that was not adapted to the soil, the use of ferment and wine of barley. He first built temples, and was a lawgiver and king (Diod. Sic.).—Bryant, ii. 60.

Chin-nong (vide also Bunsen, supra, p. 63) "was a husbandman, and taught the Chinese agriculture, &c., discovered the virtues of many plants. He was represented with the head of an ox, and sometimes only with two horns."—Comp. Bryant, iii. 584.

Manco Capac.—Peru, vide infra, ch. xiii.; very curious.

Strabo, 3, 204, says of the Turditani in Spain (Iberia), "They are well acquainted with grammar, and have many written records of high antiquity. They have also large collections of poetry (comp. ch. vii.), and even their laws are described in verse, which they say is of six thousand years standing."

Deucalion, according to Lucian, was saved from the Deluge on account of his wisdom and piety—"εὐβουλιης τε και εὐσεβιης είνεκα." [εὐβουλια—literally, "good counsel."]

Mercury gave Egypt its laws—"Atque Egyptiis leges et literas tradidisse."—Cicero, "De Natura Deorum," iii. 22.

Apollo.—Cicero says the fourth Apollo gave laws to the Arcadians (comp. infra, p. 331): "Quem Arcades Νομιον appellant, quod ab eo se leges ferunt accepisse," id. iii. 23; vide also Plato, "Leges," i. 1.

CHAPTER XI
DILUVIAN TRADITIONS IN
AFRICA AND AMERICA

Boulanger (1722–59), a freethinker, and the friend and correspondent of Voltaire, was so dominated by his belief in the universal Deluge as a fact, that he made its consequences the foundation of all his theories. Writing in the midst of a scepticism very much resembling that of the present day, he says, "What! you believe in the Deluge?" Such will be the exclamation of a certain school of opinion, and this school a very large one. Nevertheless, this profound writer, by the exigencies of his theory, was irresistibly brought to the recognition of the fact. "We must take," he continues, "a fact in the traditions of mankind, the truth of which shall be universally recognised. What is it? I do not see any, of which the evidence is more generally attested, than those which have transmitted to us that famous physical revolution which, they tell us, has altered the face of our globe, and which has occasioned a total renovation of human society: in a word, the Deluge appears to me the true starting-point (la veritable epoque) in the history of nations. Not only is the tradition which has transmitted this fact the most ancient of all, but it is moreover clear and intelligible; it presents a fact which can be justified and confirmed." He proceeds, and the drift and animus of the writer will be sufficiently apparent in the passage—"It is then by the Deluge that the history of the existing nations and societies has commenced. If there have been false and pernicious religions in the world it is to the Deluge that I trace them back as to their source; if doctrines inimical to society have been broached, I see their principles in the consequences of the Deluge; if there have existed vicious legislations and innumerable bad governments, it will be upon the Deluge that I lay the charge." It is, then, only in attestation of the fact that I adduce this author; and in his proof he has accumulated a large mass of indirect evidence, which a certain school of opinion find it convenient altogether to ignore in reference to this subject. In this class are the various institutions among different nations to preserve the memory of the Deluge, as for instance, the "Hydrophories ou la fête du Deluge à Athenes," and at Ægina, the feast of the goddess of Syria at Hierapolis, both having strange resemblances with the Jewish feasts of "Nisue ha Mâim, or the effusion of waters," and the tabernacles, in their traditional aspects, i.e. in their observances not commanded by Moses; the "effusion des eaux a Ithome ... et de Siloe" the feast of the Deluge (of Inachus) at Argos; a feast, the effusion of water, in Persia, anterior to its Mahometanism; similar festivals in Pegu, China, and Japan; in the mysteries of Eleusis; in the "peloria," "anthisteria," and "Saturnalia;" and finally in the pilgrimages to rivers in India[201] and other parts of the world; "of the multitude of traditions preserved in the diluvian festivals and commemorative usages of the gulphs, apertures, and abysses which have at one time or another vomited forth or absorbed waters" (i. 84); again, the pilgrimages to the summits of mountains in India, China, Tartary, the Caucasus,[202] Peru, &c. "It is easy to see," he adds (p. 320), "that this veneration is based upon a corrupted tradition, which has taught these people that their fathers formerly took refuge on the top of this mountain at the time of the Deluge, and subsequently descended from it to inhabit the plains."

I shall have occasion to refer again more in detail to some of these customs[203] when drawing attention to the resemblances which I shall presently point out; but I wish previously to give, more in extenso, his description of the Hydrophoria at Athens:—

"This name denoted the custom which the Athenians had on the day of this feast of carrying water in ewers and vases with great ceremony; in memory of the Deluge, they proceeded each year to pour this water into an opening or gulf, which was found near the temple of Jupiter Olympus, and on this occasion they recalled the sad memory of their ancestors having been submerged. This ceremony is simple and very suitable to its subject; it was well calculated to perpetuate the memory of the catastrophe caused by the waters of the Deluge. Superstition added some other customs.... They threw into the same gulf cakes of corn and honey; it was an offering to appease the infernal deities.... The Greeks placed it in the rank of their unlucky days (also 'un jour triste et lugubre'); and thus they remarked that Sylla had taken their city of Athens the very day that they had made this commemoration of the Deluge. Superstition observes everything, not to correct itself, but to confirm itself more and more in its errors. It was, according to the fable, by the opening of this gulf that the waters which had covered Attica had disappeared; it was also said that Deucalion had raised near to this place an altar which he had dedicated to Jove the Preserver. 'Tradition also attributed to Deucalion the temple of Jupiter Olympus,' in which these mournful ceremonies were performed. 'This temple was celebrated and respected by the pagan nations as far as we can trace history back.' It was reconstructed on a scale of magnificence by Pisistratus; every town and prince in Greece contributed to its adornment; it was completed by the Emperor Adrian in 126 of our era. The antiquity of this monument, the respect which all nations have shown it, and the character of the traditions which they have of its origin, ought to establish for the festival of the Hydrophoria a great antiquity. The feasts, in general, are more ancient than the temples."— Boulanger, i. 38–40.

I will now ask the reader, if he has not read (and seen the illustrations in) Mr Catlin's "O-kee-pa,"[204] to compare the following extract with the preceding:—

"The O-kee-pa, an annual ceremony to the strict observance of which those ignorant and superstitious people attributed not only their enjoyment in life but their very existence; for traditions, their only history, instructed them in the belief that the singular forms of this ceremony produced the buffaloes for their supply of food, and that the omission of this annual ceremony, with its sacrifices to the waters, would bring upon them a repetition of the calamity which their traditions say once befell them, destroying the whole human race excepting one man, who landed from his canoe on a high mountain in the west.[205] This tradition, however, was not peculiar to the Mandan tribe, for among one hundred and twenty different tribes that I have visited in North, South, and Central America, not a tribe exists that has not related to me distinct or vague traditions of such a calamity in which one or three or eight persons were saved above the waters on the top of a high mountain. Some of them, at the base of the Rocky Mountains, and in the plains of Venezuela and the Pampa del Sacramento in South America, make annual pilgrimages to the fancied summits where the antediluvian species were saved in canoes or otherwise, and under the mysterious regulations of their medicine (mystery) men tender their prayers and sacrifices to the Great Spirit to ensure their exemption from a similar catastrophe."—P. 2.

Yet, strange to say, this is no proof to Mr Catlin of the universal Deluge recorded in Scripture. "If," he says, "it were shown that inspired history of the Deluge and of the Creation restricted those events to one continent alone, then it might be that the American races came from the Eastern continent, bringing these traditions with them, for until that is proved, the American traditions of the Deluge are no evidence whatever of an eastern origin. If it were so, and the aborigines of America brought their traditions of the Deluge from the East, why did they not bring inspired history of the Creation?"[206]—P. 3. (Vide pp. 134, 135.)

The "O-kee-pa," Mr Catlin says, "was a strictly religious ceremony, ... with the solemnity of religious worship, with abstinence, with sacrifices, with prayer; whilst there were three other distinct and ostensible objects for which it was held,—1. As an annual celebration of the 'subsiding of the waters' of the Deluge. 2. For the purpose of dancing what they call the Bull-dance, to the strict performance of which they attributed the coming of buffaloes. 3. For purpose of conducting the young men through an ordeal of privation and bodily torture, which, while it was supposed to harden their muscles and prepare them for extreme endurance, enabled their chiefs ... to decide upon their comparative bodily strength, endurance," &c.—P. 9.

The torture no doubt subserved this subsidiary purpose, but it appears to me that the original intention and idea was torture for the purpose of expiation, as in the ceremonies in ancient Greece.[207] Sundry incidents narrated by Catlin seem to establish this. They prepare themselves by fasting (p. 25); after having sunk under the infliction of these horrible tortures (and from every point of view they are truly horrible), "no one was allowed to offer them aid when they lay in this condition. They were here enjoying their inestimable privilege of voluntarily intrusting their lives to the keeping of the Great Spirit, and chose to remain there until the Great Spirit gave them strength to get up and walk away" (p. 28); and when so far recovered, "in each instance" they presented the little finger of the left hand, and some also the forefinger of the same hand and the little finger of the right hand (all tending to make them pro tanto inefficient warriors) "as an offering to the Great Spirit, as a sacrifice for having listened to their prayers, and protected their lives in what they had just gone through" (p. 28).

For the description of the bull-dance,[208] and for the subsequent history and final extinction of the Mandans, I must refer my readers to Mr Catlin's valuable testimony to the truth of Scripture, and important contributions to ethnological science.

I shall now proceed to show analogies in what will be admitted to be most unlikely ground—in the King of Dahome's celebrated "So-sin customs," described by Captain Richard Burton.

Before, however, proceeding further, I must point out the following features in the ceremonies or customs as common to Grecian and antique pagan; to the Mandan (Indian of North America), and to the tropical African. [209] In the first place they are cyclical; they are all of a mournful character; all are interrupted at intervals by processions, dances, and songs of a traditional character; they all close in scenes of rejoicing or rather in Bacchanalian (yet still traditionally [vide page 247, note Boulanger] Bacchanalian) scenes of riot and debauchery. The duration of the festivals varies from three and four to five days; the days have fantastic names, which, although different, still in their very peculiarity, and also in the drift and meaning of the names so far as it can be gathered, are suggestive of a common origin, e.g. the first day of the Anthesteria, at Athens was called "Πιθοιγια, ἀπο τοῦ πίθους οἴγειν," "because they tapped their casks." The fourth day of the King of Dahome's customs is named "So (horse) nan-wen (will break) kan (rope) 'gbe (to-day)."—Burton, ii. 8. One part of the Mandan ceremony is called "Mee-ne-ro-ka-Ha-sha," or "the settling down of the waters," which name again closely corresponds to the ceremonies at Athens and at Hierapolis in Syria (ante), where water was poured into the opening where the waters of the Deluge were supposed to have disappeared. The fifth day of the Dahome customs is named "Minai afunfun khi Uhun-jro men Dadda Gezo"=="we go to the small mat tent under which the king sits."—Burton, ii. 27. This approximates to the scene described by Catlin (p. 20) at the close of the bull-dance (fourth day), when "the master of ceremonies (corresponding to the king at Dahome) cried out for all the dancers, musicians," and "the representatives of animals and birds," "to gather again around him." He is described as coming out of the mystery lodge and collecting them round "the big canoe."

But the closest connection is in the nature and order of the ceremonies on the fourth day at Dahome and among the Mandans. Among the latter, interrupting the bull-dance on that day, there is an apparition of "the evil spirit,"[210] graphically described by Mr Catlin (p. 22), and at Dahome (Burton, ii. 18), there intervenes between the fourth and fifth days' ceremonies what is called "the evil night" (there are two "evil nights") which is the night of the horrible massacre. But on this night also, at the close of the fourth day's ceremonies among the Mandans, the infliction of tortures (very horrible, but mild in comparison with the African butchery) commence. Now, I have already ventured the opinion that these tortures were originally of an expiatory character, and this gains confirmation by the assurance made to Captain R. Burton that the victims on "the evil night" were only "criminals" and prisoners of war, the people of Dahome, on all occasions (vide infra), preferring a vicarious mode of expiation. Captain R. Burton (ii. 19) says of these massacres:—"The king takes no pleasure in the tortures and death or in the sight of blood, as will presently appear.

The 2000 killed in one day, the canoe[211] paddled in a pool of gore, and other grisly nursery tales, must be derived from Whydah, where the slave-traders invented them, probably to deter Englishmen from visiting the king. It is useless to go over the ground of human sacrifice from the days of the wild Hindu's Naramadha to the burnings of the Druids, and to the awful massacres of Peru and Mexico. In Europe the extinction of the custom began from the time of the polite Augustus," i.e. commenced with the advent of our Lord. [Vide a reference to MS. of Sir J. Acton in Mr Gladstone's address to the University of Edinburgh, 1865, from which it would appear that the final extinction was not until the triumph of Christianity.]

Without carrying rashness to the excess of disputing the interpretation of Dahoman words with Captain Burton, I may yet demur to accepting his explanation of the term "So-sin" (the "So-sin customs") absolute et simpliciter. He says (i. 315), "The Sogan ('So' = horse, 'gan' captain) opens the customs by taking all the chargers from their owners and by tying them up, whence the word So-sin. The animals must be redeemed in a few days with a bag of cowries."[212] This is certainly a very likely definition, and although secondary, is no doubt the explanation current among the present generation of Dahomans. All I shall venture to do is to supplement it. But may not the old and primitive idea still lurk in the name? At i. 242, I perceive Captain Burton says "so" and "sin" mean water,[213] and the compound word "amma-sin" means "medicine" = "leaf-water," and again at 244 the same word "Sin" is twice used to signify liquid. If so, in the very name of the feast we find the word water, which links it into connection with "the Mandan custom" and the festivals of ancient Greece.

The word, "So" = horse, will therefore still remain, and may perhaps stand in the same relation to the "water" celebration, that the "bull" does to the Mandan celebration of the Deluge. Captain Burton, for instance, tells us (ii. 15), a "So" was brought up to us (on the fourth day of the So-sin custom, and on the fourth day of the Mandan custom "the bull-dance" was performed sixteen times round "the big canoe"); but I will place the two descriptions side by side.

Captain Burton, ii. 15.

"A 'So' was brought up to us, a *bull-face mask* of natural size, painted black, with glaring eyes and *peep-holes*, the horns were hung with *red* and *white* rag *strips*, and beneath was a dress of bamboo fibre covering the feet, and ruddy at the ends. It danced with head on one side and swayed itself about, to the great amusement of the people." *Vide* also p. 93, "Four tall men singularly dressed, and with bullocks' tails," &c.

Mr Catlin,

"The chief actors in these strange scenes (bull-dance) were eight men, with the entire skins of buffaloes thrown over them, enabling them closely to imitate the appearance and motions of those animals, as the bodies were kept in as horizontal a position, the horns and tails of the animals remaining on the skins, and the skins of the animals' heads served as *masks* through the eyes of which the *dancers were looking*." The legs of the dancers were painted *red* and *white*" (plate 6.)

If we might (on the strength of so many words of primary necessity being in common) connect "So" = horse, with the Saxon "soc" or plough (as in the soc and service tenure), we could then see a way in which the same word might apply indifferently to ox or horse; and we would, moreover, see through the common relation to Noah how the water ceremony came to be associated with the worship of Ceres in the mysteries of Eleusis. Vide Boulanger, i. 70–107.[214]

The above enumeration does not exhaust the points of resemblance. Compare the following:—

Burton, ii. 23.

"Conspicuous objects on the left of the pavilion were two Ajalela or fetish pots made by the present king (according to the customs.) Vide note 16. Both are lamp black, shaped like amphoræ (amphoræ, for holding wine) about 4 feet high, and planted on tripods. The larger was solid, the smaller callendered with many small holes, and both were decorated with brass and silver crescents, stars, and similar ornaments. The second, when filled with water and medicine allows none to escape, so great is its fetish power; an army guarded by it can never be defeated, and it will lead the way to Absokuta." Compare Pongol ceremony,

Catlin,

"In an open area in the centre of the village stands the ark or 'big canoe,' around which a great proportion of the ceremonies were performed. This rude symbol, of 8 or 10 feet in height, was constructed of planks and hoops, having somewhat the appearance of a large hogshead standing on its end, and containing some mysterious things, which none but the *medicine* (mystery) men were allowed to examine."

This must be considered in connection with the following.

Burton.

In the opening procession of the third day's customs, Captain Burton tells us (ii. 2), "First came a procession of eighteen Tansi-no or fetish women, who have charge of the last monarch's grave.... They were preceded by bundles of matting, eight large stools, calabashes, pipes, baskets of water, grog, and meat with segments of gourd above and below, tobacco bags, and other commissariat articles; and they were followed by a band of horns and rattles."[215]

In another procession (ii. 47), "The party was brought up by slave girls carrying baskets and calabashes. (Query, of water?) These, preceded by six bellowing horns, stalked in slowly, and with measured gait the eight Tansino, who serve and pray for the ghosts of dead kings. (Query, eight dead kings?) In front went their ensign, a copper measuring rod 15 feet long and tapering to a very fine end; behind it were two chauris and seven mysterious pots and calabashes wrapped in white and red checks," and presently "three brass, four copper, and six iron pots, curiosities on account of their great size.... Eight images, of which three were apparently ship's figureheads whitewashed, and the rest very hideous efforts of native art."[216]

Catlin.

In Captain Burton's account of the articles paraded in the procession, the pipes (to which great mystery is attached), the horns and rattles (vide pl.), and the baskets of water are common to the Mandan ceremony. May not the eight stools be representative of the eight diluvian survivors. Vide supra, 197, Cabiri? Let us, however, confine our attention to the "baskets of water." Compare with the following account in Catlin.

"In the medicine (mystery) lodge ... there were also four articles of veneration and importance lying on the ground, which were sacks containing each some three or four gallons of water. These seemed to be objects of great superstitious regard, and had been made with much labour and ingenuity, being constructed of the skins of the buffaloes' neck, and sewed together in the forms of large tortoises lying on their backs (comp. p. 138; also p. 269), each having a sort of tail made of raven's quills and a stick like a drumstick lying on it, with which, as will be seen in a subsequent part of the ceremony, the musicians beat upon the sacks as instruments of music for their strange dances. By the sides of these sacks, which they called Ech-tee-ka (drums), there were two other articles of equal importance which they called Ech-na-da (rattles) made of undressed skins shaped into the form of gourd shells," &c. (Note the segments of gourd accompanying the water baskets in the Dahome procession, supra.) Catlin adds—"The sacks of water had the appearance of great antiquity, and the Mandans pretended that the water had been contained in them ever since the Deluge."—[217]

Burton, ii. 35.

It must be remembered that at Dahome, royalty as there represented has absorbed and monopolized the most important parts of the ceremonial:

it is natural, therefore, to expect that the conspicuous figures in the original (or in the Mandan), which conflicted or would not consort with royalty, would be thrown into the background. Accordingly I am only able to get a glimpse of the conspicuous figures opposite in the following passage:— "The jesters were followed by a dozen pursuivants armed with gong-gongs, who advanced bending towards the throne, and shouted the 'strong names' or titles. Conspicuous amongst them was an oldster in a crimson sleeveless tunic and yellow shorts: his head was red with dust, he carried a large bill-hook,[218] and he went about attended by four drums and one cymbal."

It will be remembered (if my readers have read Mr Catlin, p. 11, 12) that the first thing "the aged white man" does on entering the mystery lodge is to call on the chiefs "to furnish him with four men," and the next is to "receive at the door of every Mandan's wigwam some edged tool to be given to the water as a sacrifice, as it was with such tools that the "big canoe" was built. [219]

Catlin,

The opening scene in the Mandan customs, effectively described by Mr Catlin, begins with "a solitary human figure descending the prairie hills and approaching the village," "in appearance a very *aged* man," "a centenarian white man," dressed in a robe of four white wolves' skins." He was met by the head chief and the council of chiefs, and addressed by them as "Nu-mohk-muck-a-nah" (the *first* and only man.) "He then harangued them for a few minutes, reminding them that every human being on the surface of the earth had been destroyed by the water excepting himself, who had landed on a high mountain in the west in his canoe, where he still resided, and from whence he had come to open the medicine (mystery) lodge, that the Mandans might celebrate the *subsiding of the waters*, and make the proper sacrifices to the water, lest the same calamity should again happen to them."

Burton, ii. 38.

"The ministers ... they were conducted by a 'Lali' or half-head, with right side of his pericranium clean shaven, and the left in a casing of silver that looked like a cast or a half melon."

Burton says (ii. 87), "One of the Dahoman monarch's peculiarities is that he is double, not merely binonymous, nor dual, like the spiritual Mickado and temporal Tycoon of Japan, but two in one. Gelele, for instance, is king of the city and addo-kpon of the 'bush'; i.e. of the farmer folk and the country as opposed to the city. This country ruler has his official mother, the Dank-li-ke.... Thus Dahome has two points of interest to the ethnologist— the distinct precedence of women and the double king." — Vide also.

Catlin,

Compare with the two athletic young men (*vide* Plate XIII.) assigned to each of the young men who underwent the torture—"their bodies painted *one half red* and the other blue, and carrying a bunch of willow-boughs in one hand."

Here two or three questions suggest themselves. If this ceremony is primitive, will not dual royalty give a clue to the duality we find so commonly in mythology, assuming the basis of mythology to be historical? 2d, Is there no clue in the name, *official* name, of Dank-li-ke? What does the reader guess the meaning to be? (p. 58.) Mr Burton tells us it means, "Dank (the rainbow), li (stand), and ke (the world)." Is it a forced paraphrase to construe this to mean—The rainbow is the sign that the world shall stand?

Upon the point of the precedence of woman, to which the Dahoman ceremony testifies, but to which it gives no clue, I shall, as it is so very important in more bearings than one, give at some length the following scene from Catlin:—

> "When 'the evil spirit' enters the camp during the ceremony, he proceeds to make various attacks, which are defeated by the intervention of the master of the ceremonies. In several attempts of this kind the evil spirit was thus defeated, after which he came wandering back amongst the dancers, apparently much fatigued and disappointed.... In this distressing dilemma he was approached by an old matron, who came up slyly behind him, with both hands full of yellow dirt, which (by reaching around him) she suddenly dashed in his face, covering him from head to foot, and changing his colour, as the dirt adhered to the undried bear's grease on his skin; ... at length *another* snatched his *wand* from his hand and broke it across her knee ... his power was thus gone ... bolting through the crowd, he made his way to the prairies."—

We shall not be surprised to learn, then, that when the "Feast of the Buffaloes" (distinct from the bull-dance) commences, several old men perambulated the village in various directions, in the character of criers, with rattles in their hands, proclaiming that "the *whole government of the Mandans* was then in the hands of one woman—she who had disarmed the evil spirit ... that the chiefs that night were old women; that they had nothing to say; that no one was allowed to be out of their wigwams excepting the favoured ones whom 'the governing woman' had invited," &c. Will not this give a clue to the precedence in Dahome, *probandis probatis*, and is not the precedence in Dahome thus interpreted, and the interlude above described evidence of the tradition, that the *woman* should break the head of the *serpent*? (Gen. iii. 15). It is of great significance, and, if so many points of comparison had not occurred, ought to have been stated at the outset, that at Dahome "the Sin-kwain ("sin," water—"kwain," sprinkling), or water-sprinkling custom follows closely upon the "So-sin or Horse-tie rites."— *Vide* Burton, ii. 167.

Now, if the reader will turn to Boulanger, i. 90, 91, he will find this identical custom in Persia, Pegu, China, and Japan. But I relinquish the details, as I fear I shall have exhausted the patience of the few readers I shall have carried with me to this point; and because the King of Dahome has a custom perhaps still more demonstrably cognate to not only the ancient Grecian ceremonies on the shores of the ocean and on the banks of rivers, but with widely diffused tradition. I shall here place four writers in juxtaposition, and with this testimony I shall conclude:—

BOULANGER.

> The ancient inhabitants of Italy repaired once a year to the Lake Cutilia, where they made sacrifices and celebrated secret mysteries or ceremonies (Dion. Halicarnassus, i. 2).
>
> The pontiffs in ancient Rome also went annually to the banks of the Tiber, "là ils faisoient des sacrifices *expiatoires* à Saturne, ce Dieu chronique," &c. (Dion. Hal. i. 8.)
>
> In the kingdom of Saka in Africa their greatest solemnity was celebrated on the banks of the rivers; the king himself presides at it (Hist. Gener. des Voy., iii. 639).
>
> The same custom has been already (supra, p. 252) noticed on the Indus.
>
> In all these cases human sacrifices were offered, or substitutes.—Boulanger, i. pp. 110–11. Compare supra, p. 243, lines from Dionysius Periegesis.

BURTON.

> At Whydat the youngest brother of their triad is Hu, the ocean or sea. [Compare with Assyrian Hoa, supra, p. 194, and Chinese Yu, p. 68.] "The Hu-no, or ocean priest, is now considered the highest of all.... At times the king sends as an ocean sacrifice from Agborne a man carried in a hammock, with the dress, the stool, and the umbrella of a Caboceer; a canoe takes him out to sea, where he is thrown to the sharks. The custom for this element is made at Whydat, in a place

near the greater market, and called Hu-kpa-man. It is a round hut, with thatch and chalked walls: outside is a heap of bones, whilst skulls, carapaces of the tortoise, and similar materials, cumber the interior. The priest is a fetish woman, who offers water and kola nuts to, and expects rum from, white visitors.—ii. p. 141.

Compare also supra, in Preface, extract from Davies' "Celtic Researches" on the Celtic god Hu.

CATLIN.

The water ceremonies in Catlin's account have already been sufficiently adverted to. He thus describes the medicine or mystery lodge in which they took place. Exteriorly, with the exception of the four images, it differed only in dimensions from the other wigwams, which are thus described? "They were covered with earth. They were all of one form; the frames or shells constructed of timbers, and covered with a thatching of willow boughs, and over and on that with a foot or two in thickness of a concrete of tough clay and gravel, which became so hard as to admit the whole group of inmates to recline on their tops. They varied in size from thirty to sixty feet, and were perfectly round." For extract describing interior, vide supra, p. 257, noting (vide Plate iii. in Catlin) the four human and four ox skulls; "the sacks of water in the form of large tortoises lying on their backs."

N.B.—With reference to the tortoise, vide ante p. 257.

Compare the "Buddhist Topes" in Major Cunningham's "Bhilsa Tope," vide p. 243.

HUNTER.

Hunter ("Annals of Rural Bengal," p. 153) says of the Santals: "The only stream of any consequence in their present country—the Damouda—is regarded with a veneration altogether disproportionate to its size. Thither the superstitious Santal repairs to consult the prophets and diviners, and once a year the tribes make a pilgrimage to its banks in commemoration of their forefathers.... However remote the jungle in which the Santal may die, his nearest kinsman carries a little relic of the deceased to the river, and places it in the current to be conveyed to the far-off eastern land from which his ancestors came."

In connection with the above, it must be remembered (*vide* Appendix G, p. 480, "Santal Traditions") that they have, although confused with the Creation, an unmistakable tradition of the Deluge, the intoxication of Noah, and the dispersion.

If, then, I have shown that the custom, for the preservation of which from oblivion, so far as the Mandans (now extinct) are concerned, we are indebted to Mr Catlin, and which so plainly tells its own tale, is common to Europe, Asia, and Africa, as well as America, I shall have established it as a tradition, not of a local American, but of an universal Deluge; and if the tradition of the universal Deluge is proved, then, according to Mr Catlin's narrative itself, there is tradition of the Creation also (vide pp. 7, 13, 42). [220]

I have replied more fully, in chap. vii., to Mr Catlin's objection--that though they have a tradition of a deluge, it is not the tradition of the Deluge, because they have not also the tradition of the Creation.

Mr Catlin argues upon the view that the American race "were created upon the ground on which they were found" ("Last Rambles," p. 321, 1868); and adds, "I can find nothing in history, sacred or profane, against this."

He takes his stand (in "O-kee-pa") upon this—that there is nothing in the Mandan tradition which can be brought in proof of their migration from another continent. In reply I shall adduce their very name.

The American continent may have been peopled by way of Behring's Straits, or from Europe in the East by way of Greenland, or by the connection of the Pacific Islands from the opposite coasts of Japan, China, and the Corea, or from the Polynesian groups in the south. The population may have poured in by all these routes. It is said (Prescott, "Conquest of Mexico," ii. 473)[221] that MSS. exist at Copenhagen proving that the American coast was visited by the Northmen in the eleventh century. The Polynesian route we may leave out of consideration, as it will not probably have been the one by which the Mandans came. As to the route by Behring's Straits, Mr Catlin admits "it is a possibility, and therefore they say it is probable" (p. 217, "Last Rambles"). But if, as there appears to me reason to think, they came from the opposite coast of the Corea, it might as reasonably be conjectured that the migration took the route of Behring's Straits, or by way of the Sandwich Islands. The possibility of the former is conceded. I will confine my attention, therefore, to the latter, which Mr Catlin pronounces absolutely impossible. In the first place, the distance between the Sandwich Islands and America is not greater than between Otaheite and New Zealand.[222] Now it is admitted that New Zealand was peopled from Otaheite. Moreover (vide Sir J. Lubbock, "Pre-historic Times," p. 390), the inhabitants of the Sandwich Islands, at two thousand miles distance, belong to the same race as those of Tahiti (Otaheite) and New Zealand, and resemble them "in religion, languages, canoes, houses, weapons, food, habits, &c."[223] The canoes of the Pacific islanders generally (vide Captain Cook passim) were of considerable size, and of very perfect workmanship. But also Prescott ("Conquest of Mexico," ii. 473, quoting Beechey's "Voyage to Pacific," 1831, p. 2 Appendix, Humboldt's "Examen. Critique de l'Hist. de la Geog." and Nuov. Cont. ii. 55) says, "It would be easy for the inhabitant of Eastern Tartary or Japan to steer his canoe from islet to islet quite across to the American shore, without ever being on the ocean more than two days at a time."[224]

We may agree, then, that the Mandans might have come by this route. Is there anything which makes it probable that they came? Well, yes; in the first place their name. Mr Catlin tells us ("O-kee-pa," p. 5), "The Mandans (Nu-mak-ká-kee, pheasants, as they call themselves) have been known from the time of the first visits made to them, to the day of their destruction, as one of the most friendly and hospitable tribes on the United States frontier." It transpires, therefore, that they are called pheasants. Is the pheasant a native of America?—on the other hand, is it not common on the opposite Asiatic continent, and on the islands adjacent to it from New Guinea to the Corea? I have never heard of the pheasant in the American continent;[225] but in reading the accounts of the missionaries of the Corea (the only foreigners who have penetrated into the country), I read, "that clouds of pheasants and birds of all kinds perch at night in the branches of the trees" ("Life of Henri Dorie," translated by Lady Herbert; Burns & Oates, p. 77); and if the reader will turn to p. 79 in the same Life, and will compare the description of the Coreans, which he will find there, with the description and portraits of the Mandans in Mr Catlin's "O-kee-pa," pp. 4, 5, he will, I think, recognise a sufficient resemblance to warrant and sustain the presumption created by their name.[226]

To the peculiarity of name, and resemblance of feature, I shall now proceed to add the evidence of some traces of their peculiar customs, or at least of some trace of the tradition out of which they arose.

I am not at present in possession of evidence to show this in the Corea itself (almost totally unknown and unexplored), but in the island of Formosa the same mode of burial is observed, only that among the Formosans other customs are added, which remind one of the commemorative customs of the Mandans.

Catlin,

"Their (Mandan) dead, partially embalmed, are tightly wrapped in buffalo hides softened with glue and water, and placed on slight scaffolds, above the reach of animals or human hands, each body having its separate scaffold."

The Mandan dance was round *"the big canoe,"* and a part of their ceremony on the roof of their wigwams.

Among the Opischeschaht *Indians (vide Field,* Oct. 2, 1869) there was a dance which they called "the roof dance." "While the dance and song were going on below, leaped up and down between the roof-board, pushed aside for that purpose, making a noise like thunder.... After the dance was finished an old Seshaaht came forward, and remarked, that as it was a dance peculiar to his tribe it could not be omitted," though "very injurious to the roof."

Ogilby's Japan,

"The manner of disposing of their (Formosans') dead and funeral obsequies is thus: When any one dies, the corpse being laid out, after twenty-four hours they elevate it upon a convenient scaffold or stage, four feet high, matted with reeds and rushes, near which they make a fire, so that the corpse may dry by degrees.... They drink intoxicating liquors. One beats on a drum made *like a chest,* but *longer* and *broader,* and turning *the bottom upwards;* the women get up, and two by two, back to back, move their legs and arms in a dancing time and measure, which pace, or taboring tread, sends a kind of murmuring or doleful sound from the *hollow tree.*"

N.B.—Their boats were constructed by hollowing out a tree (vide Catlin's "Last Rambles," p. 99).[227]

Now, compare with the above, and also with the extracts from Burton and Catlin, at, remembering the prominence of the ox or bull (the ox and bull dance) in the Mandan customs, and the connection of the bull with Nin or Ninip, and other mythological figures of which I believe Noah to have been the antitype. The following description of the most curious traditional representation in Japan (Ogilby, p. 279):—

> "Moreover, besides the ox temple in Meaco, there is also to be seen the stately chapel dedicated to the Creator of all things (the ox in the above-mentioned temple is represented as breaking the mundane egg, vide supra, p. 257), who is represented in a very strange manner. In the middle of the temple is a great pot full of water surrounded with a wall, seven feet high from the ground, in the middle of

which appears an exceeding great tortoise, whose shell, feet, and head stands in the water; out of its back rises the body of a great tree, on the top of which sits a strange and horrible figure" ... [then follows a good deal which has its explanation, but must be curtailed] ... "the image hath four arms" ... in one "the hand grasps a cruse, from whence water issues continually; the other hand holds a sceptre.... The tree whereon he sits is of brass, ... about the middle of this tree an exceeding great serpent hath wreathed itself twice, whose head and body is on the right side held fast by two horrible shapes, the remaining part thereof to the tail, two kings and one of Japan sages stretch forth" [evidently representing the contending influences (as in Mandan dance), one of the kings having the duplicated Janus head, supra,][228]

there is perhaps a still more definite tradition of the Deluge (confused as usual with traditions of the Creation) in connection with the idol Topan. "Not far from Mettogamma (said the interpreter) lies an exceeding high mountain ... the top of which stand several temples which may be seen a great distance off at sea. In these temples the Bonzies worshipped that great God which formerly created the sun, moon, and stars, but also fifteen lesser deities which some ages since conversed upon the earth (compare pp. 63, 97.) Then follows their account of the Creation. "Mankind not only increased in number but also in wickedness, differing more and more from their heavenly extract, growing still worse and worse, mocking at thunder, rainbows, and fire; nay, they blasphemed the great God himself (whom when the interpreter named, he bowed his head to the ground), whereupon He called His inferior deities about Him, telling them that He resolved to destroy and ruin all things ... and make a round globe, in which the four elements should be all resolved into their former mass; and chiefly He commanded the idol Topan to make thunder balls to shoot through the air and fire all the kingdoms with lightning ... so that none were saved except one man and his family, that had entertained and duly worshipped the gods." Of the god Topan it had been previously said "that some years since he saw the temple of the idol Topan, whose image stood on a copper altar, cast like clouds, himself armed as a warrior, a coronet helmet on his head, his hand grasping a mighty club, and seeming to fly through the sky and moving his club to occasion thunder. When it thundered, a Bonzi, whose head was adorned with consecrated leaves [Query, the olive or willow?] which no thunder could harm," offered several fishes." (Comp. 197, 203.) Vide also p. 94, representation of the fish-god in the person of their "god

Canon" [where we read of their "gods Canon and Camis or Chamis;" if we were to substitute Canaan and Cham, quid vetat?][229]

To complete the circle of evidence, as regards the general tradition, I must add the following extracts from Captain Cook's voyages, i. 110 (London, 1846):—"In the island of Huahieine, thirty-one leagues from Otaheite N.-W.," Captain Cook came upon an erection, of which he says—"The general resemblance between this repository and the ark of the Lord among the Jews is remarkable; but it is still more remarkable that upon inquiring of a boy what it was called, he said 'Ewharre no Eatua,' it is the house of God. He could, however, give no account of its signification or use"."Saw (at Uliatea) several Ewharre-no-Eatua or houses of God, to which carriage poles were attached as at Huahieine.... From thence we went to a long house not far distant, where among rolls of cloth and several other things we saw the model of a canoe, about three feet long, to which were tied eight human jawbones" [eight the number saved in the ark. Compare p. 197 with Kabiri. Compare with Ogilby (Japan, 177), where the god Canon (Canaan) is represented with seven heads on his breast, eight with himself, he having been substituted for Noah as the head of the race.] Captain Cook adds, however, "We had already learnt that these, like scalps among the Indians of North America, were trophies of war," and suggests that the canoe "may be a symbol of invasion." That I must leave to the reader to decide, but the heads might be "trophies of conquest," and at the same time memorial heads,—the memorial heads having necessarily been replaced many times since the custom was first instituted.[230]

This leads me to the final question, When was this custom instituted? Up to this I have not considered whether the custom was good or bad, demoniac or only corrupted; and as to the time of its institution I have merely assumed from the fact of its universality that it was primeval.

Before expressing my opinion, I must fortify myself with an extract from the Rev. W. Smith's very able work on the Pentateuch.[231]

> "Strange, too, though it may appear, there is much in the outward ceremonial of the Levitical worship that indicates an Egyptian type. The fact need startle no one. For it is derogatory neither to the holiness of the Almighty nor to the inspiration of his delegate, that Moses should have borrowed from others rites which were good in themselves, and which became idolatrous only then, when employed in the worship of false gods. The most of external forms are in themselves indifferent and receive their determinate value from the feeling that prompts them, and the object

to which they are directed: when given to God they are divine worship—when given to idols, they are idolatry. Nor is inspiration jeopardised because the material details may have come from a human source. Care and study and observation are not dispensed with in the mind that receives the divine communications; and Moses was instructed in all the wisdom and learning of the Egyptians for the very purpose of enabling him to use it to the best advantage ... as the Church consecrated to a higher purpose the temples and the rites and festivals found among the pagan populations at their conversion. We need not then be scandalised if we find the *ark of Jehovah* to be the counterpart of the shrine of Amun. The resemblance strikes us at once on a glance at the woodcut token from Lepsius' Denkmäler, Ab. iii., Bl. 109."

Let the reader refer to the engravings in Rev. W. Smith's Pentateuch, 291, 292. Dr Smith does not discuss the point further, only he says "In Egypt it is *the canopied boat* in which the Deity is steered on the heavenly ocean; in Israel it is the covered chest, the form best adapted for holding the stone tables of the law."

But if "the canopied boat" should have corresponded among the Egyptians to "the big canoe" among the Mandans, and the other similar memorials we have come upon, what more appropriate symbol could Moses have incorporated? Was not the ark of the covenant, in which the law was preserved in the widespread inundation of corruption, the counterpart of the ark in which mankind, in the persons of Noah and his family, were saved? and in carrying on and embodying the tradition, we may see a motive why there may have been an intentional alteration of the symbol—viz. in order to wean his people from the corruption into which the whole Egyptian ceremonial had sunk?[232] And why should it not have been so? Is there not a probability and fitness in the conjecture of some such commemorative sacrifices and memorials among mankind when they lived together before the dispersion in the times immediately following the Deluge?

APPENDIX TO CHAPTER XI.
THE PONGOL FESTIVAL.

"The Pongol Festival in Southern India," by Charles E. Govat. "Journal of the Royal Asiatic Society of Great Britain and Ireland," new series, vol. v., part i. (1870.)

"I had seen the Pongol, the touching domestic festival it is now my chief object to describe. It had proved by its simple pathos that the Hindus were akin to the noblest nations of the world, and that in their antiquity they were worthy of the honour that has come to them of being the best and the least altered representatives of the 'Juventus Mundi,' which all nations count to have been the golden age." He contrasts it with the worship in the great temple at Siringham near Trichinopoly, in which there "was ample justification for every epithet employed by Ward, Dubois, or Wilberforce." "Yet the Pongol declared with equal force in favour of domestic love and chastity, of simple thanksgiving and rural contentment.... There is much reason to suppose that the Pongol is one of the most complete and interesting of these remnants of primitive life. That it is primitive is shown by the fact that the old Vedic deities are alone worshipped. Indra is the presiding deity. Agni is the main object of worship. A further proof of this point is given by the efforts that have constantly been made by the Brahmans to corrupt the ritual, and introduce Pauranic deities. Krishna is always declared by the Brahmans to be the Pongol god, but the tradition itself bears witness that the feast is older than the god. The tale is that when the great wave of Krishna worship passed over the Peninsula, the people were so enamoured of him that they ceased to perform the Pongol rites to Indra. This made the latter deity so angry that he poured down a flood upon the earth. The affrighted people ran to Krishna, who seized the great mountain Govardhanas, wrenched it from its place, and held it aloft on the tip of his little finger, like some huge umbrella. The people then ran beneath with their flocks and were saved.... The occasion of the festival is also primitive, for the Pongol is another feast of ingathering, the centre of Hebrew festivals, as this is of those of Southern India.... The Pongol is remarkable, as will be seen, for the strange combination of pastoral, hunting, and agricultural life. There are 'harvest homes' in almost every nation, but I do not know of any other example of the combination. The great days of the feast are two—one of these devoted to the new crops, the other to the cattle alone ... while the feast winds up with a grand hunt, first of the cattle themselves and next of a hare." Compare ch. vii.; compare Patagonian.

"Long before the commencement of the feast an unwonted activity pervades native society. The Pongol is *the* social festival of the year, and must be celebrated with due honour, else an ineffaceable stain will rest on the family name. It is the Christmas and Whitsuntide of England made into one.... So soon as the *rains have finished*, and this may be expected by about the first week in December, the carpenter, the builder, and the artists are in full work repairing the houses.... The sides of the road in the bazaar are heaped with 'chatties' of all sizes and shapes. Presents are bought for children. Distant relatives have no fields of their own from which to get their rice, so a sack of the new grain from the ancestral acres goes off to each. To this is added a pot of ghee, a set of brass pots, or perhaps a jewel;

that the Pongol may not lack wherewith to make it joyful." Creditors and debtors are often brought then to a compromise, or the process is postponed "till after Pongol."

"All must be ready by the early part of January, when, according to the Hindu astrologers, the sun enters the tropic of Capricorn. The feast hangs upon this, and it will be seen that the most interesting event of the celebration must exactly coincide with the passage of the sun. The festival commences on the previous day, and lasts for seven days, of which the second marks the sun's passage, and is called Mahâ (or great) Pongol, ... the next day is Bhôgi Pongol, or Pongol of rejoicing, equally well known by the name of Indra, ... bonfires and torches are illuminated (compare Boulanger, lib. i. ch. ii.) The feast is now begun, and all turn from the fire, as it is extinguished by the rising sun, to the bath, with which every religious rite must commence. No image is used during the whole course of the celebration, except that of Ganesa.... Indra is represented on ordinary occasions as a white man sitting on an elephant. In his left hand is a bow (compare ch. xv., and in his right a thunderbolt, while his body is studded with a thousand eyes. [Query, a reference to the peacock? Compare ch. xv.] Agni has also his special image, that of a stout man, red and hairy as Esau, riding on a goat [compare Bacchus, p. 214]. Sûrya is also a red man, sitting on a water lily. He has four arms and three eyes. But none of these (deities) are known at Pongol any more than they were at the time when the hymns of the Rig Veda were composed.... The gifts are laid out on trays, —a vase of sugar, or perhaps an idol, peacock or elephant, round which will be grouped smaller works in sugar for the children.... One thing may not be forgotten, that is a lime [compare 'gourd,' p. 256]. This must be as large as money can buy, and then be carefully encased in gold leaf till it looks like one of the golden apples of antiquity. The next day is Mahâ (or great) Pongol. It is often called Sûrya Pongol. At noon the sun will cross the equator, and bring the culminating glory of the feast. So great a day must commence with appropriate ceremonial, and in this instance it is bathing. In country places the women run early in the morning to the nearest tank and plunge bodily in without undressing." [This is alluded to by Mr Gover as "an innovation so uncomfortable and possibly dangerous;" but no evidence is adduced of its being an innovation, and its being the custom of the "country parts" would incline us to the contrary belief.] The men also bathe very carefully, as if the occasion were very solemn. Reference is made to the Rig Veda, i. 23, 15–24 (Wilson, i. 57); but in these verses occur the words, "waters take away whatever sin has been found in me."

"Dripping wet, the women proceed, without changing their clothes, to prepare the feast, ... new chatties, or earthen vessels had been purchased for the occasion; one of them is now taken and is filled with rice, milk, sugar, dholghee or clarified butter, grain, and other substances, calculated to produce a tasty dish.... The ingathering must be celebrated with things that have just been garnered. Usually Hindoos will not eat new rice, as it is indigestible" (refer to Leviticus xxiii. 10–14). Another incident is that—"The head of the house approaches the image (of Ganesa), and performs pûja. Then follows a procession of the young married couples to propitiate their mothers-in-law.... So a present, the best the house can provide, is carefully put together on a tray. It may be fruit, or brass pots, or ghee, or whatever else may be thought most acceptable. Then a small procession is formed. In front go three or four men, beating on tom-toms and blowing pipes. Then follows the gift, held aloft. Over it, if the family be respectable, is held an umbrella, carried by a servant who walks behind the bearer of the gift.... The nearest relative steps forward and asks that the daughter and her husband may come to the 'boiling,' to fill up the family circle. Then follows the boiling of the pot; 'as the milk boils, so will the coming year be.' The Pongol is one long series of visits, entertainments, and social joys." (Comp. Mandan Festival, *supra*.)

"The third day of the feast is Mâttu Pongol, or the Pongol *of the cattle*. It commences with a general *wash*. They betake themselves to the nearest *sacred* tank, driving or dragging with them the whole bovine possessions of the village. They are then driven home, and adornment commences; the horns are carefully painted *red, blue, green, or yellow*,—if the owner be rich, gold leaf is employed,—heavy garlands of flowers placed on the horns. Meanwhile the women have prepared another new chatty, filling it with water, steeping within saffron, cotton seeds, and mangora leaves. The master of the ceremonial, usually the head of the house, comes for it, and places himself at the head of a procession of all the men—the women may not see the rite we now describe. In solemn silence they march round each animal four times, while the first man sprinkles the bitter water upon it and the ground as often as they pass the four cardinal points of the compass.... This done, the women and children are again admitted. The patient cattle are led out one by one to receive their final adornment.... Then, at a given signal, every rope is untied, every tom-tom, pipe, and guitar is banged or blown to the extreme of its endurance, and in an instant the herd, hitherto so patient, is careering down the street in an extremity of terror.... Any one may possess himself of whatever is carried by the cattle. No little skill and a vast amount of courage are shown by the 'timid' Hindoos in this dangerous and exciting pell-mell. The next day is Kanen Pongol, or Pongol of the calves.

"On the evening of this day we find the only token of corruption in the ceremonial." ... Then follows a dance, just as is described by Catlin as *closing* the Mandan ceremonial, in which very similar scenes occur.

Before adverting to the points of contrast between the Pongol and the Mandan and Dahoman ceremonies, I will give an extract from a book recently published, giving an account of a country hitherto unexplored — viz. Northern Patagonia. Traces I think will be recognised of the same primitive custom, though with evidences of corruption.

"Three Years Slavery among the Patagonians," by Guinnard (Bentley, 1871).[233]

"At certain periods of the year the Indians keep religious festivals. The first takes place in the summer, and is consecrated to Vita-ouènetrou (the god of goodness) for the purpose of thanking him for all his past favours, and of begging him to continue them in the future. It is generally the grand cacique who fixes the date and duration of the festival.... The preparations are made with all the religious pomp of which they are capable; the Indians grease their hair and paint their faces with greater care than usual.... At the commencement of the ceremony the women move their tents provisionally to the centre of the spot chosen by the cacique. The men do not arrive until these preparations are finished, they ride three times round the place at full gallop, shouting their war cry and shaking their lances. Then, their rides ended, they range themselves in single file, and tilt their lances with such perfect regularity as to make it a striking sight. The women afterwards take the places of their husbands" (compare Catlin, sup., p. 260), "who, after dismounting and tying up their horses, form a second rank behind them."

"The dance then commences without change of place, except from right to left. The women sing in a plaintive tone [laughter being expressly forbidden during the whole continuance of the ceremonies], accompanying themselves by striking a wooden drum." Compare Catlin, sup., 257. It is also said (Guinnard, p. 198), "The drum is composed of a sort of wooden bowl, more or less large, over which a wild-cat skin is stretched, or a piece of the paunch of a horse. This instrument ... is much used by them, especially in their religious festivals and character dances." The drum is "decorated with colours and designs similar to those on their faces. The men pirouette, limping upon the opposite leg to that of the women." Compare Catlin, 254, 260. "At a signal given by the cacique presiding over the festival, cries of alarm are raised, the men spring into their saddles, abruptly interrupting the dance to take part in a fantastic cavalcade round the site of the festival, all waving their weapons, and raising the sinister cry they utter in their pillages."

"In the intervals of these exciting diversions everybody goes visiting in the hope of tasting a little rotted milk kept in a horse-hide." Compare Pongol Festival.

"At a very early hour on the fourth day, to close the ceremony, a young *horse*, an *ox*, and two sheep, given by the richest men amongst them, are sacrificed to their god. The head turned towards the east, and the heart still palpitating is hung upon a lance and inclined towards the rising sun."

"The second festival takes place in the autumn; it is celebrated in honour of Houacouvou (*director of* the evil spirits). The object of it is to conjure him to preserve them from all enchantment. As in the first festival, the Indians dress themselves in their best, and assemble by tribes only, headed by their cacique. An assemblage of *all the cattle* takes place *en masse*. The men form a double circle around, galloping unceasingly in opposite directions, so that none of these unruly animals may escape. They invoke Houacouvou aloud, throwing down, drop by drop, fermented *milk* out of *bull's horns*, handed to them *by their wives*, while they are riding round the cattle. After repeating this ceremony three or *four* times, they sprinkle the horses and oxen with whatever remains of the milk, with the view, they say, of preserving them from all maladies; this done, each man *separates his own cattle*, and *drives it to some distance,* then returns for the purpose of assembling round the cacique, who, in a long and fervid address, advises them never to forget Houacouvou in their prayers, and to lose no time in preparing themselves to please him, by carrying desolation amongst the Christians, and increasing the number of their own flocks and herds."

This festival, therefore, in its original conception would not appear to be a worship of the evil spirit, but of him who curbs him; the same idea of the subordination of the evil spirit will be seen in Catlin's account of the Mandans.

There is nothing certainly in this account which directly connects these Patagonian ceremonies with the diluvian commemorations, unless, perhaps, the sacred drum; but there is much in common with the Pongol and the Mandan which we have seen to have been commemorative.

The prominence of sun worship will not have escaped observation; but this discovery cannot militate against my position, for I have already shown that such admixture was probable, and also indicated how it was likely to have come about. Any hostile argument which would seek to deprive those ceremonies of their significance must be directed to the extrusion of the diluvian symbols.

Further trace of these diluvian ceremonies might be traced in the Buddhist systems; but it would open out too large a question for discussion here.

CHAPTER XII
SIR JOHN LUBBOCK ON TRADITION

De Maistre's View.[234]

"We have little knowledge of the times which preceded the Deluge.... A single consideration interests us, and it must never be lost sight of, and that is, that chastisements are ever proportioned to crimes, and crimes always proportioned to the knowledge of the criminal; in such sort that the Deluge supposes unheard-of crimes, and that these crimes suppose a knowledge infinitely transcending that which we possess.... This knowledge, freed from the evil which had rendered it so noxious, survived in the first family the destruction of the human race. We are blinded as to the nature and advance of science by a gross sophism which has fascinated every eye; it is to judge of times when men saw effects in their causes by those in which men painfully ascend from effects to causes, in which they are only concerned with effects, in which they say it is useless to occupy themselves with causes, and in which they do not know what constitutes a cause. They never cease repeating—'Think of the time that has been required to know such and such a thing.' What inconceivable blindness! A moment only was required. If man would know the cause of a single phenomenon of nature, he would probably comprehend all the rest. We are unwilling to see that truths, the most difficult to discover, are very easy to understand.... 'These things,' as Plato says, 'are perfectly and easily learned if any one teaches them, ει διδάσκοι τις; but,' he adds, 'no one will teach them us, unless, indeed, God shows him the road, ἀλλ' οὐδ ἄν διδαξειεν ει μὴ Θεος υφηγοῖτο.' 'I doubt not,' said Hippocrates, 'that the arts were in the first instance favours (θεων χαριτας) granted to men by the gods.'... Listen to sage antiquity in its account of the first men: it will tell you that they were marvellous men, and that beings of a superior order deigned to favour them with the most precious communications. On this point there is no disagreement, ... reason, revelation, all human tradition make up a demonstration which the mouth only can contradict. Not only, then, did mankind commence with science, but with a science different from ours, and superior to ours.... No one knows to what epoch remounts, I do not say the early commencements of society, but the great institutions, the profound knowledge, and the most magnificent monuments of human industry and human power.... Asia, having been the theatre of the greatest marvels, it is not astonishing that its people should have preserved a leaning to the marvellous stronger than what is natural to man in general, and than each one recognises in himself individually. Hence it comes that they have always shown so little taste and talent for our science of conclusions. One would say rather that they recalled something of primitive science and of the era of intuition. Would the enchained eagle ask for a balloon to raise himself into the air? No, he would demand only that his fetters should be broken. And who knows if these people are not destined yet to contemplate sights which will be refused to the cavilling genius of Europe? However this may be, observe, I pray you, that it is impossible to think of modern art without seeing it constantly environed with all the contrivances of the intellect and all the methods of art.... On the contrary. So far as it is possible to discover the science of primitive times at such an enormous distance, we see it always free and isolated, flying rather than marching, and presenting in all its characteristics something of the ærial and supernatural. [235]... But then comes the corollary.... If all men descend from the three couples who repeopled the universe, and if the human race commenced with knowledge, the savage cannot be more, as I have said to you, than a branch detached from the social tree.... Now, what matter does it make at what epoch such and such a branch was separated from the tree? It suffices that it is detached: no doubt as to its degradation; and I venture to say no doubt as to the cause of degradation, which can only have been some crime. A chief of a nation having altered the principle of morality in his household by one of those prevarications which, so far as we can judge, are no longer possible in the actual state of things, because happily our knowledge is no longer such as to allow us to become culpable in this degree; this chief of a nation, I say, transmits the curse to his posterity; and every constant force being accelerating in its nature, this degradation, weighing incessantly upon his descendants, has ended in making them what we call savages. Two causes extremely different have thrown a deceptive cloud over the lamentable state of savages: the one of ancient date, the other belonging to our century.... One cannot for an instant regard the savage without reading the curse written, I do not say only in his soul, but even in the exterior form of his body. He is an infant, robust, yet deformed and ferocious, in whom the flame of intelligence no longer throws more than a lurid and intermittent glare.... I cannot abandon this subject without suggesting an important observation: The barbarian who is intermediate between the civilised man and the savage, has been and may be again civilised by some sort of religion; but the savage, properly so called, has never been so except by Christianity. It is a prodigy of the first order, a species of redemption, exclusively reserved to the true priesthood. [236]... For the rest, we must not confound the savage with the barbarian.

"No language could possibly have been invented, either by a single man, who could not have extorted obedience, or by many who would not have made themselves understood to each other.... But I would wish, before concluding this subject, to recommend to your notice an observation which has always struck me. Whence comes it that in the primitive language of every ancient people, we find words which necessarily suppose a knowledge foreign to these people? Whence, for instance, have the Greeks, three thousand years ago at least, found the epithet 'physizoos' (giving or possessing life), which Homer sometimes gives to the earth?.... Where have they taken the still more singular epithet of 'philomate' (liking or thirsting for blood), given to this same earth in a tragedy? (Euripides, Phœn. v. 179). Æschylus had alluded before 'to the earth drinking the blood of the two rival brothers, the one slain by the other.'[237] Humboldt ('Monum. des Peuples Indigènes de l'Amerique,' Paris, 1816) has said: 'Many idioms which at present belong only to barbarous nations seem to be the remains of rich and flexible languages, which indicate a high culture.... But tell me, I pray you, how it entered the heads of the ancient

Latins, at a time when they were only acquainted with the arts of war and of tillage, to express by the same word the idea of prayer and of punishment? Who taught them to call fever the "purifier," or the "expiator"?'[238] Would not one say that there was here a judgment, a veritable knowledge of the cause, by virtue of which the people affirmed the name so justly? But do you believe that these sorts of judgments could possibly have belonged to a time when they scarcely knew how to write, when the Dictator dug his garden, and in which they composed verses which Varro and Cicero no longer understood?... The Greeks had preserved some obscure traditions in this regard—[Mr Gladstone has shown them to be neither few nor obscure],—and who knows if Homer does not attest the same truth, perhaps without knowing it, when he speaks of certain men and certain things 'which the gods called after one manner, and men after another?'"—Count Joseph de Maistre, "Soirées de St Petersbourg," i. Deux: Entretien.[239]

Against this view of De Maistre, which I consider to be indirectly sustained by the testimony of all antiquity, stands the theory of Sir John Lubbock. There is the constant historical tradition and testimony of the human race on one side, and there is the history of "Pre-historic Times" on the other. Nevertheless, I venture to say, that the author of "Pre-historic Times" only takes up with man at the point where De Maistre leaves him.

Of course I do not seek to detach Sir John Lubbock from the evidence he has collected; neither do I forget that he is the representative of an opinion and a school; at any rate, that there is an opinion of which he is the most conspicuous exponent.

So far as my limited acquaintance with the special subjects with which Sir John Lubbock deals extends (and with these I am only indirectly concerned), he appears perfectly straightforward and candid; and, moreover, I must acknowledge my obligations to him, for he has written with remarkable breadth and ability; and it is with the aid of the interesting matter which he has accumulated,[240] expressly in disparagement of tradition, that I venture to undertake to reinstate it in honour.

Neither do I wish to ignore that Sir John Lubbock's main argument is the geological argument derived from the discovery of the fossils and implements in the drift. But on this point I beg to be allowed to say a word in protest.

As a geologist Sir John Lubbock may be entitled to rely mainly upon the geological evidence of a palæolithic age;[241] but as an ethnologist dealing with history and writing on the subject of tradition, his argument, however incontrovertible he may deem it, sinks to the second rank; and secondary I shall take the liberty of considering it. On the same grounds, though I think with more reason, that Sir J. Lubbock seeks to be relieved from "the embarrassing interference of tradition" ("Pre-historic Times," p. 336), I protest, when tradition is the subject-matter of the discussion, against a geological argument being brought to take the ground from under our feet!

In the first place, I beg to urge that if Sir J. Lubbuck's argument be well founded, Professor Rawlinson's reconstruction of Assyrian history cannot be true. Now I assume that the one order of facts is as well established as the other.

If Professor Rawlinson takes back Assyrian history and corroborates history and tradition by the evidence of recent excavations to B.C. 2234, identifies the Erech of Scripture with the Huruk of the cuneiform tablets and the modern Urka; similarly identifies the other three cities of Nimrod; and, finally, identifies Nimrod himself as Bil-Nipru; and if, further, bronze implements are found (Rawlinson, i. 101, 123, 211), along with flint doubtless (but this was common throughout the bronze age, as Sir John himself admits), at an early period;—and bronze, though comparatively rare, yet exists among the very early Assyrian remains—there seems no good reason to suppose that the knowledge of metals, which we know (Gen. iv. 22) to have existed before the Deluge, and which the construction of the ark presupposes, was ever lost.

A stone age, exclusive of metals, common to the whole world and to all mankind, is therefore an untenable hypothesis according to the testimony of history. If it existed anywhere it must have been only partially, locally, and contemporaneously with this traditional knowledge of metals, which seems to be historically proved.[242] I may at least be permitted to believe in the accuracy of Professor Rawlinson's conclusions, and to regard them as the verdict of history: and if the historical arguments so pronounce, why should the geological or palæontological argument override it? Is not history supreme on its own ground—and if Scripture is always found in perfect consistency with history, is it not as much as in strictness we should have a right to expect? "Tradidit mundum disputationi eorum" (Eccles. iii. 11).

Now, secondly, as it happens that bronze is only a combination of copper and tin in certain proportions, and as neither existed on the spot (in the Mesopotamian valley), it is a curious question how they could have hit upon the discovery through actual experiment. Tin, for instance, is only found in Cornwall, Banca (between Sumatra and Borneo), Spain, Saxony, and Siberia. Now, how did it enter the heads of even these wise Chaldæans to go to these distant countries in search of this metal unless they knew beforehand through tradition, that if procured along with copper it would produce the useful amalgam they sought? True, it might have been brought to them through commerce, but in that case there must have been some other race more advanced in civilisation than themselves. If the Phœnicians, much the same argument will recur. If some race in the countries where tin was procured, where is it now? If it exists it must be represented by some race at present or historically known to have been in a state of barbarism. This, however, at this stage of the argument, would be too precipitate an admission of degeneracy!

Now, in a certain modified sense, I should be quite prepared to admit a stone age. Nothing more probable than that in the dispersion certain families would have taken only what came readiest to hand. Those who made long marches, and came to countries where minerals were scarce, would have been in the way of losing the knowledge of metals altogether, except in so far as they preserved the tradition of them; and this would much depend upon how far they preserved other traditions.[243] Some instance should be given us—and as there are savages who are still using nothing but flint, there is still the chance—of some set of savages who have spontaneously hit upon the plan of fusing different metals, or even of smelting metals which were under their eye? Certainly not our supposed flint ancestors, who, as Professor Nillson and Sir J. Lubbock agree, must have got their knowledge of bronze from Asia: Sir J. Lubbock inclining to an Indo-European, Professor Nillson to a Phœnician "origin of the bronze age civilisation." ("Pre-historic Times," p. 49.) All this perfectly coincides with the view I have indicated, that the contrast arose through the divergence of the lines of the dispersion, leading the tribes to varied fortunes, some losing and others retaining the tradition; and those who retained it eventually communicating it to those who had lapsed. But then there are those unfortunate Bashkirs, who, Professor Nillson tells us, are still in their stone age, and who have remained Bashkirs since Herodotus described them as such 2300 years ago. As they have resisted the contact of civilisation so long, one can only watch with careful curiosity the transitionary process by which they will pass by internal development from their stone to their bronze age.[244]

I must now revert to what I at present wish to limit the discussion, viz. Sir J. Lubbock's views on the subject of tradition.

Sir John says that history can throw no light upon the question of the stone and bronze age, "because the use of metals has in all cases preceded that of writing." I should like to know whether Sir John is prepared to adhere to this "dictum" under all circumstances, inasmuch as, if he does, he must allow me to trace the use of metals in Assyria even beyond the date at which Professor Rawlinson seems actually to have found evidence of their use; for (pp. 80, 198) "in the ruins of Warka, the ancient Huruk or Erech" (the city of Nimrod) we find inscriptions on bricks of the date of the reign of Urukh or Orchamus, who, according to classical tradition, was the seventh in succession from Bel or Nimrod; which tradition, says Rawlinson (p. 189), "accords very curiously with the information derived from the inscriptions." There is nothing to indicate that the bricks here discovered were the first bricks ever inscribed; on the contrary, wherever we find bricks and metals there will be a prima facie presumption as to their previous use. [245] Only upon Sir John Lubbock's "dictum," finding evidence of writing at this date, we must necessarily conclude that the use of metals preceded it. This would bring us well up the seven reigns, and into close contact with the time of Nimrod.

> "Nor," says Sir J. Lubbock, "will tradition supply the place of history. At best it is untrustworthy and shortlived. Thus in 1770 the New Zealanders had no recollection of Tasman's visit. Yet this took place in 1643, less than one hundred and thirty years before, and must have been to them an event of the greatest possible importance and interest.... I do not mean to say that tradition would never preserve for a long period the memory of any remarkable event. The above-mentioned facts (De Soto's expedition is also referred to) prove only that it will not always do so; but it is unnecessary for us to discuss this question, as there is in Europe no tradition of the Stone Age, and when arrow-heads are found the ignorant peasantry refer them to the elves or fairies; stone axes are regarded as thunderbolts, and are used not only in Europe but also in various other parts of the world for magical purposes".

> "Relieved" then "from the embarrassing interference of tradition, the archæologist can only follow the methods which have been so successfully pursued in geology"[246]

This is partly a limitation of the question to oral tradition, and partly an anticipated denial of what I shall now venture to assert, namely, that we can only look for the savages' traditions of things known to them before they were savages, religious impressions which have not been effaced from their minds, legends connected with their race, facts which have determined their destiny. The very characteristic of the savage is that he lives only for the present; that he has little memory for the past, and no forecast for the future; that his mind is stricken with a hopeless sterility and fixedness, so that he only seems to remember things that are bred in the bone, and the tradition of which he cannot divest himself.[247]

And so the ignorant peasantry when these flints were first dug up, although they had "no tradition," rushed instinctively upon these hatchets and considered them magical, apparently on no better grounds than that they had belonged to a former race of men whom they associated with elves and fairies. Was not this their way of saying with Cicero, "Antiquitas proxime accedit ad deos."[248]

And so far from tradition supplying us with no clue to solve the problem of the stone age, does it not in this way suggest a very decided though an antagonistic view to that of Sir John Lubbock. The superstitious regard of the peasantry for these newly found relics—which I presume came under Sir John's own observation when exploring the northern coast-finds—is really very curious, because it shows that their ideas and feelings in these matters were, after the lapse of at any rate a thousand years, identical with those of their ancestors. In evidence of which I adduce the following passage from Professor Nillson, having reference to the legend of the "guse arrows" or "Orvar Odd's saga":—

> "This ancient romance shows very clearly that at the time when it was composed, neither arrows, nor other weapons of stone were in common use as weapons, but *that even then* the opinion was *generally current* that these stone weapons, which owed their existence to the dwarf race skilled in sorcery, were endowed with a magic power against witches and witchcraft which no other weapons possessed."— Professor Nillson, "Stone Age,".

But this suggests the further reflection, whether this stone age among certain tribes was not as much in rejection as in ignorance of metals. Professor Nillson shows that flint was used for *sacred* sacrificial purposes by the Jews, Egyptians, Phœnicians, and Latins, long after they were acquainted with weapons of metal. Among these the traditional idea about flint, whatever it was, was kept in due subordination; but among tribes that had sunk into savagery it is conceivable that it may have become a superstition, and dominated.

I am not sure that we do not underrate the capacity for tradition among savages where it has once taken hold; still, if it had been a question of mere savages, at the first glance I should have been disposed to agree with Sir John Lubbock. But let us take the case of Tasman, which Sir John puts forward as a sort of crucial case, and which may be accepted as such, seeing that the New Zealanders may fairly claim to be regarded as "barbarians."[249]

In the first place, I find the following in a note to "Cook's Voyages" (Smith, 1846):—"Mr Polack, in his 'Narrative of Travels and Adventures during a residence in New Zealand between the years 1831–37,' collected all the particulars relating to Cook's brush with the natives, 1769, on the spot."

Next, let us see what Cook says on the subject of Tasman ("Cook's Voyages," i. 164)—

> "But the Indians still continued *near the ship*, rowing round many times [hardly the most favourable conditions under which to recover a tradition], conversing with Tupia [the Otaheitan interpreter] chiefly concerning the traditions they had among them with respect to the antiquities of their country. To this subject they were led by the inquiries which Tupia had been directed to make, whether they had ever seen such a vessel as ours, or had ever heard that any such had been on their coast. These inquiries were all answered in the negative, *so that* tradition has preserved among them no memorial of Tasman, though by an observation made this day we find we are *only fifteen* miles south of Murderers' Bay!"

Evidently the shrewd and gallant investigator himself was not satisfied with the cross-examination, for we find at p. 170—

> "When we were under sail one old man, Topaa [a native], came on board to take leave of us; and as we were still desirous of making further inquiries whether any memory of Tasman had been preserved among their people, Tupia was directed to ask him whether he had ever heard that such a vessel as ours had before visited the country. To this he replied in the negative; but said that *his ancestors had told him* there had once come to this place a *small* vessel from a distant country called Ulimaroa, in which were *four* men, who upon coming on shore were *all killed*. Upon being asked where this distant land lay he pointed to the northward."

But what does Tasman himself say?—

> "On the 17th December these savages began to grow a little bolder and more familiar, insomuch that at last they ventured on board the Heemskirk, in order to trade with those in the vessel. As soon as I perceived it, being apprehensive that

they might attempt to surprise that ship, I sent my shallop, with seven men, to put the people in the Heemskirk on their guard, and to direct them not to place any confidence in these people. My seven men, being without arms, were attacked by these savages, who killed three of the seven, and forced the other four to swim for their lives; which occasioned my giving that place the name of the Bay of Murderers.[250] Our ship's company would undoubtedly have taken a severe revenge if the rough weather had not prevented them." — Tasman's Voyage of Discovery, Pinkerton, xi.

Now, I submit that this old man Topaa's recollection of the tradition of an event which occurred one hundred and thirty years before his time, was much more perfect than Captain Cook's, Sir Joseph Banks', Dr Solander's, and Sir J. Lubbock's recollection of the same event from geographical records.

Emboldened by this instance of the fallibility of scientific men, I now proceed to question the truth of the two following propositions of Sir J. Lubbock, after which I shall ask to be allowed to enunciate a proposition of my own.

First, Sir J. Lubbock says: "It has been asserted over and over again that there is no race of man so degraded as to be entirely without a religion — without some idea of the Deity. So far from this being true, the very reverse is the case"[251]

Second, "It is a common opinion that savages are, as a general rule, only the miserable remnants of nations once more civilised; but although there are some well-established cases of national decay, there is no scientific evidence which would justify us in asserting that this is generally the case".

In opposition to the first proposition, I maintain that there is no race of men so degraded as to be without some vestige of religion.

And in opposition to the second, I assert that if they have a vestige of religion, and nothing else, they have still that which will convict them of degeneracy.

First, To say that a savage has no idea of the Deity, is to say merely that he is a savage; and it appears to me that this extinction of all knowledge of the Deity among a people, precisely marks the point where the barbarian lapses into the savage.

Taking the range of the authorities quoted by Sir J. Lubbock,[252] I find a great concurrence of testimony to the fact that there is some vestige of religion. One only—whose authority on any other point incidental to African travel I should regard as of the highest value—Captain Richard Burton, asserts without qualification, and in language sufficiently explicit, that "some of the tribes of the lake district of Central Africa admit neither God, nor angel, nor devil." Others assert the same negatively—they did not come upon any signs of religion, any external observances, any trace of ceremonial worship. For instance, it is said that the Tasmanians had no word for a Creator (p. 468, Lubbock), which need not excite surprise, as it is also said of them that they were incapable of forming any abstract ideas at all (p. 355, Lubbock). Again, in many of those cases where it is more or less roundly asserted that there is no vestige of religion, we find it plainly intimated that there is a belief in the devil, e.g. Lubbock.

> "The Tonpinambas of Brazil had *no religion*, though if the name is applied 'à des notions fantastiques d'êtres surnaturals et puissans on ne sauroit nier qu'ils n'eussent une croyance religieuse et *même une sorte* de culte exterieur.'" — Freycinet, i. 153.

Now, although the devil may, and in many instances no doubt has,[253] made a special revelation of himself to his votaries, the ordinary channel of information concerning him is through tradition, and through the tradition of the fall of man.

But I ask further of those who dispute this, If savages are found with this fear of the supernatural world, after they have lost the idea of God, how do they get it? If not from tradition, then from reflection? But savages do not reason (Lubbock, p. 465). Moreover, Sir J. Lubbock says, what really brings us very nearly to agreement, "How, for instance, can a people who are unable to count their own fingers, possibly raise their minds so far as to admit even the rudiments of a religion?" This is said with reference to a previous allegation, "That those who assert that even the lowest savages believe in a Deity, affirm that which is entirely contrary to the evidence". But there is a great concurrence of evidence that "even the lowest savages" believe in the devil. Belief in the devil involves a realisation more or less obscure of the fallen angel, of the Spirit of Evil—and this for the savage who "cannot count his fingers" is as great an intellectual effort as would be, merely considered as an intellectual effort, a belief in the Deity. On any theory of growth or development how could he ("the lowest savage") have got the idea?

Several writers who are quoted, whilst they deny the existence of any notion of religion among a particular people, mention facts which are incompatible with that statement. I may also say, parenthetically, that to detect or elicit the sentiment of religion in others, one must have something of the sentiment in ourselves; *e.g.* there is the instance of Kolben (Lubbock, p. 469), "who, *in spite* of the assertions of the natives themselves, *felt quite sure* that certain dances *must be* of a religious character, let the Hottentots say what they will." Now I must say there is great *à priori* probability in the truth of Kolben's conviction, although he was probably led to it merely by the insight of his own mind. Let it be taken in connection with the following evidence in Washington Irving's "Life of Columbus," iii. 122–124:—

> "The *dances* to which the natives seemed so immoderately addicted, and which had been *at first* considered by the Spaniards mere idle pastimes, were *found* to be often *ceremonials of a serious and mystic character.*" Again— "Peter Martyn observes that they performed these dances to the chant of certain metres and ballads *handed down from* generation to generation, in which were rehearsed the deeds of their ancestors. Some of these ballads were of a *sacred* character, containing their *traditional* notions of theology, and the superstitions and fables which comprised their religious creeds."

Pritchard, "Researches into Phys. Hist. of Man" (i. p. 205), quoting Oldendorp, and speaking of the African negroes, says:—"At the annual harvest feast, which *nearly all* the nations of Guinea solemnise, thank-offerings are brought to the Deity. These festivals are days of rejoicing, which the negroes pass with feasting and dancing." *Vide* also "Hist. of Indian Tribes of North America, 120 portraits from the Ind. Gal. in Depart. of War at Washington, by T. M'Kenney (late Ind. Dep. Wash.) and J. Hall of Cincinnati" (Philadelphia, 1837).

> "Dancing is among the most prominent of the aboriginal *ceremonies*; there is no tribe in which it is not practised. The Indians have their *war* dance and their *peace* dance, their dance of *mourning for the dead*, their *begging* dance, their pipe dance, their green-corn dance, and their Wabana (an offering to the devil). Each of these is distinguished by some peculiarity ... though to a stranger they appear much alike, except the last.... It is a ceremony and not a recreation, and is conducted with a seriousness belonging to an important public duty."

(Lubbock) it is said, "Admiral Fitzroy never witnessed or heard of any act of a decidedly religious character among the Fuegians." Still, as Sir John admits, "some of the natives suppose that there is a great black man in the woods who knows everything, and cannot be escaped." If this is not the devil, it looks very like him. Again, Mr Mathews says, speaking of the Fuegians, "he sometimes heard a great howling or lamentation about *sunrise* in the morning; and upon asking Jemmy Button what occasioned the outcry, he could obtain no satisfactory answer; the boy only saying, 'people very sad, cry very much.'" Upon which Sir John remarks, "This appears so natural and sufficient an explanation, that why the outcry should be 'supposed to be devotional' I must confess myself unable to see".

Now, if this was not their traditional notion and mode of prayer, degraded according to the measure of their degeneracy, the degeneracy is at least proved in another way, for, being still reasonable beings, they had, according to the account, congregated together to send up a lamentation, which, if it was not prayer, could be likened only to the moonlight howling of wolves. This mode of prayer resembles what Father Loyer and the missionary Oldendorp (Pritchard, i. 197) tells us of the negroes. Father Loyer "declares that they have a belief in a universally powerful Being, and to him they address prayers. Every morning after they rise they go to the river side to wash, and throwing a handful of water on their head, or pouring sand with it to express their humility, they join their hands and then open them, whisper softly the word 'exsuvais.'" Oldendorp says: "The negroes profess their dependence on the Deity, ... they pray at the rising and setting of the sun,[254] on eating and drinking, and when they go to war." Compare also Helps' "Spanish Conquest in America," i. 285:—

> "The worship of the Peruvians was not the mere worship of the sun alone as of the most beautiful and powerful thing which they beheld; but they had also a worship of a far more elevated and refined nature, addressed to Pachacamac, the soul of the universe, whom they hardly dared to name; and when they were obliged to name this Being, they did so inclining the head and the whole body, now lifting up the eyes to heaven, now lowering them to the ground, and giving kisses in the air. To Pachacamac they made no temple and offered no sacrifices, but they adored him in their hearts."[255]

Sir John somewhat too roundly asserts that "Dr Hooker tells us that the Lepchas of Northern India have *no religion*."

Turning to Dr Hooker's "Himalayan Journal," I find (i. 135), "The Lepchas profess no religion, though acknowledging the existence of good and bad spirits.... Both Lepchas and Limboos had, before the introduction of Lama Boodhism from Tibet, many features in common with the natives of Arracan, especially in their creed, sacrifices, faith in omens, worship of many spirits, absence of idols, and of the doctrine of metempsychosis" (p. 140). We have already seen (supra, p. 224) that they had a very distinct tradition of the Deluge; indeed there is much in the account of them which reminds us of the primitive monotheism.

So, too, Sir John asserts, "Once more Dr Hooker states that the Khasias, an Indian tribe, *had no religion.* Col. Yule, on the contrary, says that they have, but he admits that breaking hens' eggs is the principal part of their religious practice."

It is true that Dr Hooker says (ii. 276), "The Khasias are superstitious, but have no religion;" he adds, however, "like the Lepchas, they believe in a Supreme Being, and in deities of the grove, cave, and stream." It seems, however, that the only outward manifestation of their religion is in "breaking hens' eggs"! What can be more ludicrous! yet here, too, would seem to be a vestige of primitive tradition. We know (vide Wilkinson, "Ancient Egyptians," second series) how primitive truth was concealed under material symbols. Gainet (i. 127) also says, "Even upon the hypothesis that these fragments of the Egyptian cosmogony were lost, one of the hieroglyphics which this people has left us would suffice to convince us of their belief in a Creator. It is the image of the god Kneph, whom they represent with an egg in his mouth; this egg being the natural image of the world taking its birth from this divinity." Again, p. 115, "In the mysteries of Bacchus[256] the dogma of the Creation was proposed under the emblem of that celebrated egg, of which the poets have so often spoken, which contained the germ of all things." "The egg," says Plutarch, "is consecrated to the sacred ceremonies of Bacchus, as a representation of the Author of nature who produces and comprehends all things in himself." There is a passage in Athenagoras to the same effect.

Superstitions were also connected with cocks and hens in Khasia. Whether these again were connected with the symbolical representation of the egg can only be conjectured. It may possibly be that the representation had a common origin with the cock of Apollo and the cock of Æsculapius, if, indeed, these were not also originally derived from the same primal conception. This would be only to renew the old classical dispute as to whether the hen proceeded from the egg, or the egg from the hen, which I take to be only the form in which the great question of the First Cause was debated by the Gentile world after their ideas of a Creator had become indistinct, and with reference to this ancient symbol. However that may be, I wish to point out that this ceremonial use of the cock may be traced in Europe, Asia, and Africa: e.g. Asia—"The Lepchas scatter eggs and pebbles over the graves of their friends.... Among the Limboos, the priests of a higher order than the Lepcha, Bijoras officiate at marriages, when a cock is put into the bride-groom's hands, and a hen into those of the bride. The Phedangbo then cuts off the birds' heads, when the blood is caught in a plantain leaf, and runs into pools, from which omens are drawn" (Dr Hooker, "Himalayan Journal," i. 238). Africa—vide Pritchard, "Phys. Hist. of Man," i. 203, 204, 208: "Even the dead are not buried without sacrifices. A white hen is slain by the priest before the corpse comes to the grave, and the bier whereon the body lies is sprinkled with its blood. This custom was introduced by the nation of Kagraut." Europe—If any one will turn to the Illustrated London News of Nov. 14, 1868, he will find an account and illustration of a local ceremony peculiar to the village of Gorbio in the Maritime Alps, in which the priest, on a particular day in the year, is solemnly presented with four cocks hung upon a halberd—together with an apple by the bachelors and spinsters of the village—from which it would seem to have had originally some connection, as we have seen above, with a marriage ceremony. Wilson ("Archæologia") remarks that the custom of "Easter, or, in the north, Paste eggs (Pasch), was very prevalent in the north."[257]

It strikes me that it would be difficult to assign a Christian origin for the custom. It must then have been a custom which the Church diverted or sanctioned in giving it an innocent or Christian application; in which case, in so far as it is pagan, it may possibly be traced to a common origin with the practices in Khasia among the Lepchas.

It would extend the inquiry too far to follow Sir J. Lubbock through all the cases adduced by him. I will conclude, therefore, with his account of the Andaman islander—who, with the Australians, Esquimaux, and Fuegians, dispute the point of being considered the lowest of mankind. It is said of the Andamans, "that they have no idea of a Supreme Being, no religion, or any belief in a future state of existence". It is, however, casually mentioned that, "after death, the corpse is buried in a sitting posture." Now this mode of burial is common to them with Esquimaux, the Australians, the Maories, and the natives of the Feegee Islands, among whom we seem to get a clue to this strange mode of burial; "the fact is, they (the Feegee islanders) not only believe in a future state, but are persuaded that as they leave this life, so will they rise again." Sir J. Lubbock, in his "Introduction to Prof. Nillson" (xxxiii.), says that this was the common mode of burial in the Stone Age; and Prescott ("Hist. of Mexico," ii. 485) says, "Who can doubt the existence of an affinity, or at least an intercourse, between tribes, who had the same strange habit of burying the dead in a sitting position, as was practised to some extent by most if not all of the aborigines from Canada to Patagonia?"[258] But not only may it be presumed that they had an affinity and intercourse, but a common religious idea. It may be doubted then whether even the naked Andaman is so entirely destitute of all religious impressions as he is supposed to be.

I have already urged that if any vestiges of religion remain they must be considered as evidence of tradition and proof of degeneracy. I think the following reflection will tend to clench this argument.

Although it is obscure and disputed to what extent certain savages do retain glimmerings of religion, it is certain and admitted that some savages have religion and a religious ceremonial. Now, as Sir J. Lubbock says, "How, for instance, can a people who are unable to count upon their fingers possibly raise their minds so far as to admit even the rudiments of religion." It is clear, then, that the lowest grade of mankind did not invent it, how then did the higher grade get it, "assuming always the unity of the human race"?

Finally, if man commenced with the knowledge of the devil, how did they proceed on to the idea of God? "The first idea of a God is almost always as an evil spirit" (Lubbock, p. 468). How then did they advance to the knowledge of the God of purity and love, or even of "the Great Spirit" of the Indians?[259]

Let us at least know whether it is supposed that this was the order of knowledge ordained by Divine Providence, or whether it is believed that man in this manner developed the idea of God out of his own consciousness, his primitive, or perhaps innate, idea being, the conception of evil and of the evil spirit.[260] Sir John says, "There are no just grounds for expecting man to be ever endued with a sixth sense." But why not? If by his own mental vigour he can out of the primitive idea of evil generate the idea of good— what may we not expect?

Yet, if any one will compare the evidence which Sir John has collected, he will come, I think, to the conclusion, that the invention and adaptability of the savage is very slight indeed. He will find that the inhabitants of Botany Bay had fish-hooks, but no nets; those of Western Australia, nets but not hooks; that those who had the throwing-stick and boomerang, were ignorant both of slings and bows and arrows; that those who had retained the knowledge of the bow did not pass on to the use of the bola; that the northern tribes visited by Kane were skilful in the capture of birds with nets, yet were entirely ignorant of fishing (452); that the nearest approach to the South American bola is among the Esquimaux (450); that the throwing-stick is common only to the widely distant Esquimaux, Australians, and some of the Brazilian tribes (*id.*); that the "sumpitan" or blowpipe of the Malays occurs only in the valley of the Amazons. Does not this point to a traditional knowledge of these things? Nevertheless, this mass of evidence seems to have produced the very opposite conviction with Sir J. Lubbock.

"On the whole, then, from a review of all these and other similar facts which *might have been* mentioned, it seems to me most probable that many of the simpler weapons, implements, &c., have been invented independently by various savage tribes, although there are no doubt also cases in which they have been borrowed by one tribe from another". Instances in which they have been borrowed from each other are not infrequent, but then neither are they inconsistent with the theory of tradition; but the instances of invention *are limited to one.* (See for instance p. 394.) At p. 394 we find—"Although they (the Esquimaux) had no knowledge of pottery, Captain Cook saw at Unalashka vessels "of flat stone, with sides of clay, not unlike a standing pye." We here obtain an idea of the manner in which the knowledge of pottery *may have been* developed. After using clay to raise the sides of their stone vessels, it *would* naturally occur to them, that the same substance would serve for the bottom also, and thus the use of stone *might be* replaced by a more convenient material."

Recollecting how roast pig came to be discovered, it cannot be said to be impossible that pottery may thus have been invented; but in this instance it might equally have been the rough substitute for the pottery of their recollection. Besides, the proof is wanting that they ever did pass on to the invention of pottery. It may, for anything we know to the contrary, be in this inchoate state amongst them still.

Now, until further evidence is forthcoming, I shall take the liberty of maintaining that savages seem to show no inventive faculty or power of recovery in themselves.[261] Whatever they possess seems to be limited to what they have retained of primitive civilisation, and what they have retained of civilisation seems exactly in proportion to what they have retained of primitive religion.

In supporting this proposition I shall hardly have occasion to go beyond the four corners of Sir J. Lubbock's "Pre-historic Times."

It is indeed a moot point with the travellers and ethnologists who have given their attention to the subject, which race of savages is "the lowest in the scale of civilisation." In this competitive examination a concurrence of opinion seems to decide in favour of the Fuegian, who at any rate is miserable enough, living, when better food fails him, on raw and putrid flesh, eked out with cannibalism; and whose clothing (in Central Fuego) consists "in a scrap of otter skin, about as large as a pocket handkerchief, laced across the breast with strings, and shifted according to the wind" (Darwin, *apud* Lubbock). Their religion, as we have just seen, consists in a vague apprehension of the black man who lives up in the woods—and their prayer is something slightly elevated above the howl of the wolf. Their civilisation, therefore, like their religion, may be considered to be at a "minimum." The Australians have been called "the miserablest people in the world". They are said to have "no religion or any kind of prayer, but most of them believe in evil spirits, and all have a dread of witchcraft". Here again we see their civilisation degraded *pari-passu* with their religious belief—so, too, with the Andaman (*vide supra*) and the Tasmanian.

When, however, we come to the inhabitants of the Feegee Islands, not greatly different from the people surrounding them, their characteristics, manners, and customs being partly Nigrito and partly Polynesian, although in the matter of cannibalism they are simply horrible, and eat their kind, not on any high notion that they are appropriating the spirit and glory of him whom they devour (vide Lubbock, 371), but from a repulsive preference; yet they have a distinct notion of religion, with temples, and ceremonies, and we are told they look down upon the Samoans because they had no religion. Well, we find the Feegeeans in a state of material civilisation exactly corresponding—they live in well built houses, 20 to 30 feet long and 15 feet high, in fortified towns, with earthen ramparts, surmounted by a reed fence, &c. "Their temples were pyramidal in form, and were often erected on terraced mounds like those of Central America". They had efficient weapons, agricultural implements, well-constructed canoes, and pottery.[262]

When, however, we come to the Tahitians we find a very high state of civilisation. Of their religion it is said—"That though they worshipped numerous deities," and sometimes sacrificed to them, "yet they were not idolators." "Captain Cook found their religion, like that of most other countries, involved in mystery and perplexed with apparent inconsistencies." They had a priesthood. "They believed in the immortality of the soul, and in two situations of different degrees of happiness somewhat analogous to our heaven and hell, though not regarded as places of reward and punishment; but the one intended 'for the chief and superior classes,' 'the other for the people of inferior rank.'" This is substantially Captain Cook's account of the Tahitians, and allowing it to be exact, although I have a suspicion that a missionary would have put it somewhat differently,[263] it shows a comparative state of religion very much elevated above anything we have yet seen. They had besides curious customs, such as that of eating apart. "They ate alone," they said, "because it was right, but why it was right they were unable to explain"—a custom which is common to them with the Bachapins (p. 384), (who, by the way, are also among the races classified as "of no religion"). Although the inhabitants of Tahiti present to us a much higher standard of religion and morality than we have yet met with, also "they, on the whole, may be taken as representing the highest stage in civilisation to which man has in any country raised himself, before the discovery or introduction of metallic implements" (Lubbock, p. 372).

It is impossible within these limits to investigate every case. I have taken the more salient cases, as instanced by Sir J. Lubbock, and contrasted them. I now wish to present the contrast in somewhat livelier form, and I do not see that I can do better than to present to the reader two scenes precisely similar, as to substance, yet under different conditions, in different parts of the world. The first shall be a description of "a whale ashore," by Sir J. Lubbock, among the Australians; and the second, a description of the same scene by Catlin ("Last Rambles, &c., among the Indians of Vancouver's Island").

I must preface that Sir J. Lubbock says that the Australians "have no religion nor any idea of prayer, but most of them believe in evil spirits, and all have great dread of witchcraft"

The following is the scene to which I refer:—

> "They are not, so far as I am aware, able to kill whales for themselves, but when one is washed on shore it is a real godsend to them. Fires are immediately lit to give notice of the joyful event.... For days they remain by the carcase, rubbed from head to foot with the stinking blubber, gorged to repletion with putrid meat, out of temper from indigestion, and therefore engaged in constant frays, suffering from a continuous disorder from high feeding, and altogether a disgusting spectacle."—*Capt. Grey, apud Lubbock,*

This is one picture; now for the other. It may be said that it is only the different idiosyncrasies of the writers transferred to their pages—that one is the narrative of *Jean qui pleure,* &c., or of the *médicin tant pis,* &c.; but I do not think so.

Mr Catlin premises by telling us that the scene occurred when on a visit with the chief of the Klah-o-gnats, of whom he says that he knew at first sight by his actions that he was "a chief, and by the expression of his face that he was a good man," and whom his companion described as "a very fine old fellow; that man is a gentleman; I'd trust myself anywhere with that man." Of their religion, the chief himself told Catlin that on that western coast of Vancouver's Island "they all believed in a Great Spirit, who created them and all things, and that they all have times and places when and where they pray to that Spirit, that he may not be angry with them."

One day came the startling announcement that a whale was ashore.

"The sight was imposing when we came near to it, but not until we came around it on the shore side had I any idea of the scene I was to witness. Some hundreds, if not thousands of Indians, of all ages and sexes, and in all colours, were gathered around it, and others constantly arriving. Some were lying, others standing and sitting in groups; some were asleep and others eating and drinking, and others were singing and dancing." The monster was secured by twenty or thirty harpoons, to which ropes were attached. "These were watched, and at every lift of a wave moving the monster nearer the shore, they were tightened on the harpoons, and at low tide the carcass is left on dry land, a great distance from the water.... The dissection of this monstrous creature, and its distribution amongst the thousands who would yet be a day or two in getting together, the interpreter informed us, would not be commenced until all the claimants arrived."

Several immense baskets had been brought in which to carry away the blubber. The possession of these baskets made all the difference in the scene which followed. To some this will be a sufficient explanation. How, then, did the others come to know nothing of baskets? Truly there are people who cannot be made to see the effect of "character upon clover." I rely, however, upon the broad lines of the contrast. The absence in this latter scene of the disgusting sights above so graphically described—their quick use of the harpoons—and the general order and equity of the distribution. "A whale ashore," Mr Catlin says ("Last Rambles," p. 105), "is surely a gift from heaven for these poor people, and they receive it and use it as such."

Whilst quoting from Catlin, I must be allowed to refer my readers to the very striking proof he incidentally affords of the theory of degeneracy in his comparative illustration of the heads of the alto and bas Peruvian, and of the Crow and modern Flathead:—

"The Crow of the Rocky Mountains and the alto-Peruvian of *the Andes*, being the two great original fountains of American man, to whom all the tribes point as their origin, and on whom, of course, all the tribes have looked as the *beau ideals* of the Indian race. The Flathead (letter *c*), aiming at the Crow skull (like the copyists of most fashions), has carried the copy into a caricature; and the Bas-Peruvian (*d*), aiming at the *elevated frontal* of the mountain regions, has squeezed his up with circular bandages to equally monstrous proportions." Also *vide* Prescott's "Mexico," ii. 493, 6th ed., 1850. "Anatomists also have discerned in crania disinterred from the mounds, and in those of the inhabitants of the high plains of *the Cordilleras* an *obvious difference* from those of the more barbarous tribes. This is seen especially in the *ampler forehead*, intimating a decided intellectual superiority.... Such is the conclusion of Dr Warren, whose excellent collection has afforded him ample means for study and comparison."

Before quitting this subject I must revive a question which I think Sir John Lubbock will admit, if he turns to the evidence dispersed in his pages, is at present involved in some obscurity. It is simply this, "How did the savage come by the knowledge of fire?" Sir John Lubbock suggests "that in making flint instruments sparks would be produced; in polishing them it would not fail to be observed that they became hot, and in this way it is easy to see how the two methods of obtaining fire may have originated.... In obtaining fire two totally different methods are followed; some savages, as for instance the Fuegians, using percussion, while others, as the South-Sea Islanders, rub one piece of wood against another.... Opinions are divided whether we have any trustworthy record of a people without the means of obtaining fire" To this point I shall recur. I will now give Sir John's quotation from Mr Dove: "Although fire was well known to them (the Tasmanians), some tribes at least appear to have been ignorant whence it was originally obtained, or how, if extinguished, it could be relighted. In all their wanderings," says Mr Dove, "they were particularly careful to bear in their hands the materials for kindling a fire. Their memory supplies them with no instances of a period in which they were obliged to draw upon their inventive powers for the means of resuscitating an element so essential to their health and comfort as flame. How it came originally into their possession is unknown. Whether it may be viewed as the gift of nature or the product of art and sagacity, they cannot recollect a period when it was a desideratum" ("Tasmanian Journal of Natural Science," i. 250, apud Lubbock, p. 355).[264]

Now, if it is a tenable opinion—and at least these are the statements of Father Gobien, and of Alvaro de Saavedra, and of Commodore Wilkes, to whose testimony I shall revert, that there are some tribes who are unacquainted with fire—that there are some who have and some who have not the art of rekindling fire, then arises the question whether those who have it not have lost the art, or whether those who now possess it invented it. If they did not invent it, they must have held it as a tradition, until, reaching a lower point of degradation still, they lost it. Mr Dove's testimony to this effect is very strong. What an emblem that never-extinguished torch of primitive tradition! We find the same tradition among the American Indians. "The Chippeways and Natchez tribes are said to have an institution for keeping up a perpetual fire, certain persons being set aside and devoted to this occupation" (Lubbock, p. 421). Freycinet certainly declares that Peré Gobien's statement, that the inhabitants of the Ladrone were totally unacquainted with fire until Magellan burnt one of their villages, to be "entirely without foundation." "The language," he says, "of the inhabitants contains words for fire, burning, charcoal, oven, grilling, boiling, &c." Again, as against Commodore Wilkes' assertion as an eye-witness, that he saw no appearance of fire in the island of Fakaafo, and that the natives were very much alarmed when they saw sparks struck from flint and steel, we are told that "Hale gives a list of Faakaafo words in which we find asi for fire" (Lubbock, p. 454). However, Sir John does not attribute to this argument the same force that Mr Tylor does, as asi is evidently the same word as the New Zealand ahi, which denotes light and heat as well as fire.[265] If, then, we have positive evidence that they have not the thing (Wilkes), and also evidence that they have the word (vide note), does not this prove that it is a tradition which they have lost? and is there not the presumption that they have lost it through degeneracy?

APPENDIX TO CHAPTER XII.

Compare the following account of the New Zealanders:—

"Shut out from the rest of the world, without any to set them a pattern of what was right or to reprove what was wrong, is it surprising that morally they should have degenerated, even from the standard of their forefathers? They were not always addicted to war, neither were they always cannibals; *the remembrance of the origin* of these horrid customs is *still preserved amongst them*. If the progressive development theory were true, aboriginal races should have progressively advanced; every successive generation should have added some improvement to the one which preceded it; but experience proves the contrary. A remarkable instance of this may be adduced in the fact, that the New Zealanders have retrograded, even since the days of Captain Cook; they then possessed large double canoes, decked, with houses on them similar to those of Tahiti and Hawaii, in which, traditionally, their ancestors arrived; it is now more than half a century since the last was seen. Tradition also states that they had finer garments in former days and of different kinds; that, like their reputed ancestors, they made cloth from the bark of trees—the name is preserved, but the manufacture has ceased. There are remains also in their language which would lead us to suppose that, like the inhabitants of Tonga, they once possessed a kingly form of government, and though they have now no term to express that high office, still they have words which are evidently derived from the very one denoting a king in Tonga. Their traditions, which are preserved, also establish the same fact, and perhaps one of the strongest proofs is their language; its fulness, its richness, and close affinity not only in words but in grammar to the Sanscrit, carries the mind back to a time when literature could not have been unknown." From "Te Ika a Maui," or "New Zealand and its Inhabitants," by the Rev. Richard Taylor, M.A., F.G.S., a Missionary in New Zealand for more than thirty years,

CHAPTER XIII
NOAH AND THE GOLDEN AGE

Taking as the basis of this theory that the law of nations forms part of a tradition, that the stream of this tradition has never ceased to flow, and that the diffusion of its waters has ever been the source and condition of fecundity; and further, that this tradition in its main current has run in the channels which Dr Newman (infra, p. 338) has indicated—for although there are other reservoirs, they have become stagnant, and exist like the fresh-water lake, the Bahr-i-Nedjig (vide Rawlinson's "Ancient Monarchies," i. 18), whose waters are "fresh and sweet" so long as they communicate with the Euphrates, but when they are cut off become "unpalatable," so that those "who dwell in the vicinity are no longer able to drink of it"—taking these various facts as the basis, we come inevitably to the question—Whence this tradition arose, and upon what authority and sanction it rests?

In answer to this I do not hesitate to affirm that presumptively it goes back to the commencement of human history, and more demonstrably to that commencement—which for historical and practical purposes is sufficient—the era of Noah.

I propose now to inquire how near this theory can be brought to the facts.

A fairer opportunity could hardly have been afforded for ascertaining the force and fulness of primitive tradition than the discovery of the American continent; yet this opportunity was totally disregarded by the Spanish conquerors,[266]—rough men, and for the most part the offscourings of Spain,—and its evidences were but sparsely and negligently collected by the explorers of a different character who followed at a later date.

Something, however, of primitive tradition has been thus preserved (*vide* Help's "Spanish Conquest of America," i. 278, 286, 290; Prescott, "Mexico," i. 54). Indeed, the approximation to the biblical narrative is so close that the suspicion would be quite reasonable that missionaries of whom we have no record had found their way to these people before the continent became known to us; or that the people themselves were of Jewish descent; or that they had left the Asiatic mainland subsequently to the preaching of St Thomas the apostle. Manco Capac (*vide infra*), according to this conjecture, may have been one of these missionaries; or it may even be that in the venerable image which the description calls up we see in vision the apostle himself.

When, however, the description is compared with the traditions I have collated of a patriarchal character—still more remote and venerable, "Him of mazy counsel—Saturn" (Hesiod), I shall ask the reader to decide whether the more improbable conjecture, measured according to time and distance, has not the greater weight of evidence.

I proceed to place in juxtaposition a recapitulation of the classical and oriental traditions, and the quotations from Helps above referred to.

"One peculiar circumstance, as Humboldt remarks, is very much to be noted in the ancient records and traditions of the Indian nations. In no less than three remarkable instances has superior civilisation been attributed to the sudden presence amongst them of persons differing from themselves in appearance and descent."

[As to the argument to be derived from colour and appearance, vide supra, p. 79.]

"Bochica, a white man with a beard, appeared to the Mozca Indians in the plains of Bogota, taught them how to build and to sow, formed them into communities, gave an outlet to the waters of the great lake [compare supra, p. 70, Chronology], and having settled the government, civil and ecclesiastical, retired into a monastic state of penitence for two thousand years.[267]

"In like manner Manco Capac, accompanied by his sister Mama Ocllo, descended amongst the Peruvians, gave them a code of admirable laws, reduced them into communities, and then ascended to his father the Sun."[268] (A confusion with the tradition of Enoch, parallel to the like confusion in the person of Xisuthrus,[269] unmistakably identified with Noah in the Babylonian tradition.)

"Amongst the Mexicans there suddenly appeared Quetzalcohuatl, the green-feathered (i.e. elegant) snake" (compare with Chaldæan fish-god, p. 199), "a white and bearded man of broad brow, dressed in strange dress, a legislator who recommended severe penances, lacerating his own body with the prickles of the agave and the thorns of the cactus, but who dissuaded his followers from human sacrifices. While he remained in Anahuana it was a Saturnian reign; but this great legislator, after moving on to the plains of Cholulas, and governing the Cholulans with wisdom, passed away to a distant country" [if this looks more like the movement among them of some apostolic missionary, it is also in keeping with the journey of Bacchus,

"travelling through all nations," &c.], "and was never heard of more."
It is said briefly of him, that "he ordained sacrifices of flowers and fruit,
and stopped his ears, when he was spoken to of war."[270] Such a saint is
needed in all times, even in the present advanced state of civilisation in the
old world."[271]—Help's "Spanish Conquest of America," i. 286.

I have shown that Calmet (and other authorities of the same date
might be adduced) identifies Saturn with Noah. Among other proofs he
points to the tradition of Saturn devouring his children (with the exception
of three), as a distorted tradition of the destruction of mankind according
to the prediction of Noah, upon the canon of interpretation, "that men are
said often to do what they do not prevent, or even what they predict." I
have also shown that this conjecture receives attestation from a fragment
of Sanchoniathon's (Phœnician),important whether regarded as a more
ancient parallel tradition, or as the same tradition nearer the fountain-head.

Without recapitulating the other points of resemblance (vide ch. x.),
let us compare what is said of Saturn with what is said of Bochica, Manco
Capac, &c.

"Under Saturn," says Plutarch, "was the golden age." "Saturn is
represented with a scythe, as the *inventor of* agriculture." Virgil (Æn. viii.
315) describes Saturn as bringing the dispersed people from the mountains
and *giving them laws*. I have also drawn attention to the *Saturnalia* as
connecting *Bacchus* with *Saturn*. Now Cicero tells us that one Bacchus was
king of *Asia*, and author of *laws called Subazian*; and Bacchus is also said
to *have travelled* through *all nations doing good*, in all places, and teaching
many things profitable to the life of man.

Noah has also been identified with Janus, and under Janus as under
Saturn was the golden age; and it is, moreover, said (vide p. 218), "that in
the time of Janus all families were full of religion and holiness." He is said
to have been the first that built temples and instituted sacred rites, and was
therefore always mentioned at the beginning of sacrifices. [This, in common
with what is said of Quetzalcohuatl is again possibly a combined tradition
of Enoch and Noah.]

Let both these traditions be compared with Berosus' account of Hoa,
or the fish-god (vide Rawlinson, "Anct. Mon." i. p. 155, and supra, p. 238).

> "He is said to have transmitted to mankind the knowledge
> of grammar and mathematics, and of all arts (or of any
> kind of art), and of the polity of cities, the construction and
> dedication of temples, the introduction of laws, to have
> taught them geometry, and to have shown them by example,

the mode of sowing the seed and gathering the fruits of the earth; and along with them to have tradated all the secrets which tend to harmonise life. And no one else in that time was found so experienced as he."[272]

In the traditions, however, which connect Noah with the Saturnian reign,[273] it appears to me that threefold confusion has to be disentangled.

I. There is a tradition of a golden and of a silver age frequently transfused.

II. When thus transfused there is often along with the tradition of a golden or silver age trace of a subordinate and incongruous tradition of a state of nature as a state of barbarism—both at the early commencement of things.

III. There is a double tradition of the succession of ages, the one ante-, the other post-diluvian.

I. The tradition of the golden age is primarily the tradition of Paradise, to which succeeded in gradation of degeneracy a silver, brass, and iron age. Of this line of tradition we have seen distinct trace in Sanchoniathon (supra, p. 127).

But there is also, as we have just seen, a tradition of another golden age connected with Saturn, Janus, &c., and of this perhaps we have the most direct testimony in the Chinese tradition.

> "The Chinese traditions," says Professor Rawlinson (Bampton Lectures, ii., quoting "Horæ Mos." iv. 147) "are said to be less clear and decisive (than the Babylonian). They speak of a 'first heaven' and age of innocence when 'the whole creation enjoyed a state of happiness; when everything was beautiful, everything was good; all things were perfect in their kind. Whereunto succeeded a *second heaven, introduced by a great convulsion,* in which the pillars of heaven were broken, the earth shook to its foundations, the heavens sank lower towards the north, the sun, moon, and stars changed their motions, the earth fell to pieces, and *the waters enclosed within its bosom burst forth with violence and overflowed,'"* &c.

Here, then, is a tradition of a second heaven, or a Saturnian reign, following a convulsion which will perhaps be conceded to be a tradition of the universal Deluge (vide p. 223), and which links the tradition of the Saturnian reign with the patriarch Noah?[274]

I ask now to be allowed to look at the same tradition from a different point of view.

I have elsewhere shown that according to the operation of natural causes everything in the primitive ages would have led to dispersion, but however probable or even certain these conjectures may be, we know as a fact that they did not operate (Gen. xi. 1, 3, 8) for some three hundred years or more, probably until after the death of Noah. Does not this look as if mankind were kept together for a period, in order that they might become settled in their ideas and confirmed in their maxims, under the influence and direction of the second father of mankind, whose direct communications with the Most High had been manifest, and whose authority necessarily commanded universal respect—"Him of mazy counsel, Saturn?" (Hesiod, "Theog.")[275]

If this theory appears far-fetched and fanciful, let it be recollected, on the other hand, that there has long subsisted a tradition among mankind of a code of nature as connected with a state of nature, which has to be accounted for (vide chap. ii.)

And when we consider how the impulsion which a nation receives at the commencement of its history continues—how much, for instance, at the distance of a thousand years we resemble our Saxon ancestors of the eighth century, and even our ancestors of the German forest in identity of character, sentiment, and institution—we must not make the lapse of centuries an impassable barrier to a belief in the traditions of mankind in the early periods of history.

Let us also, in regarding the golden or silver age, glance beyond it to that iron age which ultimately followed it, in which the world, becoming crowded and also corrupted, many families and tribes collected together for warfare, and in which one nation swallowed another until all came to be absorbed, at least on the Asiatic continent, into one or two great empires, which again contended for supreme dominion. An age of universal war, of many sorrows, of great perturbations, but one in which the process of dispersion was stayed, and mankind settled down within certain definite lines of demarcation, which in great part have continued to this day.

No wonder, then, that men turned to each other in these dark days, and talked with regret of the simple agricultural and pastoral age which had passed, and which came variously to be called, in their recollection, the second heaven, the Arcadian era, the Saturnia regna,[276] the golden age. Neither is it surprising that the idea of a state of nature misconceived as to the facts, and of a law of nature dimly remembered and distorted by human perversity, has so often obtained among mankind in modern times and also in antiquity. This is a point which I shall discuss with reference to the historical evidence in another chapter.

II. The conception of the state of nature (chap. ii.) as a basis of theory and belief arose in the main out of the speculations of lawyers and philosophers; yet it is curious that we frequently come upon a concurrent yet always subordinate tradition of equality associated with the tradition of a golden age which, if the age of Noah, we know aliunde to have been a state of hierarchical subordination to a patriarchal chief; and, along with a reminiscence of a time of peaceful prosperity at the commencement of things, the tradition of the primitive age as one of great barbarism and privation, man living on acorns, &c.

That these testimonies of tradition are incongruous and confused, I am bound to admit; but then, looked at from the point of view of tradition, they seem to me to have their explanation. If this happens to be deemed somewhat fanciful, I contend that the test in all these cases must be—(1.) Does the key fit the lock? (2.) Is there any other key producible?[277] I venture, then, to suggest that the notion of the primitive equality may be traced through the Bacchanalian traditions; and the tradition of a primitive age of great privation I believe to be the recollection of that brief but probably sharp period of suffering during which mankind clung to the mountains in distrust of the Divine injunction and promise, until brought into the plains by Noah.[278] (Vide p. 137.)

Moreover, the characteristics of this subsequent period, when mankind were living together in groups of families under the mild sway of the patriarch, when "all families were good" and when

... "With abundant goods midst quiet lands,
All willing shared the gatherings of their hands."

was just that semi-state of nature which it only required the Bacchanalian tradition on the one side to transform into the fiction of the state of savage and absolute equality, or the touch of poetry to convert into the golden reminiscence on the other.

In this way, in the person of the patriarch Noah, the fiction of a state of nature was brought into contact with the tradition of a law of nature and a law of nations, regarded as the law of mankind "when men were nearest the gods."

III. I have already noticed the double tradition of the succession of ages, the tradition from the fragment of Sanchoniathon, upon which Mr M'Lennan relies, being ante-, that of Hesiod partly ante- and partly post-diluvian. The following lines of Hesiod, for instance, bearing allusion to the confusion of tongues and the shortening of life, being plainly post-diluvian:—

"When Gods alike and mortals rose to birth,
The immortals formed a *golden race* on earth
Of *many-languaged men*; they lived of old,
When Saturn reigned in Heaven; an age of gold.

"The Sire of Heaven and earth created then
A race the third, of *many-languaged men*,
Unlike the silver they; of brazen mould,
Strong with the ashen spear, and fierce and bold."[279]

And again, of the iron race which followed them, he says—

"Jove on this race of many-languaged men
Speeds the swift ruin which but slow began;
For scarcely spring they to the light of day
E'er age untimely strews their temples grey."

I must here, too, point out how curiously the testimonies of tradition and science coincide.[280] Both are agreed as to the transition from a brass (bronze) to an iron age; but in one it is referred to as evidence of degeneracy— in the other, the transition is adduced in proof of progress. But the fact is established by the evidence of tradition, as certainly as by the conclusions of science, and is referred to accordingly by Sir John Lubbock ("Pre-historic Times," p. 6).

The lines of Lucretius are certainly remarkable—

"Arma antiqua, manus ungues dentesque fuerunt,
Et lapides, et item sylvarum fragmina rami
Posterius ferri vis est, ærisque reperta,
Sed prior æris erat, quam ferri cognitus usus.
Quo facilis magis est natura et copia major
Ære solum terræ tractabunt, æreque belli
Miscebant fluctus." —*De Rerum Natura*, lib. 5.

But here I cannot help thinking the tradition has reference rather to the use than to the knowledge of metals. We have seen, for instance, that the cultivation of the ground commenced with Noah—the fact being attested both by Scripture and tradition. Now, in the above passage, although the primitive weapons are referred to, as of stones, yet it is said "æreque solum terræ tractabunt," an averment which no doubt has reference to the brazen age; yet nothing forbids the construction, which on other grounds seems the more natural that the land was from the first so cultivated,[281] and that in strictness the commencement of the brazen age was identical with the commencement of cultivation, although in the mind of the poet it had reference to the introduction of bronze weapons and implements of war. Moreover, the sylvarum fragmina rami may point to the period immediately preceding cultivation, when the human race clung to the mountains. The testimony of Scripture to the point seems plain. Not only does the construction of the ark appear to imply the use of metals, but the reference to Tubalcain, "who was a hammerer and artificer in every work of brass and iron" (Gen. iv. 22), seems to put the antediluvian knowledge of metals beyond question.

In the first commencement after the Deluge, unless miraculously supplied, there would have been no grain or bread food until time had been allowed for its production. During this interval acorns, &c., may have been the only food. Perhaps it was so ordained to incite to the new permission to eat flesh meat. On the other hand, I ask, in those ages when men were supposed to live exclusively on acorns, was not flesh meat eaten,—were there no hunters? Had man no control over the domestic animals?

That in a peaceful period, and the intercommunication of families previous to the dispersion implies a state of peace (ch. xiii.), in a period in which, if we follow the other traditions, "all families were good," and were under the rule of an old man, "who held his hands to his ears when they spoke to him of war," it is not surprising to learn either that they had no weapons, or that they were of the simplest description. It is characteristic of an age which piques itself upon the perfection of its artillery, and whose greatest triumphs and inventions have been in the science of destruction, to look back upon a totally different age which happened only to have stone weapons, as necessarily an age of barbarism. But from our point of view it must be regarded not as an age of barbarism, but of prosperity,—not as a state of equality, but of the subordination of the members of the family to each chief, and of families relatively to each other; an age of much mental vigour and spiritual intuition, and, so far from being a period of misery, it left reminiscences of happiness such as lingered long in the memory of mankind.

CHAPTER XIV
SIR H. MAINE ON THE LAW OF NATIONS

Dr Newman in his inaugural discourse as Rector of the Dublin University ("On the Place held by the Faculty of Arts in the University Course"), which I think never received the attention it deserved, has with a few masterly touches sketched the history of Western civilisation, which in its main lines may be considered to run into, and be found identical with, the tradition I am now regarding—with this difference, that Dr Newman regards Western civilisation in its progressive, whereas we are concerned with its traditive aspects. Dr Newman says: "I take things as I find them on the surface of history, and am but classing phenomena (I have nothing to do with ethnology). Looking, then, at the countries which surround the Mediterranean seas as a whole, I see them from time immemorial the seat of an association of intellect and mind such as to deserve to be called the intellect and mind of human kind. Starting and advancing from certain centres, till their respective influences intersect and conflict, and then at length intermingle and combine, a common thought has been generated, and a common civilisation defined and established. Egypt is one starting-point, Syria another, Greece a third, Italy a fourth (of which, as time goes on, the Roman empire is the maturity, and the most intelligible expression), North Africa a fifth, ... and this association or social commonwealth, with whatever reverses, changes, and momentary dissolutions, continues down to this day.... I call it, then, pre-eminently and emphatically Human Society, and its Intellect the Human Mind, and its decisions the sense of mankind and its humanised and cultivated states— civilisation in the abstract; and the territory on which it lies the orbis terrarum, or the world. For unless the illustration be fanciful, the object which I am contemplating is like the impression of a seal upon the wax; which rounds off and gives form to the greater portion of the soft material, and presents something definite to the eye, and pre-occupies the space against any second figure, so that we overlook and leave out of our thoughts the jagged outline or unmeaning lumps outside of it, intent upon the harmonious circle which fills the imagination within it." ("There are indeed great outlying portions of mankind, ... still they are outlying portions and nothing else, fragmentary, &c., protesting and revolting against the grand central formation of which I am speaking, but not uniting with each other into a second whole.") The same orbis terrarum, which has been the seat of civilisation, has been the seat of the Christian polity. "The natural and the divine associations are not indeed exactly coincident, nor ever have been." "Christianity has fallen partly outside civilisation and civilisation partly outside Christianity; but on the whole the two have occupied one and the same orbis terrarum.... The centre of the tradition is transferred from Greece to Rome.... At length the temple of Jerusalem is rooted up by the armies of Titus, and the effete schools of Athens are stifled by the edict of Justinian.... The grace stored in Jerusalem, and the gifts which radiate from Athens, are made over and concentrated in Rome. This is true as a matter of history. Rome has inherited both sacred and profane learning; she has perpetuated and dispensed the traditions of Moses and David in the supernatural order, and of Homer and Aristotle in the natural. To separate these distinct teachings, human and divine, is to retrograde; it is to rebuild the Jewish temple and to plant anew the groves of Academus; ... and though these were times when the old traditions seemed to be on the point of failing, somehow it has happened that they have never failed.... Even in the lowest state of learning the tradition was kept up;" ... and this experience of the past we may apply to the present, "for as there was a movement against the classics in the Middle Ages, so has there been now.... Civilisation has its common principles, and views, and teaching, and especially its books, which have more or less been given from the earliest times, and are in fact in equal esteem and respect, in equal use, now, as they were when they were received in the beginning. In a word, the classics and the subjects of thought and study to which they give rise, or to use the term most to our present purpose, the arts have ever on the whole been the instruments which the civilised orbis terrarum has adopted; just as inspired works, and the lives of saints, and the articles of faith and the Catechism have been the instrument of education in the case of Christianity. And this consideration you see, gentlemen (to drop down at once upon the subject of discussion which has brought us together), invests the opening of the schools in arts[282] with a solemnity and moment of a peculiar kind, for we are but engaged in reiterating an old tradition, and carrying on those august methods of enlarging the mind, and cultivating the intellect and ripening the feelings, in which the process of civilisation has ever consisted."—Dr Newman on Civilisation.

Before examining Sir H. Maine's view on the Law of Nature and the Law of Nations, it will perhaps facilitate the inquiry if I gather up, out of the evidence which has accumulated in the previous chapters, such conclusions as will show how we stand in regard to Sir H. Maine's general theory.

I. Accepting Sir H. Maine's dictum that "the family and not the individual was the unit of ancient society;" and, in a certain sense, the further position, that it is difficult "to know where to stop, to say of what races of men it is not allowable to lay down that the society in which they are united was originally organised on the patriarchal model,"[283] I venture to maintain against Sir H. Maine the continuance of family life in a quasi state of nature, before either the development or creation of the State.

II. But in maintaining that there was a period in human history anterior to the formation of governments, I am far from asserting—on the contrary, I distinctly repudiate the notion—that there was ever an ante-social state. Society is complete within the family circle;[284] and society in any wider organisation is only the requirement and consequence of imperfection and corruption within the family, or of collision between families. Undoubtedly, there were instances in which the State grew up imperceptibly out of the extension of the family into the patriarchal system;[285] but these instances will probably have occurred among the families who remained stationary, whether by right of seniority, or by virtue of superior power, at the central point from which the Dispersion commenced. So long, however, as family government sufficed, there would have been nothing but the family; but when mankind increased, and actual relationship died out, disputes must have multiplied and become complicated—not only between individuals but between families; hence the necessity of State government—hence the necessity of an appeal on the part of individuals from the family to some supreme authority. This would be the first mode in which governments would have arisen among those who came under the action of the Dispersion. But even here—assuming the family groups to have descended from the same progenitor—we see first the family, first property, then the State. The second mode would be where several families, differing in language and race, came together and formed States.[286] Although they would have come together on unequal and varying conditions, yet they would necessarily have come together on some conditions, and for the mutual protection of their rights, their property, and their personal security. In all such cases there would have been something of a recognition and adjustment of rights, something of the nature of a compact more or less explicit, but much more formal and explicit in this mode than in the former. In any case, the end and intention of the formation of States and governments would have been the security of rights, as Cicero tells us:—"Hanc enim ob causam maxime ut sua tuerentur respublicæ civitatesque constitutæ sunt. Nam etsi, duce naturæ, congregabantur homines, tamen spe custodiæ rerum suarum urbium præsidia quærebant." But does not Sir H. Maine himself supply similar testimony? Referring to the notions of "primitive antiquity," he says:—

> "How little the notion of injury to the community had to do with the earliest interferences of the State, through its tribunals, is shown by the curious circumstance, that in the original administration of justice the proceedings were a close imitation of the series of acts which were likely to be gone *through in private life* by persons who were disputing, but who afterwards suffered their quarrel to be appeased. The magistrate carefully simulated the demeanour of a *private arbitrator, casually called in.*"—Chap. x. 374; *vide* also pp. 375, 376.

III. We come to the conclusion that the collation of the sentiments and maxims, as preserved in tradition by the families who had coalesced into States, would have formed the basis of the morality and of the jurisprudence of the States so constituted; and that in every case of oppression appeal would have been made to their pre-existing and natural rights.

IV. That whilst certain traditions—the tradition of religion, for instance—would have been perhaps more faithfully preserved in the patriarchal governments of the East, and we find evidence of this in the monotheism of the Persians; on the other hand, if there was a tradition of a law common to all nations, it would be more likely to be preserved in States formed by the amalgamation of many distinct families and races.[287]

V. That such was the origin and history of the Greeks and Romans—the two nations which formed the nucleus of the orbis terrarum within which, as Dr Newman tells us (supra, p. 339), is found the centre of Christianity and the seat of civilisation.

VI. That, whether the Roman law goes back in tradition, or, as Sir H. Maine will say, in fiction only—the fact remains, that it does so trace itself back to remote antiquity, and that the Roman law subsists to this day as the foundation of most of the codes of Europe, and has extended its ramifications to all; and that outside the circle of its influence other nations equally retrace their codes to remote antiquity, and, as a rule, to revelations made to their earliest founder. That nothing is more striking in ancient times than the manner in which their codes, which are the embodiment of laws previously in tradition, were held as a sacred deposit. This was the reason why the laws of the Medes and the Persians might not be altered; and that, according to the laws of the Visigoths, no judge would decide in any suit unless he found in their code a law applicable to the case; and perhaps we may find trace of it in the phrases familiar to us—*nolumus leges Angliæ mutari, stare super vias antiquas*, and so, too, in the *ita scriptum est*, which, as Sir H. Maine says, silenced all objections in the Middle Ages.

VII. That the fact of a tradition of "a law common to all nations" and of "a lost code of nature," is in accordance with the historical and scriptural evidence which would render such a tradition probable.

Sir H. Maine, with whose argument I now propose to deal, is, as far as I am aware, the most conspicuous opponent of the common belief in the "Law of Nations;" and yet it appears to me that we shall find testimony to the tradition even in the very terms in which he repudiates it. I must at least consider this a recognition on his part of the strength and inveteracy of the opposite view. In the following extracts I shall suppose my readers fresh from the perusal of Sir H. Maine.

Sir H. Maine says ("Ancient Law," pp. 7, 8), that the further "we penetrate into the primitive history of thought, the further we find ourselves from the conception of law of any sort." And again, "It is certain that in the infancy of mankind, no sort of legislation, not even a distinct author of law, is contemplated or conceived of." Now if Sir H. Maine had said nothing more, I should have felt bound to take this assertion upon his authority; but Sir H. Maine adds:—"Law has scarcely reached the footing of custom; it is rather a habit. It is, to use a French phrase, 'in the air,'" [Is not Sir H. Maine here hunting for a phrase which shall not imply that it is in tradition?] "The only authoritative statement of right and wrong is a judicial sentence after the facts, *not one presupposing a law which has been violated*, but one which is breathed for the first time by a higher power into the judge's mind at the moment of adjudication."

This passage may be adduced in evidence of the tradition of Noah and his heavenly-inspired judgments, but apparently it is in contradiction to the view of a law of nature, since it supposes the judge to decide through direct inspiration, or in the way of stet pro ratione voluntas, and not with reference to a "law which has been violated." Now, Sir H. Maine comes to his conclusion upon the ground of the "Themistes" of the Homeric poems. "The earliest notions connected with the conception ... of a law or rule of life are those contained in the Homeric words 'Themis' and 'Themistes'" (p. 4). "The literature of the heroic ages discloses to us law in the germ under the 'Themistes,' and a little more developed in the conception of 'Dike'" (p. 9).If this were so, law according to the conception of "Themistes" and law according to the conception of "Dike" were never contemporaneous, but necessarily successive, or rather progressive; but at page 8 we read, "The Homeric word for a custom in the embryo is sometimes 'Themis' in the singular, more often 'Dike,' the meaning of which visibly fluctuates between 'a judgment' and a 'custom' or 'usage.' 'Νομος,' a law ... does not occur in Homer."[288]

Well, allow that there need not be as yet the metaphysical conception of law, or law as a positive enactment, embracing indifferently a variety of cases. Eliminate the word "law." Instead of the phrase "law of nature" substitute "natural justice," and "the sense of right and wrong;" and it suffices that we detect "usage," "custom," right; for even if it were conceded that right is a post-Homeric rendering of δικη, yet "custom" and "usage" in their definition would have been in recognition of pre-existing right. This becomes more clear if we consider the alternative opinion. Sir H. Maine says that "under the patriarchal despotism," "every man was practically controlled in all his actions by a regimen not of law but of caprice".The judgments, then, of the patriarchal times were mere "caprice," and rights were defined without reference to any sense of justice. From "Themistes" of caprice they would proceed to legislation upon "caprice," and, ultimately, to codes which would represent nothing but a digest of the precedents of "caprice." It is difficult, then, to understand in what way and at what point the sense of justice, the conception of "dike," originated, and most of all, if this is true, it is difficult to account for the "Themistes" being regarded as akin to inspiration, as well as for the veneration with which, we have the authority of Sir H. Maine (vide infra) for saying, that Archaic law was held, and, moreover, for the persistent tendency to revert to the past.[289]

If, however, we follow Sir H. Maine in his illustration taken from English law, we shall find ourselves reinstated in our original convictions. Sir H. Maine says "An Englishman should be better able than a foreigner to appreciate the historical fact that the 'Themistes' preceded any conception of law;" but he says, "Probably it will be found that *originally* it was the received doctrine that somewhere *in nubibus* [Q. "in the air"], or in *gremio magistratuum* there *existed* a complete, coherent, symmetrical body of English law, of an amplitude sufficient to furnish principles which would apply to any conceivable combination of circumstances." If, then, we take the analogy of the English law, we come also to the identical conclusion for which I contend—viz. that the "Themistes," whether they partook of the character of commands or of judgments, *were* still in recognition of a "law which was violated."

If the "Themistes" had no reference to a law which was violated; if they were mere caprice, I have already asked, whence arose the regard for ancient law among the nations of antiquity? and I may add, how came it about that their ideas of justice were inseparably connected with the notions of morality? Does Sir H. Maine deny either of these facts? On the contrary, he affirms them:—

> "Quite enough, too, remains of these collections ['ancient codes'] both in the East and in the West, to show that they mingled up religious, civil, and merely moral ordinances *without any regard* to differences in their essential character; and this is consistent with all we know of ancient thought from other sources, the *severance* of law from morality, and of religion from law, belonging very distinctly to the later stages of mental progress"

> "Much of the old law which has descended to us, was preserved merely *because it was old*. Those who practised and obeyed it did not pretend to understand it; and in some cases they even ridiculed and despised it. *They offered no account of it except that it had come down to them from their ancestors.*"

Does Sir H. Maine dispute the persistency of tradition in general? No. vide supra, I have quoted a passage in which he explicitly maintains it.

I must observe further, that in the very passages in which he repudiates the notion of a "law of nature," two things irresistibly transpire—(1.) That there was a persistent tradition in ancient society of a law of nature; (2.) That this tradition was invariably associated with the golden age, *e.g.*:—

> "After nature had become a household word in the mouths of the Romans, the belief gradually prevailed among the Roman lawyers,[290] that the old jus gentium was in fact the lost code of nature, and that the prætors, in framing an

edictal jurisprudence on the principles of the jus gentium, were gradually restoring a type from which law had only departed to deteriorate" "But then, while the jus gentium had little or no antecedent credit at Rome, the theory of a law of nature came in surrounded with all the prestige of philosophical authority, and invested with the charms of association with an elder and more blissful condition of the race" "The law of nature confused the past and the present. Logically it implied a state of nature which had once been regulated by natural law; yet the juris-consults do not speak clearly or confidently of the existence of such a state, which indeed is little noticed by the ancients except when it finds a poetical expression in the fancy of a golden age" "Yet it was not on account of their simplicity and harmony that these finer elements were primarily respected, but on the score of their descent from the aboriginal reign of nature" "Yet it is a remarkable proof of the essentially historical character of the conception that, after all the efforts which have been made to evolve the code of nature from the necessary characteristics of the natural state [i.e. à priori] so much of the result is just what it would have been if men had been satisfied to adopt the dicta of the Roman lawyers without questioning or reviewing them. Setting aside the conventional or treaty law of nations, it is surprising how large a part of the system is made up of pure Roman law" [Because the Roman law was in the main stream of the tradition.][291]

I now come to what I may call the exposition of Sir H. Maine's argument proper, and, although I feel the full difficulty of doing this, in the case of so subtle and able a writer, I shall endeavour to condense into as short a space as possible whatever is material to Sir H. Maine's position. Sir H. Maine says

"I shall attempt to discover the origin of these famous phrases, Law of Nations, Law of Nature, Equity, and to determine how the conceptions which they indicate are related to one another. The most superficial student of Roman history must be struck by the extraordinary degree in which the fortunes of the Republic were affected by the presence of foreigners under different names on her soil. The causes of this immigration are discernible enough at a later period, for we can readily understand why men of all races should flock to the Mistress of the World; but the same phenomenon of a *large population of foreigners* and denizens meets us in the *very earliest* records of the Roman State—no doubt the instability of society in ancient Italy.... It is probable, however, that this explanation is imperfect, and it could only be completed by taking into account those active commercial relations, which though they are little reflected in the military traditions of the Republic, Rome appears certainly to have had with Carthage and with the interior of Italy in pre-historic times.... In the *early Roman Republic* the principle of the absolute exclusion of foreigners pervaded the civil law no less than the constitution. The alien or denizen could have no share in any institution supposed to be coeval with the State. He could not have the benefit of the Quiritarian Law, &c.... Still neither the interest nor the security of Rome permitted him to be quite outlawed.... Moreover, at no period of Roman history was foreign trade entirely neglected. It was therefore probably half as a measure of policy and half in furtherance of commerce that jurisdiction was first assumed in disputes to which the parties were either foreigners or a native and a foreigner. The assumption of such a jurisdiction brought with it the immediate necessity of discovering some principles on which the questions to be adjudicated upon could be settled.... They refused, as I have said before, to decide the new cases by pure Roman civil law. They refused, no doubt, because it seemed to involve some kind of degradation, to apply the law of the particular State from which the foreign litigant came. The expedient to which they resorted was that of selecting the rules of law common to Rome, and to the different Italian communities in which the immigrants were born. In other words, they set themselves to form a system answering to the primitive and literal meaning of *jus gentium, i.e.* law common to all nations. *Jus gentium* was, in fact, the sum of the common ingredients in the customs of the old Italian tribes, for they were *all the nations* whom the Romans had the means of observing, and who sent successive swarms of immigrants to the Roman soil.... The *jus gentium* was, accordingly, a collection of rules and principles determined by observation *to be common* to the institutions which prevailed among the various Italian tribes. The circumstances of the origin of the *jus gentium* was probably a sufficient safeguard against the *mistake of supposing* that the Roman lawyers had any special respect for it. It was the fruit in part of their disdain of all foreign law, and in part of their disinclination to give the foreigner the advantage of their own indigenous *jus civile*. It is true that we, at the present day, should probably take a very different view of the *jus gentium*.... We should have a sort of respect for rules and principles so universal.... But the results to which modern ideas conduct the observer, are, as nearly as possible, the reverse of those which were instinctively brought home to the primitive Roman. What we respect or admire, he disliked or regarded with jealous dread. The points of jurisprudence which he looked upon with affection were exactly those which a modern theorist leaves out of consideration as accidental and transitory— the solemn gestures ... the endless formalities, &c.... The *jus gentium* was merely a system forced on his attention by a political necessity. He loved it as little as he loved the foreigners from whose institutions it was derived, and for whose benefit it was intended. A complete revolution in his ideas was required before it could challenge his respect.... This crisis arrived when the Greek theory of a law of nature was applied to the practical Roman administration of the law common to all nations." — *Sir H. Maine's Ancient Law*, 46–52.

Sir H. Maine's theory may be summarised as an attempt to identify the "Law of Nations" with the history of Roman law, leaving out of sight the tradition of it which may be traced in other nations. Now, although there is nothing, as Napoleon used to say, which one nation hates more than another nation—and this certainly holds true of the Roman people—yet it is scarcely possible to point to any which, from the circumstances of its origin, would have been less predisposed to look in the abstract with disdain upon the laws and customs of surrounding nations, however much they may have hated them as concrete nationalities; and least of all would they have had this feeling for the institutions of the Latins, a people whom, from their peculiar connection with themselves, they would principally have had as residents among them. Sir H. Maine seems unable to shake off the prepossession, which the analysis of Roman law, to the exclusion of other evidence, would tend to lead him, viz. that the Romans were a homogeneous people, and we have just heard him speak of their "own indigenous jus civile." This indigenous jus civile was compounded, as was their nationality, of many miscellaneous elements. Whatever truth may be attached to the legends as to the foundation of Rome, and they are various, it cannot well be disputed that there was a strong trace of Sabine[292] and Etruscan,[293] in addition to the original miscellaneous Roman, or, if not miscellaneous, pure Latin element; to which, in any case, in the subsequent reigns a large Latin immigration must be added, when Rome, through the conquest of Alba Longa, became the head of the Latin league, and the infusion of a Greek in addition to an Etruscan element in the dynasty of the Tarquins. The Latin league has its significance over and above its bearing upon the present argument; and to this I shall presently revert. But to go no further, does not the existence of the Latin league[294] sufficiently account for the large influx of strangers into Rome, on account of which Sir H. Maine sees the necessity for an extension of the Roman jurisprudence? But, if this be so, his theory must fall to the ground; for, if the Roman element was distinctive at all, and was a pure Latin population, miscellaneously collected by Romulus, and not a miscellaneous population of various tribes—it was Latin quâ Roman. How then, supposing the Roman element to have become predominant, did it come to contemn the Latin element and the law of the Latins? That it excluded them is another thing, or that they were kept in a subordinate position, and not admitted to the full privileges of naturalisation, is quite conceivable on other grounds; but that there should have existed a feeling of contempt for the laws and customs of the people among whom, if their legends were true (and at any rate we have nothing else to go upon), was found the cradle of their race, is hard to understand, yet this assumption is essential to Sir H. Maine's position.

Again, the Roman family and tribal system, with their principle of agnatic relationship, was in all probability part of their organisation for war: it was the secret of their strength. Grant that they shrank from applying the principles of their domestic law, which in their application would have involved in time an organisation in conformity with it, we can at once see why they withheld the principles of their jurisprudence without withholding it in mere scorn of an alien nationality.

We rather see influences which would have predisposed them to look with reverence on the laws and customs of a people among whom they must have known that they had sprung, even if there had been no tradition of a law common to all nations "of the lost code of nature," a notion which the edicts of the prætors of the later period would hardly have generated if it had had no foundation in tradition.

If you change the *venue* to Etruria, the same arguments will apply. In proof, I quote the following passage from a competent, if somewhat antiquated (1837) authority—(Pastoret, "Hist. de la Legislation," xi. 355)— more especially as it mentions a circumstance to which I do not remember that Sir H. Maine adverts, and which would make it a matter of some difficulty for the prætors to introduce laws and principles of their own making: "Peu amis de la guerre, Ancus Martius voulut du moins ajouter à l'art de la faire quelques formalités *pour la declarer; elles étoint d'usage avant lui* chez des *peuples voisins;* ce sont les lois féciales, lois que nous avons déjà fait connoître (c. iii. 286). L'adoption des lois étrusques par les Romains reçoit une force nouvelle d'un fait conservé par Dénys et Halicarnasse (Liv. ii. § 27); c'est que *après* l'abolition de la monarchie on exposa dans la place publique de Rome *à la vue de tous les citoyens* toutes *les lois et coutûmes* de la patrie, avec les lois étrangeres nouvellement *introduites, afin* que le droit publie ne changeât pas en même temps que les pouvoirs du magistrat."

Sir H. Maine says, "The prætors early laid hold on *cognation* as the *natural* form of kinship, and spared no pains in purifying their system from the older conception [*i.e.* older according to Roman law]. Their ideas have descended to us, but still traces of agnation are to be seen in many of the modern rules of succession after death."

The reader will find[295] in Sir H. Maine the distinction between cognation and agnation very completely and lucidly stated. I may say roughly, however, that cognation is the form of relationship which we acknowledge and which is familiar to us, descending in graduated degrees, including males and females alike, from common ancestors. Agnatic relationship is rigidly confined to the male lines, excluding the connections and descendants of females, upon the maxim, Mulier est finis familiæ, though including unmarried females on the side of the father.

Now, I venture to think that the argument which may be drawn from the passage which I have quoted ought not lightly to be dismissed as a mere *argumentum ad hominem.*

Sir H. Maine says that the prætors early laid hold on cognation as the natural form of kinship. Either, then, they did this really detecting this principle as inhering in the natural law which was in tradition, or as detecting it as the "law common to all the nations known to the Romans." In the latter case, it shows that, whereas cognation was common among the surrounding nations, agnation obtained among the Romans. The latter was therefore their peculiar institution, which sustains the argument which I have just put. If, on the contrary, they detected cognation underlying the institutions of all nations, and as part of their traditional law of nature, we cannot wish for a better and clearer instance of the natural law cropping up. And it is an instance, too, of the advantage at which those argue who have on their side the authority of Scripture, indicating the landmarks. Knowing that mankind sprang from a single pair, we can see that cognation must have been the law from the commencement: for it stands to reason that commencing with common ancestors the normal and natural mode would be to include all the relations according to degrees of descent, until there was some object in excluding them. With some political necessity or expediency for the limitation to males and the exclusion of females would agnation have commenced. If we require a case in point we have it in the relationship of Laban to Jacob. According to agnatic relationship they were second cousins, but according to cognatic relationship Laban was his maternal uncle, and such accordingly he is called in the sacred text (Gen. xxviii. 2). But in the seventh century before Christ, in the thickness of Paganism, men would scarcely have come to this conclusion, since they had apparently lost, as far as we know, the knowledge of their origin; although, as we have already seen, they retained dimly the tradition of many things of which they had forgotten the specific history. From the information we derive from Sir H. Maine, the memory of cognation, as the earliest and most natural scheme of kinship, must somehow have subsisted in tradition. It was not certainly in their power to verify the truth of the tradition as we can by a reference to revelation, and yet it would seem as if, having come to this conclusion, that it was almost within the grasp of human reason to have inferred from it the origin from a single pair, and thus to have recovered the knowledge they had lost from the tradition they had preserved.[296]

A few points in Sir H. Maine's argument (supra, p. 352) remain to be noticed. I must take exception, for instance, to his averment "that what we respect and admire," viz. "principles so universal," the Roman "regarded with jealous dread." "The parts of jurisprudence which he looked upon with affection, and the solemn gestures, &c., were the parts which a modern theorist leaves out of consideration," for he seems to have recognised their justice, and allowed them to operate so effectually that his whole system of jurisprudence, which was originally based on agnatic kinship, came round to the principle of cognation.[297] In the process, and through the action so skilfully evolved and unfolded in Sir H. Maine's pages, two principles, equally to our mind, were brought into gradual recollection, viz. the comity of nations and equality before the law. The "solemn gestures," "the nicely-adjusted questions and answers of the verbal contract," "the endless formalities," are at least in evidence of the tradition.

And this suggests a reflection upon the basis of Sir H. Maine's argument, viz. that the Romans could only draw their induction from "the customs of the old Italian tribes, as these were all the nations whom the Romans had the means of observing." Now, if we attach the weight which is due to Dr Newman's remarkable view (vide supra) as to the course and confines of civilisation, we shall be, I think, struck with the fact that the two nationalities of Greece and Rome, which were destined to form its heart and centre, had as their common substratum a very peculiar people, whose characteristics exactly adapted them to retain traditions, and to carry out the scriptural saying about the people, "And they shall maintain the state of the world" — a people who were the first occupiers of the soil of Greece and Italy, and who, if not directly and historically, can through philology be traced back to the most primitive times;[298] a people tenacious of customs and traditions,[299] who were the guardians of the worship and tradition of the Dodonæan Jupiter,[300] and in possession of his shrine when the worship of Jupiter was only the thinly-disguised corruption of the worship of the true God;[301] a people to whom, according to Mr Gladstone, the Greek religion owed its sacerdotal and ceremonial development,[302] and who also inclines to the opinion, which has a more especial significance, and bearing on the present argument, that the Amphictyonic Council was a Pelasgian institution.

Now, let us consider this special significance of the Amphictyonic Council. On the one hand, it is attributed to Amphictyon, the son of Deucalion; on the other hand (as I shall presently show), we see the almost identical institution in Italy in contact with Roman law. What, then, was the Amphictyonic Council? Those who have written upon it appear to me to have endeavoured to regard it too much as a federation. Hence a double error. On the one side it was found that, instead of being a federation of all Greece, at most it was only a federation of twelve cities; it was further found that it had no external action, and that on occasions, as, e.g. the Persian war, in which the whole nation of Greece acted as one people, it made no appearance.[303] A feeling of disappointment necessarily supervened, and it was asked, if not a federation, what was it? On the other hand, although not a federation for the purposes of government or war, it would be an equal error to deny that it was a federation for certain purposes, more or less invisible to the eye, and which for such purposes retained sufficient vitality to assemble deputies twice a year, and during several centuries, for it is certain that it subsisted to the close of Grecian history, when, indeed, we are astonished to find that when faith in everything else had died out, belief in the Amphictyons again flickers into life. It is true that we know little, but the little that has transpired implies so much more. Were it not for a casual passage in a speech of Æschines, we should hardly have known more than of their existence. As it is, we are thrown back upon conjecture, and upon what we can recover indirectly from tradition. Now, if we suppose the Amphictyonic Council to have tradited down, and to have been a federation for the purposes of tradited down from primitive times, even in their rudimentary form, the rules and principles of the laws of nations, much that is strange and mysterious in its history will disappear.[304] It will at once account for its duration and prestige, in spite of its inactivity and merely passive existence, even supposing that it is reduced in our estimation to a sort of convocation, powerless for action, and merely keeping alive a tradition of the past. From this point of view, the fact of its merely being a federation of twelve States, which is generally adduced to reduce it to unimportance, taken in connection with another fact which I shall presently substantiate, really militates in favour of my argument. It shows that instead of being the one typical institution of the sort, it is only the one which stands out most prominently in history, and merely handed down a tradition which was common to many others. I have already alluded to the Latin league, through which, apparently, the Romans recovered their tradition of the law common to all nations. If all these isolated federations retained their tradition of a law common to all nations—although practically limited to the members of their own confederation—is it not at once in evidence of the action of the Dispersion and at the same time of a tradition anterior to the disruption? Without pretending to have gone over the ground necessary to present an exhaustive catalogue of such federations, I may present the following facts in evidence and illustration.

Outside the Amphictyonic union there were other federations, even within the confines of Greece itself:—

"Qui avoient le même caractère, et peut-étre un caractère plus intime d'association entre des etats voisins, pour honorer ensemble des dieux, ou pour se prêter, dans certains cas, un appui necessaire. Il s'en reunissoit une non loin de Trezime ou Argolide, une autre à Corinthe, une autre à Onchiste en Beotie; on en trouve de semblables encore dans plusieurs îles de la Grece, et dans les colonies de l'Asie Mineure.[305] Ces associations, au reste, ne seconderent pas moins la civilisation generale que n'auroit pu le faire un Amphictyonat universel."—Pastoret, Hist. de la Legis., v. 27.

We find the same federations when we come to Italy:—

"Among the other works of Servius Tullius was a temple of Diana, which he erected on the Aventine, apparently near the present church of Sta. Prisca. This temple, in imitation of the Amphictyonic confederacy, was to be the common sanctuary and place of meeting for the cities belonging to the Latin league, of which Rome had become the chief through the conquest of Alba Longa; and her supremacy was tacitly acknowledged by the temple being erected with money contributed by the Latin cities. It is said to have been an imitation of the Artemisium, or temple of Diana at Ephesus. (Liv. i. 45; Dionys. iv. 26; Varro, L. L. v. § 43; Val. Max., vii. 3, § 1.) The brazen column containing the terms of the league, and the names of the cities belonging to it, was preserved in the time of Dionysius." —Dyer's *Hist. of City of Rome,*

Compare this with Niebühr, Hist. ii. chap. ii. (Travers Twiss' "Epitome.")

"So long as Latium had a dictator, none but he could offer sacrifice on the Alban mount, and preside at the Latin holidays, as the Alban dictator had done before. He sacrificed on behalf of the Romans likewise, as they did in the temple of Diana on the Aventine for themselves and the Latins.... The opinion that the last Tarquinius or his father constituted the festival is quite erroneous, as its antiquity is proved to have been far higher. It is true that Tarquinius converted it into a Roman festival, and probably, too, by throwing it open to a larger body, transformed the national worship of the Latins into the means of hallowing and cementing the union between the states. The three allied republics had each its own place of meeting—at Rome, at the spring of Ferentina, and at Anagnia, where the concilium of the Hernican tribes was held in the circus; that the sittings of the diets were connected with the Latin festival, seems to be evinced by the usage, that the consuls never took the field till after it was solemnised; and by its variableness, which implies that it was regulated by special proclamation. Like the Greek festivals it ensured a *sacred truce.*"

In these extracts we come upon a federation resembling the Amphictyonic league, whose union is also cemented at a religious festival, the origin of which must be sought for in remote antiquity, and which festival has a direct connection with questions of peace and war. We also catch glimpses of similar federation among the Hernici and Marsi.

Now, let us go to quite an opposite point; and, if we find the same stratification cropping up, may we not conjecture it to have been once the same throughout.

"When the Europeans made their first settlements in America, six such nations had formed a league, had their Amphictyons or states-general, and by the firmness of their union, and the ability of their councils, had obtained an ascendant from the mouth of the St Lawrence to that of the Mississippi. They appeared to understand the objects of the confederacy as well as those of separate nations; they studied a balance of power.... They had their alliances and treaties, which, like the nations of Europe, they maintained or they broke upon reasons of state, and remained at peace from a sense of necessity or expediency, and went to war upon any emergency of provocation or jealousy."[306]

In Mexico also there was "that remarkable league, which indeed has no parallel in history (?) It was agreed between the States of Mexico, Tezcuco, and the neighbouring little kingdom of Tlascopan, that they should mutually support each other in their wars, offensive and defensive, and that in the distribution of the spoil one-fifth should be assigned to Tlascopan, and the remainder be divided — in what proportions is uncertain — between the two other powers.... What is more extraordinary than the treaty itself, however, is the fidelity with which it was maintained." —*Prescott's Mexico,* i. p. 17. And in the republic of Tlascala, it is said (*id.* i. 378) "after the lapse of years, the institutions of the nation underwent an important change [they had previously separated into three divisions, of which Tlascala was the largest]. The monarchy was divided, first into two, afterwards into four separate states, bound together by a sort of federal compact, probably not very nicely defined. Each state, however, had its lord or superior chief, independent in his own territories, and possessed of co-ordinate authority with the others in all matters concerning the whole republic. The affairs of government, especially *all those relating to peace and war*, were *settled* in a *senate* or *council*, consisting of the four lords, with their inferior nobles." The Tlascalans subsequently incorporated the Othonius, or Otomius (p. 378).

Here, as in the Greek and Latin Leagues, the primary objects of the law of nations seem to have been secured within the limits of their confederation, or of what they would have deemed the pale of civilization. The requirements of their horrible worship (*i.e.* the necessity of procuring human victims for their sacrifices) seems, however, to have overridden every other consideration, and to have impelled them to frequent wars with the nations outside the pale. In the case of the Tlascalans, the traditional lines seem more clearly defined. I have already hinted, in a note, with reference to the Greek and Latin Leagues that the Atlantis of Plato was, as indeed it professes to be, an embodiment of tradition, and not, as it is commonly regarded, as a figment of the imagination; but this strikes me still more forcibly when the League of the Ten Kings in the Atlantis is compared with the League of the Tlascalans.

Plato says: "The particulars respecting the governors were instituted from the beginning as follows. Each of the ten kings possessed absolute authority, both over the men and the *greater part* of the laws in his own division and in his own city, punishing and putting to death whomsoever he pleased. But the government and communion of these kings with each other were conformable to the *mandates given by Neptune;* and this was likewise the case with their laws. These mandates were delivered to them by their ancestors on a pillar of orichalcum, which was erected about the middle of the island, *in the temple of Neptune.* These kings, therefore, assembled together every fifth, and alternately, every sixth year, for the purpose of distributing an equal part both of the even and the odd; and when they assembled they deliberated on the public affairs, inquired if any one had acted improperly ... a sacrifice of *bulls* was made in the temple of Neptune, at the foot of the pillar of orichalcum.... But on the pillar, besides the laws, there was an oath, supplicating mighty imprecations against those who were disobedient.... There were also many *other laws* respecting *sacred* concerns, and such as were peculiar to the several kings; but *the greatest* were the following: that they should *never wage war against each other,* and that all of them should give assistance if any one person in some one of their cities should endeavour to extirpate the royal race. And as they consulted in common respecting war, and other actions, in the same manner as their ancestors, they assigned the empire to the Atlantis family." — *Plato's Works,* Sydenham and Taylor's tr., ii. 589.

I think it will then be conceded, that whether or not there was a tradition "of a law common to all nations," there were at any rate channels provided, well adapted to conduct and disseminate it, and that these channels everywhere converge upon the most primitive times. Before proceeding to ascertain whether anything has in fact been transmitted, I must draw attention more particularly to the circumstance that the tradition of all law is everywhere closely connected with the traditions of religion, has been handed down in a similar manner; and, so far as it retains the purity of primitive truth, under the same sanction. From this point of view the following passages from Cicero appears to me to be very significant:

"Hanc igitur video sapientissimorum fuisse sententiam legem neque hominum ingeniis excogitatum, neque scitum aliquod esse populorum, *sed æternum quiddam* quod universum mundum regerat imperandi, prohibendique sapientiâ.... Quæ non tum denique incipit lex esse, cum scriptum est, sed tum cum orta est; orta autem simul est cum mente divina." "Jam ritus familiæ patrumque servari, id est *quoniam antiquitas proxima accedit ad Deos,* a Deis quasi *traditam,* religionem tueri." — *Cicero de Legibus,* ii. 4, 11.

There is another curious passage which seems to prove that the oracles originally existed simply for the preservation of the primitive tradition; and, although mixed up with imposture, that they seem to have had the knowledge, or at least the instinct, that their prestige and power of influence was within the limits of the traditions which they had corrupted or preserved.[307]

"Deinceps in lege est, ut de ritibus patriis coluntur optimi, de quo cum consulerent Athenienses Apollinem Pythium, quas potissimum religiones tenerent, oraculum editum est eas quæ essent in more majorum. Quo cum iterum venissent, majorumque morem dixissent, sæpe esse mutatum, quæsivissentque quem morem potissimum sequerentur, e variis respondit, optimum. Et perfecto ita est ut id habendum sit antiquissimum et a Deo proximum quod sit optimum."[308]—Cicero de Legibus, ii. 16.

But this sentiment and tradition was not only common to the people of Greece and Rome, but to the yet uncivilised tribes of Germany.

"Or les dispositions, où la coutume barbare et la loi romaine s'accordent, sont encore celles qui semblent faire le fond des législations grèques: non que les douze tables aient été copiées, comme on l'a cru, sur les lois de Solon, mais à cause de l'étroite parenté des peuples de la Grèce et du Latium. A travers l'obscurité des siècles héroïques, on découvre un sacerdoce puissant qui a ses premiers établissements en Thrace, en Samothrace, à Dodone, et qui perpétuera son autorité par l'institution des mystères. On voit aussi la resistance d'une race belliqueuse."—*Ozanam, "Les Germains avant le Christianisme,"* vol. i. chap. "Les Lois."

"Au premier abord rien ne semble plus contraire aux mœurs barbares que la loi romaine, si subtile, si précise, si bien obéie. Cependant si l'on en considère les origines, on n'y trouve pas d'autres principes que ceux dont la trace subsistait dans les vieilles coutumes de la Germanie. Le droit primitif du Rome, comme celui du Nord, est un droit sacré."—*Ib.* p. 148.

"Il existait chez les Germains une autorité religieuse, *dépositaire de la tradition*, et qui y trouvait l'idéal et le principe de tout l'ordre civil. Cette autorité avait créé la propriété immobilière en la rendant respectable par des rites et des symboles, ... elle l'engageait dans les liens de la famille légitime, consacrée par la sainteté du mariage, par le culte des ancêtres, par la solidarité du sang: elle l'enveloppait dans le corps de la nation sédentaire, ou elle avait établi une hierarchie de caste et de pouvoir, à l'exemple de la hierarchie divine de la création" (p. 147). "Dans cette suite de scènes dont se compose pour ainsi dire le drame judiciaire, on reconnaît un pouvoir religieux, qui cherche *à sauver la paix, à désarmer la guerre* et qui s'y prend de trois façons différentes"

Now, if we are agreed that fitting channels for the diffusion of the tradition existed; if, further, we find that all law seems to trace itself back to a common source of supernatural revelation; if the resemblances in the traditions concerning the lawgivers of antiquity—and, with the exception of Lycurgus, the agreement in the fundamentals of their codes—in the great lines of the family, property, and the external relations of life, seems to require the supposition of some common fountain-head at which they all filled the pitcher—we shall, I think, when we come to the question of public law, only require further some evidence of a tradition of maxims, rules, and precedents of procedure in war, founded on and appealing to natural right, and claiming the sanction of the gods, to establish the existence of a law common to all nations different from that which would have arisen from the judgment of the prætors, merely applying the rules and maxims common to the Romans and the adjoining nations, in case of conflict where the law of the State was not allowed to be applied (*supra*, Maine).

I shall, doubtless, be reminded that this was only part of Sir H. Maine's argument, and that it was this, taken in connection with the influence of the Stoics on Roman law, and the stoical conception of nature,[309] which created the fiction of a law of nature, and of a law common to all nations.

Let it then be granted that the theories and maxims of the Stoics had their influence on Roman society and Roman law. It was only part of the influence which stole over and everywhere impregnated the field of primitive tradition. Sir H. Maine shows us how it at once seized upon the element of law, which, be it in fiction only, was said to be common to all nations. Would it the less have seized upon it if, instead of being a fiction, it had been a reality?—*à fortiori*, it would have done so. Therefore Sir H. Maine leaves the question as to the belief among the ancients in a "law common to all nations" still open, or rather, so far as there is an argument, it is only with the previous part of his theory that it is necessary to deal; for all that Sir H. Maine's finely-drawn reasoning and subtle detection of the influence of Grecian stoicism on Roman law accounts for—so far as the present argument is concerned—is the greater attention and respect which was henceforward paid to the fiction, supposing that it had not heretofore and always been paid to the fact, that there was a traditional law common to all nations.

I have previously pointed out the distinction between the law of nations and international law, and I am under the impression that I made the distinction before the publication of Sir H. Maine's work—certainly before I had become acquainted with it. The manner in which Sir H. Maine makes the distinction does not appear to me to be quite accurate. He says:—"It is almost unnecessary to add that the confusion between jus gentium, or law common to all nations, and international law, is entirely modern. The classical expression for international law is jus feciale, or the law of negotiation and diplomacy" The Fecial College was very far from corresponding with our Corps Diplomatique, neither was its law a law of negotiation and diplomacy; and the distinction between the law of nations and international law was made in modern times, precisely because in antiquity treaty law was subordinate to, and identified with, the traditional law. The Fecial College corresponded much more nearly to what our Heralds' College would be, supposing the Heralds' College invested with the authority of our Admiralty Courts, and also made the trustees of the foundation for the study of international law, which Dr Whewell's bequest had the intention of instituting at Cambridge. We should then have, as in ancient times, a body of men who would be at once the depositaries, the interpreters, and the heralds of a tradition, though, to complete the picture, we should have to invest them with a sacred character, and in some way to give to their decisions the sanction of religion. Dionysius of Halicarnassus tells us that they were priests chosen from the best families at Rome, and that their special intention was to see that the Romans never made an unjust war. "The seventh part of the Sacred Laws was devoted to the college of the Fecials, whom the Greeks call εἰρηνοδίκαι.[310] They are men selected from the most illustrious families, and are dedicated during their whole life to this priesthood.... It would take long to enumerate all the various duties of the Fecials, which were multifarious, ... but in the main they are these,—to take heed lest the Romans should ever undertake an unjust war with a city with which they were in league" (Lib. ii.); it was their duty to demand reparation, and, failing, to declare war; in case of differences with allies, they acted as mediators, and they adjudicated in case of disputes. It was for them to decide what constituted an injury to the person of an ambassador, and whether or not the generals had acted according to their oaths; to draw up the articles of treaties, truces, and the like; and to decide as to their nullity and validity, and to communicate accordingly with the Senate, which deliberated upon their report.

What Cicero tells us is not less to the point:—

"There are certain peculiar laws of war also, which are of all things most strictly to be observed.... As we are bound to be merciful to those whom we have actually conquered, so should those also be received into favour who have laid down their arms.... Our good forefathers were most strictly just as to this particular, the custom of those times making him the patron of a conquered city or people who first received them into the faith and allegiance of the people of Rome. In short, *the whole right and all the duties of war* are most rigorously set down in the *fecial laws*, out of which it is manifest that no war can be justly undertaken *unless satisfaction has been first demanded*, and *proclamation* of it made *publicly beforehand.*"—Cicero, *Offices*, i. xi.; again, also, *vide* iii. xxxi.

Compare these passages with Mr Gladstone's account of the Homeric age:—

"In that early age, despite the prevalence of piracy, even that idea of political justice and public right, which is the germ of the law of nations, was not unknown to the Greeks. It would appear that war could not be made without an appropriate cause, and that the offer of redress made it the duty of the injured to come to terms. Hence the offer of Paris in the third Iliad is at once readily accepted; and hence, even after the breach of the act, arises Agamemnon's fear, at the moment when he anticipates the death of Menelaus, that by that event the claim to the restoration of Helen will be practically disposed of, and the Greeks will have to return home without reparation for a wrong, of which the corpus, as it were, will have disappeared."—Iliad, iv. 160–62.[311]

It is certainly not within the scope of this chapter to indicate the multiform applications of the law of nations, which it would require a legist's special knowledge (to which the writer can lay no claim) to determine with any exactness. My object has been merely to sustain the traditional belief against those who deny it. I shall indeed, for the purposes of illustration, go into detail on one point, viz. the declaration of war; but I may mention incidentally that the Fecial and Amphictyonic law presumably extended to many other points, such as treaties, trophies,[312] truces,[313] hostages, and the like. Moreover, the maritime law of Rhodes and the islands of the Ægean, known to the Romans long before it was embodied in their code (which was not probably until they had extended maritime relations), presents, as Pastoret (ix. 118) informs us, "analogies et rapprochemens multipliés" with modern maritime legislation from the time of the Romans to the "ordonnance de la marine" drawn up by order of Louis XIV.

In an article on "Belligerent Rights at Sea" (in the *Home and Foreign Review*, July 1863), in which there will be found a nice discrimination of these questions, Mr E. Ryley says:—

"The very largest rule of belligerent rights limits the voluntary destruction of life and property by the necessity of the occasion and the object of the war. Bynkershock and Wolf insist that everything done against the enemy is lawful, and admit fraud, poison, and the murder, as we should call it, of non-combatants, as permissible expedients for attaining the object of the war. But these are the writers who lay the foundations of the law of nations in reason and custom, and ignore that perception and judgment of right and wrong which God has communicated to man. It is true that for the most part, and practically, we know the law of nations by reason and usage; but this law is founded not on that by which we know its decisions, but on justice; and reason must admit, and usage must adopt, whatever is clearly shown to be just and right, however this may be against precedent, and what has hitherto been held to be sound reason. There is no law without justice, nor any justice without conscience, nor any conscience without God. Grotius thus admirably expresses himself:—'Jus naturale est dictatum rectæ rationis, indicans actui aliqui, ex ejus convenientiâ aut disconvenientiâ cum ipsa naturâ rationali, inesse moralem turpitudinem, aut necessitatem moralem, ac consequenter ab auctore naturæ, Deo, talem actum vetari aut præcipi. Actus, de quibus tale extat dictatum, debiti sunt aut illiciti per se, atque ideo a Deo necessario præcepti aut vetiti intelliguntur.'[314] And this principle obtains greater force from the objections which have been made to it, and the efforts to establish another foundation for the law of nations. Thus the principle of utility is only a feeble attempt to give another name to the law of justice which God has implanted in His creatures; and to pretend to found a law on general usage and tacit consent is to mistake the evidence of justice for justice itself."

At first sight the passage quoted from Mr Ryley's article would seem to militate against my position; in reality we merely take up different weapons against Bynkershock and Wolf. If custom means merely precedent, it may or may not be in accordance with "that perception of right and wrong which God has communicated to man;" but if there is a tradition of a law of nations, the fact creates so great a presumption in favour of its pronouncements, that what is of usage and custom will be the criterion of what is right until the human intellect has shown that what has hitherto been held to be permissible was founded in a precedent of iniquity. On the other hand, we are agreed that the law of nations must be such as to stand the test of the "perception and judgment of right and wrong." As this perception, however, has never wholly died out among mankind, whatever is of general acceptance carries with it an assurance that it has stood this test; and "general usage and the tacit consent" is so much "the evidence of justice," that it has practically been taken, or mistaken by mankind "for justice itself," and the law of nations has always been discussed on the basis of usage. This, I contend, would not have been the case if there had not been behind usage the immemorial sanction and tradition, or if the tacit consent had been only acquiescence in wrong. I am the more confirmed in this view on perceiving that Mr Ryley, after stating his own opinion as to the right of blockade, finds his conclusions, when he has discriminated such precedents as were of an exceptional and retaliatory character, to be in conformity with usage and the decision of legists.

From this point of view those who contend for the basis of tradition and those who contend for the basis of natural justice mean the same thing. They both affirm that there are limitations to human passion even in war. They are both opposed to precedents based on force, and are equally hostile to "the principle of utility," for if, as Mr Ryley puts it, "the principle of utility" is only "another name for the law of justice which God has implanted in His creatures," the phrase is an understatement of the truth, liable to misconstruction, and tends to lower the standard of right; and if it means something different or distinct from this, it means that against which the tradition of mankind protests.

I have already said that international law, as distinguished from the law of nations, requires to be constantly discriminated by the intellect or the conscience of mankind, and more especially now that diplomatists are no longer legists.

There was a certain indirect and collateral influence arising out of the tradition of a law of nations from the fact that a body of men existing as its interpreters, or at least as its depositaries, which it appears to me was destined to operate powerfully in the interests of peace. The existence of such a body of men perpetuated a public opinion in these matters, they fostered an *esprit de corps* stronger even than the spirit of nationality which then reigned supreme and dominated society. When a violation of treaties or an unjust aggression took place there was thus found a body of men who would stigmatise or at least recognise it as such. The sentiment thus sustained was not all-influential for the purposes of peace, but it was operative to the extent of arresting the attention and perturbing the consciences of mankind. In like manner I venture to say that the diplomatic body, although the depositaries only of a bastard tradition, subserve this purpose also after a fashion, and I much doubt whether many well-intentioned men, in striving to compass its abolition would not, as matters stand, destroy the last breakwater which secures the peace of Europe.

In ancient times the comity of nations was virtually restricted to groups of cities or nations of kindred descent, or which had become confederate by reason of contiguity. This circumstance has been adduced by Sir G. C. Lewis to stop in limine the theory of a law of nations;[315] as if it was necessarily in denial of a tradition of morality common to all nations. Yet, I think that I shall be able to show instances of its recognition as between the groups, but it is precisely in its restricted application within the groups, and in the channels thus provided, that I think we shall find common features, and dimly and obscurely, though certainly, catch glimpses of the tradition.

If I may complete my thought, these confederations were so many types and anticipations of that Amphictyonic Council, which, if things had not persistently gone wrong in the world, might have been formed in mediæval times by Christendom under the presidency of the Popes,[316] and which may yet be realised in the triumph of religion which seems to be signified in the motto lumen in cœlo, as attaching to the successor of the present Pope, whose pontificate has been so singularly prefigured in the indication crux de cruce.[317]

In the *Times*, November 29, 1867, it was said, "If this theory ['the states of Christendom constituted as a species of commonwealth'] could be rendered effectual, international law would be furnished at once with its greatest need, a court to enforce its behests; but nothing is plainer than that for such arbitration *the arbitrators must be fetched from another planet.*"

But, inasmuch as Abraham Lincoln practically remarked, you cannot have "a cabinet of angels" in this world, the thing is to discover the arbitrator who is the furthest removed from sublunary influences. Now, how strong soever may be our national mistrusts and prejudices, we cannot refuse to recognise that the Papacy ostensibly satisfies these conditions, and this irrespective of the belief of the preponderant section of the Christian world that he is the infallible guide, and the divinely appointed interpreter of the tradition of morals.

Its representatives being always old men naturally inclined to peace,[318] the sovereign of a small state which a general war would imperil—professing maxims and therefore pledged to a programme of peace—(so that any deviation from it, as in the case of Julius II., would render glaring and abnormal acts which would have been unnoticed in an ordinary sovereign), a sovereign without a family (and whatever may be said of nepotism, it must be conceded that a man who has only collateral relatives is less tempted to found a family than one who has sons), a sovereign, in fine, representing the oldest line of succession in the world,[319] in the oldest city, in the centre of tradition, and like Noah in the traditional symbols (ante, p. 220), linking the new world with the old.

This, I find (I quote from a series of important papers on "English statesmen and the independence of Popes," *Tablet*, November 1870), was fully recognised by our greatest minister, Mr Pitt. In 1794, "Pitt suggested, through François de Conzié, Bishop of Arras, that the Pope should put himself at the head of a European league." "On more than one occasion," he wrote, "I have seen the continental courts draw back before the divergences of opinion and of religion which separate us. I think that a common bond ought to unite us all. *The Pope alone can be this centre....* We are too much divided by personal interests or by political views. Rome alone can raise an impartial voice, and one free from all exterior preoccupations. Rome, then, ought to speak according to the measure of her duties, and not merely of her good wishes, which no one doubts."

There have been at different periods of the world various projects of universal pacification;[320] but it is worthy of remark that they have almost all, from that of Henri IV. to the one recently broached by the Professor of Modern History at Cambridge, taken the traditional lines of a confederation of states more or less circumscribed with an amphictyonic council. This has its significance from the point of view I am indicating, but I do not see that it is satisfactorily accounted for on any other view.[321]

It would seem, then, that there has always existed in the world the tradition, and since the triumph of Christianity, the conditions by which, if it had so willed, it might have recovered the golden age of peace and happiness of which it has never entirely lost the tradition.

Until this consummation we must fall back upon the law of nations,[322] though even here it must be borne in mind that Christianity has exercised an indirect influence, and has raised the standard of morality for the world at large.[323] But when all is abated the law of nations remains the lex legum, deeply founded in the maxims, sentiments, and usages of mankind. These maxims in their tradition have been concurrently interpreted, adapted, and in a certain sense moulded by the intellect of legists, whose discriminations or conclusions have received the tacit approbation of mankind. Rarely has the production of any profane writer received such an unanimous ratification as the great work of Hugo Grotius, mainly, as we have seen (ante, p. 4), based on tradition. Again, the agreement and correspondence among the legists of different nationalities is substantial, and is only to be accounted for upon the supposition that each in his own groove faithfully incorporated and elaborated a tradition; and if you say that this was only an argument among the separate traditions of the Roman law, you only put back the argument one remove, as I have attempted to demonstrate. If conversely you say that the law of nations as we find it is purely the work and elaboration of legists, and the conclusions of abstract reason, put it to this test, bring all the legists of the world into a congress—such a congress is much needed just now—with instructions to create a new code on abstract principles, and upon the basis of the rejection of what is of custom and tradition, and see what they will accomplish! Do not all our difficulties begin exactly where, owing to the complications of modern civilisation, tradition ceases? For the rest we shall presently see what the Congress of Paris, in 1856, was able to effect in this kind.

CHAPTER XV
THE DECLARATION OF WAR

I think we have already distinct evidence that the Fecial Law was something more than our Treaty and Diplomatic Law. Let us examine it more particularly in action. If the law of nations ever was appealed to, and, if over and above, there was a tradition of a Divine revelation, or even of a prescriptive law founded on natural right, and having reference to war, which was ever invoked, it would have been in the first instance of aggression, supposing, as is implied in the term, that it was without fair cause and without fair warning. The declaration of war, therefore, is manifestly the hinge upon which the whole system of the law of nations turns.[324] Accordingly, the further we go back the more solemn and formal do we find the declaration of war to be.

> "In every instance the declaration of war was accompanied by religious formalities. When the Senate believed that it had cause of complaint against a nation, it sent a Fecial to his frontier. There the pontiff, his head bound with a woollen veil,[325] exposed the griefs of the Romans and demanded satisfaction. If it was not granted, he went back to render an account of his mission to the Senate, ... and after a delay of thirty or thirty-three days they voted a declaration of war. Then the Fecial returned to the frontier, and, casting a javelin into the enemy's country, he pronounced the following formula—'Quod populus Hermundulus,' &c.... Every war which had not been declared in this manner was considered as unjust, and certain to incur the displeasure of the gods. In the course of time this solemn declaration was replaced by a vain formality."[326]

Montfauçon ("L'Antiquité Expliquée," ii. 1, p. iv., p. 35) says:—

> "Lorsqu'ils alloient parlementer, ils avoient sur la tête un voile tissu de laine,[327] et ils étoient couronnéz de vervaine: leur office étoit d'impêcher que les Romains n'entreprissent point de guerre injuste: d'aller comme legats vers les nations qui violoient les traitez, etc.... ils prenoient aussi

connaissance faits au legats de part et d'autre. Quand la paix ne se trouvoit pas faite selon les loix, ils la declaroient nulle. Si les commandans avoient fait quelque chose contre la justice et contre le droit des gens, ils reparoient leur faute et expioient leur crime, ... à cause du violement des traites faits devant Numance, dit Ciceron par un décret du Senat le Patrapatratus livra, C. Mancinus aux Numantins."[328]

We must content ourselves, of course, with what evidence we may get of similar institutions elsewhere; but what strikes me as strange in the contrast of modern civilisation with barbarism, is, that whereas our advances, whether in the sense of peace and war (whenever they are formally made), are commonly understood, the corresponding demonstrations on the side of barbarism are invariably misconstrued.

When, for instance, Captain Cook approached the shores of Bolabola, he describes the following scene, which reads to me very like the account we have just been reading of the Roman herald:—

"Soon after a single man ran along the shore armed with his lance, and when he came abreast of the boat he began to dance, brandish his weapon, and call out in a very shrill tone, which Tupia [a native of an adjacent island who was on board] said was a defiance from the people.... As the boat rowed slowly along the shore back again, another champion came down, shouting defiance, and brandishing his lance. His appearance was more formidable than that of the other, for he wore a large cap made of the tail feathers of the topia bird, and his body was covered with stripes of different coloured cloth, yellow, red, and brown.... Soon after a more grave and elderly man came down to the beach, and hailing the people in the boat, inquired who they were, and from whence they came.[329]... After a short conference they all began to pray very loud. Tupia made his responses, but continued to tell us they were not our friends" (i. 119).

Let this be taken in connection with the following narrative:—[330]

"The large canoes came close round the ship, some of the Indians playing on a kind of flute, others singing, and the rest blowing on a sort of shells. Soon after, a large canoe advanced, in which was an awning, on the top of which sat *one* of the natives holding some *yellow* and *red* feathers in his hand. The captain having consented to his coming alongside, he delivered the feathers, and while a present was preparing for him, he put back from the ship, and *threw the branch* of a cocoa-tree in the air. This was doubtless the *signal* for an onset, for there was an instant shout from all the canoes, which, approaching the ship, threw volleys of stones into every part of her."

Here the question appears to me to be whether this act of throwing the branch, so analogous to the throwing the javelin, which was the final act in the Roman declaration of war (and to which our throwing down the glove or the gauntlet has analogy), was merely the signal to themselves, or whether it was not also the *notice* of attack to the enemy. Upon this will depend whether we are to consider it a treacherous "ruse" (and the presentation of the feathers has that aspect), or whether it was their traditional mode of declaration of war, and construed to be a treacherous attack, because the gallant navigator belonged to a nation more ignorant of the laws of nations than the savages they encountered.

From the very fact of their having enacted this comedy or ceremonial, it must be inferred either that they attached some superstitious importance to its performance, and expected some good effects from it to themselves, or that they thought that it would be understood by their adversaries, in which case they must implicitly have believed it to be common to all nations.

In either case it is just possible that after the manner of savages, they may have confused the symbols of peace and war, and ran into one what the Romans had carefully distinguished—the "caduceatores",[331] who went to demand peace, and the "fecials," who were sent to denounce war.

The red and yellow colours of the feathers in the above account may afford a clue, when it is remembered (vide note), that they coincide with the colour used by the Otaheitans to testify fidelity and friendliness; but, to appreciate this in its full significance, it will be necessary to show how commonly the traditional symbols of peace among the ancients had reference to the diluvian traditions, more especially the Dove and the Rainbow.

Assuming for the moment that Bryant is right in his derivation of the names of Juno and Venus from Jönah (Hebrew), and Οινας (Greek) = Dove,[332] I ask attention to the following, in connection with the red and yellow feathers of the Polynesians, and the tail feathers of the topia bird mentioned by Cook (supra, p. 388).[333] (Bryant, ii. 345), "As the peacock, in the full expansion of his plumes, displays all the beautiful colours of the Iris (the rainbow), it was probably for that reason made the bird of Juno, instead of the dove, which was appropriated to Venus. The same history was variously depicted in different places, and consequently as variously interpreted." (Compare p. 279.)

If this is true, if the rainbow is the symbol of peace, and the peacock is the symbol of the rainbow, will it absolutely surprise us to find feathers of various colours presented as tokens of peace? I am prepared for the reply, that Bryant's etymology is now considered obsolete; but I shall fall back upon the argument which I have urged elsewhere, that in cases where tradition renders the transmission of certain words probable, there is a presumption which overrides the ordinary canons of philological criticism. Philologers very properly lay down, *e.g.* Mr Max Müller's "Chapter of Accidents in Comparative Theology," *Contemp. Rev.*, April 1870, p. 8:—

> "Comparative philology has taught us again and again that when we find a word exactly the same in Greek and Sanscrit, we may be certain that it cannot be the same word; and the same applies to comparative mythology ... for the simple reason that Sanscrit and Greek have deviated from each other, have both followed their own way, have both suffered their own phonetic corruptions, and hence, if they do possess the same word, they can only possess it either in its Greek or in its Sanscrit disguise."

This is of course only upon the assumption that the languages have gone their own way, have followed their own corruptions; but if it can be shown that certain words, &c. &c., were preserved in tradition, and so guarded as not to come under the laws of deviation which philology traces out, or to come under them on different conditions, then, on the contrary, it is exceedingly probable that we should find them identical, or at least recognisable; in any case, this is a point which must be decided according to the evidences of tradition, and not according to the laws of philology. This will be better understood from a case in point. I append the evidence respecting the traditions of the Dove and the Rainbow—which are just the incidents which are likely to have impressed the imagination and memory of mankind.[334]

The digression we have just made involves some risk of distracting attention from the point it was intended to enforce—viz. the traditionary character of the mode, and, by implication, the traditionary recognition of the obligation, of the declaration of war. We have already seen in Ozanam (supra, p. 371) indications of the probability of similar traditions among the primitive tribes of Germany. Will it clench the argument if we find Romans and Gauls on a common understanding in these matters, when brought for the first time into contact since their original separation?—

"The great misfortunes which befel the city from the Gauls, are said to have proceeded from the violation of these sacred rites. For when the barbarians were besieging Clusium, Fabius Ambustus was sent ambassador to their camp with proposals of peace, in favour of the besieged. But receiving a harsh answer, he thought himself released from his character of ambassador, and rashly taking up arms for the Clusians, challenged the bravest man in the Gaulish army. He proved victorious, ... but the Gauls having discovered who he was, sent *a herald* to Rome to accuse Fabius of bearing arms against them, contrary to *treaties and good faith*, and *without a declaration of war*. Upon this the Feciales exhorted the Senate to deliver him up to the Gauls, but he appealed to the people, and, being a favourite with them, was screened from the sentence. Soon after this, the Gauls marched to Rome, and sacked the whole city except the Capitol, as we have related at large in the life of Camillus." — *Plutarch's Numa.*

I venture further to think that the traditionary modes of the declaration of war may be detected among the Gauls in Cæsar's time, in the manner of their challenge. *E.g.* it so came about that Cæsar wished to draw the enemy (the Nervii) to his side of the valley and to engage them at a disadvantage before his camp. To this end he simulated fear. "Our men meanwhile retiring from the rampart, they approached still nearer, *cast their darts* on all sides within the trenches and *sent heralds* round the camp to proclaim," &c. (Duncan's Cæsar, B. v. xlii.)

We will now turn to the Greek tradition. I quote from an old author who has examined the matter more fully than I find it treated elsewhere. Rous. ("Archæologiæ Atticæ," lib. 6, s. 3, civ.) says: — "As careful and cunning as they were in warlike affairs, I cannot find but that they did 'propere signi quæ piget inchoare,' bear a great affection to peace; as may appear in their honourable receiving of ambassadors, to whom they gave hearing in no worse place than a temple.... The usual ensign carried by Greek ambassadours was κηρυκεον, caduceus,[335] a right staff of wood with snakes twisted about it and looking one another in the face.... If the peace could not be kept, but they must needs have war, yet they would be sure to give warning and fair play, and make proclamations of their intentions before they marcht. The manner in proclaiming war was to send a fellow of purpose either to cast a spear or let loose a lamb into the borders of the country, or into the city itself whither they were marching (which Hesychius rather thinks to have been the signal before a battel), thereby showing them, that what was then a habitation for men, should shortly be a pasture for sheep."[336] I should rather have thought that it had analogy with the Jewish scapegoat; but, whatever the idea, it was apparently symbolled and commemorated in the woollen veil prescribed to the Roman pontiff in the declaration of war. It would seem, however, that the signal for battle (chap. v.) was "instead of sounding a trumpet, they had fellows whom they called πυρφορους, that went before with torches, and throwing them down in the midst between the two armies, gave the sign.... Now, this business they might do safely and without any danger, ... for the torch-bearers were peculiarly protected by Mars, and accounted sacred."[337]

The sense of national responsibility in war, and the reluctance of kings to involve themselves without the consent of their people would appear from Œschylos' "Supplicants" (v. 393, 363).

I have referred to the Peruvian traditions of Manco Capac's laws of war, and that "in every stage of the war the Peruvian was open to propositions for peace."

From the Hindoo tradition, apparently, Manu's code was conceived in an identical spirit. (Vide "Hist. of India," "The Hindu and Mahometan Periods," by the Hon. Mountstuart Elphinstone; Murray, 1866, ch. ii. p. 26.) "The laws of war (Manu's code) are honourable and humane. Poisoned arrows and mischievously barbed arrows and fire arrows are all prohibited." [Dr Hooker, in his "Himalayan Journal," mentions a similar tradition among the Limboos, I think, or Lepchas.[338]] "There are many situations in which it is by no means allowable to destroy the enemy. Among those who must always be spared are unarmed or wounded men, and those who have broken their weapons, and one who says, 'I am thy captive.' Other prohibitions are still more generous.... The settlement of a conquered country is conducted on equally liberal principles. Immediate security is to be assured to all by proclamation. The religion and laws of the country are to be maintained and respected." And I have fancied (vide 395) that the recognition at least of such a tradition, if it be only the "homage which vice pays to virtue," is to be read in the devices carried by the Babylonians.[339]

There was, moreover, a law at Athens which forbade them to declare war until after a deliberation of three days—"Bellum vero antequam decerneretur, triduo deliberare lex jubebat" (Apsines, Marcell. in Hermog. ap. J. Meursii Them. Att., l. i. c. xi.); and we have seen that the Senate at Rome postponed the declaration of war for thirty days. I cannot help thinking, though it is the merest surmise, that it is in the dim recollection of some such tradition that we must account for the meaningless and superstitious delays which we occasionally read of in the warfare of barbarous nations; e.g. Cæsar (De Bello Gallico, i. xl. c.) had drawn up his troops and offered the enemy battle, but Ariovistus thought proper to sound a retreat. "Cæsar inquiring of the prisoners why Ariovistus so obstinately refused an engagement, found that it was the custom among the Germans for the women to decide by lots and divination when it was proper to decide a battle; and that these had declared the army would not be victorious if they fought before the new moon."[340] [There was also a law at Athens that it was not lawful to lead forth an army before the seventh day of the month. "Vetitum Athenis erat, exercitum educere ante diem septimum."] J. Muersii, id.

I have discussed the ancient mode of declaration of war at some length as an instance of tradition. There are some, I am afraid, to whom the discussion will appear ineffably trifling; and I may even be misconstrued to say that everything would be set right in Europe, if only a herald were sent in proper form to declare war. There are men of a certain cast of mind to whom forms are repugnant; there are others to whom they are unintelligible. It has been observed, however, that the rejection of forms is one thing, the neglect of them another. The rejection of forms may be, on some principle, good, though misapplied, often does unconscious homage when it means to spurn, and may be compensated for in other ways. The neglect of them is simply evidence of laxity. Cromwell perfectly well knew the divinity which attached to forms when he said, "Take away that bauble;" and, on the other hand, no one better than he would have judged the state of an army (not his own) in which he was told that it was the custom of soldiers not to salute their officers. The declaration of war without any solemnity, still more the commencement of hostilities without any declaration at all,[341] seems to me closely analogous—as a sign of disorganisation—to the absence of any form of salute at a parade. I am far from contending that old forms, when they have become obsolete, can be resuscitated; but I do contend for the resuscitation of ancient maxims and ideas. In any age fully imbued with the responsibility of war, in which it was considered unseemly to declare it until after a three days' deliberation in solemn conclave, and which even then protracted the declaration till the seventh or the thirtieth day, would it have been possible for two great nations to have gone to war because there had been "a breach of etiquette," if indeed there was a breach of etiquette, "at a German watering-place?"[342] Allowing that this was merely the ostensible pretext, and that the real grounds remained behind—if these long deliberations had been necessarily interposed, would there not have been a thousand chances in favour of such a European intervention as saved the peace of Europe three years before in the affair of Luxembourg? Yet, so far as we know at present, the following is the history of the commencement of the most horrible, the most destructive, and the most barbarous war[343] of modern times.

"A private letter from Paris relates that the Duc de Grammont, who has taken to spend his evenings at the Jockey Club, was lately asked there, 'How he came to blunder into such a fatal war?'[344] He replied, 'I asked the Minister of War, Lebœuf, if he was ready, and he answered, "Ready! ay, and doubly ready;" otherwise,' added the Duc, 'I should have taken care not to have counselled a war which there were twenty modes of averting.'"—Times, Sept. 1, 1870.[345]

The extent of the disorganisation and the laxity into which we have fallen, appears perhaps as strikingly as in any anything else in the frequency of the complaints of the little regard paid to "parlémentaires" and officers bearing flags of truce. But what startles us more than all is the light manner in which this transgression of the law of nations is referred to even by the parties aggrieved.

I will here place two extracts which I have made in juxtaposition:—

Carver ("Travels in North America," p. 358) says, that when a deputation sets out together for their enemy's country with propositions of peace, "They bear before them the pipe of peace, which, I need not inform my readers, is of the same nature *as a flag of truce* among the Europeans, and is treated with the greatest respect and veneration *even by the most barbarous* nations. *I never heard of an instance* wherein the *bearers of this sacred* badge of friendship were ever treated disrespectfully, or its rights violated. The Indians believe that the Great Spirit *never suffers an infraction* of this kind to go unpunished."

Count Chandordy, in his reply to Count Bismarck, dated Bordeaux, Jan. 25, 1871, says:—"Count Bismarck reproaches the French armies with having *fired on parlémentaires.*" An accusation of this nature had already been brought to the knowledge of the Paris Government, and we may quote the following words of M. Jules Favre in his circular of 12th January—"I have the satisfaction to acquaint your excellency that the Governor of Paris has hastened to order an inquiry into the facts alleged by Count Bismarck, and in announcing this to him he has brought *much more numerous facts* of the same nature to his own cognizance which are imputed to Prussian sentinels, but *which he never would have allowed to interrupt ordinary relations.*"

I do not know whether this contrast between barbarism, such as it existed in the last century, and modern civilisation, will astonish those partisans of success whom in truth nothing in all the multiform atrocities of this dreadful war seems to have astonished or shocked, so that it was at times almost ludicrous to hear these *introuvables* declare such things as the bombardment of hospitals and churches, as at Strasburg and Paris, quite right, which even the German commanders, when the matter was brought to their attention, admitted to be wrong.

This perhaps is the worst symptom of corruption we have yet seen, and yet there was a time, and that quite recent, when a different sentiment prevailed. I have just referred[346] to the declaration in the Treaty of Paris, which thought to inaugurate a new era by bringing all causes of conflict in Europe to a settlement of arbitration. But let no one be discouraged or cease to believe in the possibility of such a consummation because of the result. There never was a stronger instance of the intellect of the world vainly striving to create an international code and system for itself which was to be distinct from the law of nations; for at the same moment that the diplomatists who were collected in Paris set to work upon their tower, which was to erect itself above the waters of any future inundation, they one and all agreed to demolish, and as a first step to pull down, the cornerstone from the temple of the past. How this was brought about will best be told in an extract from the Count de Montalembert's "Pie IX. et la France en 1849 et 1859,"—

> "Let us go back to the origin of the evil, ... it dates back more especially from the Congress of Paris in 1856, from that diplomatic reunion which, after having solemnly declared that none of the contracting powers *had the right to interfere either collectively or individually in the relations of a sovereign with his subjects* (Protocol of 18th March), after having proclaimed the principle of the absolute independence of the sovereigns, for the benefit of the Turkish Sultan against his Christian subjects, thought it within its competency, in its protocol of the 8th of April, and in the absence of any representative of the august accused, to proclaim that the situation of the Pontifical States was 'abnormal' and 'irregular.' This accusation developed and exaggerated at the Tribune, and elsewhere by Lord Palmerston and Count Cavour, was equally formulated under the Presidency and upon the initiative of the Minister of Foreign Affairs in France, and it is consequently France which must bear the principal responsibility before the Church and Europe. We can recall the grief and surprise which this strange proceeding created in the Catholic world."

Thus was the game set rolling; and the policy thus indicated was pursued with the eager and unrelenting pertinacity of some, and with the tacit approval of the rest of the co-signatories.

The war declared by France against Austria, which was the precipitating cause of the storm which broke upon the Papal States, can, it is true, only be regarded as evidence of the conspiracy—inasmuch as it was declared by one of the conspirators at the instigation of another, whose ultimate aim was the seizure of the States of the Church and of the other independent

Italian sovereignties to the profit of Piedmont. So soon as the victory of the French arms was decided, the Emperor's proclamation from Milan appeared, inciting the populations to insurrection. All then followed in sequence—the revolt of the Romagnas four days after the Milan manifesto, their annexation along with the other independent states of Central Italy by Piedmont, this annexation being effected with the connivance, if not the consent, of France, and for which payment was eventually made in the cession of Nice and Savoy (all this being in contravention of the treaties of Villafranca and Zurich). But what mattered the contravention of treaties in comparison with the scenes which followed? The programme of the congress, or, if that is denied, the programme of two (if not three, for it is difficult to acquit Lord Palmerston and Lord John Russell of participation by consent) of the powers who had entered into the conspiracy against European order, and these, at that time, the powers in the highest state of military efficiency, was to be carried out per fas et nefas. Naples and the patrimony of St Peter had to be secured, and as they morally presented no vulnerable side, they were seized by the hand of the marauder in defiance of "all law, human and divine."[347] Garibaldi's descent on Sicily, effected under the cover of the English navy, was simply a brusque and flagrant act of piracy, for which no plea of justification has ever been set up. The usurpation of the Papal States, though not less ruthlessly accomplished in the end, was carried through with more regard to form in its preliminary stages; yet at the last the diplomatic mask was torn off, and the invasion was made without any pretext or justification known to the law of nations, and without even a declaration of war.

Here, again, the Imperial diplomacy and Italian intrigue went hand in hand. Lamoriciere, in reliance upon the honour of France, had made all his dispositions against Garibaldi, and had received a letter from the French ambassador as late as the 7th September (bearing the same date as the so-called ultimatum of Cavour, although the Piedmontese troops had crossed the frontier before it was delivered), which I shall here reproduce, seeing that it is not on record in the Annuaire des Deux Mondes (1860)—"I inform you by the Emperor's orders that the Piedmontese will not enter the Roman States, and that 20,000 French are about to occupy the different places of those states. Make, then, all your dispositions against Garibaldi.—Le Duc de Grammont."[348] (This letter was dated September 7, 1860, the battle of Castelgidardo was fought on the 18th September 1860.) It is needless to add that no reinforcements from France appeared, and that the assurance served no other purpose than to mislead, and to throw Lamoriciere off his guard. Indeed, in spite of various protestations and the subsequent withdrawal of the French ambassador from Turin, the Catholic world settled down into the belief, not only that the Emperor of the French had never had the intention of sending troops to the rescue, but that the whole scheme of the invasion had been deliberately devised at the ominous interview which took place on the 28th of August previous, between the Emperor, Farini, and General Cialdini. It was even said that the words used by the Emperor on the occasion transpired, "frappez fort et frappez vite," — a terse and striking phrase, which will fitly perpetuate in the human memory the most flagrant violation of the law of nations which history affords.[349]

All this was done with the undisguised satisfaction of several veteran English statesmen, who were, moreover, directly or indirectly represented at the same congress which sought to bind the European powers to call in the arbitration of a friendly power, in case of disagreement, before making an appeal to arms.

Now there is no reason why this rule, good in itself, and congruous to the spirit and maxims of the law of nations, should not have been embodied as a fundamental article in the code; for the law of nations is not a dead-letter, but, like everything that is of tradition, easily lending itself to adaptation and development according to the changing circumstances of the world.

Can we be surprised that this principle, good and according to reason, but which nevertheless presupposes certain sentiments in the world in correspondence with it, should in the actual circumstances have been barren of results? Is it wonderful that it should have miscarried in the hands of men who were parties to the invasion, without even the form of a declaration of war, of the State predestined by divine Providence to be the cornerstone of Christendom? Would it have been befitting that this beneficent arrangement should have been destined to be the work of men who, either by participation or as accessories after the fact, had set their hands to a deed which shocked every principle of morality, and made the very notion of public law in Europe ridiculous?

The early commencements of this policy cannot be studied at a more appropriate moment than now, when we are witnessing its *denouement*.

What has been the result to France of its Italian policy? To Austria? To England? To Europe?

Has any power prospered that had a hand in setting the ball rolling, or, for that matter, any power that had the responsibility of staying the parricidal hand, and held back? If Austria, the first victim, had firmly and strenuously resisted the early instigations of evil, would she ever, according to human calculations, have had to fight at Magenta and Solferino? and, in another way, was there not something dramatic in the sudden reverse and displacement of Count Buol, who had been the Austrian representative at the Congress, immediately after he had hurled the fatal *ultimatum*? The retort will be triumphant. Did not France, the great culprit of all, who both cast its own responsibility to the winds and sowed the hurricane, conquer at Solferino? Truly she did; but *respice finem*, or rather, we may say, we have lived to see the end. Did not Solferino, after some ten years of delusive prosperity, lead up to Sedan? Of England I do not wish to say more than that since that date she has unaccountably fallen in the esteem of men; has, in her turn, met with injustice, and no longer maintains the same relative position which she held during the fifty years preceding the Congress.

Everything, in fine, since that date, seems to have gone in favour of that European power which remained in the background, and which, if it did no good act at the Congress, at least had the worldly wisdom to fold its arms and refrain from sacrilege. Yes, Prussia has had her victory; but by all accounts there never was a victory which has made a nation so sad and mournful, and which was greeted with fewer manifestations of joy. It was peace rather than victory which was welcomed home. Here, too, we seem to see the subtle and nicely-measured retaliation. Again, was there no significance in the unlooked-for disasters at Forbach and Woerth, occurring coincidently with the final abandonment of Rome by France?

These are things which strike the eye, but which are difficult of demonstration, and it would appear a hopeless errand to convince a generation which has witnessed the burning of Paris, if not without emotion, at any rate without serious reflection, and, in spite of manifest prediction, has refused to see in it "the finger of retribution and the hand of God."

And yet belief in this retribution of heaven is at the foundation of the law of nations. Previously to the astounding experiences of the recent war, during those years so fruitful "in pledges and perjuries," it was a common phrase, and most frequently used with reference to France, that war was no longer an affair of divine Providence, but that Providence was always on the side of the big battalions.

With one word as to the significance of this phrase, which is tantamount to a negation of the law of nations, I shall conclude.

It may certainly happen, that in a contest one party may be consciously hypocrite, whilst the other is conscious of its rectitude; but presumedly, and until the contrary is manifested, both parties must be supposed to believe themselves in the right, and to run the tilt like knights in the mediæval tournament. Nevertheless, as Dr Johnson said, there are arguments for a "plenum" and for a "vacuum," but one conclusion only can be true; and in some way in every conflict, which is true and which is just is known only to the inscrutable judgment of the Most High. We do not know all the secrets of courts, neither could we exactly determine the point if we had before us all the deliberations of councils, it is sufficient for us to know that victory is not always on the side of the big battalions, as witness, *inter alia*, Marathon, Morgarten, Bannockburn, Lepanto, Mentana. Will any Englishman maintain the proposition that victory is always on the side of the big battalions? Then, beginning with Cressy and Poictiers, and following Marlborough through the fields of Blenheim, Ramilies, and Malplaquet, and the Duke of Wellington through the Peninsular War, we must renounce that which gives "the *éclat* to all our victories." Doubtless, then, the quality of troops will in some instances weigh far more than numbers. You allow it? We now introduce an element of great uncertainty, and about which there will always be much dispute, and moreover it will always be a matter concerning which religion and morality will have much to say. It is no longer an affair of big battalions, it is no longer reduced to a matter of calculation, on which side the victory is to be. Let me further remark, that whilst there is one set of writers who will be ready to say that Providence is on the side of the big battalions, there is another set of writers, and these the men who are more conversant with the details, who will with great acuteness undertake to prove to you that it is so much an affair of Providence that in each case the victory was scarcely a victory, and only such because some casualty on the other side intervened to convert what would otherwise have been a victory into a defeat. It is unfortunately true that this latter class of historians and strategists do not, as a rule, trace in the turn of events the retribution of Providence. Still, the presumption will always be that victory favours the righteous cause, although it may be only *pro hac vice*, and ultimate success may not crown the career of the victorious nation, because its virtues may not have merited more than a signal and single success;—or it may even be that its merits may be of a kind such as to gain it a reward which transcends the rewards of earthly victory; or, again, the career of victory must be explained and measured by the depths of the final catastrophe and discomfiture.

In any case, it is a great thing for a nation to have won a victory in a rightful cause. The reward of virtue remains and gladdens the heart in the day of disaster and distress. Whatever may chance to us, there will always lie in store for us the consolation of reading the history of the battle of Waterloo; not, let us say, as the victory of one nation over another nation, but as the great and final triumph of a righteous over an unrighteous cause, gained by England. It is, thank God! impossible alike for the conqueror and the revolutionary multitude to destroy the Past.

INDEX

operation as a curse,

Blackstone on primitive life and a state of nature,

Boat, philology of the word,

Bochica,

Bolabola, declaration of war at,

Bonzies, the,

Book of Genesis, the,

Book of Sothis,

Bougainville on divinities of the Tahitians,

Boulanger, M., quoted,

on diluvian tradition,

on the Golden Age,

Brace, Mr, his "Ethnology," quoted,

"Breach of etiquette," a, consequences of,

the ostensible pretext of Franco-German war,

Brigham Young and the Mormons,

British Medical Journal on explosive bullets,

Bronze Age, the,

its commencement,

Bryant, Mr J.,

on creation of man,

on the symbol of the bull,

on Dionusus,

on Noah and Janus,

his derivation of Juno and Venus,

on the dove,

Buddhist legend,

Buffaloes, Feast of the,

"Bull-dance," the,

parallel accounts of, by Burton and Catlin,

Bunsen, Baron,

Plutarch on,

traditionary modes of,

importance attached to forms of,

consequences of the violation of forms of,

Deities of the Chaldæan Pantheon,

"De Legibus" quoted,

De Quincey, quoted,

Deluge of Deucalion, the,

Deluge of Ogyges, the,

anterior to that of Deucalion,

its date,

Deluge, the—traditions of, localised in China,

commemorative monument of,

traditions of, in Egypt,

in Cashmir,

among Sioux Indians,

among Tartar tribes,

L'Abbé Gainet on,

Phrygian legend of,

Phœnician legend of, localised,

Santal legend of,

Etruscan monument commemorative of,

connection of Saturn with,

of Ogyges and Deucalion,

traditions of, among Indian tribes,

Sanscrit story of,

its date,

traditions of, among Greeks,

Frederick Schlegel on,

traditions of, in Africa and America,

Boulanger on,

his views of human progress,

Donoughmore, Earl of,

Dove, the bird of Venus,

traditions of,

Duc de Grammont, the,

Dyaks and Javanese, contrast in colour,

Dyans,

Dyer, Dr, on the Sabines,

the temple of Diana,

Dynasties of Egypt,

Dynasty of the Popes,

Eastern Islanders, tradition among the,

Egg, the mundane, tradition of,

an emblem of the Creation,

the Mahabarata account of,

Egypt, chronology of,

its Chronicles,

dynasties of,

commemorative festival of the Deluge in,

Egyptian chronology, Palmer on,

Egyptians, the, canopied boat of,

Jewish rites and ceremonies borrowed from,

Ellis's "Polynesian Researches" quoted,

on Tahitian relics,

Endogamy,

English socialists,

Enoch, result of his disappearance regarding Nimrod,

embodied traditionally in Chaldæan gods Ana and Enu,

Enu or Bil, a Chaldæan deity,

a reduplication of Enoch,

*Epi*metheus (afterthought) and *Pro*metheus (forethought),

the unit of ancient society,

Family tradition, confusion of,

Fatimala, the,

Feast of the Buffaloes, the,

Feathers, coloured, emblematic of peace and war,

Fecial College, the,

correspondence of, with Herald's College,

Federal union between Romans and Latins,

Feegees, the, religion among,

their characteristics and civilisation,

Fergusson, Adam, on the Six Nations,

Festivals, commemorative, of the Deluge,

in Cashmir,

among various nations,

the Hydrophoria at Athens,

the "O-kee-pa,";

the Panathenæa,

the Dionysia,

in Egypt,

among the Mandan Indians,

the "So-sin" customs of Dahome,

at Sanchi,

the "Bull-dance,";

the "big canoe,";

the baskets of water,

the gourds and calabashes,

the "first man,",

among the Santals,

among the Japanese,

at Huaheine,

among the Egyptians,

Assyrian, see Assyrian mythology.

Myths connecting man with the monkey,

Myths, their importance,

Natchez tribes, institution of perpetual fire among,

Nations, law of. *See* International Law, Law of Nations.

Natural right,

Nature, law of. *See* Law of Nature.

Nature-worship,

Nazarians, the, a curious Gnostic sect,

Nebo, a Chaldæan deity,

resemblance of, to Shem,

Necessities of the pastoral life,

Negro, the, persistency of colour in,

subserviency of,

Ner, soss, and *sar,* Chaldæan periods of time,

Nergal identified with Mars,

Newman, Dr,

on history of Western civilisation,

New Zealanders, curious tradition among,

their degeneration and retrogression,

Nicolas, Mon. A.,

Niebühr, quoted,

Nillson, Professor, on the Stone Age,

quoted,

Nimrod, a powerful chieftain,

in the Chaldæan mythology,

identity with Belus,

his apotheosis confounded with Enoch's disappearance,

Nin or Ninip, the true fish-god,

identification with Noah,

emblem of, in Assyria,

Ogyges and Deucalion, traditional connection of, with Deluge,

"O-kee-pa," the, a religious ceremony of Mandans,

Old Chronicle of Egypt, the,

analysis of,

Opischeschaht Indians, ceremonies among the,

"Oracula Sybillina," the, quoted,

Oral transmission of tradition,

H. N. Coleridge on,

Orbis terrarum, the,

nucleus of,

Ordeals among the Indians,

Ordinances of Menu,

Oriental religions, Cardinal Wiseman on the,

"Origin and Development of Religious Belief," Mr Baring Gould on,

Origin and growth of International law,

"Origin of Laws," Goguet's, quoted,

Origin of Mosaic law,

Orpheus and Euridike,

"Orvar Odd's saga,",

Osiris, the judge of the soul,

Over-population, Malthus' views regarding,

Ox Temple of Meaco, ceremony in the,

Ozanam, on Laws,

Pachacamac, the Peruvian deity,

Pagan view of the social compact,

Pall Mall Gazette, the, on the Darwinian theory of conscience,

on laws,

on utilitarianism,

on European radicalism,

on the custom of the Manx Thing,

Palmer, Mr William, on Egyptian chronology,

Phoroneus, the father of mankind,

Phrygian legend of the Deluge,

Pinkerton's account of religion of the Samoides,

Plato, tradition of condition of families recorded by,

his Atlantis, an embodiment of tradition,

Plough, etymology of the word,

Plumtre's Æschylus,

Plutarch's "Numa," quoted,

Polyandry, regulated and rude,

Polygamy,

"Polynesian Researches," quoted,

Polytheism and monotheism,

Pongol festival of Southern India,

Pontifical power, the,

Poole, Mr,

Pope, the, centre of a European league,

Pope's Odyssey quoted,

Poseidon,

Positivism, Huxley's definition of,

Posterity of Ham, the,

Precedence of women in Dahome,

Pottery, the art of, an evidence of progress,

Pre-historic Archæology divided into four epochs,

Prayer and Punishment, expressed by same word by Latins,

Prescott's "History of Mexico" quoted,

Prevost, Sir G.,

Primary objects of Law of Nations,

Primitive condition of mankind, traditions regarding, from Sanchoniathon,

Primitive life,

the family,

Races, primitive,

Radicalism, European,

Radien, the deity of Scandinavian mythology,

"Rain and Rivers," the, of Col. G. Greenwood, quoted,

Rainbow, the symbol of peace,

tradition of the,

Ra or Il, the Chaldæan deity,

account of, by Rawlinson,

Ravana,

Rawlinson, Professor,

on Babylonian chronology,

on good and evil personifications,

identification of Nergal with Mars,

on deities of Chaldæan Pantheon,

on Nin or Ninip,

on Noah,

corroboration of Assyrian history,

the use of metals,

Reduplication and confusion of deities,

Reduplications—of Yao and Hoang-ti,

of Enoch,

of Bacchus,

Relics of Scriptural tradition in Greece,

Religion and philosophy, divergence between, 108.

Religion of the Samoides,

among savage races,

the Tonpinambas of Brazil,

the Feegees,

among Indians,

in Guinea,

among the Fuegians,

tendency of, to uncertainty and distortion,

confusion of family tradition,

persistency of local,

unity of Scripture with,

Duke of Argyll on,

testimony of Eusebius to value of,

oral transmission, the main channel of,

Schlegel on,

Sanchoniathon on,

concordance and divergence in,

truth and persistence of,

of the creation of man,

intellectual strictures upon,

opposition of Baring Gould's views,

relics of scriptural, in Greece,

of the man-bull,

of the Deluge among American Indians,

among Santals and Lepchas,

the *Saturday Review* on Indian,

Sir John Lubbock on,

De Maistre's view,

untrustworthiness and uncertainty of, according to Lubbock,

a Lapland,

capacity of savages for transmission of,

evidences of, in religion of savage nations,

of the mundane egg,

of fire,

the discovery of America a proof of,

of Bochica among Mozca Indians,

Peruvian, compared with classical and oriental,

transfusion and intermixture of,

Usage the basis of law of nations,

Untenable hypothesis of a Stone Age,

Urquhart, Mr D.,

Utilitarianism and international law,

"Utility," Bentham's peculiar crotchet,

the basis of his juridical system,

Vaivaswata,

Valdegamas, Marquis de,

Vancouver's Island, scene on,

Vaux, Mr, on metallurgy of the ancients,

Vega, Garcilasso de la, on Peruvian religion,

Venus,

myths of,

Vestiges of religion among savage races,

Vigne, Mr G. G.,

Violation of treaties, the,

Virgil, lines of, on Saturn,

his Æneid quoted,

the Eclogues,

Virtue and vice personified as white and black in the Zendavesta,

Voltaire, the intellect of,

Voltairean prejudices against primitive records,

Vul, the son of Ana,

Wallace, Mr,

on man,

Wallis, Captain,

Wallis, Mr J. E.,

War and peace, symbols of,

War, the Declaration of, . *See* Declaration of War.

Warburton, E., on oral transmission of past events among the Indians,

Waring, Mr J. B.,

Footnotes

[1] It has curiously happened that I have never seen the work which, after Bryant, would probably have afforded the largest repertory of facts—G. Stanley Faber's "Dissertation on the Mysteries of the Cabiri;" and it is only recently, since these pages were in print, that I have become acquainted with Davies' "Celtic Researches" and "The Mythology and Rites of the British Druids." The Celtic traditions respecting their god Hu, are so important from more than one point of view, that I cannot forbear making the following extracts from the latter author, which I trust the reader will refer back to and compare in chap. ix. with the Babylonian Hoa, at p. 66 with the Chinese Yu, and at p. 262 with the African Hu.

Davies' "Celtic Researches," p. 184, says, "Though Hu Gadarn primarily denoted the Supreme Being [compare chap. ix.], I think his actions have a secondary reference to the history of Noah. The following particulars are told of him in the above-cited selection:—(1.) His branching or elevated oxen [compare p. 205 and chap. xi.] ... at the Deluge, drew the destroyer out of the water, so that the lake burst forth no more [compare chap. iv.] (2.) He instructed the primitive race in the cultivation of the earth [compare p. 239]. (3.) He first collected and disposed them into various tribes [compare p. 239]. (4.) He first gave laws, traditions, &c., and adapted verse to memorials [compare p. 239]. (5.) He first brought the Cymry into Britain and Gaul [compare p. 66], because he would not have them possess lands by war and contention, but of right and peace" [compare chaps. xiii. and xv.] It is true that these traditions come to us in ballads attributed to Welsh bards of the 13th and 14th centuries A.D.; but, as the Rev. Mr Davies said, "that such a superstition should have been fabricated by the bards in the middle ages of Christianity, is a supposition utterly irreconcileable with probability." And I think the improbability will be widely extended if the readers will take the trouble, after perusal, to make the references as above.

[2]   I have appended a short biographical notice of Colonel G. Macdonell, which I venture to think may contain matter of public interest.

[3]   Sir H. Lytton Bulwer, in his "Life of Lord Palmerston," says, i. p. 62, "There has seldom happened in this country so sudden and unexpected a change of Ministers as that which took place in March 1807."

[4]   W. James, "Military Occurrences of Late War," i. 56, says, 1450 regular troops; Murray, "History of British America," i. 189, says, 2100 troops.

[5]   The following corrections have been supplied to me by the Hon. L. D.:—"Lieut.-Colonel George Macdonell was born on the 12th August 1780, at St Johns, Newfoundland, where his father, Captain Macdonell, was stationed. He was the second son of Captain Macdonell (who had been one of the body-guard of Prince Charles), by his wife, Miss Leslie of Fetternear, Aberdeenshire. George was rated on the navy by the Admiral of the station, who was a personal friend of Captain Macdonell, and his name accordingly remained on the list for years, but he never joined. I believe he entered in 1795 the regiment raised by Lord Darlington, and afterwards served with the Duke of York in the war in Holland. He was, I know, at one time in the 8th infantry, for I remember Sir Greathed Harris saying that he was always a well-remembered and honoured officer in that regiment. He ultimately had the post of Inspecting Field-Officer in Canada."

[6]   Pall Mall Gazette, April 12, 1871; article, "Mr Darwin on Conscience."

[7]   This article, and perhaps four or five others on miscellaneous subjects, written within a few weeks of the above date, were my only contributions to the Tablet, at that time owned and edited by my friend Mr J. E. Wallis, who, during some ten or twelve eventful years, continued to uphold the standard of Tradition, with singular ability and at great personal sacrifice.

[8]   "All that Bentham wrote on this subject ("International Law") is comprised within a comparatively small compass (Works, vol. ii. 535–560, iii. 200–611, ix. 58–382). But it would be unpardonable to omit all mention of a science which he was the means of revolutionising, and which, previously to his taking it in hand, had not even received a proper distinctive name." —

John Hill Burton, "Benthamiana," p. 396. From Bentham's point of view, "International Law" is the proper distinctive name.

[9]   Montalembert, Correspondant, Aout, 1861.

[10]   C'est une des plus admirables choses de ce monde que jamais nul empire, et nul succès n'ont pu s'assujetir l'histoire et en imposer par elle à la posterité. Des generations de rois issus du même sang se sont succédé pendant dix siècles au gouvernement du même peuple, et malgré cette perpetuité d'intérêt et de commandement, ils n'ont pu couvrir aux yeux du monde les fautes de leurs pères et maintenir sur leur tombe le faux éclat de leur vie.—Lacordaire: vid. Correspondant, Nov. 1856.

[11]   Vide "Sentiment de Napoleon I. sur Le Christianisme," d'apres des temoignages recueillis par feu le Chevalier de Beauterne. Nouvelle edition, par M. — —; Bray, Paris, 1860.

[12]   Neue Freie Presse of Vienna. Pall Mall Gazette, May 4, 1871.

[13]   "Utiles esse autem opiniones has quis neget, quum intelligat quam multa firmentur jure jurando, quantæ salutis sint fœderum religiones? quam multos divini supplicii metus a scelere revocaverit? quamque sancta sit societas civium inter ipsos diis immortalibus interpositis tum judicibus tum testibus?"—Cicero, De Legibus, ii. 7.

[14]   "From utility, then, we may denominate a principle that may serve to preside over and govern, as it were, such arrangements as shall be made of the several institutions, or combinations of institutions, that compose the matter of this science." Bentham's "Fragment on Government," xliii., and at p. 45, the principle of utility is declared "all-sufficient," ... that "principle which furnishes us with that reason, which alone depends not upon any higher reason, but which is itself the sole and all-sufficient reason for every point of practice whatsoever."

[15]   Bentham speaks of his enunciation of "the greatest happiness principle" in the following terms:—"Throughout the whole horizon of morals and of politics, the consequences were glorious and vast. It might be said without danger of exaggeration, that they who sat in darkness had seen a great light." With reference to this Lord Macaulay says, "We blamed the utilitarians for claiming the credit of a discovery, when they had merely stolen that morality (the morality of the gospel) and spoiled it in the stealing. They have taken the precept of Christ and left the

motive, and they demand the praise of a most wonderful and beneficial invention, when all they have done has been to make a most useful maxim useless by separating it from its sanction. On religious principles it is true that every individual will best promote his own happiness by promoting the happiness of others. But if religious considerations be left out of the question it is not true. If we do not reason on the supposition of a future state, where is the motive? If we do reason on that supposition, where is the discovery?"—Vide Lord Macaulay's Essays on "Westminster Reviewer's Defence of Mill," and "The Utilitarian Theory of Government" in Lord Macaulay's "Miscellaneous Writings."

[16] There was a way in which the argument was formerly stated by utilitarians which was much more plausible, but which I observe is now seldom if ever resorted to by the modern exponents of this theory. The Pall Mall Gazette, April 12, 1871, says: "The now prevailing doctrine" that there is no absolute standard of right and wrong, but "that the right and wrong of an action or a motive depend upon the influence of the action, or the motive upon the general good." The argument to which I refer is thus stated by Mr W. O. Manning in his "Commentaries on the Law of Nations," 1839:—"Everything around us proves that God designed the happiness of His creatures. It is the will of God that man should be happy. To ascertain the will of God regarding any action, we have, therefore, to consider the tendency of that action to promote or diminish human happiness," p. 59. It is perfectly true that man was created by God for happiness, and that ultimate happiness, if he does not forfeit it, is the end to which he is still destined. It is moreover true that even in this world he may enjoy a conditional and comparative happiness. How it is that this happiness cannot be complete and perfect here below is precisely the secret which tradition reveals to him. It is important, from the point of view of happiness, both for individuals and nations, that the truth of this revelation should be ascertained, and that the conditions and limitations within which happiness is possible should be known, otherwise life will be consumed in chimerical pursuits of the unattainable, and in the case of nations will be certain to end, at some time or another, in catastrophes such as we have recently witnessed in Paris. In an enlarged sense it is therefore true to say that the divine will has regard to utility; but the view

has this implied condition, that what we regard as utility should in the first place be conformable to what is directly or indirectly known to be the divine precept and command; and, on the other hand, if no advertence is made to revelation or the tradition of the human race, what is called utility, however large and disinterested the speculation may be, it can never be more than the view of an individual or of a section of mankind, which it is highly probable that other individuals and sections of mankind, looking at the same facts, from a different point of view, will see reason to contradict.

[17] If "the magnificent principle" is thus stated, "mankind ought to pursue their greatest happiness," it must be borne in mind that there are persons whose interests are opposed to the greatest happiness of mankind. Lord Macaulay's opponent replies, "ought is not predicable of such persons; for the word ought has no meaning unless it be used in reference to some interest." Lord Macaulay replied, "that interest was synonymous with greatest happiness; and that, therefore, IF the word ought has no meaning unless used with reference to interest, then, to say that mankind ought to pursue their greatest happiness, is simply to say that the greatest happiness is the greatest happiness; that every individual pursues his own happiness; that either what he thinks his happiness must coincide with the greatest happiness of society or not; that if what he thinks his happiness coincides with the greatest happiness of society, he will attempt to promote the greatest happiness of society whether he ever heard of the "greatest happiness principle" or not; and that, by the admission of the Westminster Reviewer, IF his happiness is inconsistent with the greatest happiness of society, there is no reason why he should promote the greatest happiness of society. Now, that there are individuals who think that for their happiness which is not for the greatest happiness of society, is evident.... The question is not whether men have some motives for promoting the greatest happiness, but whether the stronger motives be those which impel them to promote the greatest happiness."—Lord Macaulay's "Miscellaneous Writings," Utilitarian Theory of Government, pp. 177–9.

[18] It will be seen, later on, in what this view differs from Sir Henry Maine's.

[19] In all the Diluvian commemorative festivals, to which I shall draw attention (ch. xi.), there is one day set apart for the

commemoration of this primitive equality, accompanied with Bacchanalian festivities and ceremonials.

[20] Sir H. Maine ("Ancient Law," p. 95) says, "Like all other deductions from the hypothesis of a law natural, and like the belief itself in a law of nature, it was languidly assented to, until it passed out of the possession of the lawyers into that of the literary men of the eighteenth century, and the public which sat at their feet. With them it became the most distinct tenet of their creed, and was even regarded as the summary of all the others."

[21] "The earlier advocates of the doctrine of the social compact maintained it on the ground of its actual existence. They asserted that this account of the origin of political societies was historically true. Thus Locke, &c."—Sir G. C. Lewis, "Meth. of Reasoning in Pol." i. p. 429.

[22] "The only reliable materials which we possess, besides the Pentateuch, for the history of the period which it embraces, consist of some fragments of Berosus and Manetho, an epitome of the early Egyptian history of the latter, a certain number of Egyptian and Babylonian inscriptions, and two or three valuable papyri."—Rawlinson, Bampton Lectures. Oxford, 1859, ii. 55.

[23] I indicated this view in a pamphlet, "Inviolability of Property by the State, by an English Landlord." 1866.

[24] Again Esau and Jacob separated, after the death of the patriarch Isaac, because their stock in herds and flocks had so increased that, according to the scriptural phrase, "it was more than they might dwell together," and further, "the land would not bear them because of their cattle."—Gen. chap, xxxvi.; Vide "Pinkerton, Voy." i. 528.

Writing with reference to the Hamitic dynasty, founded at Babylon by Nimrod (vide Rawlinson, Anc. Mon.), and the conquests of Kudur-Lagamer, identified by Rawlinson as Chedor-Laomer, Mr Brace adds ("Ethnology," p. 28):—"This at a period, as Professor Rawlinson remarks, when the kings of Egypt had never ventured beyond their borders, and when no monarch in Asia held dominion over more than a few petty tribes and a few hundred miles of territory."—Vide ch. xiii. "A Golden Age."

[25] Such seems, at a comparatively recent period (1762), to have been the state of things at a widely different point among the Samoides:—"The real spot where the habitations of the

Samoides begin,—if any case be pointed out among a people which is continually changing residence,—is in the district of Mozine, beyond the river of that name, three or four hundred wersts from Archangel. The colony, which is actually met with there, and which lives dispersed according to the usage of those people, each family by itself, without forming villages and communities, does not consist of more than three hundred families, or thereabouts, which are all descended from two different tribes, the one called Laghe and the other Wanonte—distinctions carefully regarded by them."—Vide "Pinkerton, Voy." i. 524. It is also said (p. 582) of certain moral observances amongst them (vide infra, p. 155):—"All these customs, religiously observed among them, are no other than the fruits of tradition, handed down to them from their ancestors; and this tradition, with some reason, may be looked upon as law." It is a common idea amongst us that the word home is a peculiarly English word, and, I confess, it was my own impression, but I am set musing by finding among these same Samoides the word "chome" as their word for their tents, to which they cling so closely.—Vide Pinkerton, i. 63.

"I visited four other villages or *goungs*, and there may be as many more in Assam, each containing about three or four hundred people. Every community is under the patriarchal government of a chief, from whom the village takes its name.... The chiefs of villages would combine against a common enemy, but are as independent of each other as the old Highland heads of clans.... I was curiously reminded of the clan distinctions, by observing that the home-grown cotton cloths differed in pattern in the different villages. In all cases chequered patterns were worn, presenting as various combinations of colours and stripes as our own tartans, and each village possessed a pattern peculiar to itself, generally, though not universally, affected by the inhabitants."—*Travels in Northern Assam*, Field, i., 1870; *vide also Hunter's "Rural Bengal,"* 1868, p. 217.

[26]   "Hunter's Memoir of his Captivity (from childhood to the age of nineteen) among the Indians," p. 180, 181. He also adds (p. 307):—"The Indians do not pretend to any correct knowledge of the tumuli or mounds that are occasionally met with in their country.... One tradition of the Quapaws states that a nation differing very much from themselves inhabited the country many hundred snows ago, when game was so plenty that it

required only slight efforts to procure subsistence, and when there existed no hostile neighbours to render the pursuit of war necessary." And Stephen's "Central America" (i. 142) notices the absence of all weapons of war from the representations in sculpture at Copan, and says:—"In other countries, battle scenes, warriors, and weapons of war, are among the most prominent subjects of sculpture; and from the entire absence of them here, there is reason to believe that the people were not warlike, but peaceable, and easily subdued."

[27]   III., ch. xxxvii. Leges, 337.

[28]   I find incidental corroboration of this view in "The Archæology of Prehistoric Annals" of Scotland, by Dr Wilson—"The infancy of all written history is necessarily involved in fable. Long ere scattered families had conjoined their patriarchal unions into tribes, and clans acknowledging some common chief, and submitting their differences to the rude legislation of the arch-priest or civil head of the commonwealth, treacherous tradition has converted the story of their birth into the wildest admixture of myth and legendary fable."—Introd., p. 12.

Even in the plain of Sennaar (Shinar) we see something of this fusion of tribes—"Besides these two main constituents of the Chaldæan race there is reason to believe that both a Semitic and Aryan element existed.... The subjects of the early kings are continually designated in the inscriptions by the title of 'Kiprat-arbat,' which is interpreted to mean 'the four nations' or 'tongues'" (Rawlinson's "Ancient Monarchies," i. p. 69). Professor Rawlinson is also of opinion, that "the league of the four kings in Abraham's time seems correspondent to a four-fold ethnic division."

Does not the above also correspond to the four-fold ethnic division of the Vedas?—Vide infra, p. 39. Compare also the four-fold division of the world or of Peru, according to various Indian traditions, between Manco Capac and his brothers.—Vide Hakluyt Society's edition of Garcilasso de la Vega, i. 71–75. If these are not traditions of fusions of races, they can only be diluvian traditions of the four couples who came out of the ark, which was the conjecture of the Spaniards in the case of Manco Capac.

[29]   This view will be found in the first chapter of Mr J. S. Mill's "Principles of Political Economy," ch. i. p. 6. "There is perhaps

no people or community now existing which subsist entirely on the spontaneous produce of vegetation." [Whether mankind ever lived "entirely on," &c., may be questioned, but it is implied in Gen. ix. 3 that man did not subsist on animal food until after the Deluge, a fact which lies at the foundation of Porphyry's work, "De Abstinentia."] "But many tribes still live exclusively, or almost exclusively, on wild animals, the produce of hunting or fishing.... The first great advance beyond this state consists in the domestication of the more useful animals: giving rise to the the pastoral or nomad state.... From this state of society to the agricultural, the transition is not indeed easy (for no great change in the habits of mankind is otherwise than difficult, and in general either painful or very slow), but it lies in what may be called the spontaneous course of events."

[30]   Mr Hepworth Dixon's "New America," vol. i. p. 113.

[31]   Vide Sir S. Baker; vide note, ch. xiii., Noah.

[32]   The following passage, inter alia, from Herodotus seems to sustain this—"To the eastward of those Scythians, who apply themselves to the culture of the land, and on the other side of the river Panticapes, the country is inhabited by Scythians who neither plough nor sow, but are employed in keeping cattle."— Herod., iv., Mel.

[33]   These legends, shown to be aboriginal, are very curious. They are, however, too long to be extracted here. They would repay perusal.

[34]   Mr Max Müller also says ("Chips," ii. p. 41)—"It should be observed that most of the terms connected with the chase and warfare differ in each of the Aryan dialects, while words connected with more peaceful occupations belong, generally, to the common heirloom of the Aryan language," which proves "that all the Aryan nations had led a long life of peace before they separated, and that their language acquired individuality and nationality, as each colony started in search of new homes,— new generations forming new terms connected with the warlike and adventurous life of their onward migrations. Hence it is that not only Greek and Latin, but all Aryan languages have their peaceful words in common." Also vide p. 28, 29.

[35]   I find this conjecture confirmed in the pages of the most recent authority on the subject, Mr Brace, "Ethnology," p. 13,

14—"On the continent of Asia the Turanians were probably the first who figured as nations in the ante-historical period. Their emigrations began long before the wanderings of the Aryans and Semites, who, wherever they went, always discovered a previous population, apparently of Turanian origin, which they either expelled or subdued." According to Max Müller's hypothesis there were two migrations, one northern and one southern [corresponding to the migration as above], "the latter settling on the rivers Meikong, Meinam, Irrawaddy, and Bramapootra," ... "a third to the south [probably an advance of the previous one] , is believed to tend toward Thibet and India, and in later times pours its hordes through the Himalaya, and forms the original population of India." Analogy may be discovered in "the two streams or lines of Celtic migration," which, says Bunsen ("Philosophy of Univ. Hist." i. 148) "we may distinguish by the names of the Western and Eastern stream, the former, although the less direct, seems to be historically the more ancient, and to have reached this country (Britain) several centuries before the other."

[36] I am throughout assuming acquaintance, on the part of my readers, with the third and fourth of Cardinal Wiseman's "Lectures on Science and Revealed Religion;" for although my argument is distinct from that of the Cardinal, yet I everywhere regard his argument as the background and support of my position; and it is, moreover, part of the aim and intention of this work to show that the general ground and framework (this is, in fact, understating the truth) of Cardinal Wiseman's argument remains intact. There is, I think, somewhere in the Cardinal's works, a passage to the above effect, but I have not been able to recover it.

[37] If space allowed, I think the traditional lines might be indicated as plainly from the philological as from the ethnological point of view.

[38] "According to the sacred law-book, entitled the Ordinances of Menu, the Creator, that the human race might be multiplied, caused the Brahmin, Cshatriya, the Vaisya, and the Sudra (so named from Scripture, protection, wealth, and labour), to proceed from his mouth, arm, thigh, and foot." —Brit. Ency. The "Fatimala," a Sanskrit work on Hindu castes, says, "the other, i.e., the Sudra, should voluntarily serve the three other tribes,

and therefore he became a Sudra; he should humble himself at their feet."

[39]   Homer's expression (Od. i. 23, 24), that the Ethiopians divided in twain, were the most remote of men —

"Ἀθίοπας, τοὶ διχθὰ δεδαιαται ἔσχατοι ἀνδρῶν,

Οἱ μεν δυσομγένοι Ὑπερίονος οἱ δ' ἀνίοντος,"

approximates to the scriptural phrase, and seems to imply a wider dispersion than is suggested by Professor Rawlinson, i. 59.

[40]   Tylor ("Primitive Culture," i. p. 44) says, "The Semitic family, which represents one of the oldest known civilizations of the world, includes Arabs, Jews, Phœnicians (?), Syrians, &c., and may have an older as well as a newer connection in North Africa. This family takes in some rude tribes, but none which would be classed as savages. The Aryan family has existed in Asia and Europe certainly for several thousand years, and there are well known and marked traces of early barbaric condition, which has perhaps survived with least change among secluded tribes in the valleys of the Hindu Kush and Himalaya." [Query, What is the nature of the evidence that they have survived, and have not degenerated?]   Mr Tylor continues, "There seems, again, no known case of any full Aryan tribe having become savage. The gipsies and other outcasts are, no doubt, partly Aryan in blood, but their degraded condition is not savagery. In India there are tribes Aryan by language, but whose physique is rather of indigenous type, and whose ancestry is mainly from indigenous stocks, with more or less mixture of the dominant Hindu." Compare infra, ch. v., and De Maistre, p. 272.

[41]   Just as Hercules (vide Hercules, p. 180), who embodied in another line the tradition of Adam, is said by Mr Grote, "Hist. of Greece," i. p. 128–9, "to have been the most renowned and most ubiquitous of all the semi-divine personages worshipped by the Hellenes," so that "distinguished families are everywhere to be traced who have his patronymic, and glory in the belief that they are his descendants." To whom would they trace back more naturally than to Adam?

[42]   This must be taken in connection with what I have said, ch. x.

[43]   At p. 88, Mr M'Lennan sees evidence of the "form of capture" and the fact of capture among the Jews; but he will at least allow

the appeal to be made to the Scriptures, as their most authentic history. What do we find at the commencement? In the first marriage contract recorded, i.e. of Isaac and Rebecca? Why, the reverse of capture. Genesis xxvi. 8, "But if the woman will not follow thee thou shalt not be bound by the oath." Also v. 39, 40.

Mr M'Lennan (p. 29), with reference to the hurling "stones and bamboos at the head of the devoted bridegroom in Khondistan," says, "*the hurling of old shoes* after the bridegroom among ourselves *may be* a relic of a similar custom." But this custom would seem to be much more directly traced to the custom among the Jews of taking the shoes from the man who refused to marry his brother's widow (Deuteronomy), and which is more generally stated in Ruth iv. 7, as a token of *cession of right*—"the man *put off his shoe*, and gave it to his neighbour, *this was the testimony of a cession of right in Israel*" (Ruth iv. 7).

[44] "Dr Latham would invert the order of development by producing the ruder fact—polyandry—from the less rude obligation. But clearly this is an inversion of the order of nature, which is progressive," &c.—M'Lennan, "Prim. Marriage," p. 206.

[45] It seems to me that Turner's account of polyandry in Tibet, quoted by Mr M'Lennan, p. 193, gives plain evidence of the transition from the Jewish custom to the "regulated" polyandry. It is said "that the choice of a wife is the privilege of the elder brother."

[46] "Instead of endogamy we might, after some explanations, have used the word caste. But caste connotes several ideas besides that on which we desire to fix attention. On the other hand, the rule which declares the union of persons of the same blood to be incest has been hitherto unnamed", and he terms it exogamy; and he says, "in all the modern instances in which the symbol of capture is most marked we have found that marriage within the tribe is prohibited as incest."

[47] Mr M'Lennan says, "We shall endeavour to establish the following propositions:—1. That the most ancient system in which the idea of blood relationship was embodied, was the system of kinship through females only. 2. That the primitive groups were, or were assumed to be homogeneous. 3. That the system of kinship through females only, tended to render the

exogamous groups heterogeneous, and thus to supersede the system of capturing wives."

[48] "Aucune des trois chronologies bibliques, là ou elles ne s'accordent pas entre elles, ne s'impose avec une autorite suffisante soit au fidele, soit au savant. L'Eglise catholique a laissé le choix libre entre ces chronologies et elles n'oblige pas même à en adopter une." — "Le Monde et L'Homme Primitif selon la Bible," par Mgr. Meignan, Evêque de Chalons-sur-Marne, 1869.

[49] 432,000 is also the figure to which Berosus extends the Assyrian chronology. Thus the Indian fabrication commences at the point where Berosus ends.

[50] Bunsen ("Egypt," iii. 405) says, "Systematic Chinese history and chronology hardly go back as far as the year 2000 B.C., i.e. to the reign of Yü (1991)." Yet upon indirect philological conclusions, he would really take their history back beyond the Egyptian — iii. p. 379. "An explanation must be given why it (the Chinese history) commences at a later period (as above) than Egyptian chronology; much later, indeed, than is generally supposed. Search must be made in other quarters than the regular extant chronology for proofs of that vast antiquity, which the numerous records of language compel us to assign to the origines of the Chinese." This vast antiquity may be measured by the fact that, ex hypothesi, it transcends the Egyptian, and for the Egyptian in his theory of progress and development, he requires at least 20,000 years before the Christian era.

[51] Martini ("Historia Sinica," p. 14, edit. Monac.) asserts that the Egyptians computed by the era of sixty years of Hoangho. See De Vignolle's "Miscellanea Berolinensia," I. iv. 37, on the cycle of months. Compare Ideler, App. ix., note from Bunsen, iii. 385. Humboldt ("Vues des Cordillères", p. 149; Prescott, Mex., i. 105) seems to say that, "among the Chinese, Japanese, Moghols, Mantchous, and other families of the Tartar race" (compare Mexican, do.), "their series was composed of symbols of their five elements, and the twelve zodiacal signs, making a cycle of sixty years duration." This is not incompatible with, the allegation that it is "the era of sixty years of Hoangho."

[52] This tradition would seem to confirm Bryant's ("Mythology," iii. 584) conjecture that Hoang-ti was Ham. But Hoang-ti as Ham, may absorb and incorporate, as we have seen in other

instances, the history of his progenitors; and, moreover, whether he is Noah or Ham, would scarcely affect the chronological argument.

[53] On the worship of the pigeon in Cashmere, vide "Travels in Kashmir," by G. G. Vigne, Esq., F.G.S., ii. p. 11, 13. 1844.

[54] The reduplication may have occurred in this way. Hoang-ti being Noah, Yao or Yu may have been his descendant under whom they settled in China at the termination of their migration. This is confirmed by Bunsen's view, iii. 405 (iv. and v.) In which case it would not be at all unnatural to suppose that the traditions appertaining to the remote progenitor, would in time settle down upon the head of the actual founder. Chevalier de Paravey (vide Gainet, i. 93), "a trouvé un hieroglyphe chinois qui nomme la femme de Hoang-ti 'Adamon' terre jaune, et si non signifie celle qui entraîne les autres dans son propre mal." This would merely be the confusion between Noah and Adam which we have seen to occur in almost every instance. Is not the Japanese god Amida = Adima, or perhaps to Adamon—i.e., confused in relationship to Hoang-ti or Noah? what confirms the impression is, that Adima's son is Canon. Query, Chanaan.

[55] Klaproth says:—"The only Sanscrit history deserving the name of the chronicle of the kings of Kashmir, Radja Paringin'i, translated by W. H. Wilson."—Klaproth, Mem. Relatif à L'Asie.

[56] Compare the following account of existing customs in Cashmir with the above extract from Klaproth and ch. xi., with commemorative festivals of the Deluge. Mr G. G. Vigne ("Travels in Kashmir," ii. 93) says:—"What has been poetically termed the feast of roses, has of late years been rather the feast of signaras or water-nuts. It is held, I believe, about the 1st May, when plum-trees and roses are in full bloom, and is called the Shakergal, from the Persian shakergan, to blow a blossom [the Mandan ceremony took place when the willow flowered.— Catlin, p. 6]   . The richer classes come in boats to the foot of the Tukt, ascend it, and have a feast upon the summit, eating more particularly of signaras (water-nuts). The feast of the No-warh (new place) takes place at the vernal equinox [compare Noah, Taurus]   , at which period the valley is said to have been drained. It is held chiefly at the But or idol stone on Hari parbut." Query—Can this be "the ark or big canoe" in the Mandan celebration? Considering the prominence of boats in

all these mysteries, and considering the resemblance of but to boat, and the like analogies in so many languages (Sanskrit, pota = boat) (vide Vicomte d'Anselme, infra, p. 196), may we be permitted the conjecture until corrected. Compare also p. 268, Ogilby's "Japan," Cook. &c., p. 271.

[57]   I have since found this identical tradition (vide p. 325) among the Mozca Indians. "Boshicha," it is said, "taught them to build and to sow, formed them into communities, GAVE AN OUTLET TO THE WATERS OF THE GREAT LAKE, &c." This seems demonstratively to prove, either that the Mozca Indians (South America) came from China, India, or Egypt—which I have contended for at p. 266—or else, which makes the argument I have in hand stronger, they have transmitted an identical tradition by a different channel.

[58]   "The Chinese who migrated before the Deluge (sic) have no reminiscences, any more than the Egyptians, of the great catastrophe which we know by the name of the Flood of Noah" (Bunsen's "Egypt," iii. 397). Palmer ("Egypt. Chron.," i. p. 38) says, with reference to a certain date—"This is only for such as know the true date of the flood, the end of the old world—an epoch by no means to be named, nor even directly alluded to, by any Egyptian."

[59]   "Principles of Geology," tenth edition, 1868, ii. p. 471.

[60]   The ground upon which Lyell pronounces this judgment is (ii. 479) "that no fragment of pottery has been found among the nations of Australia, New Zealand, and the Polynesian islands any more than ancient architectural remains, in all which respects, these rude men now living, resemble the men of the Palæolithic age; when pottery is known to all, it is always abundant, and, though easy to break, is difficult to destroy. It is improbable that so useful an art should ever have been lost by any race of man." The argument is strongly put, but many things are left out of consideration. Supposing the primitive knowledge, is not pottery one of the arts which would be most likely to be lost in a migration across the seas? Again, that they had no pottery, and that the Palæolithic age had no pottery, shows that in the interval there had been no progress. When will there be? As to the circumstance that it is the same among the Australians and Polynesians, the fact cuts both ways. You assume that there is a uniformity in progress, but may not there

be the same uniformity in the processes of degradation? and, assuming the fact, may it not simply prove that these savages have reached the same depth as the other savages?—Vide appendix to ch. xii.

[61] The following passage from M. A. Bastian's article in The Academy, June 15, 1871, "On the People of India," seems to me to afford an illustration in point—"The natural system becomes an indispensable necessity in every science, so soon as it is clearly seen that the question is not of classification, but of observation of, and insight into, law. Classification was long held to be the sole end, instead of being merely or mainly the means of study. As, in this respect, systematic botany gave place to vegetable physiology, so, in like manner, ethnology will have to look upon its classification of race—with which the school books hitherto have been almost exclusively occupied—as merely a preliminary step towards a physiology of mankind, and to a science of the laws which govern its spiritual growth." Now, if no physiology of mankind, in the sense here intended, can be traced, and if "the science of the laws which govern its spiritual growth" (vide infra, an exposition of Mr Baring Gould's theory) has come to no definite conclusion, then the only result, as far as science is concerned, will have been the revolutionising of its classifications, and the classifications of the different races of men (and, in so far as they have been accurately ascertained, their confusion will be matter of regret) is the legitimate and ultimate end of ethnology under normal conditions.

[62] Sir J. Lubbock's "Prehistoric Times," p. 313.

[63] It has almost passed into a proverb, says Morton—who is among those who know the Americans best—that he who has seen one Indian tribe has seen them all, so closely do the individuals of this race resemble each other, whatever may be the variety or the extent of the countries they inhabit." Reusch's "La Bible et la Nature," vide also Card. Wiseman's "Lect. on Science and Rev. Rel." lect. iv., vide, however, Reusch, p. 498, where "a remarkable difference in the cranium" is noticed, "sometimes approaching the Malay, sometimes the Mongol shape."

[64] That the negro has undergone modifications, seems established by the fact that we nowhere find all the characteristics of the negro united in any one case—unless, perhaps, in the case of the negroes of Guinea, to which I have alluded. Yet, in the

people who border them, there has been noticed "un retour vers des formes superieures." The Yoloss, "out le front élevé, des machoires peu saillantes, leurs dents sont droites, et ils sont en général bein constitués, mais ils sont tout à fait noirs. Leurs voisins, les Mandingues, tiennent beaucoup plus du type négre ... mais leur teint est beaucoup moins noir."—De Bur. ap. Reusch, p. 505. But under no influences of climate has the negro ever become white like the European, or the European black like the inhabitant of Guinea; if they become darker, "c'est simplement la teint particulier à leur race qui gagne en intensité."—Burminster, ap. Reusch, p. 509.

[65] Captain Burton (ii. 165) also quotes a Catholic and a Protestant missionary as to this point. M. Wallon says, "Avec leur tendance à nous considérer comme réellement supérieurs à eux, et leur croyance que cette supériorité nous est acquise par celle de notre Dieu, ils renonceraient bientôt aux leurs idoles pour adorer celui qui nous leur prions de connaître." Mr Dawson says, "Fetish has been strengthened by the white man, whom the ignorant blacks would not scruple to call a god if he could avoid death."

Assuming the identity of Bacchus and Noah, it is a striking circumstance, from this point of view, that the name of Bacchus, among the Phœnicians, was a synonymous term for mourning.— Vide Hesychius in Bryant's "Mythology," ii. 335; vide also the verses of Theocritus. Comp. p. 247, note (Boulanger).

[66] Perhaps Captain Burton's phrase (ii. 178), "the arrested physical development of the negro," may, if extended to his mental development, exactly hit the truth, the standard being fixed by the age at which we conceive the boy Chanaan's development to have been arrested.—Comp. Wallace, infra, p. 91; comp. 217.

[67] "Annales de Philos. Chret.," t. xiii. p. 235.

[68] The expressions in the latter part of this narration recall the blessing of Jacob, and suggests the possibility of the tradition having come through descendants of Esau.

[69] This is so much in tradition as to be a matter of common parlance—for instance, when the late Emperor of the French is depicted, this is the language which, upon a certain construction, appears most natural—"On the other side stands a phalanx of satirists, represented by Victor Hugo. The only colour on the palette of those artists is lamp black. Morally they paint the ex-Emperor as dark as a negro, array him in the livery of the devil,

and then invoke the execration of history."—Spectator, Sept. 17th, 1870.

[70]   The italics are mine.

[71]   The eye would be the very most apposite symbol for blackness, if we consider that blackness lingers there after the skin has become white, and, in the case of half-breeds, is the test of descent in gradations even beyond, I believe, the octoroon.

Captain King ("Narrative of a Survey of the Intertropical and Western Coasts of Australia," ii. Append.) says, "That although there is the greatest diversity of words among the Australian tribes, the equivalent for 'eye' is common to them all."

[72]   Lenormant, "Manuel d'Histoire Ancienne," i. 23, makes a similar suggestion as to this point—"La texte de la Bible n'a rien qui s'oppose formellement à l'hypothèse que Noè aurait eu, postérieurement au deluge, d'autres enfants que Sem, Cham, et Japhet, d'où seraient sorties les races qui ne figurent pas dans la généalogie de ces trois personnages." But two objections seem to me to be fatal to this view. The races about whom this difficulty would be raised would be the red and black races: why should it be surmised that the supposed posterity of Noah, after the Deluge, should have this mark of inferiority? In the second place, it does seem to be formally opposed to Gen. x. 32—"These are the families of Noe, according to their peoples and nations. By these were the nations divided on the earth after the flood."

The red races might perhaps be accounted for by Gen. xxv. 23–25.

[73]   There appears to me, however, a text to which attention might be directed. We know that the Ethiopians were black, but in Amos ix. 7, where God is expressing His anger against His people, He says, "Are you not as the children of the Ethiopians unto me, O children of Israel, saith the Lord."

[74]   Vide also ch. x., p. 239. The tradition that Phoroneus, "the father of mankind," distributed the nations over the earth, idem nationes distribuit.

[75]   Vide ante ch. iv.; and also vide Palmer, i. 49.

[76]   And yet, with the exception of Professor Rawlinson's "Manual of Ancient History," where mention is made of Mr Palmer's

work as among eight principal works to be referred to on the subject of Egyptian chronology, and of a series of articles in the Month on the same subject, I do not recollect to have seen allusion made to it. A previous perusal of the articles in the Month above referred to will greatly facilitate the study of this question.

[77]   It will be understood that, in the above scheme and throughout, Mr Palmer assumes the existence of cotemporaneous dynasties elsewhere demonstrated. It is admitted, on all hands, that cotemporary dynasties ceased with the XVIII. Dynasty; and, in the other direction, all schemes commence with Menes. If, then, this interval of time is known or determined by one part of a scheme (as it is known from the chronicle to be 477 years), and at the same time, the exigences of the case (owing to fictitious additions) require the location of other figures within the interval, then the super-additions must overlap (apparently to those who know 477 years to be the true historical figure) at one end or the other. One hundred and fifty-six years (as above) is the extent of the overlapping (the 443 years of the cycle standing apart) in the scheme of Eratosthenes.

[78]   Such appears to me to be the conclusion of Mr Allies in his learned work ("The Formation of Christendom," ii. chap. viii. 57), "Universality of false worship in the most diverse nations the summing up of man's whole history." I request attention, however, to the following passage, which has an especial bearing upon my argument:—"No doubt the Greek mind had lived and brooded for ages upon the remains of original revelation, nor can any learning now completely unravel the interwoven threads of tradition and reason so as to distinguish their separate work. However, it is certain that in the sixth century B.C., the Greeks were without a hierarchy, and without a definite theology: not indeed without individual priesthoods, traditionary rites, and an existing worship, as well as certain mysteries which professed to communicate a higher and more recondite doctrine than that exposed to the public gaze. But in the absence of any hierarchy ... a very large range indeed was given to the mind, acting upon this shadowy religious belief, and re-acted upon by it, to form their philosophy. The Greeks did not, any more than antiquity in general, use the acts of religious service for instruction by religious discourse. In other words, there was no such thing as preaching among them. A domain,

therefore, was open to the philosopher, on which he might stand without directly impeaching the ancestral worship, while he examined its grounds, and perhaps sapped its foundations. He was therein taking up a position which these priests, the civil functionaries of religious rites, scarcely any longer retaining a spiritual meaning or a moral cogency, had not occupied."

[79] Take for instance Mr J. S. Mill's peculiar views as to the status of women, "The law of servitude in marriage" ["Wives be obedient to your husbands," St Paul]   , he says, "is in monstrous contradiction to all the principles of the modern world" "Marriage is the only actual bondage known to our law," id. But at p. 49, Mr Mill says, "The general opinion of men is supposed to be, that the natural vocation of a woman is that of a wife and mother." But he then adds "It will not do to assert in general terms that the experience of mankind has pronounced in favour of the existing system. Experience cannot possibly have decided between two courses, so long as there has only been experience of one. If it be said that the doctrine of the equality of the sexes rests only on theory, it must be remembered that the contrary doctrine also has only theory to rest upon. All that is proved in its favour by direct experience, is that mankind have been able to exist under it, and to attain the degree of improvement and prosperity which we now see; but whether that prosperity has been attained sooner, or is now greater than it would have been under the other system, experience does not say."

Take in illustration, again, the communistic schemes as against the institution of property. Now, although Christianity has realised all that will ever be possible in the way of communism in its religious orders, the communistic sects have always instinctively directed their first efforts against religion as against the basis of the social order of things which they attacked. This was forcibly brought out in certain letters on "European Radicalism," in the *Pall Mall Gazette*, October and November 1869, *e.g.* "all the contests on the three capital questions ('government, property, religion') which we are now engaged in, are but continuations of the *original divergence* of opinion (before settled government), considerably modified, of course, under the influence of time, the various *traditional notions* mankind preserves under the *name of beliefs*, and the whole stock of experience it has accumulated under the name of knowledge. So like, indeed, are the ancient and modern contests on these matters," &c.... (Letter I.) Again (Letter V.), speaking of our English socialist discussing "the necessity of building social edifices upon material, not religious grounds," the writer adds, that among continental socialists "no one thinks there of the possibility of matters standing otherwise;" and that in the socialist workshops of France and Germany it is well known "that the very basis of social radicalism requires the abandonment of all kinds of religious discussion, as matter of purely personal inclination, and the abolition of all kinds of privileges as incompatible with equality." [All this has been put out of date by the deeds of the Commune and the programme of the "International Society" — viz. "*The burning of Paris* we *accept the responsibility of. The old society must* and will perish."]

The *Spectator*, December 1869, speaks still more explicitly:— "Infirm and crippled though she be, the Roman Church is still the only one who has the courage to be cosmopolitan, and claim the right to link nation with nation, and literature with literature. Such an assembly as the Council is, at least, an extraordinary testimony to the cosmopolitanism of the great Church which seems trembling to its fall; and who can doubt that that fall, whenever it comes, will be followed by a great temporary loosening of the faith in human unity — in spite of the electric telegraph — by a deepening of the chasm between nation and nation, by the loss of at least a most potent spell over the imagination of the world, by a contraction of the spiritual ideal of every church? This ideal, even Protestants, even Sceptics, even Positivists have owed, and have owned that they owed, to the Roman Church, the only Church which has really succeeded in uniting the bond between any one ecclesiastical centre and the distant circumference of human intelligence and energy. But if the consequence of the collapse of Romanism would be in this way a loss of power to the human race, think only of the gain of power which would result from the final death of sacerdotal ideas, from the final blow to the system of arbitrary authority exercised over the intellect and the conscience, from the new life which would flow into a faith and science resting on the steady accumulation of moral and intellectual facts and the personal life of the conscience in Christ — from the final triumph of moral and intellectual order and freedom. It would doubtless be a new life, subject to great anarchy at first; but the old authoritative systems have themselves been of late little more than anarchy just kept under by the authority of prescription and tradition; and one can only hope for the new order from the complete recognition that it is to have no arbitrary or capricious foundation."

[80] "It is, upon the whole, extremely doubtful whether those periods which are the richest in literature, possess the greatest shares, either of moral excellence or of political happiness. We are well aware that the true and happy ages of Roman greatness long preceded that of Roman refinement and Roman authors; and, I fear, there is but too much reason to suppose that in the history of the modern nations we may find many examples of the same kind" (F. Schlegel's "History of Literature," i. 373). See also the account of the corruption of morals in Rome in the Augustan period (Allies' "Form. of Christendom," I. Lect. I.) "It is curious to observe that the more eloquent, polite, and learned the Greeks became, in the same proportion they became the more degraded and corrupt in their national religion" (Godfrey Higgins' "Celtic Druids," 1829, p. 207).

[81] "Il n'y a, Messieurs, que deux sortes de repression possibles: l'une intérieure, l'autre extérieure.... Elles sont de telle nature que quand le thermomètre politique est élevé, le thermomètre de la religion est bas, et quand le thermomètre religieux est bas, le thermomètre politique, la repression politique, la tyrannie s'élève. Ceci est une loi de l'humanité, une loi de l'histoire." Vide Disc. de Donoso Cortes (Marq. de Valdegamas), 4th January 1849; in which he pursues this remarkable parallelism throughout history.

[82] Montalembert ("Disc. de Reception," 1852, Discours iii. pp. 614, 615, 621, 622) says of the Constituent Assembly of 1789—"It was the Assembly of 1789 which made the word revolution the synonyme of methodical destruction, of permanent war against all order and all authority.... It had that mania for uniformity which is the parody of unity, and which Montesquieu called the passion of mediocre minds.... In a word, the Constituent Assembly was wanting not only in justice, courage, and humanity, but it was also deficient in good sense. The evil which it created has survived it. It has made us believe that it is possible to destroy everything and to reconstruct everything in a day.... God has chastised it, above all, by the sterility of its work. It had had the pretence of laying the foundations of liberty for ever, and it had for its successors the most sanguinary tyrants who ever dishonoured any nation. Its mission was to re-establish the

finances, the empire of the law, and it has bequeathed to France bankruptcy, anarchy, and despotism—despotism without even the repose which they have wrongly taken as the compensation of servitude. It has done more: it has left pretexts for every abuse of force, and precedents for any excess of future anarchy. [Montalembert could hardly have foreseen the last application of its principles which we have recently witnessed in Paris by the Commune, which, too, forsooth, was to have inaugurated a new era for humanity.] But it (this Constituent Assembly) founded nothing—Nothing! The ancient society which it reversed had lasted, in spite of its abuses, a thousand years."

[83]   From a purely philosophical point of view, why should these speculations of Mr Gladstone have been received "with more surprise and unfavourable comment" than any other "portions of his Homeric studies?"

[84]   In one way, nothing is so uncertain as tradition, and, moreover, tradition is rarely positive and direct, but, on the contrary, prone to concrete into strange, fragmentary, and distorted shapes. As an instance, we may take the tradition which Genesis attests,— When Abraham's hand had been stayed by the angel from the sacrifice of Isaac, ... "He c alled the name of that place 'The Lord seeth.' Whereupon, even to this day it is said, 'In the mountain the Lord will see.'"—Gen. xxii. 14.

In illustration of the mode and manner of tradition, is the anecdote of Mr Hookham Frere, who states, that when the Maltese talk without reserve upon religious subjects, they say, "Everybody knows that Adam was the first man, but we alone know that he possessed fishing-boats;" which Bunsen says "Can be nothing but a Phœnician reminiscence."—"Egypt," iv. 215, the reminiscence of the legend of the Fisherman. Compare the Fisherman and his wife in Grimm's "Popular Stories from Oral Tradition."

[85]   Vide "Bryant's Mythology," ii.

[86]   After the exposition of his own theory, Mr Grote says—"It is in this point of view that the myths are important for any one who would correctly appreciate the general tone of Grecian thought and feeling, for they were the universal mental stock of the Hellenic world, common to men and women, rich and poor, ignorant and instructed, they were in every one's memory and in every one's mouth, while science and history were

confined to comparatively few. We know from Thucydides how erroneously and carelessly the Athenian public of his day retained the history of Pisistratus, only one century past; but the adventures of the gods and heroes, the numberless explanatory legends attached to visible objects and periodical ceremonies, were the theme of general talk, and every man unacquainted with them would have found himself partially excluded from the sympathies of his neighbours."—Hist. Greece, i. p. 608; comp. infra, ch. xi.

[87] "Ancient Law,"

[88] "Pour trouver le veritable objet de ces dernières solemnités, dont les motifs sont compliqués, nous nous attachons à analyser leur cérémoniel et à chercher l'esprit de leurs usages; et cet esprit achève de nous faire reconnaître l'objet que nous n'avions d'abord qu'entrevu ou soupçonné, quelquefois même il nous développe encore la nature des motifs étrangers et mythologiques, et ces motifs se trouvent pour la plûpart n'être que des traditions du même fait qui ont été ou corrompués par le temps, ou travesties par des allégories."—Boulanger, _"L'Antiquite devoilée par ses Usages"_, i. 31.

[89] Vide other lines of tradition indicated in B. iii., C. iii., of De Maistre, "Du Pape."

[90] Sir J. Lubbock, Intro. to Nillson's "Stone Age," xii.

[91] E.g., Mr Grote says, in his Introduction, that through the combination and illustration of scanty facts, "the general picture of the Grecian world may now be conceived with a degree of fidelity which, considering our imperfect materials, it is curious to contemplate."

The Duke of Argyll ("Primeval Man," p. 24) says—"Within certain limits it is not open to dispute that the early condition of mankind is accessible to research. Contemporary history reaches back a certain way. Existing monuments afford their evidence for a considerable distance farther. _Tradition has its own province still more remote_; and latterly geology and archæology have met upon common ground—ground in which man and the mammoth have been found together."

[92] Gibbon ("Decline and Fall," i. 353) says, "But all this well-laboured system of German antiquities is annihilated by a single

fact, too well attested to admit of any doubt, and of too decisive a nature to leave room for any reply. The Germans, in the days of Tacitus, were unacquainted with the use of letters, and the use of letters is the principal circumstance which distinguishes a civilised people from a herd of savages, incapable of knowledge or reflection. Without that artificial help, the human memory ever dissipates or corrupts the ideas intrusted to her charge." Compare with Coleridge, infra, p. 122; Ozanam, infra, ch. xiii.

[93] Eusebius ("Ecclesiastical Hist.," ch. xxxvi.) says, speaking of St Ignatius—"He exhorted them to adhere firmly to the tradition of the apostles; which, for the sake of greater security, he deemed it necessary to attest by committing it to writing." I do not remember to have seen this quoted in testimony and proof of ecclesiastical tradition.

[94] Goguet ("Origin of Laws," i. 29) says—"The first laws of all nations were composed in verse, and sung. Apollo, according to a very ancient tradition, was one of the first legislators. The same tradition says that he published his laws to the sound of his lyre; that is to say, that he had set them to music. We have certain proof that the first laws of Greece were a kind of song. The laws of the ancient inhabitants of Spain were verses, which they sung. Tuiston was regarded by the Germans as their first lawgiver. They said he put his laws into verses and songs. This ancient custom was long kept up by several nations."

E. Warburton ("Conquest of Canada," i. 214) says—"The want of any written or hieroglyphic records of the past among the Northern Indians was to some extent supplied by the accurate memories of their old men; they were able to repeat speeches of four or five hours' duration, and delivered many years before, without error, or even hesitation; and to hand them down from generation to generation with equal accuracy.... On great and solemn occasions belts of wampum were used as aids to recollection ... when a treaty or compact was negotiated."

[95] Vide H. N. Coleridge ("Greek Classic Poets," p. 38–42), in speaking of the "Dionysiacs, the Thebaids, the Epigoniads, Naupactica, genealogies, and the other works of that sort," p. 44, he adds—"Just as in the Indian and Persian epics, in the Northern Eddas, in the poem of the 'Cid,' in the early chronicles of every nation with which we are acquainted, one story follows another story in the order of mere history; and the skill and fire

of the poet are shown, not in the artifice of grouping a hundred figures into one picture, but in raising admiration by the separate beauty of each successive picture. They tell the tale as the tale had been told to them, and leave out nothing."

[96] According to the account which the Chinese themselves give of their annals, the works of Confucius were proscribed, after his death, by the Emperor Chi-Hoangti, and all the copies, including the Chu-King, were recovered from the dictation of an old man who had retained them in memory.

"The great moralist of the East" himself, Confucius, asserted— "that he only wrought on materials already existing." *Vide* Klaproth ap., Cardinal Wiseman, "Science and Rev. Religion," ii. p. 49.

In the article in the *Cornhill Magazine*, Nov. 1871, containing the valuable collection of Dravidian (South Indian) folk-songs, it is said, that "they are handed down from generation to generation, entirely vivâ voce, and from the minstrels have passed into public use."

[97] The Duke of Argyll ("Primeval Man," p. 30) says—"Knowledge, for example, or ignorance of the use of metals are, as we shall see, characteristics on which great stress is laid" (by the advocates of the "savage theory"). "Now, as regards this point, as Whately truly says, the narrative of Genesis distinctly states that this kind of knowledge did not belong to mankind at first.... It is assumed in the savage theory that the presence or absence of this knowledge stands in close and natural connection with the presence or absence of other and higher kinds of knowledge, of which an acquaintance with metals is but a symbol and a type. Within certain limits this is true."

[98] Presuming total ignorance of writing—its invention at any period seems to me much more marvellous than the discovery of printing after the invention of writing. For the rest we have seen that writing was known at an early period to the Chaldæans and Egyptians, and probably to the Chinese and Japanese, and to the Medians (ch. xii.) Plutarch tells us that a law of Theseus, written on a column of stone, remained even to the time of Demosthenes.

[99] Phil. Hist.

[100] Burke ("Regicide Peace,") says—"The practice of divorce, though in some countries permitted, has been discouraged in all. In the East polygamy and divorce are in discredit, and the manners correct the laws."

[101] This was written before the appearance of Sir J. Lubbock's chapter on "Marriage," in his "Origin of Civilization," to which reference is made.

[102] A tradition of the constellations, a proof from tradition that they were so named in the ante-diluvian period.

[103] Sanchoniatho's "Phœnician History," by the Right Rev. R. Cumberland. London, 1720, et seq. Eusebius, Præpar. Evangel. lib. i. cap. 10.

[104] Vide Grote, i.

[105] This chapter was written before I became acquainted with Mr Palmer's "Chronicles of Egypt" (vide ch. vi.) If the reader will refer to chap. i., he will there find a learned and exhaustive exposition of the ages of Sanchoniathon, identifying them with Scripture on the one side, and Egyptian tradition on the other.

[106] Is not this the meaning of the cxlvii. psalm, in the expression, "ante faciem frigoris ejus quis sustinebit"? Does not the psalm recount to the Jewish people, in rapid allusions, all that God had done for them, in contrast to the chastisements that had befallen other nations; and if it is objected that there is no allusion to the Deluge, unless in its indirect and beneficial influences, in the words, "flavit spiritus ejus et fluent aquæ," I reply that to the survivors, the Deluge, regarded largely, and in its permanent effects, was no calamity, but the commencement of a new and more favoured era.

[107] Compare ch. xiii. The successive ages of Hesiod, more especially the lines describing the iron age, parallel to the tradition, supra, "that in the fifth age men were named from their mothers."

"No fathers in their sons their features trace,

The sons reflect *no more* their father's face;

The host with kindness greets his guest no more,

And friends and brethren love not as of yore."

—Hesiod.

President Goguet ("Origin of Laws," i. 21,) had noticed the ancient allusions to "kinship through mothers," and his statement that "women belonged to the man who seized them first.... The children who sprang from this irregular intercourse scarce ever knew who were their fathers. They knew only their mothers, for which reason they always bore their name." For this statement he also quotes Sanchoniathon, ap. Eus. p. 34, as his principal authority. But Sanchoniathon's statement, as we have seen, refers to the ante-diluvian period, in which it is borne out by Genesis vi. 4.

There is one fact adduced by Goguet (i. 43), viz. that the *Assyrians* had an analogous ceremony which must be decisive for us, though not, perhaps, for Mr M'Lennan, that the custom of seizure was ante-diluvian, since the commencement of the Assyrian monarchy in the times immediately following the flood, is one of the best established foundations of history. *Vide* Genesis and Rawlinson.

"This race of many languaged man." To any one who rightly grasps the bearing of the argument, the appositeness of this quotation will, I think, be rather strengthened than diminished by the evidence that the lines of Hesiod plainly refer to post-diluvian times (vide ch. xiii.)

[108] The Phœnician cosmogony seems to me to clinch the argument. There (vide Bunsen, Egypt, iv. 234), "The son of Eliun is called by Philo, Epigeios or autokhthon, 'the earth-born,' primeval inhabitant. By the latter of these expressions we have no doubt that Adam-Tadmon ('the Kadmos of the Greeks,' p. 195), the first man, the man of God, is implied" ("Eliun, i.e. Helyun, God the Most High," p. 232).

There is an analogy in their confused tradition of the creation. "Eudemus says, according to the Phœnician mythology, which *was invented by Môkhos*, the first principle was æther and air; from these two beginnings sprang Ulômos (the eternal), the rational (conscious) God" (Bunsen, iv. 179). Bunsen, (178) adds, "as regards Môkhos the thing is clear enough; the old materialistic philosopher is matter, and that in the sense of primeval slime." [Whence it has been suggested that we derive our word Muck, Môkh, or Môkhos.]   This beginning Bunsen considers "a philosophising amplification of the simply sublime words of Genesis: 'The earth was without form, and void, and darkness was over the face of the waters.'" Here we see the human reason hampered by the tradition that confused matter or chaos was somehow at the commencement, and with the conflicting tradition and conclusion of the intellect that it was, and must have been, created by a power superior to matter ("In the beginning God created heaven and earth"), emancipating itself, so far as to identify the Creator with the æther and air, as nearer the conception of a pure Spirit, and personifying matter, and so shunting it aside as the "inventor of the mythology."

[109] Vide De Maistre (ch. xii.)

[110] Max Müller, "Chips," &c., ii. 274. The Titans were also said to be "earth-born." Bryant (iii. 445) says Berosus gives the following tradition of the Creation. Belus after deification being confounded with the Creator, as we have seen Prometheus, id. 104 — "Belus, the deity above mentioned, cut off his own head, upon which the other gods mixed the blood as it gushed out with the earth, and from thence men were formed. On this account it is that they are rational and partake of divine knowledge. This Belus, whom men called Dis, divided the darkness and separated the heavens from the earth," &c.

[111] Compare Cicero, De Legibus, i. 8: "Est igitur homini cum deo similitudo;" and with Gen. ii. 26, 27: "and God created man in his own likeness."

[112] "The Chinese cosmogony speaks as follows of the creation of man — 'God took some yellow earth, and He made man en deux sexes.'" This is the true origin of the human race. A Hebrew tradition says that it was of the red earth, which is the same idea. The Hebrew word "Adam" expresses this idea. This correspondence as to the manner in which the body of the first man was formed, between two people who have never had relations, is very remarkable. Indian and African cosmogonies relate that the name of the first man was 'Adimo,' that of his wife 'Hava,' and that they were the last work of the Creator." — Gainet, La Bible sans la Bible, i. p. 74. I must note, too, the identity of the American Indian (supra and the Hebrew tradition, which is curious, as it might naturally be supposed that the tradition of the Red Indian took its colour from his own complexion.

Max Müller ("Lect. on the Science of Language," 1st series, p. 367) says of "man" — "The Latin word *homo*, the French *l'homme*, ... is *derived from the same root*, which we have in *humus*, soil, *humilis*, humble. *Homo*, therefore, would express the idea *of being made out of the dust of the earth.*" Bunsen also ("Phil. Univ. Hist." i. 78) says—"The common word for man in all German dialects is 'manna,' containing the same root as Sanscrit 'manusha' and 'manueshya.' The Latin 'homo' is intimately connected with 'humus' and χαμαί and means *earth-born*; ἀνθρώπων χαμαιγενεων, says Pindar. But what is ἄνθρωπος?"

[113] "Last Rambles"

[114] The following tradition of the Tartar tribes seems to supply a link. In their tradition of the Deluge (vide Gainet, i. 209) it is said, "that those who saved themselves from the Deluge shut themselves up with their provisions in the crevices of mountains, and that after the scourge had passed they came out of their caverns."

And compare, again, with the tradition of Kronos (Noah, *vide* Bryant's "Mythology," iii. 503)—"He is said to have had *three* sons (Sanch. ap. Euseb. P. E., lib. i. c. 10, 37), and in a *time of danger* he formed a *large cavern in the ocean*, and in this he shut himself up, together *with these sons*, and thus escaped the danger."—*Porph. de Nymphar. Antro.*, p. 109.

Bryant ("Mythology," iii. 405) says—"I have shown that Gaia, in its original sense, signified a sacred cavern, a hollow in the earth, which, from its gloom, was looked upon as an emblem of the ark. Hence Gaia, like Hasta Rhoia Cybele, is often represented as the mother of mankind." The following is very important with reference to my argument above:—The Scholiast upon Euripides says—"Μετα τον κατακλυσμον εν ορεσιν οικουντων των Αργειων πρωτος αυτους συνωκισεν Ιναχος] . When the Argivi or Arkites, *after the Deluge*, lived *dispersed on the mountains*, Inachus first brought them together and formed them into communities."—Comp. *infra*, p. 157, 158, 193, 332.

The instances adduced of myths connecting man with the monkey are, as a rule, traditions of degeneracy, *i.e.* of men turned into monkeys (*vide* Tylor's "Primitive Culture," i. 340), and to which I would add the rabbinical tradition of men turned into monkeys at the Tower of Babel (De Quincey, Works, xiii. 235), and the classical epic of the Ceropes, "founded on the transformation of a set of jugglers into monkeys." But if compared with the above tradition, I think that the only two instances (Tylor,

i. 341) which seem to bear out the opposite theory will wear a different aspect. I quote from Tylor as above—"Wild tribes of the Malay peninsula, looked down upon as lower animals by the more warlike and civilised Malays, have among them traditions of their own descent from *a pair* of the "unka-putch" or *white* monkeys, who reared their young ones *and sent them into the plains,* and there they perfected so well that they and their descendants became men, but those *who returned to the mountains* still remained apes. The Buddhist legend relates the origin of the flat-nosed uncouth tribes of Tibet, offspring of *two miraculous apes,* transformed to *people* the snow-kingdom. Taught to till the ground, when they had grown corn and eaten it, their tails and hair gradually disappeared, they began to speak, became men, and clothed themselves with leaves. The population grew closer, the land was more and more cultivated, and at last a prince of the race of Sakya, driven from his home in India, *united their isolated tribes* into a single kingdom."—Comp. Cecrops, &c., p. 332, *infra*.

[115] It occurs to me as possible that these various traditions may have had their foundation in the recollection of hardship, at some early period of their subsequent migration, which were transferred back and connected with their tradition of the altered state of things after the Deluge, arising out of the substitution of animal for vegetable food—of which the notion that man once lived on acorns may have been only an extreme form of expression. The following tradition of Saturn (vide infra, Saturn, p. 210), seems to tend in this direction: "Diodorus Siculus gives the same history of Saturn as is by Plutarch above given of Janus—ἐξ ἀγρίου δίαιτης εἰς ἥμερον Βίον μεταρησα ἀνθρώπους.—Diodorus, 1. 5, p. 334. He brought mankind from their foul and savage way of feeding to a more mild and rational diet."—Bryant, ii. 261.

[116] This fable of the tortoise is also among the Mandans, whom, Catlin (supra, 135) says, had no other tradition of the Creation than that they were created under the ground. Their tradition is confused with the Deluge, which dominates in their tradition.

"The Mandans believed that the earth rests on four tortoises. They say that "each tortoise rained ten days, making forty days in all, and the waters covered the earth" (vide "O-kea-pa," p.

39, infra, ch. xi.) Does not this tradition of the tortoise decide the Oriental origin of the North American Mandans?

Falconer's "Palæontological Mem.," 1868, i. 297, ii. 377–573, &c., "As the pterodactyle more than realised the most extravagant idea of the winged dragon, so does this huge tortoise come up to the lofty conceptions of Hindoo mythology; and could we but recall the monsters to life, it were not difficult to imagine an elephant supported on its back"(i. 27).

The New Zealanders have a curious tradition of their ancestors having encountered a gigantic saurian species of reptile, which must have been before they arrived in New Zealand. *Vide* Shortland's "Traditions of the New Zealanders," p. 73.

[117] I have elsewhere (vide ch. iv., et seq., x., xi.) traced the tradition of the Deluge, of the chronology of the world, &c., &c.

[118] Devil-worship is based upon the hypothesis that the evil spirit exists, and is the influence from which man has most to dread. Prudence suggests that it is wise to propitiate evil when it is powerful; and if "the existence of God is not assumed," or the conception of God not yet developed, it is hard to see how the conclusion can be impugned; and (vide next page) Mr Baring Gould endorses Grimm's opinion that man's first "idea of God is the idea of a devil."

[119] The most favourable review of Mr B. Gould's work which I have seen says:—"In tracing the origin and development of religious belief, the object of Mr Baring Gould is to establish the foundation of Christian doctrine on the nature, the intuitions, and the reason of man, rather than upon traditionary dogmas, historical documents, or written inspirations. He is of opinion that the elements of true religion are to be found in a revelation naturally impressed upon the soul of man, and that the investigation of man's moral nature will be found to disclose the surest proofs of his religious wants and destination. The author holds that if theological doctrines can be inculcated by demonstrative evidence of their harmony with man's intellectual and moral constitution, they will be received with more perfect acquiescence and conviction than when appeals are made simply to man's veneration for antiquity and authority." I think I am, at any rate, right in taking Mr B. G.'s as the view most

directly opposed to tradition, and it is from this point of view that I am brought into collision with him.

[120] Vide, however, Dr Newman's "Grammar of Assent," p. 386, et seq.

[121]

> "The lively Grecian, in a land of hills,
>
> Rivers, and fertile plains, and sounding shores,
>
> ....In despite
>
> Of the gross fictions chanted in the streets
>
> By wandering rhapsodists, and in contempt
>
> Of doubt and bold denial hourly urged
>
> Amid the wrangling schools, a Spirit hung,
>
> Beautiful region! o'er thy towns and farms,
>
> Statues and temples, and memorial tombs;
>
> And emanations were perceived, and acts
>
> Of immortality, in nature's course,
>
> Exemplified by mysteries that were felt
>
> As bonds, *on grave philosopher imposed,*
>
> And armed warrior; and in every grove
>
> A gay or pensive tenderness prevailed,
>
> When piety more awful had relaxed."
>
> —Wordsworth, *Excursion*, B. iv.

[122] "Monotheisme des Peuples Primitifs," in vol. iii. of "La Bible sans la Bible."

[123] Mr B. Gould also says, p. 104—"The Semitic divine names bear indelibly on their front the stamp of their origin, and the language itself testifies against the insulation and abstraction of these names from polytheism. The Aryan's tongue bore no such testimony to him. The spirit of his language led him away from monotheism, whilst that of the Shemite was an ever-present monitor, directing him to a God, sole and undivided. 'The glory of the Semitic race is this,' says M. Renan, 'that from its earliest days it grasped that notion of the Deity which all other people have had to adopt from its example, and on the faith of its declaration.'"

[124] I append, however, the following passage from Mr Baring Gould, as it may be serviceable in tracing tradition, and to which I may have occasion to recur (p. 161):—"Among the American Indians an object of worship, and the centre of a cycle of legend, is Michabo, the great hare or rabbit. From the remotest wilds of the north-west to the coast of the Atlantic, from the southern boundaries of Carolina to the cheerless swamps of Hudson's Bay, the Algonquins are never tired of gathering round the winter fire, and repeating the story of Manibozho or Michabo, the Great Hare. With entire unanimity, their various branches, the Powhatans, &c., ... and the western tribes, perhaps without exception, spoke of this 'chimerical beast,' as one of the old missionaries called it, as their common ancestor (Brinton's "Myths of the New World," p. 162). Michabo is described as having been four-legged, monstrous, crouching on the face of the primeval waste of waters, with all his court, composed of four-footed creatures, around him. He formed the earth out of a grain of sand taken from the bottom of the ocean. It is strange that such an insignificant creature as a hare should have received this apotheosis, and it has been generally regarded as an instance of the senseless brute-worship of savages. But its prevalence leads the mythologist to suspect that some confusion of words has led to a confusion of ideas, a suspicion which becomes a certainty when the name is analysed, for it is then found to be The Great White One, or Great Light, and to be in reality the sun, a fact of which the modern Indians are utterly unaware."

If Mr Baring Gould finds that the word Michabo also signifies "The Great Light," or "The Great White One," it goes far to identify the worship of the hare with the worship of the sun, more especially when it is noted (vide Prescott's "Conquest of Mexico," i. 103) that the hare was one of the four hieroglyphics of the year among the ancient Mexicans.[A] Animal worship seems here plainly connected with sun-worship. But above and beyond it, do we not here also get a glimpse of more celestial light? "The Great Light" is also "The Great White One." He is described as "crouching on the face of the primeval waste of waters." In these phrases we seem almost to read the text of Gen. i. 3, "And God said, Be light, and light was made;" ver. 2, "Darkness was on the face of the deep, and the Spirit of God moved over the waters."

The Indians also say that he "formed the earth out of a grain of sand taken from the bottom of the ocean." Does not this not only embody the tradition that God created the world out of nothing, but also the mode of the creation by the separation of the water from the land: ver. 9, "God also said, Let the waters that are under the heavens be gathered together in one place; and let the dry land appear.... And God called the dry land earth, and the gathering together of the waters He called seas."

[A] These hieroglyphics were symbolical of the four elements. Prescott adds—"It is not easy to see the connection between the terms 'rabbit' and 'air,' which lead the respective series." Possibly he may not have been aware of the tradition of the Algonquins as above.

[125] Is not "Num" cognate to "Numen?" and their worship of trees and worn stones worship of memorials of the Deluge? Compare Boulanger, infra, ch. xi., and on the regard for boulders in India (vide Gainet, vol. i.) Bryant ("Mythology," iii. 532) says, speaking of the Egyptians—"I have mentioned that they showed a reverential regard to fragments of rock which were particularly uncouth and horrid; and this practice seems to have prevailed in many other countries." Probably for the same reason the Lapps worshipped their lakes and rivers, as is known from the names annexed to them—"Ailekes Jauvre," that is, sacred lake, &c. Vide Pinkerton, i. 468. (Leems.)

[126] This chapter was written before the publication of Mr Cox's "Mythology of the Aryan Nations." It will be seen, however, that I indulge the hope that much that is seductive, and much even that is systematic, in Mr Cox's view, will be found to be compatible with the line I have indicated.

[127] Philo. apud Eusebius, who has transmitted the Phœnician tradition (vide Bunsen's "Egypt," iv. 281), seems to me to indicate the mode in which it came about in the following words—"Now Chronos, whose Phœnician epithet was El, a ruler of the land, and subsequently after his death, deified in the constellation of Kronos (Saturn)," &c. As to Saturn, vide ch. x.

In the cosmical theory there is analogy as to the process of deification—"In the Phœnician cosmogonies, the connection between the highest God and a subordinate male and female demiurgic principle is of frequent occurrence" (Bunsen, iv. 447).

It would seemingly be more in fitness with a cosmical theory to find direct adoration of the principle, without evidence of any previous or concurrent process of deification.

Mr W. Palmer ("Egyptian Chronicles," i. 37) says—"But when we find the rulers of the first two periods in the Chronicle, its xiii. gods and viii. demigods, answering closely to the two generations of the antediluvian and post-diluvian patriarchs in number, and therefore also in the average length of the reigns and generations; and when we know, besides, as we do, that the Pantheon of the Egyptians and other nations, which they said had all borrowed from them, was peopled, in part at least, *with deified ancestors*—for even the heavenly luminaries, and the *elements*, and *powers of nature*, and *notions of the true God still remaining*, or of angels and demons, so far as they were invested with humanity and sex, *were identified with human ancestors*; we cannot doubt that Kronos," &c.

[128] "Venator contra Dominum," St Augustine; "Cité de Dieu," xvi. ch. iv.; Pastoret, "Hist. de la Legislation."

[129] Gen. v. 24, says only—"And he walked with God, and was seen no more: because God took him." (Vide also John iii. 13.) There might still have been the belief and tradition (according to appearances) that he was so raised. (Compare 4 Kings ii. 11, and Ecclesiasticus, xliv. 16.)

[130] I believe, however, that the apostasy in the Hamitic race generally was much more direct; and I entirely agree with Bryant that it must have resulted at an early period in a systematic scheme of mixed solar and ancestral worship. Therefore, in any Hamitic tradition, we shall not be startled at finding (even in the commemorative ceremonies of the Deluge) evidence of solar mythology inextricably blended with ancestral traditions. We, however, are only concerned with the ancestral traditions, and in so far as we can discriminate them, Mr Cox's evidence of solar mythology will form no barrier to our inquiry.

In the preceding page I have quoted a passage from Sanchoniathon, which seems to indicate the mode in which the mixed system arose; but there "Cronos" (Noah) is deified in the planet Saturn. As a rule, however, we find him deified in the sun (Bryant, ii. 60, 200, 220). Ham, however, is sometimes also deified in the sun; and in cases where Ham is so deified, it is not unlikely that we shall find the patriarch relegated to Saturn.

[131] "Quoniam antiquitas proxime accedit ad deos."—De Legibus, ii. 11.

[132] The adverse decision, in the matter of the ceremonies, did not, I apprehend, touch the question we are now considering, albeit the ceremonies had reference to deceased ancestors. This will be apparent, I think, from consideration of the grounds upon which the question was debated. The Jesuits relied upon the sense in which the ceremonies were regarded by the Mandarins and literary men whom they consulted, whilst their opponents supported their arguments by reference to the popular notions and the superstitious practices introduced by the Bonzes. (Vide Cretineau Joly's "Hist. de la Com. de Jesus," vol. v. chap. i.)

[133] "Notwithstanding his stature, beauty, hand, and voice, which constitute, taken together, a proud appearance, it seems as if Mars had stood lower in the mind of Homer than any Olympian deity who takes part in the Trojan war, except Venus only."— Gladstone's "Homer," ii. 225.

[134] Vide infra, next chap. ix.

[135] Mr Cox ("Mythology," p. xiv.) says—"Mythology, as we call it now, is simply a collection of the sayings by which men, once upon a time, described whatever they saw or heard in the countries where they lived. This key, which has unlocked almost all the secrets of mythology, was placed in our hands by Professor Max Müller, who has done more than all other writers to bring out the exquisite and touching poetry which underlies those ancient legends. He has shown us that in this, their first shape, these sayings were all perfectly natural, and marvellously beautiful and true. We see the lovely evening twilight die out, &c.... They said that the beautiful Eurydice," &c. (vide infra, p. 173). It would appear, however, from Mr Cox's more extended work, "The Mythology of the Aryan Nations," that the sayings of mankind in the mythic period did not extend to speculations as to their origin and destiny, or embrace the facts of their history, or the deeds of their ancestors, but that their whole converse was upon the sun and moon, and the phenomena of the outward world.

[136] Mr Max Müller makes the distinction between "primitive or organic legends;" (and it is to these I wish to limit the discussion) "and the second, those which were imported in later times from one literature to another.... The former represents one common

ancient stratum of language and thought reaching from India to Europe; the latter consist of boulders of various strata carried along by natural and artificial means from one country to another;" (ii. 245).

It is clear that Mr Max Müller looks for harmony in his system— "We naturally look back to the scenes on which the curtain of the past has fallen, for we believe that there ought to be one thought pervading the whole drama of mankind. And here history steps in, and gives us the thread which connects the present with the past;" (p. 7). Why it was that harmony was not attained seems to be disclosed, if we read the passage in our sense and with a certain transposition of parts, at p. 3—"There were at Athens then, as there have been at all times and in all countries, men who had no sense for the miraculous and supernatural, and who, without having the moral courage to deny altogether what they could not bring themselves to believe, endeavoured to find some plausible explanation by which the sacred legends which tradition had handed down to them, and which had been hallowed by religious observances, and sanctioned by the authority of the law, might be brought into harmony with the dictates of reason and the laws of nature." (Compare with infra, p. 351, Maine.)

[137] Mr Max Müller, in his essay on "Semitic Monotheism," when opposing M. Renan's view that the monotheism of the Semitic race was instinctive, seems to say this still more explicitly—"He thunders and Dyaus thunders became synonymous expressions; and by the mere habit of speech He became Dyaus and Dyaus became He;" ("Chips," i. 358). "At first the names of God, &c., were honest attempts at expressing or representing an idea which could never find adequate expression or representation.... If the Greeks had remembered that Zeus was but a name or symbol of the Deity, there would have been no more harm in calling God by that name than by any other;" (359). It must be remembered that after the name of "Zeus," or "Dyaus," = sky, had been adopted, they still retained the conception of the Divine nature and personality, as is evidenced in the words of the oracle of Dodona—"Ζεὺς ἦν, Ζευς ἐστίν, Ζευς ἔσσεται ὦ μεγαλε Ζευ,—He was, He is, He will be, O great Zeus!;"

Also (ii. 15) in the Orphic lines—

"Zeus is the beginning, Zeus the middle;

Out of Zeus all things have been made."

If we are agreed upon this, then I have no contention with Mr Max Müller; but with Max Müller as an auxiliary, I direct my argument to the attack of Dr Dollinger's position ("The Gentile and the Jew," I. B. ii. p. 64)—"The beginnings of Greek polytheism," viz., "the deification of Nature and her powers, or of particular sensible objects, *lay at the root of all the heathen religions*, as they *existed from old time*, amongst the nations now united under the Roman empire."

According to Mr Lewes ("Hist. of Phil.," i. 44), it was Xenophanes who first confused the sky with the Deity—"Overarching him was the deep blue infinite vault, immovable and unchangeable, embracing him and all things—that he proclaimed to be God." (Contrast the Peruvian tradition, infra, p. 304.) St Clement of Alexandria (Strom. v. p. 601, Max Müller, chapter i. p. 366.) says, on the contrary, that Xenophanes maintained that there was but "one God, and that he was not like unto men, either in body or mind."

[138] Granting the tendency to nature-worship, I conclude that the conspicuous luminaries of the heavens would become primary objects of such worship. In amusing illustration of this I remember a friend of mine telling me that he happened to ask a young lad, the son of one of his tenants, who had just returned from a voyage to the Northern seas, how he liked his captain? He said, "Oh, he was an awful man—he swore by the sun, moon, and stars." Still less do I deny the tendency to sun-worship. It was, as Gibbon tells us (ii. 438, iii. 150), the last superstition Constantine abandoned before his conversion, and the first to which Julian betook himself after his apostacy.

It may, moreover, be urged, that the sun figures in all these legends. I say, on the other hand, so also does the *serpent*. This serpent may be the serpent "of *darkness*," and still be the serpent of *tradition*, but how darkness or night is aptly personified by a serpent I am at a loss to perceive. Then again the sun *may* always be only the symbol of what is bright and heavenly. But when (Max Müller, ii. 171) we see this serpent Zohak, called by the Persians "by the name of Dehak, *i.e., ten evils*, because he introduced "*ten evils into the world*," we cannot help recalling the profane expressions attributed to the devil when he saw the ten commandments—proscribing the *ten* evils in question.

[139] Mr Max Müller may perhaps lay stress upon the circumstance that Baldr dies at the winter solstice. But this equally bears out the tradition noticed by Lenormant, that immediately after the Fall, there came upon the world a great cold. (Vide supra, ch. vii.)

[140] From the "Elder Edda." (Quoted from Dr Dasent's "Norsemen in Iceland." Oxford Essays, 1858.)

[141] What is still more remarkable, the same tradition is found in the "Popol Vul;" (Mexican traditions), and as it is there given, fits in still more exactly with the solution I have suggested. It is there said that the first race of men were created "out the earth," the third out "of a tree called Tzité."[B]   If   the "Popol Vul;" came under Christian or European influences in the 17th century, it would have been more likely to have been brought into harmony with the Bible, rather than with either Homer, Hesiod, or the Edda. Let us pursue the myth a little further. Mr W. K. Kelly, "Indo-Europ. Tradition and Folklore;" (vide Max Müller, ii. 197) says, "This healing virtue, which the mistletoe shares with the ash, is a long descended tradition, for the Kushtha ... a healing plant, was one that grew beneath the heavenly Asvattha," which is elsewhere called "the imperishable Asvattha or Peepul (Ficus religiosus), out of which the immortals shaped the heaven and the earth," which legend Mr Kelly further traces in the German Yggdrasil (although Mr Max Müller from his own point of view dissents); at the foot of which tree (p. 207) "lies the serpent Nidhöggr, and gnaws its roots." Neither Mr Max Müller nor Mr Kelly discuss the point with reference to the view suggested above.

[B] Tiki was the great progenitor among New Zealanders.— Shortland.

[142] Gen. i. 1, "In the beginning God created heaven and earth. 2. And the earth was void and empty, and darkness was upon the face of the deep; and the spirit of God moved over the waters. 5. And He called the light day and the darkness night; and there was evening and morning one day."

In addition to the instances adduced by Gainet, it will be remembered that the Jewish sabbath was from evening to evening, and with us the astronomical day commences at noon, and the commencement and termination of the civil day at mean midnight.

In the *second* [Chinese]   dynasty the day commenced at mid-day. Wei-Wang, the founder of the *third* dynasty, fixed it at midnight." (Bunsen's "Egypt," vol. iii. p. 390.)

In the Phœnician cosmogony "the beginning of all was a dark and stormy atmosphere," "thick, unfathomable black chaos." (*Vide* Bunsen's "Egypt," iv. 176.)

The New Zealanders have preserved the tradition with still greater distinctness. "In the *beginning of time* was Te Po (the night or darkness). In the generations that followed Te Po came Te Ao (the light);" &c., &c. (*Vide* Shortland's "Traditions of the New Zealanders," p. 55.)

Vide Gladstone, "Homer," ii. 155; Cox, "Mythology of Aryan Nations," i. 15, on the relation of Phoibos to Leto. "This is precisely the relation in which the *mythical night* stood to the day which was to be born of *her*."

Vide on this point Wilkinson's "Ancient Egyptians;" (I. chap. xiii.) "The Mygale," says Champollion, "received divine honours by the Egyptians, because it is blind, and *darkness is more ancient than light*." The Arabs have the expression "*night and day*;" (*vide* Wilkinson). Aristotle says "The theologians consider all things to have been born of night." The Orphean fragments call "night the Genesis of all things.... The Anglo-Saxons also, like the Eastern nations, began their computations of time from night, and the years from that day corresponding with our Christmas, which they called "Mother Night," and the Otaheitans refer the existence of their principal deities to a state of darkness, which they consider the origin of all things." (*Vide* Gen. i. 2, 3; *id.* p. 273–4.)

[143] "Gesta Romanorum," tale xviii. Swan. Rivingtons 1824.

[144] On this point, that Prometheus is Adam, vide M. Nicolas' "Etudes Philos. sur le Christ.," 1. ii. ch. v. 30 (19th edit.)

[145] In like manner, the Peruvians recognised "Pachacamac;" (vide infra, p. 304), in the description which the Spaniards gave of the true God; and in so far as they had retained the monotheistic belief, this was true. Garcilasso de la Vega, a most competent witness who testifies to this, adds—"If any one shall now ask me, who am a Catholic Christian Indian, by the infinite mercy, what name was given to God in my language, I should say Pachacamac."—Hakluyt Society, ed. of Garcil. de la Vega, i. 107.

[146] "This is not a mere arbitrary supposition, for it is expressly said in Holy Writ, that the first man, ordained to be 'the father of the whole earth' (as he is then called), became, on his reconciliation with his Maker, the wisest of all men, and, according to tradition, the greatest of prophets, who in his far-reaching ken, foresaw the destinies of all mankind in all successive ages down to the end of the world. All this must be taken in a strict historical sense, for the moral interpretation we abandon to others. The pre-eminence of the Sethites chosen by God, and entirely devoted to His service, must be received as an undoubted historical fact, to which we find many pointed allusions even in the traditions of the other Asiatic nations. Nay, the hostility between the Sethites and Cainites, and the mutual relations of these two races, form the chief clue to the history of the primitive world, and even of many particular nations of antiquity." — Fred. Von Schlegel's "Philosophy of Hist.," Robertson's trans., p. 152.

[147] Compare these epithets, and what was said above, of resemblance "to classical Hades," with the following verses from the "Oracula Sybillina," lib. i. 80 —

"Orcus eos cepit græco qui nomine dictus

Est *Ades*, quod primus eo descenderit *Adam*,

Expertus mortis legem," &c.

[148] Osiris also is "the judge of the soul, or the god of the world of spirits." "Osiris is never represented in an animal form, but is called the Bull" (infra pp. 203, 204), vide Bunsen's "Egypt," iv. 332. Bunsen's own view is, that "the history of Osiris is the history of the cycle of the year, of the sun dying away and resuscitating himself again." Mr Palmer ("Egyptian Chronicles," i. p. 3) says — (and I think it as well that I should state that I had come to an almost identical conclusion, and had written this and the following chapter before I became acquainted with Mr Palmer's profound and yet still neglected work, vide ch. vi.) — "The first human ('Osiris = Adam and Isis = Eve') having been thrown back into pairs of anthropomorphous deities (p. 2), the original Osiris and Isis, formed by the divine potter as parents of all, disappear in name, and are represented by Seb and Nutpe, while Osiris, Typhon, and Horus, the progeny of Seb and Nutpe, answers rather to Cain, Abel, and Seth, in the old world, and to the three sons of Noah in the new.... From Osiris-Seb (whether he be viewed as Adam or Noah) are derived

downwards all the successive generations of Egyptian, gods and demigods, patriarchs, kings, and other men" [and for a parallel exposition of the Phœnician myth, vide Palmer, p. 53 and seq., "each dynast in turn, in the early generations, being identifiable at once with Seb and Osiris, as father of those following, with Osiris again by sharing the same mortality, and with Horus as renewing his father's life and being the hope of the coming world. So each ancestor in turn went, it was said, to the original Osiris as patriarch of the dead, and to his intermediate Osirified fathers, and was himself Osirified like them, all making one collective Osiris." [I have not space to discuss the question at what stage the mythology became pantheistic.] "Waiting for that reunion and restoration which was to come through successive generations by the great expected Horus, who was to take up into himself the old, and to be himself the new Osiris."

[149] In a note to Cardinal Wiseman's "Science and Revealed Religion" on Conformity between Semitic and Indo-Europ. grammatical forms, it will be seen that Ana in Chaldaic is the pronoun of the first person singular, and corresponds with the revealed appellation of the Deity, "I Am who Am" (Exod. iii. 14) = the τὸ Ἐγω.

[150] Max Müller, Chips i. 153, refers to Dr Windischmann's ("Zoroastrian Studies") discovery that there are ten generations between Adam and Noah, as there are ten generations in the Zendavesta between Yima (Adam) and Thrâstouna (Noah), and without controverting the point. Mr Palmer ("Egypt. Chron.," i. 45) says—"And though the fancy of making the ten kings to begin only after 1058 years, and to be not all named from the same city, seems to distinguish them from Adam and the nine patriarchs his descendants, still Xisuthrus, the tenth, being clearly identified with Noah, by the flood and the ark, the very number ten, and the relation of the succession in which they stand one to the other, show that Alorus, the first of them, is no other than Adam."

[151] Gainet (i. 211) quotes as follows from "Ceremonies Relig." i. vii.: "The Mandans pretend that the Deluge was caused by the white men to destroy their ancestors. The whites caused the waters to rise to such a height that the world was submerged. Then the first man, whom they regard as one of their divinities, inspired mankind with the idea of constructing, upon an eminence, a tower and fortress of wood, and promised them that the

water should not rise beyond this point." Here seems a very analogous confused tradition of Adam and Nimrod, the Deluge and the Tower of Babel. Comp. with the distinct testimony to the Mandan tradition, infra, ch. xi.

[152] I find that the Egyptians had the same confused tradition respecting Menes, who stood to them in the same relation as Nimrod to the Assyrians (vide Bunsen's Egypt, ii. p. 65). "The statement in Manetho's lists that Menes was torn to pieces by a hippopotamus, is probably an exaggeration of an early legend, that he was carried away by a hippopotamus, one of the symbols of the god of the lower world. The great ruler was snatched away from the earth, to distinguish him from other mortals, just as Romulus was."

[153] "Etienne de Byzance dit qu'à 'Icone' ('de urbibus' voce 'Iconium') ville de Lycaonie près du Mont Taurus dans les régions occupées par les habitants antediluviens regnait Annacus dont la vie alla au-déla de trois cents ans. Tous les habitants d'alentour demandèrent à un oracle jusqu'à quelle époque se prolongerait sa vie. L'oracle répondit que ce patriarche étant mort, tout le monde devait s'attendre à périr. Les Phrygiens à cette ménace jetèrent les hauts cris, d'où est venu le proverbe: 'Pleurer sous Annacus, ce que l'on dit de ceux qui se livrent à des grands gémissements. Or le Déluge étant survénu tous périrent.... Dans ces récits tout est conformé à la Bible. Annacus a vécu trois cents ans avant le Déluge. Il a averti ses concitoyens: il est entouré du même respect que le patriarche Noë lui-même. Annacus parait venir d'Enoch; tout announce une identité de personnages." (Gainet, Hist. de L'Anc. et Nouv. Test. i. 94, 95.) The connection between the death of Enoch and the destruction of mankind may accord as well with the traditional belief in his reappearance at the end of the world.

Compare the Grecian tradition of Inachus, son of Oceanus (*vide* Bryant, ii. 268), and with it, Hor., Od. 3, lib. ii.:

"Divesne, prisco et natus ab Inacho,

Nil interest, an pauper, et infimâ

De gente," &c

[154] Vide his other epithets, infra, p. 239; also Rawlinson (Herod. i. p. 600), says that "upon one of the tablets in the British Museum there is a list of thirty-six synonyms indicating this god (Hoa).

The greater part of them relate either to "the abyss" or to "knowledge."

Compare this with the following verses from the "Oracula Sybillina," i. ver. 145—

"Collige, Noë, tuas vires ...

... Si scieris me

Divinæ te nulla rei secreta latebunt."

Now, without entering into the question of the authenticity of the Sybilline verses, I may at least quote them in evidence of the current tradition concerning Noah in the second century of the Christian era, supposing them to have been forged at that period.

[155] "Comment le nom du premier navigateur connu, tel qu'il se prononça en Hébreu et qu'il nous est transmis par la Génese, 'Noh, Naus, Noach,' serait-il devenu le nom d'une arche flottante, d'un navire, en Sanscrit et en vingt autres langues? Nau, sanscrit; Naw, armenien; Naus, grec; (Navis, latin); Noi, hibernien; Neau, bas breton; Nef, nav. franc; Noobh, irlandais; Naone, vanikoro; Nacho, allemand vieux; Naw, timor; Nachen, allemand; _S'nechia_, islandais; _S'naeca_ ou Naca, anglo-sax.; _S'nace_, ancien anglais; Sin-nau, cambodge, &c.

"Enfin nous demandons comment le nom Hébreu de l'arche de Noë. Tobe, prononcé comme on écrivait généralement en Orient, en sens inverse, donne le nom d'un vaisseau dans vingt langues qui sont des dialectes du Sanscrit? L'écriture boustrophedone, qui fait les lignes alternativement à droite et gauche sans interruption a pu donner naissance à cette manière de dire:—*Boat*, anglais; *boite*, français; *bat*, anglo-saxon; *boot*, hollandais; *bat*, suedois; *baat*, danois; *batr*, islandais; *bad*, breton; *bote*, espagnol; *boar*, persan; *batillo*, italien; *pota*, sanscrit." *Vide* other similar proofs from Vicomte d'Anselme's "Monde Païen," &c. In Gainet, i. 223, a curious additional instance of the same word having connections with "boat" and arc (*tobe*) might be discovered in Kibotos, the name of a mountain in Phrygia, where the ark is said to have rested (Gainet, i. 220). Also we have almost the same words—ark and arc—to express (though according to a different etymology) these dissimilar objects.

"The words oar and rudder can be traced back to Sanskrit, and the name of the ship is identically the same in Sanscrit (naus, nâvas), in Latin (navis), in Greek (naus), and in Teutonic, Old High Germ. (nachs), Anglo-Saxon (naca)."—Max Müller, "Comp. Mythol.," p. 49.

I may draw attention, as having reference to other branches of this inquiry, to a possible affinity with the name of the patriarch, in the term *Noaaids*, applied by the Laplanders to their magicians (Pinkerton, i. 459, &c.); and to the term Koader*nicks*, applied by the Samoids to the same (*id*. 532). I own there might be danger in pushing the inquiry further, as I might even bring the patriarch Noah into contact and connection with Old Nick!

I may also refer to the term "Janna" (Janus), as applied to the officer "who had the office of entertaining ambassadors" at the court of Kenghis Khan (id. v. 7, p. 40; Rubruquis's Embassy, A.D. 1253, also 56).

[156] Comp. "Traditions of the New Zealanders."

[157] Do not the seven richis or sages correspond to the seven (or eight) (Phœnician) Kabiri. (There were seven or eight persons in the ark, accordingly as we take separate account or not of Noah.) As regards the Kabiri, their number (seven or eight, accordingly as we include "Æsculapius") must be the clue to the solution of "the most obscure and mysterious question in mythology." Bunsen ("Egypt," iv. 229) says of an astral explanation:—"It does not enable us to explain the details of those representations which do not contain the number seven (or eight), and, in fact, seven brothers." It will suffice, from our point of view, if there are numerically seven persons. Bunsen (iv. p. 291) says—"It is quite clear that the fundamental number of the gods in the oldest mythologies of Phœnicia, and all Asia, as well as Egypt, was seven. There were seven Kabiri, with the seven Titans. There are also seven Titans mentioned in other genealogies of the race of Kronos. Of the latter, one dies a virgin and disappears." But as with the Kabiri we have seen the number seven, or eight, accordingly as Æsculapius is included or not, so (vide p. 314) we see the primitive gods of Egypt either seven or eight, accordingly as Thoth, "the eighth," or Horus, figure as the "last divine king" (p. 319). When Horus so figures, "he is frequently represented as the eighth, conducting the bark of the gods, with the seven great gods," &c. Moreover, it is elsewhere (p. 347) said that "the Phœnicians, in their sacred books, stated that the Kabiri embarked in ships, and landed near Mount Kaison.

This legend was corroborated by the existence of a shrine on that coast in historic times." [Query, The tradition of the Deluge localised, and the shrine commemorative of that catastrophe (vide Boulanger, &c., infra, p. 244); and supposing that the tradition of the number saved in the Flood had been preserved down to a certain date, we should then expect that the number would become rigid and fixed. But that if the tradition of the actual survivors had become indistinct, what more natural than that the eight principal characters of ante-diluvian, or even post-diluvian, history should be substituted for them, and that the same confusion and agglomeration of legend should take place as we shall see occurring in the tradition of Noah?]

In the Persian or Iranian legend of Shâh-nâmeh, "the three sons of Ferêdûn—Ireg, Tur, and Selm—are mentioned as their patriarchs, and among them the *whole earth was divided*." But in the more ancient Gâthâs there is mention of "the *seven*-surfaced or *seven*-portioned earth." [*Query*—apportioned by *the eighth*?]   *Vide* Bunsen's "Egypt," iii. 478.

For the Indian tradition compare the following from Hunter's "Bengal" (i. p. 151)—"Another coincidence—I do not venture to call it an analogy—is to be found in the number of children born to the first pair. As the Santal legend immediately divides the human species into *seven* families, so the Sanscrit tradition assigns the propagation of *our race after the flood* to *seven rishis*." I also find in F. Schlegel's "Philosophy of History" (p. 150, Robertson's trans.)—"The Indian traditions acknowledge and revere the succession of the first ancestors of mankind, or the holy patriarchs of the primitive world, under the name of the *seven great rishis*, or sages of hoary antiquity, though they invest their history with a cloud of fictions."

[158] Syncellus, quoting Berosus (vide Abbé de Tressan, "Mythology," p. 10), says that Oannes (the mysterious fish, vide ante) left some writings upon the origin of the world. These, no doubt, correspond to the "Liber Noachi." I do not disguise that this statement is probably derived from what is called the false Berosus. The reference, however, which I have made to these writings at p. 139 may raise doubt whether they did not embody true traditions.

[159] I fancy it might be traced also in the Phœnician fish-god, Dagon. The Saturday Review (June 4, 1870) in its review of

Cox's "Mythology," says—"Dagon cannot be divided Dag-on, the fish 'On,' for a Semitic syllable cannot begin with a vowel; and if the necessary breathing 'aleph' were inserted (which it is very unsafe to do), it would then mean 'the fish of On,' which is not the signification required." But it is the signification which would fit in here; moreover, might not the terminal "aon," or "haon," suggested, have been originally, i.e. before displacement by "boustrophedon"—Noa or Noah? I give this suggestion with all proper diffidence, and with some genuine misgiving as to the "breathing aleph." I find that Bryant ("Mythology," iii. p. 116) makes a similar suggestion.

Bunsen ("Egypt," iv. 243) says—"Dagon is Dagan, i.e. corn. This is also implied by the Greek form of it—Sitôn, wheat-field (comp. p. 219). We have in the Bible, Dagon, a god of the Philistines, a name usually supposed to be derived from 'dag,' fish; the god has a human form ending in a fish, like the fish-shaped goddess, Derketo-Atergatis. It is clear, from Philo's own account, that the Phoenician Poseidon was a god of this kind, and it is difficult to find any other name for him. Yet we cannot say that Dagon is very clearly explained. Here is a god of agriculture, well authenticated, both linguistically and documentally, Dagan, i.e. wheat, and he is the *Zeus of agriculture.*" *Vide* p. 219. P. 261 says Dagon must not be confounded with "Dagan," but without reconciling it with the above at p. 243, on the contrary, we find "Dagon, Dagan = corn (the fish-man)." At p. 241, quoting from the *text* of Philo, it is said still more pointedly—"Dagon, after he *had discovered corn and the plough,* was called Zeus Arotnios." Comp. p. 204.

Believing (vide ch. xii.) in the tradition of mythology, even among savages, I could not but be much struck on coming upon the following passage in Roggeveen's voyage, to find—in his account of the Eastern Islanders—the same conjunction of the bull and fish implied in the traditional names of their idols:— "The name of the largest idol was called Taurico, and the other Dago; at least, these were the words they called to them by, and wherewith they worshipped them. These savages had great respect for the two idols, Taurico and Dago, and approached them with great reverence ... and to supplicate for help against us, and to call upon with a frightful shout and howling of Dago! Dago!" ("Historical Account of Voyages Round the World," 1774, i. 469, 470.)

After showing the resemblance of a feast at Argos to other commemorative feasts of the Deluge, Boulanger (*vide infra,* i. 83) says—"Les Argiens avoient encore une autre fête pendant laquelle ils précipitoent dans un abîme un agneau.... ils étoient armés de javelines, ils appelloient *Bacchus* au son des trompettes et l'invitoient _à semontrer hors de l'eau_; cette apparition n'arrivoit pas fréquemment sans doute" (comp. *supra,* 197, and 237). "Plutarque remarque que lors qu'ils précipitoient l'agneau, ils avoient soin de cacher leurs trompettes et leurs javelines. Nous ne prétendons point expliquer tous ces mystères." Is it that they feared, with armed weapons in their hands, to evoke the apparition of the old man "whose conquests were all peaceful" (p. 216), and who, as Manco Capac (p. 326), "shut his ears when they spoke to him of war."

[160] This closely corresponds to the description of Oannes given by Sanchoniathon, "Ap. Euseb." (Bryant, ii. 301), i.e. with two heads (comp. infra, p. 220), the human head being placed below the head of a fish:—"ἄλλην κεφαλην ὑποκατω της τοῦ ἰχθυος κεφαλης."

[161] Vide similar traditions of the man-bull in India and Japan. Bryant, iii. 589, who adds, "We shall find hereafter that in this (Parsee) mythology there were two ancient personages represented under the same character, and named L'Homme Taureau; each of whom was looked upon as the father of mankind." Compare pp. 158, 189, the two Menus and the two Osiris.

[162] The prayer used in the worship of Dionysos at Elis, preserved by Plutarch, ended with "Ἄξιε Ταυρε—Ἄξιε Ταυρε," worthy bull! (vide Bunsen's "Egypt," iv. 446.) Compare p. 215 with Dionysius = Bacchus = Noah; also of the three Samothracian names of the Kabiri—viz., Axieros, Axiokerse, Axiokersos. Bunsen says, "the syllable Axi or Axie which is found in all three, cannot be anything but the Greek word 'Axios,' which was used in the worship of Dionysos at Elis" (id., vide infra).

On this symbol of the bull in connection with Noah and the Ark vide Bryant (ii. 416, et seq. 439). He says, "Every personage that had any connection with the history of the Ark was described with some reference to this hieroglyphic ... that the Apis and Mnenis (Menes) were both representations of an ancient personage is certain; and who that personage was may be known from the account given of him by Diodorus. He speaks of him by the name of Mnenes, but confines his history to Egypt, as the history of Saturn was limited to Italy; Inachus and Phoroneus to Argos; Deucalion to Thessaly ... the same person who in Crete was styled Minos, Min-nous, and whose city was Min-Noa; the same who was represented under the emblem of Mentaur, or Mino-taurus (Minotaur). Diodorus speaks of Mnenes as the first lawgiver," &c., &c.... [Mnenes or Menes may embody traditions of Noah and Misraim, as Osiris does of Adam and Noah.]   At p. 422–435 [plate]   , we find Menes represented as a bull with the sacred dove.... Plutarch (Isis and Osiris) says the bulls, Apis and Mnenes, were sacred to Osiris ... and Eustath. (in Dion. v. 308) says of the Tauric Chersonese, "that the Tauric nation was so named from the animal Taurus or bull, which was looked upon as a memorial of the great husbandman Osiris, who first taught agriculture, and to whom was ascribed the invention of the plough." ... Lycophron (v. 209 and scholia) says, Ταυρος, Διονυσος. Plutarch says Dionusus (vide supra, p. 203) was styled Βουγενης, or the offspring of a bull, by the people of Argos, who used to invoke him as a resident of the sea, and entreat him to come out of the waters. The author of the Orphic hymns calls him "Taurogenes." Ταυρογενης Διονυσος ευφροσυνην πορε Θνητοις. Ταυρογενης, is precisely of the same purport as Θηβαιγενης [ark-born]   , and the words of this passage certainly mean "that the ark-born deity Dionusus restored peace and happiness to mortals." [Noah's name in Scripture signifies "peace and consolation"— Νωε εβραισϊαναπαυσις (rest), Hesychius.]   ... The title given to Diana—viz. Taurione, is remarkable, for "Taurus was an emblem of the Ark, and by Taurione was signified the arkite dove." Taurus, and ione from Οινας of the Greeks, and Ionas of the eastern nations = dove, and curiously in an inscription in Gruter, Diana is at the same time called "Regina undarum," and "decus nemorum" (Bryant, ii. 434). The connection of Diana, Juno, and Venus with the dove and rainbow is very striking, but would lead to too long a digression. So, too, would a discussion as to how Noah or the Ark (secondarily) came to be associated with the bull, as a hieroglyphic. Compare the above with the ox-heads and bull dance in the Mandan commemoration of the Deluge, infra, ch. xi.

[163] Since writing the above I have found the following note in Rawlinson's "Herodotus," i. 623, on Ninip:—"There is, however, another explanation of the name Bar-sam or Bur-shem, of which some notice must be taken. It has been already stated that if the Noachid triad be compared with the Assyrian, Ana will correspond with Ham, Bel-Nimrod with Shem, and Hoa with Japhet."

The following passage, also from Rawlinson's "Herodotus," i. 609, appears to me valuable in proof of the transition from ancestral to solar worship, or at least of their interfusion:—"The sun was probably named in Babylonia both San and Sanei, before his title took the definite Semitic form of Shamas, by which he is known in Assyrian and in all the languages of that family." Now, standing by itself, this might not appear very significant; but compare it with the following passages connecting Ham with the sun:—"By the Syrians the sun and heat were called ... Chamba; by the Persians, Hama; and the temple of the sun, the temple of Ammon or Hammon." Mr Bryant shows that Ham was esteemed the Zeus of Greece and the Jupiter of Latium. Mr G. Higgins' "Anacalypsis," p. 45. Bryant says, "the worship of Ham, or the sun, as it was the most ancient, so it was the most universal of any in the world." These passages may possibly be so interpreted as to support a solar theory, but is it not at least suspicious to see the name of the central luminary so apparently identified with historical characters whose memory is distinctly preserved aliunde in the traditions of their descendants? Compare Nimrod, ch. viii. 164, et seq.

[164] Rawlinson says that there is no doubt that Nebo represents the planet Mercury, and between the attributes of Mercury or Hermes, the epithets of Nebo, and the traditions concerning Shem, there is something in common. He is the god of eloquence and persuasion—the god of alliances and peace. "He contributed to civilise the manners and cultivate the minds of the people." "He united them by commerce and good laws." The Egyptian Mercury or Thaut first invented landmarks. Finally, "He was consulted by the Titans, his relations, as an augur, which gave occasion to the poets to describe him as interpreter of the will of the gods."—_L'Abbe de Tressan, "Mythology."_

[165] "Notwithstanding the difficulty of ascending to so distant a period, there will always be found some traces by which truth may be discovered.... The historian Josephus relates that

the Chaldæans from the earliest times carefully preserved the remembrance of past events by public inscriptions on their monuments. He says they caused these annals to be written by the wisest men of their nation." — _L'Abbe de Tressan, "Hist. of Heathen Mythology."_ London, 1806.

[166] I had come to the above conclusion upon the perusal of Rawlinson, and before I had read Bryant, who, I find, had already come to this identical conclusion. ("Mythology," iii. 109.) Speaking of Berosus' account of Oannes and Xisuthrus, he says, "The latter was undoubtedly taken from the archives of the Chaldæans. The former is allegorical and obscure, and was copied from hieroglyphical representations which could not be precisely deciphered.... In consequence of his borrowing from records so very different, we find him, without his being apprized of it, giving two histories of the same person. Under the character of the man of the sea, whose name was Oannes, we have an allegorical representation of the great patriarch; whom in his other history he calls Sisuthrus."

[167] Bochart also says (Geog. Sacra, lib. i.) "Noam esse Saturnum tam multa docent, ut vix sit dubitandi locus."

[168] "Cum falce, messis insigne." — Macrobius, "Saturn."

[169] Sanchoniathon, vide supra M'Lennan (ch. vii.)

[170] Bryant (Mythology, ii. 261) says: — "He is by Lucian made to say of himself οὐδεις ὑπ' ἐμοῦ δοῦλος ἦν. The Latins in great measure confine his history to their own country, where, like Janus, he is represented as refining and modelling mankind, and giving them laws. At other times he is introduced as prior to law; which are seeming contrarieties very easy to be reconciled." There were traditions also of Saturn in Crete and Sparta. — Bryant, iii. 414.

[171] Vide supra, p. 211.

[172] An indirect argument in proof of the identity of Saturn and Noah might be adduced if I had space to incorporate Boulanger's evidence of the ceremonies among the ancients' commemoration of the Deluge, ("Vestiges d'usages hydrophoriques dans plusieurs fêtes anciennes et modernes"). This being assumed, is it not of some significance that when the Roman pontiffs proceeded to the banks of the Tiber to perform their annual (commemorative) ceremonial, that they should make their

expiatory sacrifices to Saturn? The points that Bryant takes (ii. 262) are very striking:—"He was looked upon as the author of time, 'Ipse qui auctor temporum' (Macrob. i. 214). [His medals had on the reverse the figure of a ship.]   They represented him as of an uncommon age, with hair white as snow; they had a notion that he would return to second childhood. 'Ipsius autem canities primosis nivibus candicabat; licet etiam ille puer posse fieri crederetur.'—Martianus Capella. Martial's address to him, though short, has in it something remarkable, for he speaks of him as a native of the former world—

'Antiqui rex magne poli, *mundique prioris,*

Sub quo prima quies, nec labor ullus erat.'—l. 12, E. 63.

I have mentioned that he was supposed, καταπινειν, to have swallowed up his children; he was also said to have ruined all things; which, however, were restored with a vast increase."— Orphic Hymn, 12, v. 3. Compare Calmet, supra.

Martianus Capella and Varro de Ling. Lat. lib. i. 18, call him *Sator*, a sower, "Saturnus Sator." Now it is curious that the ancient Germans had a god "of the name of *Sator*." He is described by Verstegan as "standing *upon a fish*, with a wheel in one hand, and in the other a *vessel of water* filled with fruits and flowers."

N.B.—I was surprised to find in Carver's "Travels in North America" the phrase among the North American Indians, of things being done at the instigation "of the Grand *Sautor*."

[173] "Saturn is by Plato supposed to have been the son of Oceanus."— Bryant, ii. 261.

[174] Vide Autochthones, ch. vii.

[175] "The Scriptures tell us that Noah cultivated the vine; and all profane historians agree in placing Bacchus in the first ages of the world" (in proof of early cultivation of the vine).—Goguet, "Origin of Laws," i. 116. Compare supra, p. 213, "Saturnus Sator." Bryant says, "The history of Dionusus is closely connected with that of Bacchus, though they are two distinct persons." He supposes Dionusus to be Noah, and Bacchus Ham. But he may very well have embodied the traditions of both. Pausanius (lib. iii. 272) says Dionusus was exposed in an ark and wonderfully preserved. He was also said to have been twice born, and to

have had two fathers and two mothers, in allusion to the two periods of his existence separated by the Deluge.

Dionusus (Orphic Hymn, 44, 1) is addressed as ἔλθε, μακαρ Διονυσε, πυρισπορε ταυρουμετωπε.

[176] The phrase "Father Bacchus," current among the ancients (vide Hor. Odes. i. xviii.) has always struck me as singular. It is perfectly congruous with the tradition of Noah; but who will tell us its appropriate solar or astral application?

[177] Montfauçon, from whom I have quoted, was simply an antiquarian — a very erudite and laborious antiquarian, but one whose sole concern was to discriminate facts without reference to their bearings, and who would have had, I have little doubt, a supreme contempt for the speculations in which I have indulged. He says in his preface — "I have a due regard for those great men who have excelled in this sort of learning, but must own at the same time I have no taste for it.... It signifies very little to us to know whether they who tell us Vulcan was the same with Tubalcain, or they who say he was the same with Moses, make the best guess in the matter." Though the general opinion may not incline any more now than then to the biblical interpretation, yet I think a great change has taken place in public opinion as to the importance of the inquiry.

Triptolemus was also said to have been "the inventor of the plough and of agriculture, and of civilisation, which is the result of it," and to have instituted the Elusinian mysteries. Like Bacchus he is also said to have "ridden all over the earth, making men acquainted with the blessings of agriculture." — Smith. Myth. Dict.; vide also infra, p. 224: "Deucalion."

[178] Dionusus like Bacchus came to India from the west. — Philostratus, lib. ii. 64; Byrant, ii. 78. The Indian Bacchus "appears in the character of a wise and distinguished oriental monarch; his features an expression of sublime tranquillity and mildness." — Smith, Myth. Dic.

[179] This appears to me still more apparent in the 26th Idyll of Theocritus, where, when the Bacchanals were at their revels,

"Perched on the sheer cliff Pentheus would espy

All....

(For profaning thus "these mysteries weird that must not be profaned by vulgar eyes," Pentheus is torn to pieces by the Bacchanals)....

"Warned by this tale, let no man dare defy

Great Bacchus; lest a death more awful should he die.

And when he counts *nine* years or scarcely *ten*

Rush to his ruin. May I pass my days

Uprightly, and be loved by *upright* men.

And take this motto, all who covet praise

('Twas ægis-bearing Jove that spoke it first),

The godly seed fares well, *the wicked is accurst*."

—*Caverley's Theocritus*, xxvi.

This seems to bear out what is perhaps only vaguely implied in the sacred text that the curse was on Chanaan—the boy and his posterity—and not on the whole race of Cham.—*Vide ante*: also compare the "Bacchæ" of Euripides, in the following passage from Grote's "Plato" (iii. 333):—"So in the 'Bacchæ' of Euripides, the two old men, Kadmus and Teiresias, after vainly attempting to inculcate upon Pentheus the belief in and the worship of Dionysus, at last appeal to his prudence and admonish him of the danger of unbelief;" which, if it be tradition, would look as if Chanaan's offence was only the final and overt expression of previous unbelief.

[180] Vide Dr Smith's "Myth. Dict." art. Janus:—"Whereas the worship of Janus was introduced at Rome by Romulus, that of Sol was instituted by Titus Tatius."

[181] If Janus is allowed to have been identified with Saturn (supra) we may see through the analogy of Saturn how these secondary functions came to be attributed to him—Saturn was also Chronos [that Chronos = Noah, vide Palmer's Egypt. Chron., i. p. 60]   ; "but," as Dr Smith says, "there is no resemblance between the deities, except that both were regarded as the most ancient deities in their respective countries." As Chronos simply personifies antiquity itself, this only means that Saturn was the most ancient deity. When subsequently he became merged in "Chronos," his ancient sickle became converted into a scythe. Dr Smith ("Dict. Myth.") says, "He held in his hand a crooked pruning knife, and his feet were surrounded with a

woollen riband;" and Goguet ("Origin of Laws," i. 94) says, "All old traditions speak of the sickle of Saturn, who is said to have taught the people of his time to cultivate the earth."—Plut. i. p. 2, 275; Macrob. Sat., lib. i. 217.

Goguet ("Origin of Laws," i. 283) says, "Several critics are of opinion that the Janus of the ancients is the same with Javan the son of Japhet, Gen. x. 3."

It may afford a clue if I advert to the circumstance that whilst in the Phœnician alphabet (vide Bunsen's Egypt. iv. 290, 293, 297), Dagon, Dagan = Corn (the Fish-man, vide supra, p. 200), stands for the letter D. "The door" is its hieroglyphic equivalent. Thus we get in strange juxtaposition what we may call symbols, connecting Janus with the Fish-god and with the god of agriculture.—Vide supra, p. 200, and infra.

[182] Bryant ("Mythology," ii. 254) says, "Many persons of great learning have not scrupled to determine that Noah and Janus were the same. By Plutarch he is called Ιαννος, and represented as an ancient prince who reigned in the infancy of the world.... He was represented with two faces, with which he looked both forwards and backwards; and from hence he had the name of Janus Bifrons. One of these faces was that of an aged man; but in the other was often to be seen the countenance of a young and beautiful personage. About him ... many emblems.... There was particularly a staff in one hand, with which he pointed to a rock, from whence issued a profusion of water. In the other hand he held a key.... He had generally near him some resemblance of a ship.... Plutarch does not accede to the common notion" (that it was the ship that brought Saturn to Italy), "but still makes it a question why the coins of this personage bore on one side the resemblance of Janus Bifrons, and on the other the representation of either the hind part or the fore part of a ship.... He is said to have first composed a chaplet, and to him they attributed the invention of a ship. Upon the Sicilian coins (at the temple) of Eryx his figure often occurs with a twofold countenance, and on the reverse is a dove encircled with a crown, which seems to be of olive. He is represented as a just man and a prophet (comp. pp. 207–208), and had the remarkable characteristics of being in a manner the author of time and the god of the year."

[183] "Megasthenes stated that the first king (of India) was Dionysus. He found a rude population in a savage state, clothed in skins,

unacquainted with agriculture, and without fixed habitations. The length of his reign is not given. The introduction of civilization and agriculture is a natural allusion to the immigration of the Aryans into a country inhabited by Turanian races.... Fifteen generations after Dionysus, Hercules reigned.... Now all this is obviously pure Indian tradition. Dionysus is the elder Manu, the divine primeval man, son of the Sun (Vivasvat). He holds the same position in the primeval history of India as does Jima or Gemshid, another name of the primeval man in the Iranian world.... The first era, then, is represented by Megasthenes as having fourteen generations of human kings, with a god as the founder and a god as the destroyer of the dynasty, in all fifteen or sixteen generations."—Bunsen's Egypt, iii. 528. Compare those fifteen generations with Palmer. Compare the confusion of Dionysus and Hercules with Deucalion and Prometheus, &c., p. 232. Pelasgus among the Arcadians passed for the first man and the first legislator (Boulanger, i. 133). Of Cadmus, too, it is said—"Greece is indebted to him for alphabetical writing, the art of cultivating the vine, and the forging and working of metals."—Goguet, ii. 41.

[184] Vide supra, Oannes, ch. ix.; vide Smith, "Myth. Dict."

[185] "All nations have given the honour of the discovery of agriculture to their first sovereigns. The Egyptians said that Osiris (vide supra, p. 204) made men desist from eating each other, by teaching them to cultivate the earth. The Chinese annals relate that Gin-Hoang, one of the first kings of that country, invented agriculture, and by that means collected men into society, who before had wandered in the fields and woods like brute beasts." (Goguet, "Origin of Laws.") I need not remind the reader that Goguet's learned work is not written from our point of view. Compare infra.

[186] Vide, chap. xiii. Golden age, Mexican tradition.

[187] Although the greater number of these traditions have been localised, yet in almost every case we shall find embodied in them some one incident or other of the universal Deluge, as recorded by Moses. Kalisch ("Hist. and Crit. Commentary on the Old Testament") says:—"It is unnecessary to observe that there is scarcely a single feature in the biblical account which is not discovered in one or several of the heathen traditions; and the coincidences are not limited to desultory details, they

extend to the whole outlines, and the very tenor and spirit of the narrative; ... and it is certain that none of these accounts are derived from the pages of the Bible—they are independent of each other.... There must indisputably have been a common basis, a universal source, and this source is the general tradition of primitive generations."

It is not, I think, generally known how widespread these traditions are. L'Abbé Gainet has collected some thirty-five ("La Bible sans la Bible"); but Mr Catlin (vide infra, p. 245) says he found the tradition of a deluge among one hundred and twenty tribes which he visited in North, South, and Central America. This accords with Humboldt's testimony (Kalisch, i. 204), who "found the tradition of a general deluge vividly entertained among the wild tribes peopling the regions of Orinoco." To these I must add the evidence of the indirect testimony of the commemorative ceremonies which I have collected in another chapter (vide p. 242). It has been said that the Chinese tradition is too obscure to be adduced, but we shall see (p. 65) whether, when in contact with other traditions, it cannot be made to give light; and I shall refer my readers to the pages of Mr Palmer (supra, p. 71) for evidence of the tradition in Egypt, where it had heretofore been believed that no such evidence was to be found. In India (vide ch. ix.) the tradition is embodied in the history of Manu and the fish; and Bunsen ("Egypt," iii. 470) admits "that there is evidence in the Vedas, however slight, that the flood does form a part of the reminiscences of Iran." Vide also p. 68, evidence of the tradition in Cashmere. I wish also to direct attention here to two recent and important testimonies to the existence of the tradition in India and the Himalayan range. Hunter's "Bengal," it will be seen that the Santals have a distinct tradition of the Creation, flood, intoxication of Noah, and the dispersion; and of the Vedic evidence, which Bunsen (supra, 223) calls slight, Mr Hunter says:—"On the other hand, the Sanscrit story of the Deluge, like that in the Pentateuch, makes no mystery of the matter. A ship is built, seeds are taken on board, the ship is pulled about for some time by a fish, and at last gets on shore upon a peak of the Himalayas." Dr Hooker ("Himalayan Journal," ii. 3) says:—"The Lepchas have a curious legend of a man and woman having saved themselves on the summit of Tendong (a very fine mountain, 8613 feet) during a flood which once deluged Sikhim," which he authenticates on the spot. Here, as in many of Mr Catlin's instances of local tradition, I may observe that the event as recorded proves the universality of the Deluge for the rest of the world, or at least all the world below the level of Tendong. In speaking, however, of the universal Deluge (universal as far as the human race are concerned), I do not enter into the geological argument, or exclude the view (permissible I believe, vide Reusch, p. 368, and note to Rev. H. J. Coleridge's fourth sermon on "The Latter Days") that it was not geographically universal. I merely adhere to the testimony of tradition, and from this point of view it would suffice (vide Reusch) that it was universal so far as the horizon of the survivors extended.

[188] Mr Grote certainly says—"Apollodorus connects this deluge with the wickedness of the brazen race in Hesiod, according to the practice general with the logographers of stringing together a sequence out of legends totally unconnected with each other." One would have thought in one's simplicity that if any two legends linked well together, uniting in common agreement with the scriptural account, it would be the legends of the Deluge and the brazen age.

[189] Let the significance of the following coincidence be considered in connection with the evidence at p. 244, Boulanger, "Ces fêtes (Atheniasmes, 'Anthisteries') avoient pour objet une commémoration (of the Deluge) et l'on en attribuoit la fondation à Deucalion; elles étoient aussi consacrées à Bacchus, ce qui les a fait nommés les anciennes ou les grandes Bacchanales."— Comp. ch. xi. p. 244, also supra, 213.

[190] It is the fashion to deride Bryant's etymology, and no doubt he did not write in the light of modern science; but I find ("Mythology," iii. 534) that he had already given this information. "Main, from whence mœnia, signified in the primitive language a stone, or stones, and also a building."

[191] Mr Max Müller, in his "Lectures on the Science of Language," first series, says of "Man":—"The Latin word 'homo,' the French 'l'homme' ... is derived from the same root, which we have in 'humus,' soil, 'humilis,' humble. Homo, therefore, would express the idea of being made of the dust of the earth.... There is a third name for man.... 'Ma,' in the Sanscrit, means to measure.... 'Man,' a derivative root, means to think. From this we have the Sanscrit 'Manu,' originally thinker, then man.

In the later Sanscrit we find derivations such as 'Mânava, Mânasha, Manushya,' all expressing man. In Gothic we find both 'man,' and 'Maunisk,' the modern German 'maun,' and 'mensch.' There were many more names for man, as there were many names for all things in ancient language." As an instance of the correspondence of Old Egyptian and Welsh, Bunsen's "Philosophy of Univ. Hist.," i. 169, gives "Egyptian, 'man' = rockstone; Welsh, 'maen;' Irish, 'main' (coll. Latin, 'mœnia;' Hebrew, 'e-ben')." And (p. 78) Bunsen says—"The divine Mannus, the ancestor of the Germans, is absolutely identical with Manus, who, according to ancient Indian mythology, is the God who created man anew after the Deluge, just as Deucalion did."

[192] The Saturday Review, Nov. 14, 1868 (reviewing "The Indian Tribes of Guiana," by the Rev. W. Brett), says of the Indian traditions:—"The 'old people's stories' of the creation and the deluge are highly characteristic.... Under the rule of Sigu, son of Maikonaima, the tree of life was planted, in whose stem were pent up the whole of the waters which were to be let forth by measure to stock every river and lake with fish. Twarrika, the mischievous monkey, forced open the magic cover which kept down the waters, and the next minute was swept away with all things living by the bursting flood. The re-peopling of the world, as described by the Tamanacs of the Orinoco recalls the legend of Deucalion. One man and one woman took refuge on the mountain Tamanacu. They then threw over their heads the fruits of the Mauritia (or Ita) palm, from the kernel of which sprang men and women who once more peopled the earth."

[193] "Essay on Primæval History."

[194] "According to the calculations of Varro, the deluge of Ogyges occurred 400 years before Inachus, i.e. 1600 years before the first Olympiad, which would bring it to 2376 years before the Christian era; now, according to the Hebrew text, the Deluge of Noah took place 2349 B.C., which makes only a difference of 27 years. It is true that many other authors have reconciled these epochs." Hesiod and Homer are silent on the subject of both Deucalion and Ogyges.... "It results from these considerations that the traditions of the ancient nations of the world confirm the narrative of Genesis, not only as to the existence, but even as to the epoch, of this catastrophe as fixed by Moses. Mersius (apud Gronovium, iv. 1023) cites more than twenty ancient authors

who speak of Ogyges as appertaining in their eyes to what was most primitive in Greece. He is son of Neptune. He is the first founder of the kingdom of Thebes. Servius represents him as coming immediately after Saturn and the golden age [which directly connects Noah with Saturn, and the golden age with Noah] . Hesychius says of Ogyges that he represented all that was most ancient in Greece. That, indeed, passed into a proverb; they said, 'old as Ogyges,' as if they said, 'old as Adam'" (Gainet, i. 229).

[195] In the same way we find "Mentuhotep," or "Sesortasen I." named, "when all other ancestors are omitted, as the sole connecting link between Amosis (xviii. dynasty) and Menes." Vide Palmer's "Egyptian Chronicles," i. 385.

So, too, are Fohi (whom I believe to be Adam) and Shin-nong (Noah) connected and linked together in Chinese chronology. "I. Fohi the great Brilliant (Tai-hao), cultivation of astronomy and religion as well as writing. He reigned 110 years. Then came fifteen reigns. II. Shin-nong (divine husbandman). Institution of agriculture [compare ante, ch. x.] The knowledge of simples applied as the art of medicine."—Bunsen's "Egypt," iii. 383, chap. on Chinese Chronology. Vide ante, 61; chap. on Tradition, p. 129; Prometheus.

[196] Kenrick says:—"The fact of traces of the action of water at a higher level in ancient times on these shores is unquestionable; under the name of raised beaches such phenomena are familiar to geologists on many coasts; but that the tradition (in Samothrace) was produced by speculation on its cause, not by an obscure recollection of its occurrence, is also clear; for it has been shown by physical proofs that a discharge of the waters of the Euxine (Black Sea) would not cause such a deluge as the tradition supposed" (Cuvier, Disc. sur les Revolutions du Globe, ed. 1826).

If these speculations were made at the commencement of Grecian history, and the speculations had reference to evidence of diluvian disruption along the highway by which they passed into Greece, should we not expect that theories of the violent rather than the gentler and gradual action of water would dominate in their geological tradition? Colonel George Greenwood, in "Rain and Rivers," p. 2, says on the contrary—("with reference to the theory that valleys are formed by 'rain and rivers'")—"There is, perhaps, no creed of man which, like this, can be traced up to the most remote antiquity, and traced down from the most remote antiquity to the present day. Lyell has himself quoted Pythagoras for it, through the medium of Ovid:—

'Eluvie mons est deductus in æquor

Quodquo fuit campus *vallem decursus aquarum*

Fecit.'

But Pythagoras only enunciates the doctrine of Eastern antiquity; that is, of the Egyptians, the Chaldæans, and the Hindoos. But since Pythagoras introduced this doctrine in the West, if it has ever slumbered, it has perpetually *re*-originated. Lyell shows that among the Greeks it was taught by Aristotle; among the Romans by Strabo; among the Saracens by Avicenna; in Italy by Moro, Geneselli, and Targioni; and in England by Ray, Hutton, and Playfair."—*Rain and Rivers*, by Col. George Greenwood. Longmans, 1866. 2d edit.

[197] Gen. vi. 18; viii. 15; vi. 13; ix. 8; viii. 20; ix. 20; and Ecclesiasticus xliv. 1, 3, 4, 19, "The covenants of the world were made with Him."

[198] I feel justified in bringing in attestation also the following verses of the "Oracula Sybillina," for, as I have already said, even if they be forgeries of the second century A.D., they at any rate represent the tradition at that date (i. v. 270):—

"Noë fidelis amans æqui servata periclis

Egredere audenter, simul et cum conjuge nati

Tresque nurus: et vos terræ loca vasta replete,

Crescite multiplice numero, *sacrataque jura*

Tradite natorum natis....

Hinc nova progenies hinc *ætas aurea* prima

Exorta est hominum....

... ast illo se tempore regia primum

Imperia ostendent terris quum *fœdere facto*

Tres justi reges, divisis partibus æquis,

Sceptra diu populis imponent *sanctaque tradent*

Jura viris."...

Compare also the following verses (Orac. Sybil, i. 145) with the Vedic tradition (infra, p. 238) of the promise made to Satiavrata, and the Babylonian tradition respecting Hoa (infra):

"... Collige, Noë, tuas vires ...

... Si scieris me

Divinæ te nulla rei secreta latebunt."

[199] I only instance this as evidence that laws of some sort were attributed to Bacchus, whom the traditions also speak of as King of Asia: to judge of these laws by what we know of the Subazian mysteries, would be as if we were to form our opinion of the Mandan ceremonies (vide infra, ch. xi.) by the last day's orgies only. In this matter we may say with Cicero, De Legibus, ii. 17—"Omnia tum perditorum civium scelere ... religionum jura polluta sunt."

[200] Layard ("Nineveh and Babylon," p. 343) says, "We can scarcely hesitate to identify this mythic form (at Kosyundik) with the Oannes or sacred man-fish, who, according to the traditions preserved by Berosus, issued from the Erethræan sea, instructed the Chaldæans in all wisdom, in the sciences and the fine arts, and was afterwards worshipped as a god in the temples of Babylonia.... Five such monsters rose from the Persian Gulf at fabulous intervals of time (Cory's "Fragments," p. 30). It has been conjectured that this myth denotes the conquest of Chaldæa at some remote and pre-historic period by a comparatively civilised nation coming in ships to the mouth of the Euphrates.... The Dagon of the Philistines and of the inhabitants of the Phœnician coast was worshipped, according to the united opinion of the Hebrew commentators on the Bible, under the same form." The five apparitions at long intervals may have been the confusion of the previous revelations to the patriarchs with those made to Noah—or they may be reduplications (vide supra, p. 157).

[201] Dionysius Periegesis says the women of the British Amnitæ celebrated the rites of Dionysos:—

"As the Bistonians on Apsinthus banks

Shout to the clamorous Eiraphiates;

Or as the Indians on dark-rolling Ganges

Hold revels to Dionysos the noisy,

So do the British women shout Evoë." (v. 375.) (Qy. Enoë.)

Vide "The Bhilsa Topes," by Major A. Cunningham, p. 6.

[202] I would specially draw attention to the instances of temples constructed upon the model of ships, concerning which vide Bryant's "Mythology," ii. 221, 226, 227, 240; and compare with Plate XVIII. in Montfauçon, ii.

[203] Compare Bryant.

[204] "O-kee-pa, a Religious Ceremony, and other Customs of the Mandans," Trübner & Co. London, 1867. Mr Catlin's statements are attested by the certificates of three educated and intelligent men who witnessed the ceremonies with him, and is further corroborated by a letter addressed to Mr Catlin by Prince Maximilian of Neuwied, the celebrated traveller among the North American Indians, who had previously referred to them (he spent a winter among the Mandans).

[205] I read in the Times, March 6, 1871, that "The American papers state that workmen in Iowa, excavating for the projected Dubuque and Minnesota railroad, in the limestone at the foot of a bluff, discovered recently some caves and rock chambers, and, on raising a foot slab, a vault filled with human skeletons of unusual size, the largest being seven feet eight inches high. A figured sun on the walls is taken as indicating that the skeletons belonged to a people who worshipped that luminary [compare supra, p. 152]   and the representation of a man with a dove stepping out of a boat, as an allusion to a tradition of the Deluge. The fingers of the largest skeleton clasped a pearl ornament, and traces of cloth were found crumbled at the feet of the remains. Many copper implements were found, and it is thought that the Lake Superior mines may have been worked at an early period. The remains were to be removed to the Iowa Institute of Arts and Sciences at Dubuque."

[206] Compare account of Mandan tradition of the Creation, from "Hist. des Ceremonies Religieuses," supra, p. 191.

[207] Supra, These tortures have their exact counterpart in India, e.g. the ceremony of the Pota (compare Sanscrit, "pota" = boat), thus described by Hunter ("Rural Bengal," 1868, p. 463):— "Pota (hook-swinging), now stopped by Government, but still practised (1865) among the Northern Santals [who have the distinct tradition of the Deluge and dispersion referred to, supra]   in April or May. Lasted about one month. Young

men used to swing with hooks through their back [as seen in Catlin's illustrations], as in the Charak Puja of the Hindus. The swingers used to fast the day preceding and the day following the operation, and to sleep the intermediate night on thorns."

"On pleuroit et l'on s'attristoit dans les fêtes *les plus gayes et plus dissolues*; les cultes d'Isis et d'Osiris, ainsi que ceux *de Bacchus, de Céres*, d'Adonis, d'Atys, &c., étoient *accompagnés de macérations et de larmes*." —*Boulanger*, iii. 355.

[208] Bryant ("Myth." ii. 432) says, "There were many arkite" (i.e. commemorative of ark) "ceremonies in different parts of the world, which were generally styled Taurica sacra" (from taurus = bull). These mysteries were of old attended with acts of great cruelty. Of these "I have given instances, taken from different parts of the world; from Egypt, Syria, Cyprus, Crete, and Sicily."

[209] Let the following points of resemblance be noted also in the "Panathenæa." The lesser, and it is supposed the annual festival, was celebrated on the 20th of Thargelion, corresponding to the 5th May (compare Catlin). Every citizen contributed olive branches and an ox (vide Catlin) at the greater festival. "In the ceremonies without the city there was an engine built in the form of a ship, on purpose for this solemnity;" upon this the sacred garment of Minerva "was hung in the manner of a sail," "the whole conveyed to the temple of Ceres Elusinia." "This procession was led by old men, together, as some say, with old women carrying olive branches in their hands." "After them came the men of full age with shields and spears, being attended by the Μετοίκοι or sojourners, who carried little boats as a token of their being foreigners, and were called on that account boat-bearers; then followed the women attended by the sojourner's wives, who were named υδριαφοροι, from bearing water pots." —Compare Burton, Catlin. Then followed select virgins, covered with millet, "called basket-bearers," the baskets containing necessaries for the celebration. "These virgins were attended by the sojourner's daughters, who carried umbrellas (vide Pongol Festival, appendix), little seats, whence they were called seat-carriers." —Compare Burton (vide Potter's "Antiquities," i. 419.)

Compare also the following in the "Dionysia" or festivals in honour of Bacchus (ante, p. 215) with Catlin. "They carried thyrsi, drums, pipes, flutes, and rattles, and crowned themselves with garlands of trees sacred to Bacchus, ivy, vine, &c. Some imitated Silenus, Pan, and the Satyrs, exposing themselves in comical dresses and antic motions;" and in this manner ran about the hills "invoking Bacchus." "At Athens this frantic rout was followed by persons carrying certain sacred vessels, the first of which was filled with water."

Bryant ("Mythology," ii. 219) speaking of Egypt ("the priests of Ammon who at particular seasons used to carry in procession a boat," concerning which refer to page 254), says—"Part of the ceremony in most of the ancient mysteries consisted in carrying about a kind of ship or boat, which custom upon due examination will be found to relate to nothing else but Noah and the Deluge." He adds that the name of "the navicular shrines was Baris, which is very remarkable; for it is the very name of the mountain, according to Nicolaus Damascenus, on which the ark of Noah rested, the same as Ararat in Armenia." Herodotus speaks of "Baris" as the Egyptian name of a ship, l. 2, 96; Eurip. "Iphig. in Aulis," v. 297; Æschylus, Persæ, 151; Lycophron, v. 747, refer to names of ships in connection with Noah. Sup., p. 196. Query—is our word barge a corruption of baris? or perhaps of baris in connection with "argus," also a term for the ark. (With reference to this etymology vide my remark, p. 116, and d'Anselme, p. 196, and Bryant, ii. 251.)

[210] Compare the "Bhain-sasur" or buffalo-demon at Usayagiri, carrying a trident. Vide "The Bhilsa Tope," Major Alex. Cunningham, 1854.

[211] It is as well to note, however, that the Dahomans have recently altered their customs. The one Captain Burton witnessed (ii. 34) was a "mixed custom," and elsewhere allusion is made to "the new" ceremony.

[212] Analogies may perhaps be discovered in the representations of the procession escorting a relic casket on the architraves of the western gate at Sanchi. (Vide "The Bhilsa Tope," by Major Alex. Cunningham, p. 227.)

"Street of a city on the left, houses on each side filled with spectators,... a few horsemen heading a procession, ... immediately outside the gate are four persons bearing either trophies or some peculiar instruments of office. Then follows a *led horse*, ... a soldier with a bell-shaped shield, two fifers, three *drummers*, and two men blowing *conches*. Next comes the king on an elephant, carrying the holy relic casket on his head and supporting it with his right hand. Then follows two peculiarly dressed men on horseback, perhaps prisoners. They wear a kind of cap (now only known in Barmawar, on the upper course of the Ravi) and boots or leggings. The procession is closed by two horsemen (one either the minister or a member of the royal family) and by an elephant with two riders."

It may have had connection with the *Aswarnedha* or horse sacrifice (Cunningham, p. 363.) Boulanger (i. 109) says, "That after the winter solstice the ancient inhabitants of India descended with their king to the banks of the Indus; they there sacrificed *horses* and *black bulls*, signs of a funeral ceremony; they then threw a bushel measure into the water without their assigning any reason for it." Compare the throwing the cakes into the gulf at Athens, and the hatchets into the water at the Mandan custom. Could it be that at the Dahoman ceremony the horses were redeemed because the wretched victims were substituted, carrying out the idea of vicarious sacrifice and expiation?

Sir John Lubbock ("Origin of Civilization," p. 199) says, speaking of water worship, "The kelpie or spirit of the waters assumed various forms, those of a man, woman, horse, or bull being the most common." Compare supra, pp. 196, 202, 204, Manou, Bacchus.

Homer (Hom. Il., Heynii, xxi. 130, Lord Derby, 145), says—

"Shall aught avail ye, though to him (the river Scamander)

In sacrifice, the blood of countless *bulls* you pay,

And living *horses* in his waters-sink;"

and (210) Asteropœus is called "river-born," because the son of Pelegon, who "to broadly flowing Axius owed his birth." Remembering the belief of certain tribes of Indians (supra, p. 137) that they were "created under the water," which I have construed to mean, that they were created on the other side of the Deluge, so we may take in a similar sense the traditions of these Homeric heroes that they were "river-born;" and does the expression, son of Pelegon (compare "son of Prometheus," supra, p. 232), imply more than that he was the descendant of Phaleg, or, if not in the line of descent, the descendant of progenitors who had retained the tradition that Phaleg was so

called, "because in his days the earth was divided"?—Gen. ch.
x. 25. Compare ancient Welsh ballad (Davies' "Mythology of
British Druids," p. 100)—

"Truly I was in the ship

With Dylan (Deucalion), son of the sea....

When ... the floods came forth

From heaven to the great deep."

[213] The name for river in the Chitral or Little Kashghar vocabulary
(Vigne, "Travels in Kashmir") is river = sin; also in the Dangon,
on the Indus, voc. (id.) river = sin; in the Affghan (Kalproth) the
sea = sind. Sindhu is the Sanscrit name for river (Max Müller,
"Science of Lang.," 1st series, 215); and has also its equivalent
in ancient Persian. In Danish, river or lake = so; in Icelandic, sjor
(sjo); in Bultistan, touh; German, see; English, sea; in Kashmir,
sar = marse; Icelandic, saus. Compare Rivers Saar, Soane, Seine,
Irish Suir; perhaps also Esk and Usk (Vigne, "Trav. in Kashmir").
Horse = shtah, in Bultistan. Has not so analogy with eau, augr
(Chittral), water? Sara = water in Sanscrit (Max Müller, "Chips,"
ii. 47); Sanscrit, vari, more generic term for water; Latin,
mare; Gothic, marie; Slavonic, more; Irish and Scotch, muir
(id.) Compare Chinese "ma" = horse; Mongol, "mon" = horse;
German, machre; English, mare. Conclusion, either there is the
same word for horse and water in certain languages, which may
have occurred in the way of secondary derivation from these
"mysteries," or if so means water, then "So-sin" may only be
a reduplication, as in the names of some of our rivers—e.g.
Dwfr-Dwy = water, of Deva = Dee-river (Archæol. Journal, xvii.
98). Bryant ("Myth." ii. 408) says "The ίππος, hippus (horse),
alluded to in the early mythology was certainly a float or ship,
the same as the ceto." There is, moreover, the analogy in the
Latin of aqua and equus. Another Sanscrit word for water, "ap"
(Max Müller, Sc. of L., 103) has analogy with the Greek ίππος =
horse. It appears (Sc. of L., 2nd series, p. 36), that the Tahitians
have substituted the word "pape" for "vai" = water; but both
words "pape," to ap, "vai," to vari, seem to have analogies to
Sanscrit as above. Plato ("Cratylus," c. 36, Sc. of L., 1st series, p.
116) mentions that the name for water was the same in Phrygian
and Greek. At p. 235, 1st series, Mr Max Müller says that Persian
Harôya is the same as Sanscrit Saroya; which latter "is derived
from a root 'sar' or 'sri,' to go, to run; from which 'saras,' water,

'sarit,' river, and 'Sarayu,' the proper name of the river near Oude."

Here at any rate in the Sanskrit "sar," to run, we may, if the above conjecture is rejected, start the words "horse" and "water" from a common root.

[214] Compare (Klaproth, "Mem. Asiat." ii. 12)—Eng. ox; Mongol, char; Hebrew, chor; French, charrue (plough.) Klaproth, ii. 405, "Les cheveux en Thou Khin (whom he identifies with the Turks) portaient le nom de Sogo ou soko; cest le même nom que le Turc sâtch ou sadg." Can it have affinity with Chinese sa (Chinese szu = bœuf sauvage); German, säen; Swedish, sá; French, semer; English = to sou; Peruvian, sara = maize; also French, coudre, to sow with English corn; Sanscrit, go; High German, chus; Sclavonic, gows (Max Müller, "Chips," ii. 27); and Kashmir and Dongan, gau; Icelandic, ku? In Affghan a bull = sakhendar and soukhandar. In the extinct Tartar Coman (vide Klaproth) ox = ogus or seger = Turkish, okus; Sanscrit, oukcha; German, ochse. Plough = Sanscrit, sinam; Irish, serak; Persian, siar. Horse = asp, Persian; ess, Sclavonic = English ass; and in Chittral on Indus (vide horse or bull used in ceremonies on banks of Indus, infra) horse = astor. (Has not tor here affinity with taureau.) Corn = Aslek (Kirghish) and Ashlyk (?) Turkish. Max Müller (Science of Language, p. 231), says—"Aspa was the Persian name for horse, and in the Scythian names, Aspabota, Aspakara, and Asparatha, we can hardly fail to recognise the same element." Also, p. 242, "The comparison of ploughing and sowing is of frequent occurrence in ancient language." Eng., plough; Sclav., ploug = Sanscrit, plava, ship = Gk. πλοιον, ship. "In English dialects, plough is used as a waggon or conveyance. In the Vale of Blackmore, a waggon is called a plough, or plow, and Zull (A.-S., syl) is used for aratrum."—Barnes, "Dorset Dialect," p. 369, ap. Max Müller.

[215] Compare the procession in the Panathenæa and Dionysia, supra.

[216] "Eight men representing eight buffalo bulls," in Mandan celebration, "took their positions on the four sides of the ark or 'big canoe.'"—Catlin, p. 17. "The chief actors in these strange scenes were eight men with skins of buffaloes," &c. p. 16. Four images were suspended on poles above the mystery lodge.

[217] In the Japanese (vide p. 269) version of the legend of the bull breaking the mundane egg (vide p. 396), a gourd or pumpkin is also broken which contained the first man. — Vide Bryant's "Mythology," iii. 579. "I have mentioned that the ark was looked upon as the mother of mankind, and styled Da-Mater, and it was on this account figured under the semblance of a pomegranate," "as it abounds with seed" — Bryant, ii. 380. Vide also plate (Bryant, ii. 410), where Juno (vide, p. 395) holds a dove in one hand and a pomegranate in the other.

[218] Compare alsosup, with Saturn. "Ipsius autem canities," &c., and "cum falce messis insigne."

[219] Compare again these two figures, one figuring in the Dahoman procession, the other in the Mandan bull dance.

[220] I allude to the opening of the ceremony by the centenarian white man, "the first and only man." Mr Catlin is of opinion that this incident was introduced and superadded by some missionaries, though he adds it would be still more strange if the (Jesuit) missionaries had instructed them "in the other modes." This, however, is understating the case. It is conceivable that missionaries should have come among them, but in this case we should have expected some trace of Christian practices and dogmas; it is difficult to conjecture what set of missionaries could have indoctrinated them with the recondite pagan mysteries of Eleusis and Hierapolis.

[221] Vide also Giebel, "Tagesfragen," p. 91; apud Reusch, p. 500.

[222] Vide "Cook's Voyages," i. 199; Prescott, ii. 476.

[223] "There have been recent instances of Japanese vessels having been thrown by shipwreck upon the coasts of the Sandwich Islands, and even on the mouth of the Columbia." — Reusch, "La Bible et la Nature,"

"Since the north-west coast of America and the north-east of Asia have been explored, little difficulty remains on this subject.... Small boats can safely pass the narrow strait. Ten degrees farther south, the *Aleutian* and Fox islands form a continuous chain between Kamschatka and the peninsula of Alaska in such a manner as to leave the passage across a matter of no difficulty." — Warburton's "Conquest of Canada," i. 194.

Ellis ("Polynesian Researches," ii. 46) says: "There are also *many* points of *resemblance* in language, manners, and customs between the South Sea Islanders and the inhabitants of Madagascar in the west; the inhabitants of the *Aleutian* and *Kurile* islands in the north, which stretch along the mouth of Behring's Straits, and forms the chain which connects the old and new worlds," &c.

[224] "The Sandwich Islands, with a population of 500,000, are more than two thousand miles from the coast of South America. How did the population of those islands get there? Certainly not in canoes over ocean waves of two thousand miles. But I am told 'the Sandwich islanders are Polynesians;' not a bit of it; they are two thousand miles north of the Polynesian group, with the same impossibility of canoe navigation, and are as different in physiological traits of character and language from the Polynesian, as they are different from the American races. — "Last Rambles" (Catlin), p. 317. 1868.

Captain King, "Transactions on returning to Sandwich Islands," &c., continuation of Cook's voyages, Pinkerton (xi. 730) says on the contrary: "The inhabitants of the Sandwich Islands are undoubtedly of the same race with those of New Zealand, the Society and Friendly Islands, Easter Islands, and the Marquesas. This fact, which, extraordinary as it is, might be thought sufficiently proved by the *striking* similarity of their *manners* and *customs,* and the general resemblance of their *persons* is established beyond all controversy by the *absolute identity* of their language."

Shortland says that the New Zealanders, "when speaking of any old practice, regarding the origin of which you may inquire, have the expression constantly in their mouths, 'E hara i te mea poka hou mai; no Hawaika mai ano.'—It is not a modern invention; but a practice brought from Hawaiki, Sandwich Islands)." — Shortland's "Traditions of the New Zealanders,"

[225] As far as I can ascertain, the pheasant is not a native of America. Yarrell speaks of it as Asiatic, and that it has been domesticated "in all parts of the old continent." So also Gould. Of the American writers, neither Wilson, Audubon, Bonaparte, Nuttall, Richardson, or Jameson include the pheasant. Mr Catlin, however, says, "From the translation of their name, already mentioned (Nu-mah-ká-kee, pheasants), an important inference may be drawn in support of the probability of their having formerly lived much farther to the south, as that bird does not

exist on the prairies of the Upper Missouri, and is not to be met with short of the hoary forests of Ohio and Indiana, eighteen hundred miles south of the last residence of the Mandans. In their familiar name of Mandan, which is not an Indian word, there are equally singular and important features. In the first place, that they knew nothing of the name or how they got it; and next, that the word Mandan in the Welsh language [Mr C.'s theory is that they are the survivors of Prince Madoc's expedition from Wales in the fourteenth century]   means red dye, of which further mention will be made." On the legend of the Welsh expedition, vide Warburton's "Conquest of Canada," ii., Appendix iv.

[226]   "The Indians resemble the people of north-eastern Asia in form and feature more than any other of the human race; their population is most dense along the districts nearest to Asia; and among the Mexicans, whose records of the past deserve credence, there is a constant tradition that their Aztec and Toltec chiefs came from the north-west." — Warburton's "Conquest of Canada," i. 195.

Brace ("Manual of Ethnology," p. 115) says, after noting that whereas the prominence in the head "is anterior in the Chinese rather than lateral, as in the American Indians and the Tangusic tribes," adds, "The peculiar distinguishing characteristics are the smallness of the eyes and the obliquity of the eyelids. The nose is usually small and depressed, though sometimes, in favourable physical conditions, natives are found with a slightly aquiline nose, *giving the face a close resemblance to that of the American Indians or New Zealanders."*

Refer to argument with reference to the Mozca Indians.

[227]   Compare what Ogilby says: "Near Firando (Japan) at an inlet of the sea stands an idol, being nothing but a chest of wood, about three feet high, standing like an altar [the big canoe was placed on end among the Mandans, whither women, when they suppose they have conceived, go in pilgrimage, offering on their knees rice or other presents." at Jado, it is said, "somewhat farther stands a temple dedicated to all sorts of animals with a very high double roof." (Query, Noah's ark?)

In the Illustrated London News, January 13, 1872, its correspondent from Yokohama gives a short account of the Japanese religious festivals, in which among other coincidences I note the following: "The most absurd," he says, "is one in which the foul fiend is simultaneously expelled from every house by dint of pelting him with boiled peas. The devil is chased out of the town with a dance of derision, by young fellows in grotesque costumes, for the public mirth." Compare with the scene in the Mandan ceremonies, described by Catlin, vide supra,

[228] Compare in "Flint Chips," (E. T. Stevens). "The Omahas possess a sacred shell, which is regarded as an object of great sanctity by the whole nation. It has been transmitted from generation to generation, and its origin is unknown. A skin lodge is appropriated to it, and in this lodge a man, appointed as a guard to the shell, constantly resides. It is placed upon a stand, and is never suffered to touch the earth. It is concealed from sight by a number of mats made of strips of skin plaited. The whole forms a large package, from which tobacco" (comp. Stevens' "Flint Chips," p. 315, and Catlin, supra) "and the roots of trees" (comp. supra, p. 155), "and other objects are suspended," &c. &c.

[229] Vide Japanese tradition of the Deluge (Bertrand, "Dict. des Relig.," Gainet, i. 208; also id.), it is said that the Japanese commemorate this event in their third annual festival, which takes place on the fifth day of the fifth month. Compare with Mandan's, supra.

[230] Captain Cook, speaking of their dances, says, "Between the dances of the women the men performed a kind of dramatic interlude, in which there was dialogue as well as dancing; but we were not sufficiently acquainted with their language to understand the subject. Some gentlemen saw a much more regular entertainment of the dramatic kind, which was divided into four acts."

Vide Abbe Gainet, "La Bible sans la Bible," i. 213, quotes l'Abbe Domenech, who speaks of "the dance of the Deluge among many nations of the north and west of America." Gainet also says that there were two distinct traditions of the Deluge in the east and west groups of the Society Islands (Otaheite).

L'Abbe Gainet (i. 211) gives an account of the *Mandans* from "Ceremoníes Religieuses," i. 7, which it will be interesting to compare with Catlin, as it was written a century previous to his visit. "The Mandans pretend that the Deluge was formerly raised up against them by the white men to destroy their ancestors.... Then the *first man*, whom they regard as one of their divinities, inspired mankind with the idea of constructing upon an eminence a *town* and fortress in wood, and promised them that the water should not pass that point. They followed his advice and constructed the ark on the banks of the Heart river. It was of a very large size, so that a part of their nation found safety there whilst the rest perished. In memory of this memorable event they place in each of their villages a small model of this *edifice* [which may account for the erect position of 'the big canoe'] , this model still exists. The waters abated after that, and to this day they celebrate, in memory of this ark, the fête of the '*Okippe*,' which lasts *four days*."

[231] Longmans, 1868, i. 290.

[232] Cardinal Wiseman in his letters to John Poynder, Esq. ("Essays on Various Subjects," i. 257), says, "Dr Spencer, a learned divine of the Established Church, published two folio volumes replete with extraordinary erudition, entitled 'De Legibus Hebræorum ritualibus et eorum ratione,' which has gone through many editions both here and on the Continent. Now, the entire drift and purport of this work is manifestly twofold—first, to prove that the great design of God, in giving rites and ceremonies to the Jews, was to prevent their falling into idolatry; secondly, to demonstrate that almost every practice, rite, ceremony, and act so given was directly borrowed from the Egyptian heathens; ... that whether we speak of the more solemn and especial injunctions, or of the minutest details of the ceremonial law, of circumcision and of sacrifice in all its varieties, and with all its distinctive ceremonies of purification and lustrations and new moons; of the ark of the covenant and the cherubim; of the temple and its oracles; of the Urim and Thummim, and the emissary goat; of them all Spencer has endeavoured to prove, and that to the satisfaction of many learned men, that they pre-existed among the Egyptians and other neighbouring nations."

I have not met with Dr Spencer's work. I may mention, however, the pomegranates in the Levitical robe as an instance. Vide references in this chapter and appendix.

[233] Much doubt has been expressed as to the veracity of M. Guinnard's narrative, but the scenes and customs referred to are not likely to have been invented; and on the supposition of a fictitious narrative (although I see nothing incredible) they will probably have been imported from true narratives of other tribes. In either case they supply additional evidence.

[234] I need not remind my reader that these speculations of De Maistre anticipated by many years the analogous, though at the same time independent, conclusions of Archbishop Whately, in his lecture "On the Origin of Civilisation," published in 1854.

[235] "We ought then to recognise that the state of civilisation and of science is, in a certain sense, the natural and primitive state of man. Thus, all oriental traditions commenced with a state of perfection and light, and, I repeat it, of supernatural light; and Greece—lying Greece, which 'has dared everything in history'—renders homage to this truth, in placing its Golden Age at the beginning of things. It is no less remarkable that it does not attribute to the following ages, even to the iron age, the state of savagery, so that all that it has told us of those primitive men living on acorns, &c., puts it in contradiction with itself, and can only have reference to particular cases, i.e. to some races degraded, and then reclaimed to a state of nature, which is a state of civilisation."—De Maistre's "Soirées de St Petersbourg" i. Deux: Entretien, p. 98.

[236] I consider that this remark has been fully substantiated in Marshall's "Christian Missions."

[237] Compare with Gainet, i. 92, 93.

[238] "Now it is clear that the train of thought which leads from purification to penance, or from purification to punishment, reveals a moral and even a religious sentiment in the conception and naming of pœna, and it shows us that in the very infancy of criminal justice punishment was looked upon (Mr Max Müller is speaking with reference to what I may call briefly the Sanscrit epoch) not simply a retribution or revenge, but as a correction, as a removal of guilt. We do not feel the presence of these early thoughts when we speak of corporal punishment or castigation; yet castigation too was originally chastening, from 'castus,' pure; and 'incestum' was impurity or sin, which, according to Roman law, the priests had to make good, or to punish by a 'supplicium,' or supplication or prostration before the gods."

[239] Compare with Max Müller, "Chips," ii. 256.

[240] Vide chapter on Savage Life in "Pre-historic Times."

[241] It may perhaps be doubtful to what extent Sir J. Lubbock maintains his theory of a Stone Age; although Sir John formally excludes China and Japan from the argument, he nevertheless appears to me to assume the existence of universal transitional periods through which the human race necessarily passed. "It would appear that pre-historic archæology may be divided into four great epochs. Firstly, that of the Drift: when man shared the possession of Europe with the mammoth, &c. This we may call the 'palæolithic period.' Secondly, the later or polished Stone Age; a period, &c. Thirdly, the Bronze Age, &c. Fourthly, the Iron Age." Sir John adds, certainly—"In order to prevent misapprehension, it may be well to state at once, that for the present I only apply this classification to Europe, though in all probability it might be extended also to the neighbouring parts of Asia and Africa. As regards other civilised countries, China and Japan for instance, we as yet know nothing of their pre-historic archæology. [I should rather say, as we as yet have no reason to suppose that they have ever lost the knowledge of metals.] It is evident also that some nations, such as the Fuegians, Andamaners, &c., are even now only in an age of stone. But even in this limited sense, the above classification has not met with general acceptance; there are still some archæologists who believe that the arms and implements—stone, bronze, and iron—were used contemporaneously."—Pre-historic Times, pp. 2, 3. I think that the concluding sentence makes it quite clear that Sir John assumes the existence of universal progressive periods as above. In any case it may be proved in this way. Sir John argues upon the hypothesis of the unity of the human race; and I also think that he will not refuse the unbroken testimony to the fact of the civilisation of Europe from Asia. Either, then, the first colonisation took place when Asia was in the state of the "Drift," or in the "later polished Stone Age," or else the migration left Asia with the knowledge of bronze or iron. On the latter supposition the argument I contend for is conceded, and original civilisation and subsequent degeneracy is established. To escape this alternative the universality of a Stone Age in Asia as well as in Europe, must be proved or assumed. This assumption I maintain is essential to Sir John's argument.

[242] Wilson ("Archæologia of Scotland," 360) says, "But after all it is to Asia we are forced to return for the true source of nearly all our primitive arts, nor will the canons of archæology be established on a safe foundation till the antiquities of that older continent have been explored and classified." Not only bronze but iron has been found in the East in use at an early period (vide Layard, "Nineveh and Babylon," 178–9, 194). At Nimroud, Dr Percy (id. 670) says the iron was used to economise the bronze; if so it must have been cheaper, and therefore probably more abundant; and he is of opinion that "iron was more extensively used by the ancients than seems to be generally admitted." Philology seems also to establish an early common knowledge, and subsequent tradition of the use of metals. Mr Max Müller (ii. 45) says, "That the value and usefulness of some of the metals was known before the separation of the Aryan race can be proved only by a few words; for the names of most of the metals differ in different countries. Yet there can be no doubt that iron was known, and its value appreciated, whether for defence or attack. Whatever its old Aryan name may have been, it is clear that Sanscrit 'ayas,' Latin 'ahes,' in 'ahencus' and even the contracted form 'æs, æris'; the Gothic 'ais,' the old German 'er,' and the English iron, are names cast in the same mould, and only slightly corroded even now by the rust of so many centuries." The Swedish Gothic race had no tradition but of weapons of iron. (Professor Nillson's "Stone Age," p. 192.) I find in Captain Cook's Voyages that in Otaheite their word for iron is "eure-eure." Germans (apud Tacitus) called their iron lances "framea," which has great resemblance to ferrum. (Vide Wilson, 195.) The following passage from Wilson's "Archæologia" seems to prove this common terminology still more extensively — "The Saxon 'gold' differs not more essentially from the Greek 'χρυσος' than from the Latin 'aurum'; iron from 'σιδερος' or 'ferrum'; but when we come to examine the Celtic names of the metals it is otherwise. The Celtic terms are: Gold: Gael, 'or,' golden, 'orail'; Welsh, 'aur'; Latin, ' aurum.' Silver: Gael, 'airgiod,' made of silver, 'airgiodach'; Welsh, 'ariant'; Latin, 'argentum' — derived in the Celtic from 'arg,' white, or milk, like the Greek 'ἀργος,' whence they also formed their 'ἀργυρος.' Now, is it improbable that the Latin 'ferrum' and the English 'iron' spring indirectly from the same Celtic root? Gael, 'iarunn'; Welsh, 'haiarn'; Saxon, iron; Danish, 'iern'; Spanish, 'hierro,' which last furnishes no remote approximation to 'ferrum.' Nor with the older metals

is it greatly different, as bronze, Gael, 'umha' or 'prais'; Welsh, 'pres,' whence our English 'brass,' a name bearing no very indistinct resemblance to the Roman 'æs.' Lead in like manner has its peculiar Gaelic name 'luaidha,' like the Saxon 'læd' (lead), while the Welsh 'plwm' closely approximates to the Latin 'plumbum.' It may undoubtedly be argued that the Latin is the root instead of the offshoot of these Celtic names, but the entire archæological proofs are opposed to this idea," p. 350.

Sir J. Lubbock, "Pre-historic Times" says, "The tools of the Tahitians when first discovered were made of stone, bone, shell, or wood. Of metal they had no idea. When they first obtained nails they mistook them for the young shoots of some very hard wood, and hoping that life might not be quite extinct, planted a number of them carefully in their gardens."

Captain Wallis, however, speaking of the islands within the Polynesian group, remarks "as an extraordinary circumstance that although no sort of metal was seen on any of the lately discovered islands, yet the nations were no sooner possessed of a piece of *iron*, than they began to *sharpen it*, but did not treat copper or brass in the same manner." — "Voyages of English Navigators round the World," iii. 108.

Would not these different appreciations of iron and brass be accounted for if we suppose iron to be the *last* metal they had been traditionally acquainted with? iron being the more common and inexpensive metal.

[243] "Mr Vaux of the British Museum has added the following interesting note on the metallurgy of the ancients. 1st, The earliest form of metal work appears to have been employed in the ornamentation of sacred vessels for temples, &c.... Occasionally the floor or foundation of some temples was of brass: thus χαλκεος οὐδὸς (Soph. Œd. Col.), perhaps like the room at Delphi called λαïνος οὐδὸς, itself also a treasury." — Layard, "Nineveh and Babylon,"

Boulanger, "L'antiquité dévoilée par ses usage," (iii. 359), says, "Ce sont les mystères qui out tiré les hommes de la vie sauvage pour les ramener à la vie sociale et policée. Ces mystères étoient un composé de cérémonies religieuses ... *leur origine remonte* au temps des héros et des demi-dieux."

[244] "Of all the different phases of civilisation, those which a nation must pass before it attains the highest grade of development, the first rude state is the most enduring and the most difficult to get over." —Professor Nillson's "Stone Age," 191.

"The evidence of the transition from a stone to a bronze age among the Egyptians *appears merely to be* the use of a stone knife found in their catacombs, and used for the *sacred* incision into the dead, although they used bronze and iron knives for ordinary purposes, and whereas the *stone* knife was used by the early *Hebrews* in circumcision, and by the priests of Montezuma as instruments of human sacrifice." —Wilson's "Archæologia,"

[245] It amounts to this, that we are requested first of all to discard and absolutely exclude all that we do know through direct historical evidence of our origin, and to determine it merely by scientific induction.

Sir J. Lubbock says in his introduction to Professor Nillson's "Stone Age" (which is a summary of the whole question), "I have purposely avoided all reference to history, all use of historical data, because I have been particularly anxious to show that in archæology we can arrive at definite and satisfactory conclusions, on independent grounds, without any assistance from history; consequently regarding times before writing was invented, and therefore before written history had commenced" (p. xlii.) Compare with supra, ch. vii.

[246] "It must not be forgot to the honour of the Babylonians that they are acknowledged, by all antiquity, to have been the first who made use of writing in their public and judicial acts, but at what period it is not known." —Goguet, "Origin of Laws," i. 45.

Diodorus, however, says of the Egyptians (vide p. 48), "Menes without doubt has been esteemed the first legislator of Egypt, because he was the first who put his laws in writing. For before him Vulcan, Helius, and Osiris (vide ante, p. 189) had given laws to Egypt." —Diod. l. 1, 17–18.

But also it must be recollected that the copper mines of Egypt were worked from the earliest period.

[247] But there are savages and savages; or rather there are savages who are strictly such, and savages who have still the germ of life

and who are more properly distinguished as barbarians. Vide ante, De Maistre's definition of the barbarian.

[248] I find curious testimony to the belief in M. Maupertius' (Pinkerton, i. 252–4) account of an expedition of thirty leagues which he was induced to make into the interior of Lapland, by the accounts which he had received of a monument which the Laplanders "looked upon as the wonder of their country, and in which they conceived was contained the knowledge of everything of which they were ignorant." In the end a monument was found bearing on it the appearance of great antiquity, and an inscription which M. Celsius, his companion ("very well acquainted with the Runic"), could not read. M. Maupertius indeed says, "If the tradition of the country be consulted, all the Laplanders assure us that they are characters of great antiquity, containing valuable secrets; but what can one believe in regard to antiquity from those people who do not even know their own age, and who for the greater part are ignorant who were their mothers." Without supposing that the mysterious stone actually concealed any valuable and recondite knowledge, I am still struck by this attestation to the belief that antiquity shrouded such secrets; and if, which does not altogether accord with other accounts, the Lapps are as ignorant as they are here represented, then it would seem to be true that when mankind lose the knowledge of everything else, they still retain the tradition of their loss and the knowledge of their degradation. Concerning the superstitious veneration for stone arrow-heads very generally diffused, vide Mr E. T. Stevens' "Flint Chips" (Salisbury, 1870, p. 89.)

[249] Vide Sir George Grey's "Polynesian Mythology," p. xiii.; F. A. Weld's (Governor of Western Australia) "Notes on New Zealand,"

[250] This was a recognition on Tasman's part that there was a violation of the law of nations, which he evidently considered ought to have been recognised by these people. For killing unarmed men he does not stigmatise them as savages, but as murderers, which name has clung to the spot and to the transaction to this day.

[251] I am aware that what I have opposed to Sir J. Lubbock is only the contrary and not the contradictory of his proposition. I find, however, that a very competent authority, Wilson,

"Archæology and Pre-historic Annals of Scotland," says: "No people, however rude or debased be their state, have yet been met with so degraded to the level of the brutes as to entertain no notion of a Supreme Being, or no anticipation of a future state." "All polytheism is based on monotheism; idolatry implies religious feeling."—Bunsen's Egypt, iv. 69. But in truth it was not a priest or a missionary who first enunciated the contradictory of Sir John Lubbock's proposition—it was Cicero. "Itaque ex tot generibus nullum est animal, præter hominem, quod habeat notitiam aliquam dei: ipsisque in hominibus nulla gens est, neque tam immansueta, neque tam fera, quæ non etiam si ignoret qualem habere deum deceat, tamen habendum sciat." De Legibus; i. 8.

[252] I should not have considered it necessary to have entered so elaborately into this argument, if I had previously read the chapter on Animism in Mr Tylor's "Primitive Culture." The instances, however, which follow will stand as supplementary.

[253] Sir J. Lubbock says of the Feegee islanders: "They did not worship idols, but many of the priests seem to have really thought that they had been in actual communication with the Atona; and some of the early missionaries were inclined to believe that Satan may have been permitted to practise a deception upon them, in order to strengthen his power. However extraordinary this may appear, the same was the case in Tahiti."

[254] After all, is there not something in their mode of prayer which recalls the language of Psalm cxl., "Dirigatur oratio mea sicut incensum in conspectu tuo: elevatio manuum mearum sacrificium vespertinum."

If the reader will refer to Bunsen's "Egypt," &c. vol. i. p. 497, he will find "a man with uplifted arms" as the ideographic sign (19) for "to praise, glorification," which is in evidence not only that it was the natural but the traditional mode.

[255] Garcilasso de la Vega's authority is so unimpeachable, and at the same time his testimony is so unmistakable on this point, that it will be as well to give his own words, as he was well acquainted with the Peruvian traditions, through his mother, who was one of the Yncas. He adds: "When the Indians were asked who Pachacamac was, they replied that he it was who gave life to the universe, and supported it; but that they knew him not, for they had never seen him, and that for this reason

they did not build temples to him, nor offer him sacrifices; but that they worshipped him in their hearts (mentally), and considered him to be an unknown God.... From this it is clear, that these Indians considered him to be the maker of all things." Hakluyt ed. of Garcil. de la Vega's "Royal Commentaries of the Yncas," ed. C. Markham, 1869, i. 107. He further remarks that, whereas they hesitated to pronounce the name of Pachacamac, "they spoke of the sun on every occasion."

Compare the accounts we have of the Guanches. M. Pegot Ogier, "The Fortunate Isles" (Canaries), 1871, says (p. 283), that a comparison of the Chronicles of the Conquest shows that, "far from being idolaters, the Guanches worshipped one God, the Creator and Preserver of the world," and that (p. 282), "in their worship, they *raised their hands* to heaven, and sacrificed on the mountains by pouring milk on the ground from a *height*; their milk was carried in a sacred vase called *ganigo*." The name of their god, "Achoron Achaman" = "He who upholds the heaven and earth," and "Achuhuyahan Achuhucanac" = "He who sustains every one," has resemblances with "Pachacamac" = "Pacha," the earth; and "camac" participle of "camani," "I create." — (C. Markham, Hakluyt ed. of Garcil. de la Vega, i. 101.)

[256] Compare with.

[257] Compare the following passage in the Bishop of Chalons' "Le Monde et l'Homme Primitif" (with reference to Gen. i. — the Creation). At p. 11 the Bishop says, "That when the Book of the Law of Manou and the Mahabarata relate that God, who contains within Himself his own principle in the first instance, the water, and gave it fecundity, and that the produce of this fecundity became an egg, ... can we see in this anything else than the fantastic translation of this phrase of Scripture, 'L'esprit de Dieu couvait la surface des eaux — Rouha Elohim meharephet hal pene hammaïm.'" Vide also p. 11 (as to universality of tradition) and p. 34 as to text also. J. G. Vance ("Archæol." xix.) says, upon the mundane egg "the whole system of ancient religion was based" (J. B. Waring, "Stone Monuments of Remote Ages," p. 5, 1870).

[258] I find, in Archæological Journal, No. 89, 1866, p. 27, that corpses in a sitting posture were found under the long cromlechs in South Jutland.

[259] Vide Dr Newman's "Grammar of Assent," p. 386, et seq.

[260] Per contra, I invite Sir J. Lubbock's attention to the following passage from Mr Gladstone's "Homer" (ii. 44), "As the derivative idea of sin depended upon that of goodness, and as the shadow ceases to be visible when the object shadowed has become more dim, we might well expect that the contraction and obscuration of the true idea of goodness would bring about a more than proportionate loss of knowledge concerning the true nature of evil. The impersonation of evil could only be upheld in a lively or effectual manner as the opposite of the impersonation of good; and when the moral standard of Godhead had so greatly degenerated, as we find to be the case even in the works of Homer, the negation of that standard could not but cease to be either interesting or intelligible. Accordingly we find that the process of disintegration, followed by that of arbitrary reassortment and combination of elements, had proceeded to a more advanced stage with respect to the tradition of the evil one than in the other cases."

[261] Sir J. Lubbock ("Pre-historic Times," p. 337) says, "The largest erection in Tahiti was constructed by the generation living at the time of Captain Cook's visit, and the practice of cannibalism had been recently abandoned." For these statements he refers to Forster, "Observations made during a Voyage round the World," p. 327, a work I have not at hand, and also Ellis, "Polynesian Researches," ii. p. 29. I have made the reference to the latter, but I do not find a syllable about cannibalism; and as to the other point Ellis says, "In the bottom of every valley, even to the recesses in the mountains ... stone pavements of their dwellings and courtyards, foundations of houses and ruins of family temples, are numerous.... All these relics are of the same kind as those observed among the nations at the time of their discovery, evidently proving that they belong to the same race, though to a more populous era of their history." I draw attention to this inadvertence, as the above instances (two) are the most important of the four which Sir J. Lubbock adduces in support of his view. Vide Appendix.

[262] The Duke of Argyll, balancing the conclusions of Archbishop Whately and Sir J. Lubbock ("Primeval Man," p. 139), says, "Whately defies the supporter of Development to produce a single case of savages having raised themselves. Sir J. Lubbock replies by defying his opponent to show that it has not been

done and done often. He urges, and urges as it seems to me with truth, that the great difficulty of teaching many savages the arts of civilised life, is no proof whatever that the various degrees of advance towards the knowledge of those arts which are actually found among semi-barbarous nations may not have been of strictly indigenous growth. Thus it appears that one tribe of red Indians called Mandans practised the art of fortifying their towns. Surrounding tribes, although they saw the advantage derived from this art, yet never practised it, and never learned it." So far as to the fact. The Duke of Argyll continues the argument on the side of Sir J. Lubbock. But what I wish to indicate is that this crucial instance of the Mandans may be triumphantly adduced in support of my proposition. Why, these are the very Mandans among whom Catlin and the Prince Maxmilian of Neuwied discovered the curious commemorative ceremony of the Deluge! Vide ch. xi.

[263] Since writing the above, I have referred to Wallis and Bougainville. Wallis could not discover "that these people had any kind of religious worship among them." Bougainville says "that their principal deity is called 'Ein-t-era,' i.e. 'king of light' or 'of the sun'; besides whom they acknowledge a number of inferior divinities, some of whom produce evil and others good; that the general name for these ministering spirits is Eatona; and that the natives suppose two of these divinities attend each affair of consequence in human life, determining its fate either advantageously or otherwise. To one circumstance our author speaks in decisive terms. He says, when the moon exhibits a certain aspect which bears the name of 'Malama Tamai' (the moon is in a state of war), the natives offer up human sacrifices.... When any one sneezes, his companions cry out 'Eva-rona-t-eatona,' i.e. 'May the good genius awaken thee,' or 'May not the evil genius lull thee asleep.'"

Captain King ("Journal of Transactions on returning to the Sandwich Islands," &c., Pinkerton, xi. 737) says of the Sandwich Islanders, "The religion of these people resembles in most of its principal features *that of the Society and Friendly Islands.* Their morais, their whattas, their idols, their sacrifices, and their sacred songs, *all of which* they have in common with each other, are *convincing proofs* that their religious notions are derived *from the same source.*"

[264] The "Popul Vul" (pp. 223–227, Paris, 1861, vide Baring Gould, "Origin and Development of Religious Belief," p. 383) gives an instance—or embodies a reminiscence—of a people who had lost the tradition of fire.

"Then arrived the tribes perishing with cold, ... and all the tribes were gathered, shivering and quaking with cold, when they came before the leaders of the Iniches.... Great was their misery. 'Will you not compassionate us,' they asked; 'we ask only a little fire. Were we not all one, and with one country, when we were first created? Have pity on us.' 'What will you give us that we should compassionate you,' was the answer made to them.... It was answered, 'We will inquire of Tohil'" (their fire-god); and then follows the horrible condition of human sacrifices to be offered to their fire-god Tohil, with reference to which Mr B. Gould quotes it. Vide supra, p. 81, tradition among the Sioux Indians, of fire having been sent to them from heaven after the Deluge.

In Colden's "Five Indian Nations," p. 167, I find an Indian chief says: "Now before the Christians arrived, the general council of the Five Nations was held at Onondaga, where there has from *the Beginning* a *continual fire* been kept burning; it is made of two great logs, *whose fire never extinguishes.*"

[265] I find, in Falkner's "Description of Patagonia," &c., 1774 (Falkner resided near 40° 7′ in those parts), "that in the vocabulary of the Moluches, although the word for 'fire' is 'k'tal,' the word for 'hot' is 'asee,' 'cold' 'chosea.'"

But Sir J. Lubbock admits "asi" is the same word as "ahi," and if "ahi" denotes light and heat, *it also* signifies fire.

Should we not expect, at least ought it to cause surprise, that the word for "fire," where poverty of language may be presumed, should stand also for light and heat? In the Andaman vocabulary (Earl's "Papuans") "ahay" is their word for the sun—in which the two senses seem to combine. In Shortland's "Comp. Table of Polynesian Dialects" (Traditions of the New Zealanders"), I find *ahi* means fire, and not light.

	New Zealand.	Raratonga.	Navigator's (Savaii).	Sandwich Islands (Hawaii).
Fire =	Ahi.[C]	Ai.	Afi.	Ahi.

[C] And as would appear from Shortland (id. pp. 55, 56, "ao," a seemingly cognate though not identical word with "ahi," is the New Zealand word for light. But in Bougainville's "Vocabulary of Faiti (Otaheite) Island," I find again "eaï," i.e. their word for fire, whereas their word for light, not darkness, is "Eouramaï" and "Po" = day light), whilst they have a distinct word for "hot" = "Ivera"—"Era" being the sun. Compare Sanscrit "aghni" = ignis, fire.—Vide Card. Wiseman, "Science and Revealed Religion," p. 40, 5th ed.

[266] The works of Garcilasso de la Vega, Valera, P. de Cieza, and De Sahagun must be excepted. As an instance of the neglect which we have reason to regret, the former gives an account of one only (the Raymi) of the four annual festivals of the Peruvians.— Hakluyt Soc. ed. ii. 155. He gives the name, however, of another—namely, the Situa.

[267] Probably a tradition of the penitence of Adam.

[268] Here, the admixture of sun-worship, as identifying the mythology at any rate with the Hamitic and "Cuthite," directly militates in favour of my view against the conjecture that Manco Capac was a missionary.

[269] Vide also the like confused tradition of Nimrod (Assyria) and Menes (Egypt), Bunsen, p. 192.

[270] If an identity has been established between Quetzalcohuatl and Manco Capac (vide Prescott "Conquest of Peru," i. 9), it will appear that this legislator, who shut his ears when he was spoken to of war, did nevertheless leave them admirable maxims (compare with Indian (Aryan) maxims, p. 400) and laws of war, e.g. Prescott, "Peru," p. 69. Compare extract from Davies—vide supra, preface.

"The Peruvian soldier was forbidden to commit any *trespass on the property* of the inhabitants whose territory lay in the line of march. From the moment *war was proclaimed,*" &c., "in every stage of the war he was open to *propositions for peace,* and although he sought to reduce his enemies by carrying off their harvests and destressing them by famine, the Peruvian monarch allowed his troops to commit no unnecessary outrage on person or property." It is not to the point that these rules were not always observed.

[271] Compare supra, p. 201, note to Manou (Bacchus).

[272] Compare with Gen. vi. 18, viii. 15, "And God spoke to Noe, saying"; also vi. 13, ix. 8; and Gen. viii. 20—"And Noe built an altar unto the Lord, and taking of all cattle"; and ix. 20—"And Noe, a husbandman, began to till the ground, and planted a vineyard." Also Ecclesiasticus xliv. 1, 3, 4, 19, "The covenants of the world were made with him." Compare also with the "Oracula Sybillina," supra, p. 237.

[273] It may be well here to recall to recollection the well-known lines of Virgil—

"Ultima Cumæi venit jam carminis ætas:

Magnus ab integro seclorum nascitur ordo,

Jam redit et Virgo, redeunt Saturnia regna

Jam nova progenies cœlo dimittitur alto."

Eclogues IV.

[274] Boulanger ("L'Antiquité Devoilée," i. 10), recognises, although it perplexes him, the tradition which places the gold and silver age after the Deluge—"à la suite de cet évenement, les traditions de l'age d'or, et du regne des Dieux paroissent encore plus bizarres;" also id. iii. 338; also 308. Also 328, "Ce n'est donc point un état politique qu'il faut chercher dans l'age d'or, ce fut un état tout religieux. Chaque famille pénétrée des jugemens d'en haut, vecut quelque temps sous la conduite des pères qui rassembloient leurs enfans." It is thus that Seneca depicts the golden age. Vide p. 231.

[275] It might be a sufficient answer to say that they did not operate because a miraculous intervention ordained it otherwise; but if we seek the explanation in natural causes they will be found such as will exactly confirm the theory. The causes which lead to dispersion are the necessities of the pastoral life. If there, then, was no dispersion, the conclusion is that during the three or four centuries after the Deluge mankind were mainly engaged in husbandry—"and Noe, a husbandman, began to till the ground." But husbandry is the first and essential condition of civilisation. We have seen that Mr Mill, Mr Hepworth Dixon, &c., believe that mankind slowly arrived at this stage through the intermediate stages of shepherd and hunter. On the contrary it would appear that they started in this career. Again, given the conditions which Genesis describes—families living in patriarchal subjection to a chief who had the knowledge of

husbandry—cultivation would be the natural consequence; for the one and only hindrance to cultivation, supposing the knowledge, is insecurity. "Most critical of all are the causes which conduce to agriculture, agriculture at once the most fruitful and the most dangerous expedients for life. He who tills the soil exposes his valuable stores to the malice or enmity of the whole world. Any marauder," &c. ("Miscell." by Francis W. Newman, 1869). But as the conditions described in Genesis exclude the probability of such interruption—agriculture would have been the preferable resource of life—and so it would have continued until circumstances led to the extension of the pastoral mode. So far, then, as we are brought to regard the different modes of life as progressive or successive (I believe that even at this early stage they were contemporaneous), the order of the succession according to the theory now in vogue must be reversed; and we must regard mankind as first a community of husbandmen, gradually extending themselves as shepherds, to be finally still more dispersed in some of their branches as hunters.

[276] "And truly there is a sap in nations as well as in trees, a vigorous inward power, ever tending upwards, drawing its freshest energies from the simplest institutions, and the purest virtues and the healthiest moral action.... And if of nations we may so speak, what shall we say of the entire human race, when all its energies were, in a manner, pent up in its early and few progenitors; when the children of Noah, removed but a few generations from the recollections and lessons of Eden, and possessing the accumulated wisdom of long-lived patriarchs, were marvellously fitted to receive those strange and novel impressions, which a world, just burst forth in all its newness, was calculated to make?"—Card. Wiseman, "Science and Revealed Religion," Lect. ii.

It is to this period that I am inclined to refer the belief in an age of high chivalry and virtue, with subsequent degeneracy, widely diffused in the legends of King Arthur. I will surrender my opinion whenever the historical information respecting that monarch shall have been more exactly determined.

[277] "The evidence, therefore, of the meaning of this part of the Homeric system is like that which is obtained, when, upon applying a new key to some lock that we have been unable to open, we find it fits the wards and puts back the bolt."— Gladstone, "Homer and the Homeric Age," ii. 30.

[278] Plato's testimony to this tradition is remarkable (Plato de Legibus, lib. i.) Boulanger extracts the passage with reference to the golden age (iii. 296). (Vide also Grote's Plato, iii. 337.) Plato says—"That it is a tradition that there was formerly a great destruction of mankind caused by inundations and other general calamities [are not these calamities those to which Horace alludes, I. Ode iii.,

"Semotique prius tarda necessitas

Lethi corripuit gradum,"

from which only a few escaped?] those who were spared led a pastoral life on the mountains. We may suppose," he adds, "that these men possessed the knowledge of some useful arts, of some usages to which they had previously conformed." Plato indeed goes on to tell how this knowledge must have been lost, and one reason he gives is, "mankind remained many centuries on the summits of the highest mountains—fear and remembrance of the past did not permit them to descend into the plains." Strabo (apud Boulanger, iii. 301) also discusses this question. He says that mankind descended into the plains at different periods according to their courage and sociability (lib. xiii.) Varro (De re Rustica, lib. xiii. cap. i.) says they were a long time before they descended." Now, in these passages from Plato, Strabo, and Varro, there is distinct testimony to the fact of mankind remaining on the mountains after the Deluge, and their subsequent inferences are drawn from the fact that they supposed them to have remained there a long time. Is not this merely that they have recorded one tradition to the exclusion of another—viz., that mankind were brought into the plains by Saturn, in accordance with the indications in Genesis ix. 20, "and Noe, a husbandman began to till the ground." Compare supra, Bryant, "Mythology," iii. p. 22, following [St] Epiphanius, says the descendants of Noah remained 659 years in the vicinity of Ararat—i.e. five generations.

[279] With reference to the stone age, vide p. 288.

[280] Concerning the evident tradition of the dispersion in Hesiod, "Theog." v. 836, vide Bryant's "Mythology," iii. 51, et seq.

[281] This appears to me to be borne out by the Sanscrit root "ar, to plough," being seemingly cognate with "æs, æris," and with the produce corn = "arista," aroum, aratrum, Greek ἀϱσμηα, &c.

Sanscrit, "ar, to plough," *vide* note 1 in Brace's "Ethnology." *Vide* also Max Müller, "Science of Language," *id*. *Vide* also Max Müller, "Chips," ii. p. 45.

"The name of the plough (in Egypt) was ΖΗβιξ, *ploughed land*, appears to *have been* αϱτ, a word still traced in the Arabic 'hart,' which has the same import; and the Greek ἀϱητϱον and Roman *aratrum* appears to indicate, like the αϱουϱα, an Egyptian origin." —*Wilkinson's Ancient Egyptians*, i. 45.

If "ar," as in "αϱιστος," should be proposed as the primitive root, it must be after rejection of the evidence of secondary derivation; but does not our common parlance still run to the comparison of virtues with metals, "good as gold," "hard as iron," "true as steel." Why then at a later period should not brass have become the expression for best in the brazen or warlike age, when courage was the virtue principally regarded? If this is accepted, "Ἀϱης," or Mars, so far from being the root, would be a tertiary derivation—the embodiment and deification of what was regarded as best in the brazen age. Gladstone ("Homer," ii. p. 225), shows that Mars was a deity of late invention, and not one of the traditionary deities. Rawlinson, vide supra, p. 164, identifying Ares with Nimrod.

Bunsen ("Egypt," iii. 466), says in a note, "Arya" in Indian means lord. Its original meaning was equivalent to "upper noble." The popular name "Arja" is derived from it, and means "descended from a noble." I will only add that "Ari" in Egyptian means "honourable" (in Nofruari). But "ar" might mean to plough; for the Aryans were originally and essentially an agricultural, and therefore a peasant race. Agriculture at the time we are contemplating would have been the most honourable employment (supra, p. 329), it would not have been "an agricultural and therefore peasant" employment till insecurity brought about the state of dependence and vassalage. The Aryans would have been noble as being of the Japhetic race.

[282] I.e., "The teaching and government of the University remained in the Faculty of Arts," and not in the faculty of theology or law or modern philosophy. I have for my own purposes of condensation been obliged to take certain unpardonable liberties of transposition in the above abstract, for which I can only plead my necessity. I should not in any case have so exceeded in quotation, were this very masterly address at all accessible, but,

as far as I know, it is only to be found in the Catholic University Gazette, November 16, 1854.

In order to show the full significance of these extracts from Dr Newman, and also their bearing on points still to be discussed, I will append the following suggestive passage from Sir H. Maine's "Ancient Law," —"It is only with the progressive societies that we are concerned, and nothing is more remarkable than their extreme fewness. In spite of overwhelming evidence, it is most difficult for a citizen of Western Europe to bring thoroughly home to himself the truth that the civilisation which surrounds him is a rare exception in the history of the world. The tone of thought common among us, all our hopes, fears, and speculations, would be materially affected, if we had vividly before us the relation of the progressive races to the totality of human life. It is indisputable that much the greatest part of mankind has never shown a particular desire that its civil institutions should be improved since the moment when external completeness was first given to them by their embodiment in some permanent record.... There has been a material civilisation, but instead of the civilisation expanding the law, the law has limited the civilisation."

I must also express my belief that if Mr Lowe had read the lecture of Dr Newman, he would have very much modified the views he enunciated in his lecture on "Primary and University Education," at the Philosophical Institution at Edinburgh.— *Times*, November 4, 1867.

[283] "Ancient Law," p. 123.

[284] It by no means follows that God does not will, and did not foreordain society in its wider organisation, according to the conditions and circumstances out of which it arose.

[285] Sir H. Maine says:—"The points which lie on the surface of history are these: the eldest male parent—the eldest ascendant—is absolutely supreme in his household. His dominion extends to life and death, and is as unqualified over their children and their houses as over his slaves. The flocks and herds of the children are the flocks and herds of the father." [This is not borne out by what we read of Abraham and Lot, Esau and Jacob—e.g., "But Lot also, who was with Abraham, had flocks of sheep, and herds and tents. Neither was the land able to bear them, that they might dwell together" (Gen. xiii.). "And the possessions

of the parent, which he holds in a representative rather than a proprietary character, are equally divided at his death among his descendants in the first degree, the eldest son sometimes receiving a double share, under the name of birthright, but more generally endowed with no hereditary advantage beyond an honorary precedence." The separation then commenced with the division of the inheritance; and whether it was ever an equal division, and not proportioned to the respective ages of the sons, or determined by other motives, or again, a division of different kinds of property, may be open to question; but at any rate a division took place, and a separation of families was consequent upon it. The division was not only the sign and token, but the efficient cause of the separation; and so not only the dispersion of families, but separate ownerships commenced with the descendants in the first degree.

[286] Compare Plato, "Leges;" Grote's "Plato," iii. 337.

[287] "In that old heathenism of the Roman world, into which it was the will of God that the Christian religion should be introduced by the apostles, there were then diverse and often conflicting elements. There was a good element, which came from God; there was a thoroughly bad element, which came from Satan; and there was a corrupt element, which was the fruit of the workings of unregenerate human nature upon society, and upon the objects of sense and intelligence with which man is placed in relation. The good element we see embodied in great part of the laws and institutions of the ancient world, as also in much of the literature, the poetry, the philosophy of Greece and Rome, which literature consequently—after having been purified, and as it were baptized—has always been used by the Christian Church in the education of her children. This element, I say, was originally the gift of God, the Author of nature, to man, the offspring of reason and conscience, the tradition of a society of which God was Himself the founder. It enshrined whatever fragments of primeval truth as to God, the world, and man himself, still lingered, in whatever shape, among the far-wandering children of Adam. St Paul alludes to this element (Acts xvii. 22); ... and his words altogether seem to imply that God watched over it, supported it and fostered it, as far as men were worthy of it, and that it might even have been expanded into a perfect system of natural religion and of reasonable virtue, had men been grateful enough to earn larger measures of grace

from God, who left not Himself without witness in His daily providence, and was not far from 'any one of His children.'" — "Four Sermons," by the Rev. Henry J. Coleridge, S. J. Burns & Oates. 1869. P. 52. (48.)

[288] The word 'νόμος' is found in the Hymn to Apollo, v. 20, attributed to Homer [the term θεμιστες also, v. 391] — and in Hesiod, Op. et Dies, v. 276.—Goguet, ii. 78. In the Hymn to Apollo it is only applied to song. The Greeks had the same word, however—viz. νομοι, as for laws, songs, and pastures— that is to say, the term law, νομος, is applied to the instrument of its transmission, and to what would then have been its most ordinary subject matter. This seems to me in evidence of its primitive use.

Take, moreover, the following passage in the First Book of the Iliad, v. 233:—

Ἀλλ' ἐκ τοι ἐρεω, και ἐπι μεγαν ὅρκον ὀμοῦμαι

ναι μα τοδε σκῆπτρον, το μεν οὑποτε φυλλα καὶ ὀζους

φυσει, ἐπειδη πρῶτα τομην ἐν ὀρεσσι λελοιπεν,

οὐδ' ἀναθηλησει· περι γαρ ῥα ἑ χαλκος ἐλεψε

φυλλα τε καὶ φλοιον· νυν αὐτε μὶν υἱες Ἀχαιων

ἐν παλαμης φορεουσι, δικασπολοι, οἱτε Θεμιστας

προς Διος εἱρυαται· ὁ δε τοι μεγας ἐσσεται ὅρκος.

—Heyne's Homer, i. v. 233–239.

"But this I say, and with an oath confirm,
By this my royal staff, which never more
Shall put forth leaf nor spray since first it left   ¬
Upon the mountain side its parent stem,
Nor blossom more; since all around, the axe
Hath lopped both leaf and bark, and now 'tis borne,
Emblem of justice, by the sons of Greece,
Who guard the sacred ministry of law
Before the face of Jove! a mighty oath.
The time shall come when all the sons of Greece
Shall mourn Achilles' loss," &c.

—*Lord Derby's Translation,* 275–285.

Here we have the term "dike" not merely in embryo, but in the compound word "dikaspoloi," administrators of justice, implying something akin to judges, and a condition of things in which law was reduced to a state in which there was something to guard and administer. Not only so, but the staff, the "emblem of justice," is borne by them when they *guard* the "Themistes" before the gods.

It will not only be curious to discover, but the discovery of vestiges in modern times of the old traditional modes and ceremonial will throw light upon the administration of justice in ancient times. I dare say many other instances may be indicated. I will adduce the following:—If my readers will turn to the *Pall Mall Gazette* (July 12, 1870), they will find an account of "The Manx Thing," or "the ancient custom of the Ruler, his Council, and the Commons meeting together in the open air to proclaim the law to the people standing around." "The Lieutenant-Governor is the representative of the King, and takes an oath to deal truly and uprightly between our sovereign lady the Queen and her people," "and as indifferently betwixt party and party *as this staff now standeth*." "He is assisted by two demesters or supreme judges, who must deem the law truly, as they will answer to the Lord of the Isle." Here, as in Homer, there is reference to an emblem and a ceremonial repugnant to the notion that (*infra*) "every man under the patriarchal despotism was practically controlled by a regimen not of law but of caprice."

Mr Adams describes the following scene in one of the islands in the archipelago off the mainland of Korea—"The chief, who really has something very noble and majestic about him, as is generally the case with men in high authority among the natives of these islands.... The demeanour of those of his countrymen who surrounded him was as free and independent as his own was reserved and dignified.... In his hand he held his badge of office, a wand of ebony with a green silken cord entwined about it like the serpent of Æsculapius."—"Travels of a Naturalist in Japan and Manchuria," by Arthur Adams, F.L.S. 1870. Compare also with infra.

[289] I feel very much supported in my argument by the following passage from Mr Gladstone's "Homer" (ii. 420): "Mr Grote says that 'the primitive import' of the words ἀγαθὸς, ἐσθλὸς, and

κακός, relates to power and not to worth; and that the ethical meaning of these is a later growth, which 'hardly appears until the discussions raised by Socrates, and prosecuted by his disciples.' I ask permission to protest against whatever savours of the idea that any Socrates whatever was the patentee of that sentiment of right and wrong which is the most precious part of the patrimony of mankind. The movement of Greek morality with the lapse of time was chiefly downward and not upward.... But as to the words ἀγαθὸς and κακὸς, the case is far more clear; and here I ask, Can it be shown that Homer ever applies the word ἀγαθὸς to that which is morally bad? or the word κακὸς to that which is morally good? If it can, cadit quæstio; if it cannot, then we have advanced a considerable way in proving the ethical signification.... In the word δικαιος, however, we have an instance of the epithet never employed except in order to signify a moral or a religious idea. Like the word righteous among ourselves, it is derived from a source which would make it immediately designate duty as between man and man, and also as it arises out of civil relations. But it is applied in Homer to both the great branches of duty. And surely there cannot be a stronger proof of the existence of definite moral ideas among a people, than the very fact that they employ a word founded on the observance of relative rights to describe also the religious character. It is when religion and morality are torn asunder, that the existence of moral ideas is endangered."

[290] Either, then, the Roman lawyers fell back upon the old traditions, or else the lawyers introduced the superstition of the law of nature, and then became victims to the superstition they had invented. In any case, the "belief" in "the lost code of nature gradually prevailed." I am presently going to discuss with Sir H. Maine how far in the latter case such a belief is likely to have prevailed.

[291] Vide also Sir H. Maine, p. 77: "It is important, too, to observe that this model system, unlike many of those which have mocked men's hopes in later days, was not entirely the product of imagination. It was never thought of as founded on quite untested principles. The notion was that it underlay existing law, and must be looked for through it. Its functions were, in short, remedial, not revolutionary or anarchical. And this unfortunately is the exact point at which the modern view of a law of nature has often ceased to resemble the ancient."

[292] I shall consider that Dr Dyer has fairly reinstated a large portion of early Roman history until I see his arguments refuted. Without endorsing his opinion I may quote what Dr Dyer says ("Hist. of the City of Rome," p. 27) in evidence of the admixture of the Sabine element:— "The importance of the Sabine element at Rome has not perhaps been sufficiently considered. The late M. Ampere has discussed the subject with great learning and ability in his interesting work, 'L'Histoire Romaine à Rome.' He remarks that not only did the Romans borrow from the Sabines almost all their religious and much of their political and social organisation, their customs, ceremonies, arms, &c., but also that the far greater part of the primitive population of Rome was Sabine, that most of the men who played a part in Roman history were of Sabine extraction, and that what is called the Latin tongue contains a strong infusion of Sabine elements."

[293] Evidences of the Etruscan element are so marked, that Niebühr, in his first edition, asserted the Etruscan origin of the city. He subsequently, however, came to the conclusion that "there was so much in the Roman state that was peculiar to Rome and Latium, as to be incompatible with the supposition of Rome being an Etruscan colony."—_Appendix to Travers Twiss' Epitome of Niebühr._

[294] A federal union existed between the Roman people and the Latins in the reign of Servius Tullius (Niebühr, i. ch. xxv.) "The old Latin towns had retained their ancient rights, and the colonies, that together with them formed the Latin nation, had all received the full freedom of Rome, and had become municipia a full century before the Consul Junius Norbanus introduced the franchise of the Latin freedmen.... The towns on the north of the Po, inhabited by a mixed population of Italians and Celts speaking Latin,... were termed the 'Lesser Latium.'... A law which regarded Latin citizens as foreigners, and applied to them the principle that the child follows the condition of the baser parent, can only have related to this inferior Latium." (Niebühr, ii. ch. vi.)

[295] Vide also De Fresquet, "Droit Romain," ii. 25–29.

[296] "The above table shows that before the separation of the Aryan race, every one of the degrees of affinity had received expression and sanction in language, for, although some spaces had to be left empty, the coincidences, such as they are, are sufficient to

warrant one general conclusion."—Vide table, Max Müller's Essays, ii. p. 31.

Of course, I am speaking only of the actual affinity, not of laws of succession founded upon it. These must be controlled by other considerations, and by other natural rights, as, for instance, the right of testation or by reasons of State requiring hereditary succession and a Salic law, or by reasons of family compelling the agnatic rule as the only mode of preserving the ancestral domain to the family—a necessity which applies as stringently to small freeholds as to broad manors.

In illustration, I quote the following passage from the Rev. W. Smith's "Pentateuch" (above referred to, ch. xiii., "Indirect internal evidence of Mosaic authorship," vol. i. 307)—"As the journey (Exodus) proceeds so laws originate from the accidents of the way.... The laws regulating the succession to property furnish an example of the same kind. In Numbers xxvi. 32–36 it is ordained in accordance with patriarchal usage, that the family inheritance descend by the male line. But a case immediately turns up where there happens to be no male issue. Zelophahad had left no sons, but only daughters, and what was to become of the property? How was the succession to be regulated? To meet the case, Jehovah orders Moses to proclaim the law of Numbers xxvii. 8–11, in virtue of which daughters, in failure of sons, are to succeed. Shortly after, a new difficulty arises. As heiresses, the daughters of Zelophahad were now to have property of their own. But if they married out of their tribe, was the property to go with them? (Num. xxxvi. 1–9.) Such a condition would at once have upset the fundamental laws of inheritance. Hence, to avoid the evil, they are enjoined to marry within their own tribe; and a general law to the same effect is promulgated" (xxxvi. 8, 9).

[297] "We should know almost nothing about it (agnation) if we had only the compilations of Justinian to consult; but the discovery of the MS. of Gaius discloses it to us at a most interesting epoch, just when it had fallen into complete discredit, and was verging on extinction."—Ancient Law, p. 153.

[298] Gladstone's Homer, i. 305–372.

[299] Id. i. 106–108.

[300] "The Greek mythology was derived from the Pelasgians, and the oracle of Dodona belonged to them."—Niebühr, Hist. i. 28.

"The Pelasgians were a different nation from the Hellenes: their language was peculiar, and not Greek.... The Pelasgians, as well as the Hellenes, were members of the Amphictyonic association, the main tie of which was religion, in which both nations agreed." —*Niebühr, Hist.* i. (*Travers Twiss' Epitome*, ch. iii.)

"The royal laws became odious or obsolete, the mysterious deposit was silently preserved by the priests and the nobles, and at the end of sixty years the citizens of Rome still complained that they were ruled by the arbitrary sentence of the magistrate; yet the positive institutions of the kings had blended themselves with the public and private manners of the city; some fragments of that venerable jurisprudence were compiled by the diligence of antiquarians, and above twenty texts still speak the rudeness of the Pelasgic idiom of the Latins." —*Gibbon's Decline and Fall*, vol. viii. ch. xiv.

[301] Gladstone, ii. 173, &c.; Strabo.

[302] Id. i. 294.

[303] Vide, Pastoret, "Hist. de la Legislation," v. 21.

[304] "The oath taken by the deputies bound the Amphictyons not to destroy any of the Amphictyonic cities, or to debar them from the use of their fountains in peace or war; to make war on any who should transgress in these particulars ... or who should plunder the property of the god (the Delphine Apollo).... This is the oldest form of the Amphictyonic oath which has been recorded, and is expressly called by Æskines the ancient oath of the Amphictyons." —Cyclop. of Arts and Sciences.

[305] The Ionian federation, composed also of twelve cities, was almost identical. "L'association s'etoit formée d'abord entre les douze cités, en y comprenant les deux îles voisines de Samos et de Chio.... On s'assembloit dans un lieu sacré du Mont Mycale, que les Ionians avoient dediés en commun à Neptune." —Pastoret, ix. 170. There was also a confederacy of seven states, which met in the temple of Neptune, in the island of Calauria, "and which is even called by Strabo, viii. 374, an Amphictyonic Council." —Cyclop. of Arts and Sciences, art. Amphic. Council.

[306] Adam Fergusson, "Essay on Civil Society," 130. Whatever the conduct of the Iroquois or Five Nations (sometimes counted as six) may have been towards surrounding nations, the fidelity

with which they held to their compacts among themselves is fully acknowledged.

Colden ("History of the Five Indian Nations") says, "This union has continued so long that the Christians know nothing of the original of it.... Each of these nations is an absolute republick by itself, and every castle in each nation makes an independent republick and is governed by its own 'Sachems' or old men.... They have certain customs which they observe in their publick transactions with other nations, and in their private affairs among themselves; which it is scandalous for any one among them not to observe, and these always draw after them either publick or private resentment whenever they are broke."

In Plato's Republic, "It is laid down that the Greeks are natural enemies of the barbarians, but are natural friends and *allies of one another, so that all hostilities between Greek states* are to be avoided—are to be conducted on principles of mildness and forbearance, and to be considered as civil discord rather than foreign war." "The ten kings of the Atlantic island were never to make war on each other—there was a sort of Congress between them." Critias, chap. 15. Sir G. C. Lewis, "Method," &c., ii. 234. This, taken in connection with what we know of the Amphictyonic Council, reads more like tradition than fiction.

[307] The general assemblies of Greece were held at Delos, "Comme Métropole du Culte," Pastoret ix. 13. "Ce qu'il y a d'assuré, c'est que le Pontife exerçoit sur plusieurs objets une véritable administration de la justice. La décision n'en appartenoit qu' à lui. Les règles qu'il devoit suivre, le caractère et l'étendue de ses droits, étoient pareillement établis dans le recueil connu sous le nom de Jus Pontificum (Macrobe parle deux fois de ce Jus Pontificum, mais comme d'un ouvrage perdu. Saturn, vii. chap. xiii.) Un fils du pontife romain Publius Scævola est même cité dans le livre des Lois comme prétendant qu'on ne pouvoit exercer un si haut ministère sans savoir le droit civil. Quoi, tout entier? dit Cicéron, qui le refute; et qui font au pontife le droit des mers, le droit des eaux, ou d'autres droits semblables?" — Pastoret ix. 203. "Torts, then, are copiously enlarged upon in primitive jurisprudence. It must be added that Sins are known to it also. Of the Teutonic codes it is almost unnecessary to make this assertion.... But it is also true that non-Christian bodies of archaic law entail penal consequences on certain classes of acts and on certain classes of omissions, as being violations of divine

prescriptions and commands. The law administered at Athens by the senate of the Areopagus was probably a special religious code; and at Rome, apparently from a very early period, the Pontifical jurisprudence punished adultery, sacrilege, and perhaps murder. There were, therefore, in the Athenian and in the Roman states laws punishing sins." —Sir H. Maine.

The expression unwritten laws (ἄγραφοι νόμοι) first occurs in the funeral oration of Pericles (Thuc. ii. 37), when it appears to denote those laws of the state which are corroborated by the moral sanction. It next occurs.... Xenophon, Mem. iv. 4, § 19, 25, ... the expression was doubtless adopted by Socrates from popular usage. Thus Plato speaks of τὰ καλούμενα ὑπο τῶν πολλων ἄγραφα νόμιμα (Leg. vii. 793). Vide Sir G. C. Lewis, "Method of Rea. in Pol.," ii. 27. [The "laws called unwritten by the multitude" must evidently imply laws known to the multitude but in tradition.]

Cicero, "De Natura Deorum," iii., says, "Habes, Balba, quid Cotta, quid *pontifex* sentiat. Fac nunc, ego intelligam, quid tu sentias: a te enim philosopho rationem accipere debes religionis; *majoribus autem nostris etiam nulla ratione reddita credere.*" "Lex est cui homines obtemperare convenit, cum ob alia multa, tum ab eo maxime quod lex omnis inventus quidem, ac *dei munus est.*" "Lex est sanctio sancta, jubens *honesta,* prohibens contraria."

[308] This last sentence is only a gloss of Cicero's from the stoical point of view, since clearly the enunciation of the oracle would compel the conclusion, that what was most ancient and nearest the gods was the best, and not that the best, as abstractly conceived, was to be held the most ancient, &c. A moment's consideration will suffice to show that in this substitution is involved the whole extent of the difference between the principle of conservation and the principle of change.

"Demosthène qui avait en faire tant de mauvaises lois, prononçait que" toutes les lois sont l'ouvrage et le présent des dieux "et c'était à ce titre qu'il réclamit pour elles l'obéissance des hommes. Socrate professait la même doctrine." —Ozanam, "Les Germains avant le Christianisme," i., 159. Again, "Quand on étudie les lois indiennes on y voit tout un grand peuple enchaîné par la terreur des dieux. Le livre de la loi s'annonce comme une revelation.... Les prescriptions du droit sacré enveloppent pour ainsi dire toute la vie civile, et c'est là qu'on decouvre enfin la raison de tant de coutumes dont les Occidentaux avaient conservé la lettre, mais non l'esprit." — *Id.* p. 161. "If the customs and institutions of barbarians have one characteristic more striking than another, it is their *extreme uniformity*" (Maine's "Ancient Law," p. 366). "There are in nature certain fountains of justice whence all civil laws are derived but as streams; and like as waters do take tinctures and tastes from the soils through which they run, so do civil laws vary according to the regions and governments where they are planted, though they proceed from the same fountains." (Bacon, "Advancement of Learning," B. ii. W. iii. 475, ap.; D. Rowland, "On the Moral Commandments," p. 85.)

[309] "L'erreur a été de croire qu'il n'est rien de plus facile à l'homme que de suivre la nature, tandis que c'est au contraire le chef-d'œuvre de l'art que de la contenir dans les bornes que la nature lui prescrit: c'est où peuvent à peine parvenir les legislateurs les plus sages. Que de préjugés à éteindre! que d'erreurs à combattre! que d'habitudes à vaincre! toutes choses qui dans tous les temps commandent impérieusement au genre humain." — _L'Antiquité dévoilée par ses usages_, i. 1. ii. ch. iii. par Boulanger.

[310] Εἰρηνοδίκαι — "Feciales quia interpretes et arbitri sunt pacis et belli." — Lexicon, Ben-Hederic, Ernesti.

Vide also Plutarch, "Numa;" Livy, lib. i. c. 34.

Vattel, iii. c. iv., says: — "It is *surprising* to find among the Romans such justice, such moderation and prudence, *at a time too* when apparently nothing but courage and ferocity was to be expected from them."

[311] Gladstone, "Homer and the Homeric Age," iii. 4.

[312] "To demolish a trophy was looked on as unlawful, and a kind of sacrilege, because they were all dedicated to some deity; nor was it less a crime to pay crime to pay divine adoration before them, or to repair them when decayed, as may be likewise observed of the Roman triumphal arches.... For the same reason, those Grecians who introduced the custom of erecting pillars for trophies incurred a severe censure from the ages they lived in." — Potters "Archæologia," ii. c. 12. "Before the Greeks engaged themselves in war it was usual to publish

a declaration of the injuries they had received, and to demand satisfaction by ambassadors; which custom was observed even in the most early ages.... It is therefore no wonder what Polybius relates of the Ætolians, that they were held for the common outlaws and robbers of Greece, it being their manner to strike without warning, and make war without any previous or public declaration."—Id. ii. c. vii. p. 64. (Compare infra, ch. xv.)

[313] "Omnes portas concionabundus ipse imperator circumiit, et quibuscumque irritamentis poterat, iras militum accuebat, nunc fraudem hostium incusans, qui, pace petita, induciis datis, per ipsum induciarum tempus, contra jus gentium ad castra oppugnando venisset."—P. Livius, 1. xc.

[314] "De Jure Belli ac Pacis," l. i. c. l. § x. n n, 1 et 2.

[315] Sir G. C. Lewis ("Method, &c., of Reasoning in Politics," ii. 35), quotes Mr Ward, "History of Law of Nations" (i. 127), to the effect "That what is commonly called the law of nations, is not the law of all nations, but only of such sets or classes of them as are united together by similar religions and systems of morality." Sir G. C. Lewis' view is that "as there are no universal principles of civil jurisprudence which belongs to each community, so there are no universal principles of international law which are common to all communities."—Id.

[316] Since writing the above, I have read a series of papers (which commenced I think in August 1871) in the Tablet under the title of "Arbitration instead of War," and I perceive that the writer arrives by a different route at a similar conclusion. I should have had pleasure in incorporating the argument with this chapter, but I shall do better if I induce my readers to peruse and weigh it as it deserves.

[317] I allude to the ancient prophecy of St Malachy. Its authenticity as the prophecy of St Malachy may be questioned; but the antiquity of the prediction, and its existence in print early in the sixteenth century is, I believe, fully established. The copy which lies before me will be found in Moreri's Dictionary of 1732, in the Pontificate of Innocent XIII. Twelve mottoes given in prediction from that date, fits the motto "crux de cruce," to the 12th successor of Innocent, viz. Pius IX. Ten other mottoes follow commencing with "lumen in cœlo."

[318] "The pontifical power is, from its essential constitution, the least subject to the caprices of politics. He who wields it is, moreover, always aged, unmarried, and a priest; all which circumstances exclude ninety-nine hundredths of all the errors and passions which disturb states."—De Maistre, Du Pape, B. II. chap. iv.

[319] "The history of that Church joins together the two great ages of human civilisation. No other institution is left standing which carries the mind back to the times when the smoke of sacrifice rose from the Pantheon, and when the cameleopards and tigers bounded in the Flavian amphitheatre. The proudest royal houses are but of yesterday when compared with the line of the supreme Pontiffs. That line we trace back in an unbroken series, from the Pope who crowned Napoleon in the nineteenth century, to the Pope who crowned Pepin in the eighth; and far beyond the time of Pepin the august dynasty extends, till it is lost in the twilight of fable.... The Catholic Church is still sending forth to the farthest ends of the world missionaries as zealous as those who landed in Kent with Augustine, _and still confronting hostile kings with the same spirit with which she confronted Attila."—Macaulay's Essays, "Review of Ranke's Popes._"

[320] Sir G. C. Lewis, "Method, &c.," ii. 285, enumerates several.

[321] In De Quincey's Works, xii. 140, there is a disquisition on Kant's scheme "of a universal society founded on the empire of political justice," where it is competent that as the result of wars man must be inevitably brought "to quit the barbarous condition of lawless power and to enter into a federal league of nations, in which even the weakest number looks for its rights and protection—not to its own power, or its own adjudication, but to this great confederation (fœdus amphictyonum), to the united power, and the adjudication of the collective will," and is said to be "the inevitable resource and mode of escape under that pressure of evil which nations reciprocally inflict," and which seems to contemplate a situation like the present. "Finally war itself becomes gradually not only so artificial a process, so uncertain in its issue, but also is the after-pains of inextinguishable national debts (a contrivance of modern times) so anxious and burdensome; ... that at length those governments which have no immediate participation in the war, under a sense of their own danger, offer themselves as mediators, though as yet without any sanction of law, and thus prepare all

things from afar for the formation of a great primary state-body or cosmopolitic Areopagus, such as is wholly unprecedented in all preceding ages." I am fully aware of the divergence of this view from that which I have indicated, but I wish to point out that it is only "unprecedented" in so far as it is cosmopolitic and extends to all humanity; but so extending it ought not to include the traditional notions of an "Areopagus"—fœdus amphictyonum—or confederation of states. It ought rather to talk of an interfusion of states, the only condition upon which the cosmopolitic Areopagus would be possible; yet it inevitably falls into the traditionary lines. Moreover, before mankind can attain to this inter-fusion of states, one supreme difficulty, which seems always to be over-looked, must be overcome, we must bring mankind back to be "of one lip and one speech." The scheme, on the other hand, of a federation cannot be pronounced impracticable until it has been tried; yet, although it lies latent in the idea of Christendom, and although it has had a sort of informal recognition in the theory and policy of the balance of power, there has never been any understanding from which we can gather what the results would be, if the bond of federation were ever cemented by any solemn pledge or sanction.

[322] "Historicus" (Letter in the Times, February 12, 1868) writes—"The system of international law professes to be a code of rules which ought to govern, and in fact in a great degree does govern, the conduct of independent nations in their dealings with one another.... How can one doubt that in fact such a rule exists and does operate? Let us test the matter by an example. When the news of the affair of the Trent reached England, what was the first question that every one asked? Was it not this, 'Is this act conformable to the law of nations, or is it not?' Did not the English Cabinet summon all the most distinguished jurists to advise them what the law of nations was? Was not the decision absolutely dependent on their advice.... The code of the law of nations, based on all other laws, on morality, deduced by the reasoning of jurists from well established principles, illustrated by precedents, gathered from usage, confirmed by experience, has become from age to age more and more respected as the arbiter of the rights and duties of nations, ... and now, after this system has been elaborated with so much care, and has yielded results so beneficial to the human race, we are to be told that the only real question in differences between nations is, 'Whether,

all things considered, it is or is not worth while to go to war?' not, be it observed, right or wrong to go to war. This is exactly the doctrine set forth in the celebrated Thelian controversy recorded in Thucydides." W. Oke Manning, "Commentaries on the Law of Nations" (p. 17), says, "Sir J. Mackintosh in his 'Hist. of the Progress of Ethical Philosophy' (prefixed to the 'Encyclopædia Britannica,' p. 315), speaks of Suarez as the writer who first saw that international law was composed not only of the simple principles of justice applied to intercourse between states, but of those usages long observed in that intercourse by the European race which have since been more exactly distinguished as the consuetudinary law acknowledged by the Christian nations of Europe and America. But Suarez himself speaks of this distinction as already recognised by previous writers."

[323] "La religion Chrétienne, qui ne semble avoir d'objet que la félicité de l'autre vie, fait encore notre bonheur dans celle-ci.... Que d'un côté, l'on se mette devant les yeux les massacres continuels des rois et des chefs grecs et romains, ... et nous verrons que nous devons au Christianisme, et dans le gouvernement un certain droit politique, et dans la guerre un certain droit des gens, que la nature humaine ne saurait assez reconnaître." —Montesquieu, "Esprit des Lois," i. xxiv. chap. 3.

[324] I must here do Mr Urquhart the justice to point out that he has been the principal advocate of this doctrine, that the declaration of war is the turning-point upon which everything depends, and more than any other man has laboured to enforce it. (Vide "Effects on the World of the Restoration of Canon Law," by D. Urquhart, 1869.) At p. 61, Mr Urquhart refers to the action taken by the Fecials. I have the misfortune to differ with Mr Urquhart on many points, but I have pleasure in bearing testimony as above.

[325] The Very Rev. Dr Rock ("Textile Fabrics," p. xii.) says—"The ancient British speciality was wool, and the postulants asking admission to the different castes, the sacerdotal, bardic, and the leeches or natural philosophers, were distinguished by stripes of white [Cicero (De Legibus, ii. 18) says, "Color autem albus præcipere decorus deo est quum in cateris tum maxima in textili"]   , blue, and green severally on their mantles, although the bards themselves were distinguished by some one of the colours above-mentioned (vide infra). [The significance of this will be noted at p. 391.]   I may further remark,

parenthetically, that here is an instance of national civilisation being pari passu with religious traditions. The British speciality was wool—query, because "of the heavy stress laid upon the rule which taught that the official colour in their dress," &c. (Id., vide ante, chap. xii. p. 292.)

St Paul says (Heb. ix. 19), "For when every commandment of the Lord had been read by Moses to all the people, he took the blood of calves and goats, with water, and scarlet *wool*, and hyssop, and sprinkled both the book itself and all the people" (Goguet, "Origin of Laws," ii. p. 9). The Spaniards in 1643 made a treaty of peace with the Indians of Chili; they have preserved the memory of the forms used at the ratification. It is said that the Indians killed many sheep, and stained in their blood a *branch* of the cane-tree, which the deputy of the Caciques put into the hands of the Spanish general in token of peace and alliance." Goguet also refers to Heb. ix. 19.

[326] De Fresquet, "Droit Romain," i. 48.

[327] Compare with the description of Saturn, "Saturnus, velato capite falcam gerens."—Fulgent. Mythol. i. c. 2.

[328] In the above extract from Montfauçon it should have been added, that when the Romans sent one of their fecials to declare war he went in sacerdotal habit—"Arrivant au confins de la ville, il appelloit à temoins Jupiter et les autres dieux comme il alloit demander réparation de l'injure au nom des Romains, il faisoit des imprécations sur lui et sur la ville de Rome, s'il disoit rien contre la vérité, et continuoit son chemin ... s'il rencontroient quelque citoien quelque payisan (paysan) il repétoit toujours ses imprécations," &c.

[329] A somewhat similar scene is also indistinctly traced in the following:—"Wood relates that on his visit to St Julian in 1670, in walking inland he 'met seven savages, who came running down the hill to us, making several signs for us to go back again, with much warning and noise, yet did not offer to draw their arrows. But one of them who was an old man came nearer to us than the rest, and made also signs we should depart, to whom I threw a knife, a bottle of brandy, and a neckcloth, to pacify him; but seeing him persist in the same signs as before, and that the savageness of the people seemed incorrigible, we returned on board again.'" Quoted by R. O. Cunningham, "Natural History of the Straits of Magellan and West Coast of Patagonia," 1871, p.

143. A similar scene is described by Roggerwsen in his voyage, I think, to Easter Island.

This, in connection with the scene at Bolabola, recalls the mode of procedure in the Odyssey, ix. 95 (Pope), when Ulysses reaches

"The land of Lotus and the flowering coast.

We climbed the beach and springs of water found,

Then spread our hasty banquet on the ground.

Three men were sent deputed from the crew

(A herald one) the dubious coast to view,

And learn what habitants possessed the place.

They went and found a hospitable race,

Not prone to ill, nor strange to foreign guest:

As our dire neighbours of Cyclopean birth."

[330] Vide Captain Wallis' Voyage, in "Hist. Account of all the Voyages round the World," 1773, iii. p. 79.

[331] Caduceatores—compare supra, p. 348. In connection with these latter, let us inquire more particularly as to their wand of office, the caduceus. "In its oldest form" it "was merely a bough twined round with white wool; afterwards a white or gilded staff with imitations of foliage and ribands was substituted for the old rude symbol. These were probably not turned into snakes till a much later age, when that reptile had acquired a mystic character." Müller's explanation is that it was originally the olive branch with the stemmata, which latter became developed into serpents.—Encyc. of Arts and Sciences. If, therefore, Müller's explanation is correct, the oldest form of the symbol of office of those who were the depositaries of laws of nations in the matter of peace and war, was a symbol which has a special history and significance in connection with the Deluge. Will this not tend to identify their institution with that epoch? It will, perhaps, be said that the branch of a tree is in any case a natural symbol of peace. But why a symbol or token at all? Why more than a simple gesture of salutation? unless the symbol embodied some idea which conveyed a pledge over and above? What, then, was this idea, unless the traditional idea? It may appear to us a natural emblem, but it is not so from association of ideas with the scriptural dove and olive branch? and yet consider how universal it is. Captain Cook's Voyages (i. p. 38; London, 1846) says, "It is remarkable that the chief, like

the people in the canoes, presented to us the same symbol of peace that is known to have been in use among the ancient and mighty nations of the northern hemisphere, the green branch of a tree." This occurred both in New Zealand and Otaheite. Wallis ("Voyages round the World," iii. 98) says that on an occasion when the Otaheitans wished to testify fidelity and friendliness, "the Indians cut branches from the trees and laid them in a ceremonious manner at the feet of the seamen; they painted themselves red with the berries of a tree, and stained their garments yellow with the bark of another." We have, as we have just seen, found this symbol in the caduceus, and it appears to me that the caduceus in its earlier form of a staff with foliage and ribands, is recognisable in the Gothic monuments as given in Stephens' "Central America." Vide also Cunningham's "Bhilsa Topes." Washington Irving ("Life of Columbus," iii. 214) speaks of the natives coming forward to meet them with white flags; and the same, if I remember rightly, is recorded in Cook's visit to the Sandwich Islanders. The white flag is our own symbol; but what is the white flag but the development and refinement of the staff and white wool? Again, why are stripes, in a variety of combination of colour, the characteristic symbol of flags? The reader will find the answer on returning to the text, where he will also learn the significance of the red and yellow, in the above descriptions.

[332] II. p. 317.

[333] Vide also in Carver's "North America" (p. 296), an engraving of the Indian "Calumet of Peace,"—the stem is of a light wood curiously painted with hieroglyphics in various colours, and adorned with the feathers of the most beautiful birds. It is not in my power to convey an idea of the various tints and pleasing ornaments of this much-esteemed Indian implement"(p. 359).

[334] It will hardly be denied that the tradition of the rainbow as a sign and pledge to man existed among the ancients. Vide Bryant, ii. 348. [The goddess Iris, who was sent with the messages of the gods, bore the same name as the rainbow Iris.]

E.g. Homer—

"Ἴρισσιν ἐοικότες ἅς τε Κρονίων

ἐν νεφεϊ στήριξε, τερας μεροπων ἀνθρωπων.—*Il.* xi. 27.

"Like to the bow which Jove amid the clouds

Placed *as a token to desponding man.*"

Also—Il. xvii. 547.

ἤΰτε πορφυρέην ιριν θνητοῖσι τανύσσ
Ζεὺς ἐξ οὐρανόθεν τέρας ἔμμεναι.

"Just as when Jove mid the high heavens displays
His bow mysterious for a *lasting sign.*"

And the lines (Theog. v. 700) in Hesiod, in which Iris is called the daughter of Wonder, who is sent over the broad surface of the sea when strife and discord arose among the immortals, and who is also called "the *great oath* of the gods"—["This is the token of the *covenant* between you and me, for *perpetual generations,*" Gen. ix. 12.] —who is told to bring from afar in her golden pitcher the many-named water.

Iris is called the daughter of Thaumas (which so closely approximates to the Greek Θαυμα = wonder, Bryant says to the Egyptian "Thaumus"). Bryant further thinks that Iris and Eros were originally the same term, but that in time the latter was formed into the boyish deity Cupid = Eros. According to some, Iris was the mother of Eros by Zephyrus. [There were indeed three Eroses, which mark three different lines of tradition, *vide* Gladstone on Iris (the rainbow), "Homer and the Homeric Age," ii. 156.]   Eros (Cupid), though a boy, was supposed to have been at the commencement of all things; and Lucian says, "How came you with that childish face, when we know you to be as *old as Japetus?*" The union of Cupid and Chaos (the Deluge is frequently alluded to as chaos, *vide* Bryant) "gave birth to men and all the animals." Hesiod makes Eros the first to appear after Chaos. "At this season (Deluge) another era began; the earth was supposed to be renewed, and time to return to a second infancy. They therefore formed an emblem of a child with a rainbow, to denote this renovation of the world, and called him Eros, or Divine Love," ... "yet esteemed the most ancient among the gods."—Bryant, ii. 349. (Cupid is represented with a bow, as is also Apollo and Diana, which was an allusion to the supposed resemblance of the bow and the rain*bow*.) Probably from his connection with Iris, he is represented as breaking the thunderbolts of Jupiter, and riding on *dolphins* and subduing other monsters of the sea. Smith ("Myth. Dict.") says Iris is derived from ἐρῶ εἴρω, "so that Iris would mean the speaker or messenger," ... "but it is not impossible that it may be connected with εἴρω, 'I join,' whence εἰρήνη; so that Iris, the goddess of the rainbow, would be the joiner, or conciliator, or the messenger of heaven, who restores peace in nature," It appears to me more likely that εἰρηνη = *peace* (derivation uncertain—Liddell and Scott) was derived directly from Iris, in accordance with the tradition, and that the Greek word for wool, εἰρος, was cognate to εἰρηνη, from being an emblem of peace (*e.g.* the pontiff's caduceator, woollen veil). In the same way, if we do not actually find the rainbow as the token of the herald or caduceator, may we not discover it conversely in the circumstance that *Iris* is represented as carrying in her hand a _herald's_ staff?

It is curious that we actually find, what I may call the sister emblem, viz. the Dove, used by the ancients, though just as we find, if I am right in the conjecture, the rainbow among the Polynesians, used in a perverted way as an ensign of war. It was possibly in superstitious remembrance of the tradition which we find more directly among the ancient Aryans and the Peruvians (p. 326–400), that war ought only to be made with a disposition towards peace; and that they thought to place themselves under the sanction of heaven by carrying this emblem as their ensign of war. Such, however, was the fact. Bryant (ii. 302) says:—"The dove became a favourite hieroglyphic among the Babylonians and Chaldees.... In respect to the Babylonians, it seems to have been taken by them for their national ensign, and to have been depicted on their military standard when they went to war. They seem likewise to have been styled Iönim, or the children of *the Dove;*" and they are thus alluded to by the Prophet Jeremiah, ch. xxv. ver. 38 (*id.*) Bryant says (ii. 285), "The name of the Dove among the ancient Amonians (by which term he intends the descendants of Chus) was Iön and Iönah; sometimes expressed Iönas, from whence came the Οινας of the Greeks."

I should rather put it that we find the word for the Dove common to the Hebrew and the Greek (Iönah, Hebrew; Οινας, Greek), and, as Bryant seems to imply, among other nations also—*e.g.* the Babylonians—which is precisely what we should have expected. But if this identity is allowed, we must proceed with Bryant to see in Juno, Venus, and Diana, simply embodiments of the tradition of the Dove. Bryant says that "Juno is the same as Iöna," and although, as we have seen, the peacock is said to be her bird (with reference to the other symbol, the rainbow), and although Ovid (Bryant, 344) sends her to heaven accompanied by Iris (rainbow), yet in the plate (from Gruter) p. 410, she will be seen with a dove on her wand, and a pomegranate, as symbol of the ark (*vide* p. 380), in her hand. Bryant, moreover (344), considers Juno to be identical with Venus. There was a statue in Laconia called Venus-Junonia. Of Dione and Venus Bryant says (ii. 341):—"I have mentioned that the name Diona was properly Ad, or Ada, Iöna. Hence came the term Idione; which Idione was an object of idolatry as early as the days of Moses. But there was a similar personage named Deione.... This was a compound of De Iöne, the dove; and Venus Dionœa may sometimes have been formed in the same manner.... Dionusus was likewise called Thyomus." *Vide* also Bryant, pp. 316, 317. In Genesis viii. 9, the dove returned to the ark, not having found "where her foot might rest." "In the hieroglyphical sculptures and paintings where this history was represented, the dove could not well be depicted otherwise than as hovering over the face of the deep. Hence it is that Venus or Dione is said to have risen from the sea. Hence it is, also, that she is said to preside over waters; to appease the troubled ocean; and to cause by her presence an universal calm; that to her were owing [on the retiring of the waters]   the fruits of the earth.... She was the Oenas ('Οιναϛ') of the Greeks; whence came the Venus of the Latins." The address of Lucretius to this deity concludes with two lines of remarkable significance—

"Te Dea, te fugiunt venti; te nubila cœli

Adventumque tuum; tibi rident æquora ponti;

Pacatumque nitet diffuso lumine *cœlum.*"

"In Sicily, upon Mount Eryx, was a celebrated temple of this goddess, which is taken notice of by Cicero and other writers. Doves were here held as sacred as they were in Palestine or Syria [*vide* also in Cashmere, p. 64]. It is remarkable that there were two days of the year set apart in this place for festivals, called Ἀναγωγια and Καταγωγια, at which time Venus was supposed to *depart over the sea*, and after a season to return. There were *also sacred pigeons*, which then took their flight from the island; but one of them was observed on the ninth day to come back from the sea, and to fly to the shrine of the goddess.

This was upon the festival of Ἀναγωγια. Upon this day it is said that there were great rejoicings. On what account can we imagine this veneration for the bird to be kept up, ... but for a memorial of the dove sent out of the ark, and of its return from the deep to Noah? The history is recorded upon the ancient coins of Eryx; which have on one side the head of *Janus* bifrons, and on the other the sacred dove."—Bryant, ii. 319.

Mr Cox's ("Mythology," ii. ch. ii. sec. vii.) counter-explanation, if I rightly gather it, is that "on Aphroditê (Venus), the child of the froth or foam of the sea, was lavished all the wealth of words denoting the loveliness of the morning; and thus the Hesiodic poet goes on at once to say that the grass sprung up under her feet as she moved, that Eros, Love, walked by her side, and Himeros, longing, followed after her." "This is but saying, in other words, that the morning, the child of the heavens, springs up first from the sea, as Athene is born by the water-side." But why should the morning spring first from the sea?— more particularly when the effects of her rising is noted in the springing up of flowers on the land? If the rainbow, we see the reason in her connection with the Deluge, and her connection with the subsequent renovation of nature. Mr Cox also says (p. 3):—"In her brilliant beauty she is Argunî, a name which appears again in that of Arguna, the companion of Krishna and the Hellenic Argynius." Does not this complete the chain of her connection with Juno? Mr Cox (p. 8) says:—"The Latin Venus is, in strictness of speech, a mere name, to which any epithet might be attached according to the conveniences or the needs of the worshipper.... The name itself has been, it would seem, with good reason, connected with the Sanscrit root 'van,' to desire love or favour,"—a derivation which equally accords with Bryant's view. Then there is the striking connection of Venus with Dionusos (vide p. 395). Mr Cox (p. 9) says, "The myth of Adonis links the legends of Aphrodite (Venus) with those of Dionusos. Like the Theban wine-god Adonis, born only on the death of his mother; and the two myths are, in one version, so far the same that Dionysos, like Adonis, is placed in a chest, which, being cast into the sea, is carried to Brasiæ, where the body of his mother is buried." (Comp. Kabiri, Bunsen.) Mr Cox connects Athene with Aphrodite (Venus) (p. 4). Therefore we must ask him to reconsider his explanation of "the Athenian maidens embroidering the sacred peplos for the ship presented to Athêne at the great Dionysiac festival." Compare evidence, supra, in chap. on Boulanger, &c.; Catlin.

[335] Vide ante, 391. That the entwined snakes were of late date would appear, I think, from the allusions to the suppliants' wands in Æschylus, e.g. (vide Plumtre's Æschylus, "Libation Pourers," v. 1024) when Orestes puts on the suppliants wreaths, and takes the olive branch in his hand—

"The branch of *olive* from the topmost growth,

With amplest tufts of *white wool* meetly wreathed."

and in the Supplicants (22)—

"Holding in one hand the branches

Suppliant, wreathed with *white wool* fillets."

[336] Also, "Joannis Meursii Themis Athica, sive de Legibus Alticis," i. xi. says, "Postquam vero exercitus eductus esset pugnam inire, non licebat antiquam emissum agmen hostium quis, hunc expectans accepisset."

[337] This has something in common with the fiery cross sent round by the Highlanders as the summons to war. In another aspect it has resemblances with the Indian mode of declaration of war. "The manner in which the Indians declare war against each other is by sending a slave with a hatchet, the handle of which is painted red, to the nation which they intend to break with; and the messenger, notwithstanding the danger to which he is exposed from the sudden fury of those whom he thus sets at defiance, executes his commission with great fidelity."— Carver's "Travels in North America," p. 307.

[338] That there may be limitations to the horrors of war, seems to be established by the instance of the prohibition of explosive bullets. I read in the Times (March 11, 1871):—"The British Medical Journal declares its opinion that the charges which have been put forward of explosive bullets having been used by the contending armies have been groundless; and is inclined to believe that the articles of the St Petersburg Convention

have been faithfully adhered to, notwithstanding the mutual recriminations to the contrary by both French and German Governments."

[339] Indirect evidence of the importance formerly attached to the declaration of war may, I think, be discovered in the formal addresses and invocations of the gods by the Homeric heroes previous to combat, which to us seem so forced and unnatural; and the same sentiment was noticed by the Spaniards, when they first came over, among the Peruvians, who did not neglect the punctilio of the declaration of war even in their most high-handed aggressions, e.g. Garcilasso de la Vega (Hakluyt Soc. ed. ii. 141) says—"The invaders sent the usual summons that the people might not be able to allege afterwards that they had been taken unawares."

[340] Carver ("Travels in North America," p. 301) says of the Indians—"Sometimes private chiefs make excursions.... These irregular sallies, however, are not always approved of by the elder chiefs, though they are often obliged to connive at them.... But when war is national, and undertaken by the community, their deliberations are formal and slow. The elders assemble in council, to which all the head warriors and young men are admitted, when they deliver their opinions in solemn speeches; weighing with maturity the nature of the enterprise they are about to engage in, and balancing with great sagacity the advantages or inconveniences that will arise from it. Their priests are also consulted on the subject, and even sometimes the advice of the most intelligent of their women is asked. If the determination be for war they prepare for it with much ceremony."

[341] "In ancient times war was solemnly declared either by certain fixed ceremonies or by the announcement of heralds; and a war commenced without such declaration was regarded as informal and irregular, and contrary to the usages of nations. Grotius says that a declaration of war is not necessary by the law of nations—"Naturali jure nulla requiritur declaratio," but that it was required by the law of nations, jure gentium, by which term, be it remembered, he means the usages of nations. And in this he was right, as until the age in which he lived wars

were almost invariably preceded by solemn declarations. The Romans, according to Albericus Gentilis, did not grant a triumph for any war which had been commenced without a formal declaration (De Jure Belli, c. ii. § i.); but the Greeks do not seem to have been at all regular in the observance of the custom (Bynkershock, Quæs. Jur. Pub., l. i. c. ii.) During the times of chivalry declarations of war were usually given with great formality, the habits of knighthood being carried into the customs of general warfare, and it being held mean to fall upon an adversary when unprepared to defend himself (Ward, Introd. ii. 206–230). With the decline of chivalry this custom fell into disuse. Gustavus Adolphus invaded Germany without any declaration of war (Zouch, De Judicio inter Gentes, P. ii. § x. 1); but this appears to have been an exception to the usages of the age, and Clarendon speaks of declarations of war as being customary in his time, and blames the war in which the Duke of Buckingham went to France, as entered into 'without so much as the formality of a declaration from the king, containing the ground and provocation and end of it, according to custom and obligation in the like cases.' Formal denunciations of war by heralds were discontinued about the time of Grotius; the last instance having been, according to Voltaire, when Louis XIII. sent a herald to Brussels to declare war against Spain in 1635."—W. Oke Manning's Commentaries on Law of Nations.

[342] "Looking back on the history of the autumn ... we may yet be impressed by the conviction that, had the union of the European family of nations been strengthened as it might have been before the war broke out, it might never have been begun, or would have long since terminated. The Treaty of Paris put on record a declaration in favour of arbitration, but it proved to be worthless when sought to be applied."—Times, Feb. 15, 1871. I shall have a word to say presently on the declaration of the Treaty of Paris.

[343] It must not be forgotten, however, that it was the revolution in Paris which gave this war its abnormal character, and created situations for which the law of nations had no precedents, or precedents only which were of doubtful application.

[344] Compare infra, p. 412.

[345] Compare with the following account of the declaration of war by M. F. de Champagny, de L'Acad. Fr., in the Correspondant, 25 Juin 1871:—"A government wrongly inspired proposed to us a war. Without asking it why it wished to make it, without asking if it could make it, without reflection, without discussion, without listening to the men of name and experience, who implored of us at least twenty-four hours for reflection, we accepted this war, I do not say with enthusiasm, but with frivolous levity, not as crusaders, but as children. It seemed to us sufficient to tipple in the 'cafés,' singing the 'Marseillaise,' to intoxicate the soldiers, to throw squibs into what were then called sensational journals, to cry 'à Berlin!' in order to go right off to Berlin. And when it was discovered that we were not going on at all to Berlin, but that Berlin was coming to Paris, that this enthusiasm of the 'café' did not cause armies to spring into life, what was our resource? Always the same: to overthrow a government!"

[346] Vide note 19, p. 403.

[347] These were the words which the Marquis of Bath had the courage to use in the House of Lords when everybody else was joining in a ludicrous "dirge of homage" to Cavour. I wish to put this protest, as well as the similar protests of the Marquis of Normanby and the Earl of Donoughmore on record, as there may come a time when England will be glad to recur to them.

[348] Vide "Current Events," in Rambler, 1860.

[349] "Does the faith of treaties, the right of treaties, still exist? Look at what has happened in Europe during the last twenty years. The treaties made with the Church were the first violated; they have declared that a 'concordat' is nothing more than a law of the State, which the State can alter at will—in other words, that, unlike all other contracts, conventions of this nature, inviolable for one of the parties, can be broken by the other at its pleasure; kings have thus put the Church outside the law of nations. But, in consequence, they have excluded themselves. When the most sacred of all treaties were thus trampled upon, how would they have the others respected? They have even written, or caused to be written, on a solemn occasion ('Napoleon III. et L'Italie, 1859') that treaties no longer bind when the general sentiment declares against them; in other terms, when they displease us. At this epoch, in 1859, we were disputing with Austria a

possession which all treaties had guaranteed to her, and the neutral signatories of these treaties did not protest. Victorious over Austria, we have in our turn made a treaty with her; and this treaty was violated when scarcely signed; and neither we nor the rest of Europe protested. Later on, the dissensions between Germany and Denmark ended in a treaty, which the rest of Europe guaranteed; but soon Germany broke this treaty by force of arms, and Europe did not say a word. I omit here the convention of September, ... the treaty of 1856. On all these occasions the indifference of third parties has come to the aid of the cupidity of the aggressors; and the moral sense has been so far wanting in the Cabinets that they have assisted and applauded acts of brigandage for the love of the art, and without even thinking that the brigand, when he grew strong, would fall on the morrow on themselves. Will you find in European history twelve years so fruitful in pledges and perjuries?"